MW00848674

God with Us

ANSLEY L. QUIROS

God with Us

Lived Theology and the Freedom Struggle
in Americus, Georgia, 1942–1976

The University of North Carolina Press *Chapel Hill*

This book was published with the assistance of the Authors Fund of the University of North Carolina Press.

© 2018 The University of North Carolina Press
All rights reserved
Set in Arno Pro by Westchester Publishing Services

The University of North Carolina Press has been a member of the
Green Press Initiative since 2003.

Library of Congress Cataloging-in-Publication Data
Names: Quiros, Ansley Lillian, author.
Title: God with us : lived theology and the freedom struggle in Americus,
    Georgia, 1942–1976 / Ansley L. Quiros.
Description: Chapel Hill : University of North Carolina Press, [2018] |
    Includes bibliographical references and index.
Identifiers: LCCN 2018016975 | ISBN 9781469646756 (cloth : alk. paper) |
    ISBN 9781469646763 (pbk : alk. paper) | ISBN 9781469646770 (ebook)
Subjects: LCSH: Civil rights movements—Georgia—Americus—History—20th century. |
    African Americans—Civil rights—Georgia—Americus—History—20th century. |
    Religion and sociology—Southern States. | Americus (Ga.)—Religion—20th century. |
    Americus (Ga.)—Race relations.
Classification: LCC F294.A5 Q5 2018 | DDC 323.1196/0730758913—dc23
    LC record available at https://lccn.loc.gov/2018016975

Cover illustration: Ida Berman's *Koinonia Farm Camp at Highlander* (Koinonia
Farm Photographs, Hargrett Rare Book and Manuscript Library, University of
Georgia Libraries; used by permission of Karen Berman).

A version of chapter 5 was previously published as "The Road to Charlottesville
Runs through Americus, Georgia," *The Activist History Review* (October 2017),
https://activisthistory.com/2017/10/06/the-road-to-charlottesville-runs-through-
americus-georgia/. Used here with permission.

For Amanda Paul Miller Privette, and Marilyn Miller Privette Quiros,
and all those who long for justice in the South

Contents

Illustrations and Map

Acknowledgments

Among the many things I have learned in writing this book is the common grace of generosity. So many have helped along the way, sharing documents, expertise, insight, and time. To y'all, I offer my sincerest thanks.

Many institutions and communities of scholars have supported and sustained this work over the years. Thank you to all at Furman University who fostered a love of history, especially Tim Fehler, Savita Nair, David Shi, Courtney Tollison, and Dianne Vecchio. Early stages of the work were presented at conferences at Drew University, Emory University, the University of Memphis, and the Association for the Study of African American History and Life, where conversations and questions improved it mightily. Librarians and archivists at the National Southern Baptist Archive in Nashville, the Pitts Library and Rose Library at Emory University, the Hargrett Library at the University of Georgia, and the Jimmy Carter Presidential Library in Atlanta also helped along the way, and they deserve recognition for their work in cataloguing the past. I have found historians of the South, wherever they may be found, particularly collegial and helpful, notably, Jim Auchmutey, Ed Blum, Joe Crespino, Bob Elder, Paul Harvey, and Hank Klibanoff. Steve Haynes's ecclesiastical repentance group brought together thoughtful, supportive laypeople and scholars interested in race and religion. Participating in this group, and meeting Anthony Bradley, Carolyn Dupont, Dalton Lyon, and Joe Reiff, proved to be an unmitigated blessing.

Special thanks go to Vanderbilt University for offering me an unmatched intellectual community. To Jessica Burch, Will Bishop, Courtney Campbell, Jon Hansen, Miriam Martin, Erin Woodruff Stone, Lu Sun, Amy Gant Tan, Nick Villanueva, and especially Matt Owen and Frances Kolb Turnbell: you were delightful companions, academic and otherwise. Presenting this work at the History Department's Americanist Seminar and in other workshops was invaluable in honing the argument and refining the prose. A year at the Robert Penn Warren Center for the Humanities, run by the indomitable Mona Frederick, provided needed time to write as well as a superb set of readers: Emily August, Whitney Laster, Aoife Laughlin, John Maddox, Paul Morrow, Aubrey Porterfield, and Jamie Shenton. Thank you to the Vanderbilt History Department—namely, Michael Bess, Bill Caferro, Jim Epstein, and Jane Landers, each of whom offered me consistent encouragement and good humor. My heartfelt appreciation, too, to Paul Kramer, whose keen eye reshaped the project at a key moment; to Sarah Igo, for her constant editing and advocacy; and to Dennis Dickerson, who shepherded the project with enthusiasm and expertise from the very beginning. Thanks as well to Charles Marsh, for reading this work and championing it, and to Karen, for making sure Charles got my emails. My profoundest gratitude belongs to Gary Gerstle. He read countless drafts of this work, and his ruthless blue pen improved it immeasurably. As a mentor and historian, he is unrivaled.

Over the course of writing this book, life and work have taken me on a veritable tour of the Deep South, from South Carolina to Tennessee, and always, to Georgia. My most recent stop has been to the University of North Alabama, where I have found energetic teachers, a community of scholars, and a home. My colleagues in the History Department have been readers, mentors, and friends, and I thank you all. Thanks, too, to the College of Arts and Sciences, which, in the form of its Research Award, offered critical support for the project in its final stages. My students at UNA have been, quite unexpectedly, the book's most enthusiastic backers, reminding me that the stories of race and religion in the American South are worth telling.

It has been a distinct privilege to work with the University of North Carolina Press, particularly Brandon Proia, Jad Adkins, Cate Hodorowicz, and Dino Battista. Thank you all for your thorough work and support without which there would be no book. Thank you, too, to the anonymous reviewers whose careful readings sharpened the analysis and enriched the narrative. I remember someone telling me once that Brandon Proia was the best editor out there. Now I know why. Brandon, your keen edits enhanced the book tremendously, and your good humor sustained me throughout. Thank you.

Though this story of Americus is one of conflict and struggle, what I found in my time there was nothing but kindness, openness, and support. Karl Wilson was my first friend and most ardent supporter; he made introductions for me and continued to mail me newspaper clips for years. Alan Anderson knows more about Americus than anyone and generously shared his wisdom with me. Sam Mahone has worked tirelessly to tell the story of the Americus and Sumter County Movement and has been a constant friend. Outside of town, the saints at Koinonia Farm continue their tradition of offering respite and insight. Thank you to Bren Dubay, Amanda Moore, and Bill Harris, Jr., for welcoming me to the farm and letting me see your archive. Thanks also to the many churches in Americus that shared their histories with me, especially First Baptist, First Presbyterian, Bethesda Baptist, Campbell Chapel A.M.E., and especially First United Methodist—and Jan Bird and Lyn Dozier in particular. Bill and Ann Harris are the epitome of hospitality, providing me a real home in Americus and welcoming me into their lovely family. Charles and Shirley Sherrod also deserve my deepest gratitude, for everything. Finally, to all those in Americus who opened their homes and shared their stories—often through tears, on couches, at kitchen tables over coffee, on porches with dogs underfoot—thank you. Your willingness to tell the truth about even the difficult times gives me hope for the South yet.

Frances Kolb Turnbell has earned my special thanks. She read every word, reformatted every note, and has had hundreds of conversations far outside of her chosen field. Frances, your conscientious attention and your faithful friendship sustained both the book and me. Special thanks as well to Stacy Quiros. With characteristic selflessness, she read the entire manuscript over summer mornings at Panera and returned detailed, smart comments. Thank you, mom.

Finally, the ideas in this book, about theology and race and the church, were fostered by my family, which always has my admiration and love. My great grandmother, Amanda Paul Miller Privette, and my grandmother, Marilyn Privette Quiros, were smart, gracious Southern women who longed for justice to come to the South. I think they would have enjoyed this book, and I humbly dedicate it to them and all like them who have gone before.

God with Us

Introduction
Sweet Jesus and Unbearable Madness

Beliefs always find expression in action.
—Benjamin Mays, *Seeking to Be Christian in Race Relations*, 1957

It was nearly Christmas. Holly was draped across the grand doors of the church, and its windows shone with a soft glow. A group of young people stood outside on the sidewalk, looking up. Carol Henry, whose father was inside delivering a revival message, had tears in her eyes. Collins McGee set his jaw. "I want y'all to observe something," their leader said, "You see all of this light around the church? . . . [They are] trying to light it up because they are refusing to allow God's light to shine on the inside. I want y'all to notice how much darkness there is." From outside, they could still hear the Christmas hymn: "*And in despair I bowed my head/ 'There is no peace on earth,' I said/ 'For hate is strong, And mocks the song/ Of peace on earth, good-will to men!'*"

The group had entered the First Baptist Church, received bulletins, and taken their seats near the back on a smooth wooden pew. They waited to hear about the Incarnation, the Word made Flesh, and that sacred Christmas message that God was made man and dwelt among them. After a quiet moment, an usher approached and asked them to leave. When no one stirred, the agitated usher grabbed Collins McGee, who was black, by the arm and began to push him toward the doors. "This church has authorized me to use whatever means necessary to keep niggers out of our services," he said angrily, as the group followed behind, whispering their protestations over the delicate instrumentation. The door slammed shut.

Out on the sidewalk, they listened to the muted hymn: "*Then pealed the bells more loud and deep/ God is not dead, nor doth He sleep/ The Wrong shall fail, The Right prevail/ With peace on earth, good-will to men.*" Collins McGee closed his eyes and listened.[1]

THROUGH ITS ORIGINS, its Awakenings, sects, and diverse manifestations, America and its history has always been closely bound up with the beliefs of its people. When these beliefs have clashed, Americans have engaged in a fight not only over religious orthodoxy but for the very soul of the nation. Such was the case in the civil rights struggle. The American South of the 1960s was the country's most religious region and yet the most racially divided. It was the place where people prayed most fervently and where they beat their neighbors most brutally. As one writer commented, "it was a place of Sweet Jesus and unbearable madness."[2]

God with Us contends that the civil rights struggle, rightly understood as a major social, cultural, and political conflict, constituted a theological conflict as well. Whether in the traditional sanctuaries of the major white Protestant denominations, in the mass meetings in black churches, or in Christian expressions of interracialism, Southerners resisted, pursued, and questioned racial change within various theological traditions. Indeed, Christian theology contributed both to the moral power of the civil rights movement and to the staunch opposition it encountered. But how? How could it be that integrated Christian communities, segregationist white churches, and civil rights activists all claimed to follow the tenets of Christianity? Why is it that Dr. King and the Ku Klux Klan both professed belief in God the Father, in Jesus Christ, and in the Holy Bible? Why did all boast that God was with them? As those in the struggle grappled with issues of race, they inexorably grappled with issues of religion. While many invoked Christian doctrine concerning the race question, many also invoked race concerning issues of religious orthodoxy. That struggle is the heart of this work. Uncovering the theological elements present in the conflict over civil rights clarifies not only the passion and anger felt during the 1960s, but also offers insight into the rise of the Religious Right and the continually vexing relationship between race and religion in America. Although the presence of religion in the civil rights movement is often acknowledged, a specific, community-based study of the theological motivations and hindrances operating on both sides of the movement has not yet been undertaken. *God with Us* attempts to take up this task, analyzing the theological elements of racial conflict in Americus, Georgia.

THE HISTORICAL INTERPRETATION of the civil rights movement has long stressed the courage and resilience of its leaders and participants, the political changes it wrought, and the transformation it rendered in American life.[3] The popularity of this view is evident in the social exaltation of the civil rights movement—holidays commemorating civil rights leaders, inspirational photographs adorning the cinderblock walls of classrooms across the country, and publicized anniversary celebrations. From early interpretations that focused on the national political achievements of the movement, the historiography has expanded to include the stories of grassroots organizations and local movements and to extend the chronology and scope of the larger black freedom struggle. These contributions have focused increasingly on the cultural and social implications of the movement, seeking to free it from its strict political confines and neat chronology and locate a larger narrative of struggle for change.[4]

Curiously, though, for all its expansions, the historiography has underemphasized the religious convictions of ordinary people. While certainly acknowledging the organizational role of the black church and general religious influences, scholarship of the civil rights movement has tended to offer a mostly secular account of the struggle for political and social equality. Even when the presence of religious beliefs is mentioned, the content of those beliefs is seldom explored. The theological nature of the struggle for human equality has been diluted. In addition to obscuring the motivation and inspiration driving much of the movement, the diminution of religious belief exposes, as one scholar put it, "The modernist conceit that what black people do and say in church cannot possibly be taken seriously."[5] Though certain leaders' religious views, most notably King's, have received ample, excellent treatment, the beliefs of ordinary men and women of faith have too often been trivialized or sidelined.[6] We must prioritize black voices whether they are in a pulpit or a pew.

Some have begun this important work. Historians such as Albert Raboteau and Lewis V. Baldwin have prioritized theology in the black protest tradition while David Chappell's *A Stone of Hope* attributes the revolutionary success of the civil rights movement to, among other things, the collective spiritual power of the black prophetic tradition. "It may be misleading to view the civil rights movement as a social and political event that had religious overtones," Chappell writes. Rather, the struggle was, for many black Americans, "primarily" theological, with political aims "secondary or incidental." He argues that scholars must reframe the civil rights struggle as part of America's great religious revivals, and not simply of social protest. There is ongoing work to be done, therefore, in uncovering the theological motivations and religious convictions of not only of the movement's leaders but of its grassroots participants.[7]

Just as the historiography of the civil rights movement has begun to engage the theological elements of the struggle, so, too, has much of the literature on white resistance to civil rights. The reemergence of political and evangelical conservatism in the 1970s and 1980s forced scholars to contend seriously with the ideas of Southern conservatives who were suddenly occupying the nation's central administrative offices. Historians uncovered the roots of this New Right in massive resistance, in the political battles over the role of the state in public education and private enterprise, and in the resurgence of religious fundamentalism.[8] For years, though, the theological aspects were dismissed as secondary to other political, social, or cultural forces.[9] Much of this owed to the influence of the so-called cultural captivity thesis in which white Southern churches refused to sincerely grapple with the teachings of Christ or the applications of the Gospel; instead, they unreflectively reinforced social hierarchies. As Paul Harvey has characterized this view: "compelled to choose between Christ and culture, Southerners chose culture."[10] Another reason stemmed from academic reluctance. "If religion has been and continues to be so important to those arguing in favor of segregation as well as those resisting it," legal historian Jane Dailey asks, "why have modern historians preferred to study scientific racism or white supremacist politics and ignored this more widespread and deeply held set of beliefs?"[11] The answer is provocative if not entirely surprising. "In this secular, not to say cynical, age," Eugene Genovese remarked, "few tasks present greater difficulty than that of compelling the well-educated to take religious matters seriously."[12] This secular snobbery led scholars to render theology an "archaic vestige" and not "a coherent cosmology" broad enough to provide people with a functional worldview in modernity.[13] Besides being poor scholarship, historians' marginalization of unsavory religious views has perpetuated an overly simplistic, triumphalist narrative of the civil rights movement, one that misses the heart of the struggle. When the theology of white Protestants in the South is taken seriously, it soon becomes evident how intertwined theology and segregation were in the minds of Southern Christians, as a new generation of scholars is now showing.[14]

Paul Harvey has long stressed theological commitment in Southern life, inspiring others to include belief as a major mode of analysis for the civil rights era. For instance, Joseph Crespino, in his study of conservatism in Mississippi, uncovered the importance of a certain brand of Christianity in strengthening white claims to superiority and separateness. Religious claims, he discovered, were not merely manipulative moral coverings for sinister political and hegemonic aims, as they are too often parodied. Like Crespino, Carolyn Dupont has argued that white Mississippians were legitimately religious and had religious criticisms of the civil rights movement that led them to a particular brand of political and social conservatism.[15] Even silence was a strategy. "The decision to refrain from preaching about racial justice," Charles Marsh has argued, "signaled a theological position, which stemmed from a coherent theological system." Often overlooked, this system justified segregation and created a theology of racial purity, a theology with "pervasive influence."[16] In recent years, other religious historians, such as Mark Newman, Carter Dalton Lyon, Joseph

Kip Kosek, and Steve Haynes, have likewise investigated the powerful influence of white Southerners' religious beliefs.[17]

Christian theology, in the hands of some, was harnessed to preserve the segregationist system; in the hands of others, it was used to defy it. Both sides claimed God was with them. Therefore, it is pressing for scholars to consider the civil rights struggle not only as one over competing visions for the country but also as one over what Jane Dailey has called "competing claims to Christian orthodoxy."[18] The notion of orthodoxy reframes the civil rights struggle, imbuing it with the same spiritual significance as the Council at Nicaea or the same fervor as the Inquisition. It also helps explain why both sides claimed divine authority and employed the Bible to make their case. It was not just civil rights but Christian orthodoxy that was at stake. This interpretation complicates the civil rights struggle by seeing it as one without a predestined victor. It also takes historians into the hidden realms of significance that created layered and multifaceted contestations over race and religion in the South.

While many have noted the slippery nature of metaphysical inquiry, there is a glaring need in the historical literature of both civil rights and white resistance to address the ways in which theological ideas have manifested in the lives and stories of the past.[19] In the everyday that becomes history, individuals embodied theological concepts and doctrine. They also adapted and created theologies to match their circumstances, a practice rife with consequences and significance. Certainly, it can be challenging to access these hidden realms of the soul, especially for a historian. But through oral histories and a careful examination of religious materials, sermons, and relevant theological works and trends, it is possible to recapture a sense of people's spiritual understandings and orderings, looking, like Shakespeare's poet, "from heaven to earth, earth to heaven," and "giving airy nothing a local habitation and a name."[20] Despite the difficulties, there is a need to reexamine the social and political realities of racial division and reconciliation in light of the theological. *God with Us* addresses this need, borrowing, notably, Charles Marsh's notion of *lived theology*.[21]

WHAT EXACTLY IS *lived theology*? Theology, most simply defined, is the systematic study of God—what St. Augustine of Hippo characterized as "reasoning or discussion concerning the Deity," or what Marsh himself has called the effort to "venture a word about God, who transcends human speech."[22] Although traditionally theology indicated a central discourse surrounding Christianity and the Christian tradition, from the 1500s onward it has broadened to include not only Christian theology, but also the study of other belief systems and religions. Even within these shifts, theology continues to indicate an intellectual, even grammatical, engagement with notions of the divine, occupying the realm of the mind and the soul. But, the internal, ephemeral renderings of the mind and soul find their way into the external, tangible stuff of life. As Raphael Warnock has cautioned, "Theology that is not lived is not theology at all."[23]

That brings us to *lived theology*. According to Marsh, lived theology "might be considered a probing and careful narration of life inside the movement of God in the social world."[24] It is the story people tell themselves and others about what God is doing in the world and how they are participating in that divine action. For Marsh, lived theology involves studying the "patterns and practices" as well as the "narrated accounts of faith-formed lives"; both are "communicative," "rich and generative material for theological inquiry."[25] In this way, lived theology effectively expands *what* can be categorized as theological and also *who* can be. Theology belongs not only to Barth and Aquinas but also to a "more varied cast" of "everyday saints and sinners."[26]

Lived theology stands in contrast to the idea of lived religion, also referred to as "popular religion," another field unto itself that focuses on concrete religious practices in the lives of everyday parishioners rather than on issues of belief.[27] It sometimes includes interrogations of theological beliefs, but the study of lived religion does so with "an empiricist orientation to religion," with a focus on doing rather than believing. Lived religion, Robert Orsi explained, "points us to religion as it is shaped and experienced in . . . everyday experience."[28] Simply put, lived religion examines action to understand belief while lived theology examines belief to understand action.

These methodological descriptions of lived theology are certainly helpful, but a concrete definition remains needed. "Lived theology examines practice, objects and beliefs in order to understand God's presence in human experience"; it is an exploration of belief and an examination of how those beliefs are embodied in action in the world.[29] Lived theology therefore exists not only in the unseen realms of belief, the hidden motivations and repetitions of the heart, but also in the external actions that individuals or communities believe to have theological significance. It is both the internal substance of theological beliefs and their outward performance. For instance, a woman praying may be an example of lived theology in that her act of praying demonstrates a possession of belief; that is, the act of kneeling or bowing one's head is an outward performance of theological adherence. But she also may be an example of lived theology in that her act of prayer reveals specific theological presuppositions: namely, that there is a God, that God hears prayers, and that God's hearing matters in her specific situation. Those theological tenets, like her action itself, can be subversive and can challenge the status quo. In other words, it is not only the general presence of belief that is significant, but the specific content of that belief. This approach broadens the possibilities for what actions may constitute lived theology. Theology can be lived not only in conspicuously religious actions, like prayer, but in seemingly secular ones, like marching or even standing still. There are almost no boundaries for what actions may be theological, depending on the actor's state of mind or heart.

To study lived theology in the civil rights struggle, then, is to examine marching and singing, shouting and shooting, voting and vitriol on the one hand, and the more hidden beliefs that animated those actions on the other. These are subtle prayers, internal hopes and fears, ways of imagining God and society. Though, as Marsh has cautioned, "there are no easy patterns for predicting the way religious ideas govern particular courses of action," there exists "in each case, a theological sense or inner logic in these embedded theologies."[30] What people believe influences, consciously or unconsciously, how they act. To borrow a phrase from Dorothy Sayers, "The dogma is the drama."[31]

And there is perhaps no greater instance of theological drama than the civil rights struggle. In fact, Thomas Merton, the Catholic thinker and writer, once described the civil rights movement as "the greatest example of Christian faith in action in the social history of the United States."[32] Yet, at the same time that many activists put their faith in action in the protest movement, as we have seen, many segregationists likewise invoked the divine in their attempt to maintain segregation. Therefore, we must reimagine the civil rights struggle as not only a social, political, and cultural struggle but also as a theological one.

Seen theologically, the civil rights era emerges as a temporal site of fierce conflict and as a moment of opportunity. For a fleeting instant, the movement confronted evangelical America in its own language—the language of faith. But the moment passed by. Instead of listening and turning from racism, white Southern Protestants largely retreated into old arguments, while the civil rights movement fragmented, with many abandoning the tenets of theological nonviolence. The dream that the movement espoused of the beloved community, of interracial Christian cooperation, ended in division and dissension. The possibility Christian nonviolence offered America vanished, and by the late 1960s Southern Christians were as divided as ever. Mostly lost, too, was the opportunity for white Southerners to reconsider the theological demands of Christianity in relation to the historical complexities of race in the South and in the nation. Instead, white Southerners largely embraced a form of reactive racial politics, though one still steeped in the language of religious orthodoxy. Therefore, engaging with the lived theology of the civil rights movement and its adversaries not only promises a more nuanced understanding of the past, but also reveals the power of theology in American life and politics, a power for deep schism but potentially, too, for reconciliation.

While a few scholars have begun identifying lived theology in the black protest movement, in white allies, and even in the white resistance to civil rights, these competing visions of orthodoxy have not been fully understood together. They must be placed in conversation, and, more to the point, in community.[33] For just as theological ideas are embodied in individuals they are also embodied within communities, communities that experience cooperation and conflict and exist in soil and space. *God with Us* attempts an understanding of theological community through the story of a town—Americus, Georgia.[34]

TUCKED AWAY IN the pecan orchards and cotton fields of Southwest Georgia's Sumter County, Americus was in many ways an archetypical town in the Deep South. Its 13,000 residents were almost exactly divided between black and white.[35] Agriculturally based, community oriented, deeply segregated, and devoutly religious, Americus looked a lot like many other small cities scattered throughout the South in the twentieth century. Yet, for all its ordinariness, Americus boasted a few particulars that make it an ideal place to position a theological interrogation of the civil rights struggle.

Perhaps the most noteworthy was the presence of Koinonia Farm, an explicitly Christian endeavor in interracialism on the outskirts of town. From its founding in the 1940s, Koinonia Farm existed to be a demonstration of Christian racial equality, infuriating its segregationist neighbors and infusing racial questions with religious overtones. Americus was important as well for being a key site for the Student Nonviolent Coordinating Committee's Southwest Georgia Freedom Project. During the course of this project, activists clashed with recalcitrant local institutions, generating conflicts. Harsh suppressions of demonstrations, draconian legal sentences for dissenters, and attacks of arson evidenced a brutality that drew national notoriety. The story of Americus is compelling, and it has not yet fully been told.[36]

The fierce struggles in Americus provide extraordinarily rich material through which to examine the theological dimensions of the civil rights struggle. The battle over race and orthodoxy there was particularly contentious and intensely violent. Marches downtown, votes in church boardrooms, kneel-ins and prayer rallies, the persecution of Koinonia Farm—all contributed to a charged atmosphere of conflict over race, theology, culture, and politics. The people of Americus—from J. R. Campbell, an A.M.E. minister who led the local movement, to Charles Wheatley, a racist, Presbyterian business

Selected Georgia cities and regions. (Based on a map from Stephen Tuck's *Beyond Atlanta: The Struggle for Racial Equality in Georgia, 1940–1980*, University of Georgia Press, 2001.)

magnate; from Clarence Jordan, a radically integrationist white Baptist, to Robertiena Freeman, a young black student jailed for protesting—also vividly demonstrated these contestations. Americus was a place of both profound Christian interracialism and vehement Christian segregation. Lofty ideas and clashing ideologies took on flesh and blood. Theology incarnated.

"Oh God," Flannery O'Connor once prayed, "Please help me to get down under things and find where you are."[37] In a sense, *God with Us* seeks the same goal: to get down under things in Americus, Georgia, and to there find the divine.

Uncovering the theological in the narrative of 1960s Americus requires a deep understanding of both the racial and religious stakes. Thus, Part I of *God with Us* describes the historical and theological landscape of midcentury Americus. Examining national and regional patterns as well as local peculiarities, the book takes up Koinonia Farm, Americus's established white Protestant churches, and several prominent black churches, with attention to each group's claims to theological and racial orthodoxy. Chapter 1 opens with the story of Koinonia Farm. Reflecting its founder, Clarence Jordan, Koinonia Farm possessed a considered theological foundation, one that emphasized Christian communalism, redemptive agrarianism, and racial reconciliation. After its establishment in 1942, Koinonia Farm initially appeared to be a quirky anomaly. But the farm's unflinching commitment to Christian orthodoxy and racial parity soon drew the ire (and gunshot) of the local white community. It also revealed the sharp theological conflict between the Christianity of Koinonia and that of its Americus neighbors. If the Koinonians' beliefs led them to communal interracialism, the theology of most white Protestants in Americus led them to a very different conclusion. This segregationist white Protestant establishment in Americus is the subject of chapter 2. The imposing churches on Lee Street, particularly the First Baptist Church, First Methodist Church, and First Presbyterian Church, promoted a theological worldview marked by a commitment to biblical literalism, evangelism, and congregational autonomy. In a world that evangelicals saw as besieged by modernism, communism, and secularism, they imagined themselves as protectors of piety, liberty, and orthodoxy. And, in the postwar South, they understood themselves also as protectors of segregation, a commitment no less momentous and, in their estimation, no less godly. Chapter 3 addresses the black church in Americus (with its different denominational affiliations and particularities) and its theological tenets. Inherited from generations of faithful black Christians as well as twentieth-century black religious intellectuals, this black theology often included the belief that all people were image-bearers of God, that segregation was sinful and idolatrous, that God existed on the side of freedom, and that Jesus suffered for and with his people. These beliefs not only sustained the black church throughout eras of oppression, but also imbued its freedom struggle with transcendent power. Koinonia Farm, white Southern Protestants, and the black churches of Americus represented distinct groups with particular theologies and competing claims to Christian orthodoxy and to the Christian view of race.

Part II traces how these theological contexts influenced the civil rights struggle of the 1960s. Chapter 4 locates the practice and performance of theology in the marches and demonstrations of the black freedom movement as it arrived in Americus, revealing how ideas, prayers, songs, and certain theological teachings anchored action. The theology developed over previous years was lived out in unapologetic and even confrontational ways. From attending mass meetings in churches that were later burned, to enduring horrific weeks of imprisonment, to singing hymns over the sound of police sirens, the community of black faithful in Americus joined the national struggle for freedom. Chapter 5 discusses the quiet but steely resistance of many white Southerners to the changes of the 1960s. Though much of the opposition to the civil rights movement gradually turned away from acerbic public pronouncements, overt violence, and explicit racism, it nevertheless regrouped, condemning the immorality of the movement, ostracizing dissenters, and abandoning public schools for private Christian ones. Many white Southerners changed their tactics but preserved the conservative theology that had buttressed racial oppression. Chapter 6 explores religious positions in direct conflict through the kneel-in effort in which activists attempted to integrate Americus's white churches. Kneel-ins confronted Christian segregationism directly, sparking a theological crisis over the meaning of Christian orthodoxy that rippled outward from Americus. The conclusion wrestles with questions about the significance of the theological battles of the 1960s and their enduring political and religious consequences for Americus, for Georgia, and for the nation.

THE CIVIL RIGHTS STRUGGLE brought remarkable change in the United States; it also laid the social, cultural, and theological groundwork for ongoing battles over race and religion. The fights over school vouchers, over nuns distributing contraception, over abortion and welfare, *Obergefell v. Hodges* and Black Lives Matter, have roots in the tumultuous 1960s. And, just as the civil rights era cannot be properly understood without an examination and consideration of the role of lived theology, neither can the decades that follow. By interrogating the theological contestations inherent and apparent, *God with Us* contributes to accounts of both the civil rights movement and white resistance to it, lending understanding to the befuddling, persistent intersections between race and religion. The story of Americus, Georgia, is above all an investigation of how conflicts over orthodoxy occur in communities, how "ordinary southern towns become theatres of complex theological drama."[38] It is to that drama that we now turn.

Part I

CHAPTER ONE

Demonstration Plot for the Kingdom
The Radical Orthodoxy of Koinonia Farm

When time began, the Idea already was. The Idea was at home with God, and the Idea and God were one. . . . In him was life, and the life was humanity's light. And the light shines on in the darkness, and the darkness never quenched it. . . . Well the Idea became a man and moved in with us. We looked him in the face—the face of an only son whose father is full of kindness and integrity.

—Clarence Jordan, "The Idea Made Flesh," 1969

Sumter County . . . could have gone down as the most glorious little county in all the world. It could have stood out as a shining light to the rest of the nation— for freedom, for truth, for justice.

—Meeting with Concerned Citizens, May 25, 1957

The Southern sun blazed down on the two men making their way across the scrubby soil of Southwest Georgia. It bore fiery witness as one man bent down, put his hands to the earth, grasped a handful, and let the parched dirt slide through his calloused fingertips. With a peaceful, sly smile, he turned to his friend and declared: "This is it."[1]

The man was Clarence Jordan, a Southern Baptist minister, farmer, native Georgian, and radical visionary. The place was 440 barren acres eight miles southwest of Americus, a small city in Sumter County. No one looking at the forgotten and dusty expanse of earth would have bet on Eden flourishing there. But it was a different sort of Eden that Jordan and his friend, Martin England, were pursuing.

Unable to resolve the teachings of Jesus Christ with the social customs of the time, Jordan and England sought to create a place where the doctrines of Christianity could be enjoyed in purity. They would call their theological experiment Koinonia Farm.[2] Koinonia means *fellowship* or *communion* in Greek, marking the farm as a space where a community could live and work out their beliefs about the Fatherhood of God, brotherhood of man, dignity of work, and fellowship of the Spirit together. As one Koinonia observer put it, "the ideas of the new Testament either had to be rejected or incarnated."[3] Koinonia was to be this Incarnation.

Established as a "demonstration plot for the Kingdom of God" in 1942, Koinonia imagined itself as an embodiment of Christian theology. Deriving its purpose from the New Testament gospel of Jesus, Koinonia would be characterized by unity, generosity, service, and love. In this place where the land would be redeemed, and barren places made fruitful, racial and economic barriers would be broken down too. As Martin England expressed it, "the Christian religion can reconcile differences between people of different race, class, and economic opportunity."[4] By its very existence, Koinonia would expose the hypocrisy of Southern Christians, speaking as they did of love and brotherhood while cruelly oppressing black people.

The Koinonians, as they were called, believed that, in their communal life on those acres of Georgia land, they could manifest their faith in Christ. Clarence and Florence Jordan, Martin and Mabel England, and the others who would come to live at the farm "were unified," historian Dallas Lee has written, "around the idea that the koinonia—the fellowship of believers—was the continuation in history of the incarnation, of the life and death and resurrection of Jesus."[5] The Word was made flesh; theology living and lived. Though often derided as radical, the Koinonians insisted that they practiced orthodox, biblical, even Baptist, doctrine, and that any radicalism belonged to Christ, not to them.[6] The presence of Koinonia Farm, the teachings of its founder, Clarence Jordan, its theology of radical orthodoxy, and its history in Sumter County reveal that Christian principles and race relations had been intertwined long before the demonstrations, mass meetings, and kneel-ins. Before the civil rights movement arrived in Americus, Koinonia Farm did; it was a prophetic "voice in the wilderness" in the segregated South. It was a voice that would be misunderstood and suppressed, at times heard only by the sun high above.

Clarence Jordan, a Prophet in Blue Jeans

Clarence Jordan, "tall, high-hipped, hands jammed into blue jean pockets, floppy straw hat shading a grin—dusty from the peanut rows, bespectacled from persistent study," was, in the words of Dallas Lee, a man "full of the unexpected." A walking paradox, Jordan was "a gentle man who thundered," a homegrown son who took on the established tradition, a faithful Baptist hated by many of his fellow churchgoers, "a nonviolent man who was known to have stared down a Ku Kluxer or two," an unassuming servant who believed God could use him to change the world.[7] In this one man, a traditional Southern upbringing collided with radical encounter with Jesus Christ. He was a "prophet in overalls" who sought to preserve the South's land and change its customs, committed to loving his neighbors but also just as committed to confronting them with the truth.[8]

Jordan was born on July 29, 1912, in the small town of Talbotton, Georgia, fifty-five miles northwest of Americus. His father was an "intense, puritanical" banker who founded the Bank of Talbotton as well as the Talbotton general store, working to ensure that his family enjoyed relative prosperity and privilege. The seventh of ten children, Jordan enjoyed a full, social childhood, while displaying a certain reticence, seriousness, and independence from a young age. Although he played sports and participated in school events, Jordan also spent hours by himself playing the piano, talking with his mother, and practicing typing on his father's typewriter. Clarence developed a predilection for verbal sparring with his family and friends, choosing some matter to argue for hours. His brother Frank branded the contentious Clarence "Grump," a nickname that endured throughout his childhood.[9]

Like many Southerners, the family attended the local Baptist Church faithfully. The church served as a social gathering place: the location of barbecues, picnics, choir rehearsals, and holiday celebrations. The Baptist Church also represented a place of dogmatic religious and moral instruction. Sunday school lessons, prayer meetings, stern sermons, and steamy nights at summer tent revivals—these traditional elements of Southern Baptist faithfulness marked Clarence's upbringing in Talbotton.[10]

But even in a culture where the tenets of the Baptist Church were as undisputed as the notion that chicken ought to be fried, the contrarian Clarence had moments of questioning. As a small child in church he had frequently sung the familiar melody: "*Jesus loves the little children / All the children of the world / Red and yellow, black and white, they are precious in His sight / Jesus loves the little children of the world.*"[11] "The question arose in my mind," Clarence recalled, years later, "'were the little black children precious in God's sight just like the little white children?' The song said they were. Why were they always so ragged, so dirty and hungry? Did God have favorite children?" While admitting he "could not figure out the answers to these puzzling questions" at the time, Clarence nevertheless stated that from a young age, he "knew something was wrong."[12]

Another moment occurred a few years later, when Clarence was twelve. The Talbot County Jail sat close to the Jordans' house, and Clarence would often veer past it on his way home from school. Stopping to observe the convicts on the chain gang, he felt simultaneously repulsed and enamored by their sinewy muscles, their profane language, the mystery of their punished lives. Almost all of them were black. Peering behind the barbed wire fences, Clarence watched men with chains binding their ankles, men whose spirits were worn down under shame and mistreatment, men whose bodies were scarred by the lash and bruised by the awful strain of the "stretcher," a primitive torture device.[13] So frequent were Clarence's visits to the jail that he developed friendships with the men and even received cornbread from the jail's cook on occasion. He knew their names, their faces, and their voices.[14]

One swampy night in August, Clarence and his family attended a religious revival in Talbotton, singing hymns and praying for the Holy Spirit's presence to enliven their hearts and shine through in their lives. The warden of the jail, Mr. MacDonald, participated, singing bass in the choir and becoming particularly "carried away" during a rendition of the song "Love Lifted Me."[15] With tears welling up in his eyes and his face contorted with feeling, MacDonald bellowed, "*Love Lifted Me! / Love Lifted Me! / When nothing else could help / Love Lifted Me! / . . . Love so mighty and so true, merits my soul's best song / Faithful, loving service, too, to Him belong.*" Lying in bed that night, the hymn still ringing in his ears, Clarence's sleepy reverie was interrupted by screaming. The "agonizing groans" persisted for what seemed an eternity, as a horrified Clarence lay awake in the darkness, listening intently. "I was sure I could recognize who it was, and I was sure I knew what was happening," Clarence remembered. "I knew not only who was in the stretcher, but who was pulling the rope"—Mr. MacDonald. Identifying with the tortured prisoner, Clarence burned with anger toward the warden who, only hours earlier, had proclaimed God's mercy and vowed his own loving service. "I got really mad with God," Clarence recalled, deciding, "if He [God] was love and the warden was an example of it, I didn't want anything to do with it."[16] This and other incongruities between the character of God and the reality of life in the Jim Crow South began to trouble a young Clarence, though he never mentioned this experience or revealed his growing disillusionment to his family. Rather, as Lee described, "It remained a secret, stuffed into the chemistry of his body and soul, where guilt abides, where fear is rooted, and where conviction slowly matures to action."[17]

Clarence Jordan decided to become a farmer and use the skills acquired to strike a blow against the sharecropping system. He hoped to equip black farmers with the knowledge they needed to maintain successful farms and lift themselves from poverty. With these hopes, Jordan left Talbotton in 1929 and enrolled at the Georgia State College of Agriculture at the University of Georgia (UGA) in Athens. At UGA, Clarence shed his more antisocial tendencies and embraced college life. His siblings noticed the change, and they ribbed him for it. "Still averaging seven dates a week with those debutantes?" his sister Cornelia wrote in one letter. Another warned against too much "popularity with the fairer sex." "You don't know how popular 'Grump' is until you follow him around awhile," Clarence's brother George remarked in a letter to their mother.

In addition to dating and studying, Clarence pledged a fraternity, served in the Officer's training reserves, wrote for the college's agricultural newspaper, and participated in the debate team, drama club, band, and the YMCA. He also joined and eventually led the Baptist Young People's Union, and he attended Sunday school at the local First Baptist Church.[18] For a while, his social activities and academic work overshadowed the persistent racial and religious questions of his youth. But by his senior year, Clarence's passion for farming was tempered by a mounting suspicion that agricultural know-how would not be enough to address the real issues behind the South's inequality. "Whites seemed to have the very things I wanted blacks to have," Jordan mused, "and the whites were living in such a hell. Why should I feel that blacks would be in any less of a hell if they had these things?" He concluded, "There had to be something extra somewhere." He began to seek out "spiritual resources," and soon "felt a call to the ministry." In 1933, Jordan enrolled at Southern Baptist Theological Seminary in Louisville, Kentucky.[19]

The lanky country boy initially felt out of place in such a "northern metropolis," but Clarence soon adjusted and threw himself into his studies. "I thought the work at the University was pretty hard but now I see it was only child's play compared to what it is up here," Clarence wrote to his mother in 1933, "Hebrew alone requires almost as much time as did all my subjects at Georgia, to say nothing of Greek, Biblical Interpretation, Old Testament, New Testament, Sociology and Music." In addition to theological study, Clarence served at several local churches, learning the skills of pastoral ministry and honing his preaching.[20]

Clarence's increased workload had somewhat distracted him from the romantic pursuits of his Georgia days. But one day Clarence visited the campus library and noticed among the volumes, a lovely young woman with blond hair and piercing blue eyes. Smitten, Clarence returned to the library again and again, studying the library assistant, Florence Kroeger, as much as the books. Florence was bright and opinionated, willing to speak her mind and to defend her point of view.[21] Unconcerned with traditional domesticity, she was open to an unconventional, adventurous life. Clarence and Florence dated throughout Clarence's three-year tenure in Louisville and celebrated their engagement in the spring of 1936.[22] They married in July of that year, with the consent of her German-American family.[23]

After completing his M. Div., Clarence opted to remain in Louisville, where he continued his studies of the Greek New Testament in a Ph.D. program.

Interpreting the language could be tedious, but Clarence had an insatiable desire to understand Christianity without the intervention of translation, denomination, or tradition.[24] The Jesus he had learned about in Sunday school, Clarence discovered, was a mere shadow compared to the figure he now confronted—human, confrontational, controversial, relational, sorrowful, joyful. "I had thrown Jesus out because of Mr. Mac," he later reflected, but "Mr. Mac didn't really represent Jesus. I looked at the New Testament and it read differently than before."[25] In the person and teachings of Jesus, the issues that had so troubled Clarence as a Baptist boy in the segregated South were resolved. This close reading of the Greek New Testament not only led Clarence to "discover theological foundations for the human impulses already alive in him," but it also propelled him to consider the application of the gospel for life in the United States, particularly in regard to race relations.[26]

His racial reckoning deepened in January 1939, when Jordan got involved with a ministry called the Sunshine Center (soon renamed the Fellowship Center), in Louisville's impoverished and overcrowded West End.[27] He taught Sunday school, organized community events, collaborated with local black clergy, founded a cooperative store, and distributed donations.[28] At the Sunshine Center, Jordan became convinced of the necessity of meeting people's physical as well as spiritual needs and also of the importance of equality in interracial projects.[29] "The only way . . . constructive work, agreeable to both groups, can be done," Jordan wrote, is if white workers "understand that they are *helpers* rather than bosses and put on equal footing with the other workers."[30] While many liberal Protestants before him had adopted the Social Gospel and sought to reduce the effects of poverty and ignorance, Jordan, "unlike his Social Gospel forebears," focused predominately on the issue of "racial separation."[31] Jordan noted that in the New Testament the early church's fellowship extended to both Jews and Gentiles, since Christ's resurrection nullified distinctions between racial or ethnic groups. Historical Christianity could provide a foundation for improved race relations.

With this in mind, the Jordans began attending a black church in Louisville, much to the consternation of the white Baptist establishment. "Did not Jesus respect racial boundaries," the white Baptist minister railed, upon receiving the Jordans' membership transfer request, "and did not Paul maintain that he was a Hebrew of Hebrews?" He added, irately, that "white Baptists" were paying Jordan's salary. With noticeable sarcasm and even bitterness, Clarence articulated the man's theological position: "It was unethical and unchristian to join a Negro church because it was a Christian principle to abstain from meat if it caused your brother to stumble, and surely this would cause many to stumble."

"I guess it is also a Christian principle," he continued, "to tear out of the New Testament all those pages which proclaim the universality of Christian brotherhood and which so terribly upset our complacent social traditions."[32] Clarence's racial theology did indeed upset the social traditions of Southern Seminary. During the spring of 1938, Clarence invited some seminarians from Simmons University, the historically black seminary in town, to lead a prayer meeting at Southern.[33] Typically, after these prayer meetings, visitors ate in the dormitory; Jordan assumed this hospitality extended to the black seminarians. However, days before the meeting was to occur, he was informed that some of the seminary's board members, including Florence's boss, were outraged by the thought of blacks and whites eating together. To spare the black seminarians humiliation, Clarence and Florence invited them to eat in their apartment.[34] Incidents like these exasperated Jordan, as he continued to wrestle with the principles of the New Testament and the unwritten laws of the South.

During his work with the Fellowship Center, Clarence learned that many black families in Louisville had relocated from Georgia and Alabama.[35] Their urban plight was the result of their rural one, he realized, as the suffocating oppression of sharecropping drove people to cramped cities in search of industrial work. "The city was grinding them up," he later recalled, and "it drove me to get back to the areas that were vomiting these people up and see if we couldn't reverse the trend from the farms to the city."[36] Clarence's passion for improved race relations was beginning to converge with his training in agriculture.

It was at this point that Clarence began to challenge not only racism but also materialism. Jordan discovered, particularly in his study of the book of Acts, a strong correlation between shared belief and shared possessions. He read that in the early church "no one said that any of the things that belonged to him was his own, but they had everything in common"; that the sharing of material possessions stemmed from the sharing of faith, that "those who believed were of one heart and soul." Biblically, Jordan reasoned, Christian charity should not be formulated as paternalistic righteousness that gave extra to the poor, but as the result of a total sacrifice of life to Jesus and natural sharing of all things in grace. Though in nascent form in the 1930s, Jordan's theology of shared belief and shared possessions would flourish in the rocky red soil of Koinonia.[37]

Rebelling against certain Southern Baptist traditions, Jordan pursued an older, more authentic, more orthodox Christianity. He boldly claimed he had no desire to worship God "at the shrine of our ancestors nor of Southern traditions" but, rather, in "spirit and truth."[38] By extricating the red letters of Jesus from the cross-stitched platitudes of Southern living room decor, Jordan understood them with all their powerful, uncomfortable implications. He condemned many of his peers in seminary and in the Southern Baptist church as evincing a "fervent profession of faith in Christianity on the one hand and just as fervent refusal to practice it on the other."[39] Jesus had been so "zealously worshipped, his deity so vehemently affirmed, his halo so brightly illuminated, and his cross so beautifully polished" that, Jordan claimed, he "no longer exist[ed] as a man." He had, rather, been transformed into "an exquisite celestial being" who came to humanity "momentarily and mistakenly" and then promptly ascended back into heaven. In short, Jordan accused the church of "harp[ing] on the deity of Christ in order to get rid of him" because "the church can't face him as a man because they are afraid of what kind of man he might be."[40] "By thus glorifying him," Jordan concluded, "we more effectively rid ourselves of him than did those who tried to do so by crudely crucifying him."[41] Separating Jesus from the flesh of humanity rendered him irrelevant in human relations. Instead of glorifying Christ into irrelevancy like many of his white Baptist peers, Jordan sought instead to encounter the divine man Jesus in all his biblical radicalism.

Following Clarence's graduation, the Jordans remained in Louisville, where Clarence formed a group of students who met regularly to discuss his ideas. "I think back to those mornings, gathered around the table in that huge old house in the middle of the slums when he taught us," one student remembered, adding, Clarence "opened eyes too long naive."[42] After several months, the students began to call themselves a koinonia. Though the group was small and the students busy with their classes, Clarence imagined that it could embody his theology, especially regarding nonviolence, racial reconciliation, and the common possession of wealth. During these months of the student koinonia fellowship, Clarence revealed his dream of creating an agricultural community in the South that would address poverty, deprivation, and racism.

That dream would soon become a reality. One of Clarence's former professors, Walt Johnson, published a newsletter, which he circulated among former students. In one of these newsletters, Johnson published a letter from a missionary on furlough from Burma by the name of Martin England. Along with his thoughts on the fundamental incompatibility between racial discrimination and Christianity, England proposed a solution. "Suppose there were some Christian employees and employers, whites and Negroes, farmers and merchants, illiterates and school teachers," England offered, "who were willing to enter into fellowship to make a test of the power of the spirit of God in eliminating the natural and artificial barriers that exist." Jordan immediately wrote to England: "We have to talk." These two Southerners and Southern

Baptist ministers shared a desire to see an interracial Christian farming community in the South. Jordan's clarity and his certainty were appealing to England, whereas the more introspective, measured, and experienced England was a good match for Jordan as well. With much planning and plotting and praying and without much money (they had about $57.13 when they initially pooled their savings), they envisioned the agricultural community as the embodiment of their shared theology. Soon enough, during one of these discussions, Jordan turned to England and said, with a mischievous grin, "Well, what are we waiting for?"[43]

So, in 1942, Jordan and England began to search for a place in the rural South to farm, live, and worship in interracial, intentional Christian community.[44] Though they had initially decided to pursue properties in Alabama, as it was "fairly typical of the entire South," at the last moment, Clarence's brother suggested a piece of land not terribly far from the Alabama line in Sumter County, Georgia. The 440 ordinary-looking acres of soil were "slightly eroded and virtually treeless," save for one sad pecan seedling. Even so, as soon as Jordan and England set foot on the dry expanse, they knew they had found their "demonstration plot."[45]

The Lived Theology of Koinonia Farm

From the moment they purchased the land in 1942, Jordan and England imagined Koinonia Farm as an incarnation of their beliefs. "The purposes of the farm," they stated in their initial newsletter, were to relate "the entire life of the people to Jesus Christ and his teachings," "to seek to conserve the soil, which we believe to be God's holy earth," and to "undertake to train Negro preachers in religion and agriculture" as they studied and worked together. These three stated goals—community, farming, and racial reconciliation—characterized the farm; each expressed a facet of the Koinonians' lived theology.

The first theological principle adopted by Koinonia Farm was that of *redemptive agriculture*. Koinonia shared with a number of organizations and New Deal programs the belief that improving economic and social life in the South hinged upon farming.[46] But Koinonia also possessed "an interest in the spiritual side of life."[47] Combining his theological and agricultural training, Jordan maintained that farming, "the enrichment and preservation of the soil—for the sake of the soil itself," amounted to participation in the restoration of creation.[48] Creation, the Koinonians thought, was intended to produce an abundance that would provide for people, and humanity was to have dominion over the earth. But man had fallen, and the world was broken—not just a vague spiritual brokenness, but a physical brokenness bringing famine, disease, barrenness, and blight. Work was hard and at times the soil returned only thorns and thistles.[49] Nevertheless, the Koinonians believed that Christians were called to rebuild the broken creation, empowered by God's spirit. As they tilled the soil, planted pecan trees, harvested crops, and sweated underneath the big Georgia sky, the Koinonians envisioned their work contributing not just to prosperity for their farm and community, but to the restoration of a fallen world.

The second theological premise was that of *Christian community*. The Koinonians strove to "embody the spirit of Jesus through a life together." As Jordan wrote, "Christ apart from his Church is the Word apart from the flesh. The two belong together. We thereby make our surrender to Christ a concrete, objective act by turning over everything, including ourselves, to his church-community, or koinonia." They followed the early church, undertaking a "surrender of self, vocation, possessions—everything" in order to live a common life unto God. But unlike restorationist groups, which completely mimicked the early church, the Koinonians accepted that their community was shaped by the context of the twentieth-century American South.[50]

Instead of pursuing the gleaming riches of the postwar economy or the suburban dream of nuclear families cocooned inside white picket fences, the Koinonians worked the land and lived in modest wooden cabins. Speaking of the dangers of greed and what Jordan later called "the worship of mammon," he said, "America has become so success-conscious, so status-conscious, so materialistic! We tend to measure success in terms of possessions. This," he lamented, "just devastates us." In contrast, the incarnational theology of Koinonia rejected the pursuit of material wealth and individual accolades. Though they would vehemently deny that they were communists, the Koinonians did advocate material parity and even redistribution unto that end. As Jordan reasoned, "If you're taking more than your share, somebody is left with less than his share" and likely "terribly exploited." Material equality was "the Christian spirit" in which possessions were rendered not to the state, but to God and each other. "A person who is deeply satisfied at the spiritual level and has learned the deeper secrets of life," Jordan explained, "can be happy with relatively few things." Communal sharing stemmed from spiritual joy; social arrangements derived primarily from theological commitments.[51]

The third theological aspect crucial to Koinonia Farm was *racial reconciliation*. Central to the Koinonians' doctrine was the idea that redemption in Christ meant being adopted by God as sons and co-heirs with Christ.[52] Therefore the Koinonians determined to "joyfully accept as a brother anyone whom the Father begets as a son."[53] The Koinonia community was a "family," "brothers and sisters of all variations," where all God had called were accepted as "sons and daughters of the same Father.[54] In God's family, there existed "no favorite children, whether they are blonds or brunettes, white or black."[55] The Koinonians believed that their Christian faith ruled over and above the man-made racial hierarchies of the South. "They weren't concerned with segregation or integration as such," one journalist commented, "only the Fatherhood of God and the brotherhood of man."[56] Coretta Scott King understood this theological basis for interracialism, writing after Jordan's death: "Clarence Jordan [and Koinonia Farm] had the courage to prove men and women of different races could not only work together, but live together in peace and harmony," an "example of brotherhood at work."[57] As Alma Jackson, a black man who worked at Koinonia for years, remembered: "Koinonia paid the best wages around for picking peanuts and sweet potatoes. 'And you didn't have to say 'yes sir' and 'no ma'am' and all that. We could sit down at the table and eat with them. We were one family out here."[58] This idea, embodied by the Koinonians and articulated by Alma Jackson, was both theologically orthodox and socially radical. While most Southern Protestants would have conceded that all Christians belonged to the family of God in theory, they were often unwilling to live out that theology in practice.

The doctrine of adoption into God's family was not the only theological premise that inspired the Koinonians' stance on race. They also believed that all distinctions between people collapsed once the holy God reconciled sinful humanity to himself through the incarnation, crucifixion, and resurrection of Christ. Integration was not just a familial requirement, but, as Jordan put it, a celebration of "that great fact that in Jesus Christ the 'middle wall of partition' was abolished." If God had removed the barriers between himself and his people, the people should have no divisions amongst themselves; God "allow[ed] no partition walls which divide men into race, caste, or nation." "[Jesus] integrated us and abolished the segregation patterns which cause so much hostility," Jordan wrote, such that, "by his sacrifice on the cross he joined together both sides into one body for God . . . hostility no longer exists." This racial radicalism stemmed from theological orthodoxy. "Being Christians, orthodox Baptist preachers, and native-born white Southerners," Jordan claimed, "we feel that at least we have the prerequisites to proclaim to the South the message of Jesus. We also believe that if Mr. Lincoln can give the Negro the right to go to the polls and vote, surely the Lord Jesus can break up a system that denies him the right to go to the table and eat." Reconciliation was to be first to God, through faith in Christ, and then to one another, as adopted brothers and sisters regardless of race.[59]

In practicing *redemptive agriculture, Christian community,* and *racial reconciliation,* Koinonia Farm sought to embody Christ, to be an incarnation of his likeness, presence, and Spirit, on those dusty 440 acres in southwest Georgia. They were living their theology, "devoted to the proclamation of Jesus Christ and the application of his teaching."[60]

The theological experiment began haltingly. The Jordans and Englands moved onto the farm Christmas of 1942, and for months, Clarence and Martin sweated and toiled, planning the farm, planting trees, and repairing the dilapidated property. They raised the first building, affectionately dubbed the Treehouse, in the summer of 1943.[61] Though the Englands left to go back overseas, more people arrived, including Christian missionaries, ministers, and conscientious objectors.[62] One of these was a Midwesterner named Con Browne, who, after suffering in military service and becoming a Baptist minister, sought to practice Christian pacifism. He and his wife, Ora, were overjoyed to have found a group of like-minded Christians, though, by Con's own admission, he had little experience either in agriculture or the South. "I was a real tenderfoot, slight and bespectacled," Con laughed, admitting, "I could barely cut a lawn." He joked, "I'm sure Clarence heaved a sigh of relief when we came."[63] But Clarence probably did.

His experiment in lived theology was growing. By the time the farm was ready, there were eight people willing to formally constitute the koinonia: Clarence and Florence Jordan, Howard and Marion Johnson, Gilbert Butler, Con and Ora Browne, and Norman Lory. These original eight pledged their "total unconditional commitment to seek, express and expand the Kingdom of God as revealed in Jesus Christ," as they "joyfully enter[ed] into a love union with the Koinonia" and "gladly submit[ed]" themselves to it.[64]

Over the next ten years, more were drawn to Koinonia by Clarence's message of community, pacifism, and racial equality. The farm tended to attract unique Christians like Margaret and Will Wittkamper. Will, an intelligent, serious farm boy from central Indiana, had been sentenced to a Kentucky work camp for being a conscientious objector during World War I. Upon his release at the war's end, Will attended a Disciples of Christ seminary where he refined his radical religious ideals. Conceding that others viewed him as "a queer fellow, a freak, and perhaps a fool," he stood his ground: "I am sorry but my religion stands above all to me." Will's wife, Margaret, possessed the same theological conviction. Raised in Virginia, she was a pretty, friendly blond who sold Avon products and loved children, but maintained staunch religious convictions regarding war and racial equality. She met Will while working for the Fellowship of Reconciliation in Texas, and the two soon married and had several sons. But the Wittkampers did not really feel at home in Texas, Colorado, or Louisiana, where they moved after being pushed out by "disapproving parishioners" who tired of Will's message of peace and equality. Not until they arrived at Koinonia did they feel at home. Journalist Jim Auchmutey aptly described Koinonia as "a large, extended family of religious dissidents and misfits."[65]

Koinonia members built and inhabited small wooden cabins on the property, sometimes sharing these humble lodgings among several families. They took turns cooking and ate most of their meals together in a common area. They met together daily for prayer and worship meetings, with Clarence often leading, but with everyone sharing testimonies and devotionals. Meetings to discuss farm and communal governance occurred frequently, as members voted on how money should be allocated and spent.[66] The Koinonians also worked diligently—farming, building, cooking, cleaning—often dividing tasks by gender.[67] A schedule from December 21, 1949, reveals the Koinonia daily routine: "6 A.M.: rising bell, 6:15–6:45: devotional, 8:15–11:45: work ["field work, cattle, poultry, building and maintenance, household work, and cultural"], 11:45–1:00: dinner, 1:00–4:30: work, 4:30–5:30: chores, and 6:00–7:00: supper."[68] After supper, there was usually free time to read, socialize, sing, and relax, though some nights the members conducted business meetings during that time. The Koinonians worked together, ate together, worshiped and prayed together. They also experienced conflict and forgiveness.[69] There were certainly tense moments as individual expectations collided with the decisions of the group, but there were also easier moments of staying up late discussing nonviolence and eating popcorn. It was, to quote Dietrich Bonhoeffer, simply "life together."[70]

In the late 1940s and early 1950s, the Koinonia experiment thrived. Young people visited the farm in droves, with many opting to stay.[71] In the early 1950s, for instance, Claud and Billie Nelson found themselves captivated by Koinonia's theological vision and decided to live there. "Our going to Koinonia Farm boils down to this," Claud wrote, "if we believe in the Kingdom of God as taught and lived by Jesus Christ. . . . We must make a definite attempt to realize the 'kingdom'—that is, to practice love as a way of life." He continued, "We must relate everything we do—life, work, play, fellowship—to what we believe."[72]

Con Browne estimated that during these years the farm welcomed around 8,000–10,000 visitors annually. With the extra hands, Koinonia was able to

Clarence Jordan and Bo Johnson at Koinonia Farm.
(Photographer unknown; courtesy of Koinonia Farm)

expand its operations, raising poultry, peanuts, and pecans. The farm functioned well, and the soil, treated with care and diligence, began to produce. The Koinonians purposefully planted more fruits and vegetables than they could consume, enabling them to share the excess with their poorer neighbors. They even came up with the idea of a "cow library" in which they would rent out cows to other Sumter County farmers. When the cows were all milked out, they could trade them in for fresh ones. When Clarence realized that the local hens were underproducing eggs, he researched the issue, introduced a new breed of hen, and shared the excess eggs. At a local co-op, they sold them in egg cartons that spread Koinonia's vision, symbolized by a white hand and a black hand clasped across the rippled cardboard.[73]

Most of Koinonia's neighbors were poor blacks who lived outside the Americus city limits, and they were intrigued and understandably puzzled at the experiment in Christian living on their doorstep. One such man was a former sharecropper who quickly joined Clarence and Martin as a farmhand. The three men worked side by side and even ate their meals together. Seeing that blacks were treated with unheard-of dignity, more and more black neighbors began to participate in life at Koinonia, where they could interact with whites without fear. The farm taught agriculture classes and conducted a Vacation Bible school and Sunday school for black and white locals. In the mid-1950s, one black family came to live at Koinonia. Rufus and Sue Angry lived five miles from the farm where they worked as sharecroppers. After hearing about the farm through their older boys who went over occasionally, the Angrys were intrigued. They began visiting Koinonia, and "after much soul searching, and much prayer and meditation," decided to live there. "The more we learned about the group," Sue Angry recalled, "the more we liked the way of life that the group was living." Rufus farmed with the men; Sue raised the children, worked grading eggs from the henhouse, and ran the farm's local consignment shop. Living at Koinonia, "you learn what it means to be a human being," Sue stated. "You learn to see the other person as you do yourself. You see God in everyone."[74] The farm also welcomed many black neighbors, like Collins McGee and Alma Jackson, into their fellowship more informally through its service, activities, and programs.

The most ambitious of these community programs was Camp Koinonia, begun in 1955. Usually held during the summer months following the harvest, Camp Koinonia brought together around eighty children, black and white, for a week of Bible study, craft time, singing, camping, and fellowship.[75] News of Camp Koinonia spread, with one woman writing from Orangeburg, South Carolina, that she had heard about the camp from a man at Morehouse College and wanted her eight-year-old daughter to attend for several weeks.[76] In order to get the children to the farm, Koinonians drove around in the early morning and evening, picking up and dropping off the children. They did the same thing not only for Vacation Bible School but also for public school during the year. In the absence of adequate transportation for black children, the Koinonians began to transport the children to and from school each day.[77] In hopes of fostering natural relationships, Koinonia also held interracial social events. People of all races and backgrounds came together to play sports and enjoy themselves at dances and parties at the farm, where the stifling barriers of Jim Crow did not trump the mandates of Jesus Christ. This was not merely a time to have fun and let loose; it was also a demonstration of equality, joviality, and familiarity within the family of God. This interracial fellowship and service was the vision of Koinonia. But not everyone liked it. As Martin England remembered, it "was something that just wasn't done in Southwest Georgia. [It] was slapping all the good white Southern traditions in the face. For a farmer to mess up his truck taking nigger children to a nigger school was just too much."[78]

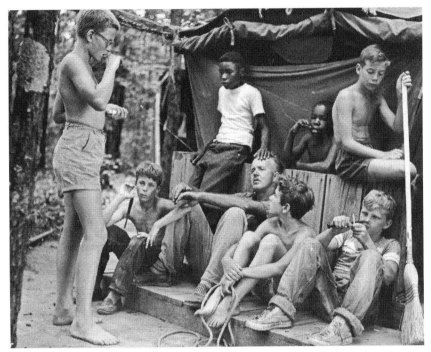

Integrated group at Camp Koinonia, Monteagle, Tennessee, 1956. (Photographer: Ida Berman; Koinonia Farm Photographs, MS 3049, Hargrett Rare Book and Manuscript Library, University of Georgia Libraries; courtesy of Karen Berman)

Radical Orthodoxy as Southern Heresy

From the beginning, Koinonia had rankled its neighbors in Americus. One evening headlights broke through the twilight, and several "utterly menacing" men stepped from a car. "We understand you been taking your meals with the niggers," a gruff voice pronounced, "We're from the Ku Klux Klan, and we're here to tell you we don't allow the sun to set on anybody who eats with niggers." Unfazed, Clarence reached forward and grasped the hand of the hostile Klansman. "I'm a Baptist preacher, just graduated from the Southern Baptist Seminary," he began, with a mischievous smile, "I've heard about people who had power over the sun, but I never hoped to meet one." Stunned and bemused, the Klansman replied that his father had also been a Southern Baptist preacher. The men then stood there, talking about being Baptist, farming, and life in the South, as the sun set over the expanse of farmland behind them. In those early days, segregationist anger could still be dispelled with a little good humor and appeals to old-time religion.[79]

Occasional visits from Klansmen aside, during the early years of the farm, the people of Americus largely dismissed the Koinonians as inconsequential crazies.[80] That dramatically changed in 1954. Following the landmark *Brown vs. Board of Education* ruling and the subsequent mobilization of massive resistance, any racial leniency was interpreted as a threat.[81] No longer a quaint Christian experiment, Koinonia was seen as a radical, subversive, un-Christian display of Southern heresy. These pacifists were refashioned as a dangerous group attempting to overthrow the social order. In some ways this was correct; the Koinonians *were* trying to overthrow the old order of things as they sought to usher in "the kingdom of God." Their theology of radical orthodoxy demanded racial equality, and it framed race as an inherently religious issue. For this reason, Koinonia's opponents desperately tried to discredit their Christianity as insincere. When that proved largely unsuccessful, they resorted to intimidation and violence. In the words of one Americus resident, Koinonia Farm "caught holy hell."[82] Even so, the presence of Koinonia Farm forced people to grapple with race as a theological issue, as well as a social, cultural, and political one.

Things would soon worsen. In 1956, anger flared when Clarence Jordan offered to "vouch for the moral character" of two young black students, Thelma B. Boone and Edward J. Clemons, who sought to enroll in the business school at the University of Georgia.[83] Jordan provided Boone and Clemons with the alumni endorsement required for applications, and even traveled with them to Athens.[84] Though this integration attempt did not succeed, Jordan's involvement earned him and Koinonia condemnation. When the *Americus Times-Recorder* ran a story under the headline, "Negroes Fail in Attempt to Enroll at Ga. College, Endorsed by Americus Man-White Minister Resident of Koinonia Farms," any hope of peaceful relations with their South Georgia neighbors dissipated.[85] At a local States' Rights Council meeting, Sumter County Solicitor General Charles Burgamy mused, "what we need now is for the right kind of Klan to start up again and use a buggy whip on some of these race mixers. I believe that would stop them."[86] Jordan himself reported that the White Citizens' Council called the farm "a cancer that would have to be cut out."[87] Georgia Representative Paul Jones said that the very existence of Koinonia Farm "seems to weaken [Georgia's] whole stand on segregation," adding, "something ought to be done about it."[88] Georgia governor Marvin Griffin even contacted the local sheriff in Americus to inquire who "this Jordan fellow was."[89] With racial tensions rising in Americus and throughout the state, segregationists hunted for a scapegoat. Koinonia gave them one.

Suddenly, Koinonia Farm epitomized, as one writer put it, "everything in the world that is foul, un-Southern and subversive."[90] Their theologically based integrationism was swiftly recast as a communist ploy or at least "damn sure suspect."[91] In this period, the mere accusation of association with anything Red became a scarlet letter of guilt.[92] The Georgia attorney general, Eugene Cook, alleged that Koinonia was known to have welcomed and harbored communists, promoted subversion, and possibly planned to overthrow the government.[93] A formal investigation in 1957 became "an excuse to look into every nook and cranny of Koinonia," culminating in a subpoena of Koinonia before the Georgia Grand Jury in the case *State of Georgia vs. C. Conrad Browne*.[94]

C. Conrad, or Con, Browne had been a resident of Koinonia since 1949, and he was in charge of the farm's interracial summer camp, which is probably the reason charges fixated on him. Though for years Camp Koinonia had seemed merely a quaint exercise in paternalistic charity, in the post-*Brown* era, it represented a subversive attempt at racial mixing. The camp received numerous injunctions from Americus authorities in the summer of 1956, including one claiming the camp was "detrimental to morals" since it would "show live pigs being born" and be "nonsegregated on the basis of sexes." These injunctions, as intended, drastically delayed the camp's operations, prompting Browne to accept the Highlander Folk School's offer of "free use of their facilities" in Monteagle, Tennessee. Highlander's known communist ties provided ample reason for the investigation of Con and thus, of Koinonia.[95]

Throughout the proceedings, Clarence Jordan and others testified about the farm's activities, and tried to use the attention to highlight the spiritual nature of Koinonia and to profess its incarnational theology. As Jordan recollected, "I tried to explain to them the difference between Christ and Marx, but soon it became clear that they didn't know anything about either one of them." To a man who pointedly inquired if the Koinonians were communists, Jordan responded, "No, unless Jesus Christ was a communist—we follow His teachings." The Koinonians presented their records and answered all charges with factual and theological justifications. "I don't think a Christian is worth his salt who hasn't been called a Communist today," Clarence Jordan reflected, adding, "Trying to refute that epithet is about like running for your birth certificate when someone calls you a son of a bitch."[96]

Following a week of testimony, on April 5, 1957, the grand jury declined to indict. However, it did issue a sixteen-page report that painstakingly documented the unproven charges. These included fabricated claims that Koinonia owed tax money, knowingly harbored communists, kept blacks in a state of "brainwashed peonage," planned conspiracy against the government, and that its Christianity was "sheer window dressing and its practice of Christianity has no precedent in the religious annals of the United States." The grand jury even alleged that Jordan himself was a deceitful and immoral man. This unsubstantiated report was published in the local newspaper, the *Americus Times-Recorder*, sent to state officials, and passed on to the U.S. attorney general. Thus, many in Americus and beyond concluded that Koinonia was a suspect organization and that its racial views were inspired by communism, not Christianity. As the Georgia revenue commissioner opined, "We think [Koinonia] neither charitable nor religious. It's simply a move to integrate the races and I think it is a disgrace." George Mathews, the chairman of County Commissions, captured the prevailing sentiment, telling an editorial writer from the *Nation*: "That farm makes a lot more money than my farm does. They must be getting help from Washington. . . . Washington wants a yellow race, anyway. As to being a religious colony, they don't have no religion at all, and you can quote me on it. We got no room for people like them here, and we don't aim to have them around much longer." Though Mathews's statement was full of false allegations—Jordan was not from the North, the farm was not making any money, and it was certainly not supported by the federal government—the most striking was the assertion that Koinonia was not really a religious community. Koinonia's insistent rebuttals, and complaints that the report was "biased and unfair," fell on deaf ears.[97]

This small Christian community met unbridled hostility. Epithets were hurled out of car windows. Menacing phone calls interrupted farm life at all hours. Members were constantly pulled over and arrested. Con Browne began having nightmares, dreaming of laying his own slain child on the Sumter County courthouse steps. Pacifism in the face of terror had profound psychological effects.[98]

The terror had profound economic effects as well. Americus residents instituted a suffocating boycott. Mechanics refused to fix the Koinonians' equipment. Unable to get the hardware supplies needed, the cotton crop could neither be processed nor even harvested. No one would buy their produce or eggs any longer, and the 4,000 laying hens that could not be given away had to be butchered. The Koinonians could no longer purchase insurance on their farm equipment, and no one in the county would sell them fertilizer or other products. The bank abruptly canceled the Koinonians' checking account and refused to make further loans, despite consistent and timely payment of loans in the past.[99] Even those sympathetic to Koinonia were intimidated if they did business with the farm. As one supplier told Jordan, "Nothing personal, understand. It's strictly business. . . . I can't afford to lose my customers." When

Jordan appealed to Christian charity, the man replied that though he was a Baptist, "that's not the point here. . . . I just can't lose the business."[100] The butane gas dealer who refused to sell to the Koinonians confessed it made him feel "like [Pontius] Pilate," saying, "I just want to wash my hands and my soul."[101] The abandonment by former friends and neighbors was especially difficult. "I would rather face the frantic, childish mob, even with their shotguns and buggy whips," a devastated Jordan declared, "than the silent, insidious mob of good church people who give assent to boycott and subtle psychological warfare."[102]

The boycott continued from June 1956 through the early 1960s, bringing Koinonia to the brink of financial ruin. The community came to depend wholly on charitable donations from sympathetic supporters through their mail-order pecan business. "You can get rid of a man just as effectively by starving him as by shooting him," Jordan mused. "Good folk who wouldn't pull a trigger helped in the boycott," he continued, adding, "I'd rather be shot at."[103] He soon would be.[104]

To challenge the mores of Southern society so starkly was to invite not only intimidation, but also outright violence.[105] Vandalism, stealing crops, tearing down fences, tampering with signs, destroying farm equipment, and dumping trash on Koinonia's property became regular occurrences in the late 1950s. In one particularly senseless episode, vigilantes chopped down nearly 300 peach, apple, and pecan trees planted on Koinonia's property.[106] Klansmen burned crosses on the lawns of Koinonia's neighbors, in a largely successful attempt to scare people away from the farm.[107] One day, a procession of seventy or eighty cars slowly drove past the farm in a silent statement of malice.[108] Seeing the motorcade of cars approaching, a Koinonia woman innocently asked whose funeral it was. A Klansman chillingly responded, "It might very well be yours."[109] One antagonist fired bullets from a heavy caliber pistol at the roadside stand the Koinonians operated several miles from the farm. The stand would later be bombed several times, until the Koinonians abandoned it altogether, leaving its wreckage "as a monument to violence."[110]

Those who aided Koinonia faced violence as well. In May 1957, opponents of the farm bombed a feed store in downtown Americus for breaking the boycott.[111] Even the *Americus Times-Recorder*, a newspaper that rarely commented on social matters, issued a statement condemning the recent violence and calling for its immediate cessation.[112] "No one," the editor asserted, "could believe that such [violence] could happen in Americus, a city of peace-loving, church-going, cultured people."[113]

Perpetrators of violence soon aimed at the farm itself, where sixty men, women, and children lived.[114] Cars speeding down the rural highway in front of Koinonia regularly unleashed bullets into the community buildings as they passed by. In the last week of March 1957 alone, the farm endured three shooting incidents.[115] During a particularly dramatic episode, assailants fired into the bedroom of the Jordans' eldest daughter, Eleanor, with bullets ripping through an armchair where Clarence Jordan had been sitting moments before, before finally lodging themselves in a children's toy closet in the next room.[116] Later, some men opened gunfire in broad daylight while children played outdoors. "We were playing volleyball," Clifford Angry remembered, and "when the gunfire started, we hit the ground."[117]

Another drive-by shooting targeted farm visitors, including a man from Michigan. The next morning, as he left for Detroit, he asked if he should leave his hat, which now boasted a clean bullet hole, as evidence. "Take it with you," Clarence replied, as "evidence of warm Southern hospitality."[118] During her visit to the farm, Dorothy Day found her station wagon was "peppered with bullets."[119] After hearing of the violence, the eccentric Baptist minister and Southern dissident Will Campbell visited Koinonia in the late 1950s. Roaming around the farm with Clarence, he "picked up a few of the 30-caliber slugs" and then headed for Albany where he had naively made an appointment with the FBI to implore them to investigate the shootings, since "not every ordinary citizen owned a 30-caliber machine gun." Campbell suspected the weapons used to attack Koinonia were "borrowed" from the National Guard and Army Reserve units in Americus. The FBI disinterestedly claimed they had been shown "no evidence which would lead them to think there had been any violation of federal law."[120] The Koinonians would face the terror campaign with neither local nor federal protection.

Some children were sent away from the danger. The Jordans' oldest son went to live in another intentional community in South Dakota.[121] The Angrys, the black family living at Koinonia, were also forced to flee the violence. They moved to Hidden Springs, New Jersey, to try to start another Koinonia with several other families, including Harry and Ailene Atkinson, who had been at Koinonia since 1945.[122] In one of the most harrowing accounts, the mother of Alma Jackson, an eighteen-year-old black man then living at Koinonia, "came weeping and mourning and crying for him to come home, not to live at Koinonia anymore." She was, the Koinonians explained, "thinking of Emmett Till, kidnapped and murdered and thrown in the river last year."[123]

Exhaustion and exasperation wore down the remaining group. A desperate Clarence Jordan even petitioned President Dwight Eisenhower in a "last resort." He wrote that Koinonia Farm was "facing annihilation unless quick, decisive action is taken by someone in authority." Jordan described the recent violence and requested federal intervention, since America "is a land where free men have the right—and the duty—to walk erect and without fear in their pursuit of peace and happiness."[124] The White House and attorney general assured the Koinonians that they would take the matter seriously, expressing a "strong aversion to acts of violence," only to hand over the matter to the governor of Georgia, the very same man who, months before, had angrily demanded to know who "this Jordan fellow was." Rather than offering protection against violence, Governor Griffin appointed the county's prosecuting attorney to take steps to "get rid of this interracial cancer in the fair community of Georgia."[125] The federal government offered no protection to Koinonia.[126]

Finally, on May 26, 1957, a delegation of prominent Americus citizens visited Koinonia and asked them to leave Sumter County.[127] Ten well-attired men, representing the power structure of the city, took their seats in dilapidated chairs among the Koinonians, dressed in blue jeans and work clothes. "We have a problem which we've got to recognize," began Frank Myers, representing the Chamber of Commerce. That problem, according to the group's official spokesman, Charles Crisp, was the existence of Koinonia Farm. While allowing that the Koinonians were "dedicated Christians," Crisp alleged that the group did not "make brotherly love in the community," which, he asserted is the "first duty of a Christian." Koinonia, he railed, "has set brother against brother; it has created bitterness; it has created hatred; it has created every emotion that is contrary to my concept of Christianity." The assembled men then stated that "unless this experiment is moved. . . . Somebody is going to get hurt. . . . That is the reality of the situation." Therefore, they stated, it would be "serving the best interests of the community and certainly the best interests of your Lord to move and leave us in peace."[128] When Jordan protested that abandoning Koinonia would be spiritually detrimental, the men responded, "Well, I hope that we're big enough to be interested in your spiritual welfare, but we're particularly, right now, interested in your physical welfare." After this terse discussion, the delegation left. As the men got in their cars to leave the farm, Clarence lamented that "Sumter County . . . could have gone down as the most glorious little county in all the world. It could have stood out as a shining light to the rest of the nation—for freedom, for truth, for justice." Instead, it was a small Georgia city with an anxious Chamber of Commerce, a city so plagued by racism that it chose to expel a radical Christian group rather than honor its religious principles.[129]

The Koinonians decided to stay. As Florence Jordan recalled, "there was never any feeling that we should leave. We knew we wouldn't be the first Christians to die, and we wouldn't be the last." Even in the midst of violence and persecution, specific theological beliefs sustained the community. Rather than capitulate to intimidation and fear, the Koinonians steeled their resolve by looking to the example of Christ. Like Jesus, who was misunderstood and persecuted, the Koinonians had to be willing to endure scorn and derision for their radical message. Even oppression was incarnational. Not only did the Koinonians believe that they were like Christ in his suffering, but they believed that the resurrection of Christ transformed their suffering. "Jesus did not remain in the tomb," Clarence taught, "so those who are seeking to follow His example . . . need not fear those who would kill the body, for they, like a mighty stream, cannot be stopped by barriers erected by men." Christians, even when they suffered, would be victorious, as Christ was. As a letter sent to the Koinonians during this period declared: "What is success after all? When Jesus was nailed to the cross, who failed? We would say that his enemies failed." In this way, the besieged Koinonia community found comfort and strength in their theology. A letter written during this period described a "real closeness" and "great joy" at Koinonia, as members shared in "glorious" times of worship together, singing "'I Need Thee Every Hour' and 'Jesus, Keep Me Near the Cross' completely unannounced." The radical Christian orthodoxy of Koinonia both prompted its persecution and sustained its members in it.[130]

It also encouraged local blacks in Americus. For young Sam Mahone, Koinonia represented "a beacon of hope."[131] Indeed, Koinonia Farm's "endurance in the face of violence and threats—especially in the middle and late fifties . . . put hope in the hearts of many South Georgia Negroes."[132] One day during a Klan rally in Americus in 1957, a group of local blacks stood and watched, noticeably undaunted by the display of hatred. "You should know," one onlooker explained, "Koinonia has taught us not to be afraid."[133] Mabel Barnum, a prominent black citizen and business owner likewise added that Koinonia proved that "you don't have to be afraid of the Klan."[134] These black residents in Americus saw that even in the midst of danger and persecution, there was an insistent good that refused to capitulate. Koinonia indeed refused to retreat from their vision of interracial Christian community, and in so doing, fostered courage that would soon transform Americus and the South.

Nevertheless, the late 1950s and early 1960s marked a period of decline for Koinonia Farm. As the number of community residents fell to only a handful, agricultural operations largely collapsed. By 1958, many members had fled to safety, particularly those with children, and only five to eight adults remained. That number fell to four by 1963. Though in one sense this was a time of suffering, even decline, for the farm, Koinonia made some extremely significant contributions during the 1960s that had a great effect on both the history of the civil rights movement and modern Christianity in America. One of these was Clarence Jordan's *Cottonpatch Gospel*.

Theological Reimaginings in the *Cottonpatch*

While Koinonia Farm incubated its residents' integrationist vision, it also contributed to the broader theological struggle for racial equality through Clarence Jordan's *Cottonpatch* translation of the Bible. For years, Jordan had been a popular speaker at colleges, universities, seminaries, workshops, and churches, as he shared his insights from the Bible and applied them to quotidian life, including, notably, race relations. Nearing the end of his life, Jordan sought to formally chronicle these ideas. Life on the farm had quieted, and Jordan began to spend more time in his little writing shack, where he penned his 1968 *Cottonpatch Translations* of the New Testament. Through his writings, and specifically the *Cottonpatch Translations*, Clarence Jordan and Koinonia Farm once more challenged the relationship between Christianity and race and left a lasting legacy to Christianity in America.

Long possessed of a deep interest in the Greek New Testament, Jordan tried to apply the truths of the New Testament to life in the segregated South, "not only in his own tongue but in his own time." The good news, or gospel, should not be relegated to "musty history," Jordan believed, but should be presented as "fast-breaking *news*." Instead of the Word becoming Flesh and dwelling among us, Jordan joked, "Too many people think that the Word became a mummy and dwelt in our archives." Jordan wanted to bring that Word to life again. By taking some creative liberty, he tried to "rescue the New Testament drama from the sanctuary and classroom" and place it "under God's skies where people are toiling and crying and wondering"; the result was a colloquial and often biting interpretation entitled *The Cottonpatch Translations*.[135]

Jordan's version of the Gospel of Luke began: "Now during the fifteenth year of Tiberius as President, while Pontius Pilate was governor of Georgia, and Herod was governor of Alabama . . . while Anna and Caiaphas were co-presidents of the Southern Baptist Convention, the word of God came . . . down on the farm." The word came to John the Baptist, who, in Jordan's rendering, traded his camel hair and asceticism for "blue jeans and a leather jacket" and his locusts and honey for "cornbread and collard greens." Jesus himself was raised in the Bethlehem equivalent of Valdosta, Georgia, baptized in the Chattahoochee River, and described as "plenty smart, and God liked him." Jordan tried to place the unfamiliar traditions and lexicon of the ancient Roman

Empire in accessible language for the people he knew in Georgia, hoping then that it would pierce their hearts and change their lives.[136]

By stressing biblical characters' similarities to the people Southerners knew, Jordan applied Jesus's teachings to the moral issues of the day. In Jordan's *Cottonpatch* rendering of the story of the Good Samaritan, the priest and the Levite became a white preacher and a gospel song leader. The Samaritan, meanwhile, was a black man who was "moved to tears" by the suffering of another and drove him to the hospital in Albany, telling the nurse on call, "You all take care of this white man I found on the highway. Here's the only two dollars I got, but you all keep account of what he owes and . . . I'll settle up with you when I make a pay-day." When he taught this passage in speaking engagements, Jordan would then ask his listeners, "If you had been the man held up by the gangsters, which of these three . . . would you consider to have been your neighbor?" When his listeners predictably said, "Why of course, the nig—I mean, well, er . . . the one who treated me kindly," Jordan would look them squarely in the eye and authoritatively say, "Jesus said, 'Well, then, you get going and start living like that.'" He affirmed that there was no place for racism in the community of Christ and declared that God "has stamped his image on every race in heaven and on earth." If Southerners persisted in enacting racism, "if you segregate," Jordan harshly warned, "you commit a sin and stand convicted under the law as a violator." In his translation of the book of Ephesians, or "The Letter to the Christians in Birmingham," Jordan stated that "thoughtless white Christians" have often tried to keep blacks "outside of Christian fellowship" to deny their "rights as fellow believers" and treated them "as though the Gospel didn't apply." Because of Christ, Jordan continued, "you who were once so segregated are warmly welcomed into the Christian fellowship."[137]

These translations directly countered the prevailing racial mores, not by celebrating the promises of democracy, civil justice, or human rights, but by directly applying the Bible to Southern life. It "just burns my heart out," Jordan claimed, that "the Supreme Court is making pagans be more Christian than the Bible is making Christians be Christians." He continued, "I can hardly stand it sometimes when the whole integration struggle is . . . about whether or not we can sit down and eat hamburgers and drink cokes together. We ought to be sitting around Jesus' table drinking wine and eating bread together. . . . The sit-ins never would have been necessary if Christians had been sitting down together and at Christ's table all these many years." Jordan believed that the true power of change was theological but that many Christians had truncated the Bible's meaning and rendered their religion ineffectual. These "white washed Christians," he exclaimed, "have had the Word of God locked up in their hearts and have refused to do battle with it." Instead of hiding truths behind "artificial piety and the barriers of time and distance," Jordan's colloquial dialect forced the application of the Bible into daily living and into the struggle for racial equality. The demands of Jesus and the words of the Scriptures confronted people shopping on Main Street, worshipping in prominent churches, and living in shacks on the outskirts of town.[138]

Through the *Cottonpatch Translations*, the theology of Koinonia Farm was made accessible to a larger audience. Excerpts appeared in many Christian journals and publications, and, with its adaption into a musical by Harry Chapin in 1981, the "Cottonpatch Gospel" was widely disseminated in song and screenplay.[139] Indeed, Jordan's colloquial presentation of the Gospels continues to challenge social mores and apply the radical teachings of Jesus to everyday life, especially life in the South.

When Clarence Jordan and Martin England walked the scorched red earth that day in 1942, they could not have anticipated the effect their small farm and experiment in Christian community would have. The lived theology of Koinonia Farm—redemptive agriculture, Christian community, and racial reconciliation—confronted the segregationist Christianity of Americus. By framing the issue of racial equality religiously, by providing a haven for both their black neighbors and white dissidents, and by articulating the teachings of Jesus with relevance for race relations, Koinonia Farm defied Jim Crow with its radical Christian orthodoxy. But Koinonia also comprised a major opportunity lost.

Twenty years before the civil rights movement arrived in Americus, Koinonia Farm did. In a familiar drawl, members spoke to their fellow white Baptists of love and peace, and of Christianity's racial demands. But Americus refused to listen. Koinonia Farm was a voice crying in the wilderness, a prophetic John the Baptist that preceded the civil rights movement in Americus and offered a foretaste of what was to follow: a bitter theological struggle over race and religion.

CHAPTER TWO

Lee Street Theology

White Southern Protestantism in Americus, 1945–1963

I would rather face the frantic, childish mob, even with their shotguns and
buggy whips, than the silent, insidious mob of good church people.
—Clarence Jordan, 1957

Maintaining segregation is a sincere Christian viewpoint arrived at after
much prayerful thought and deliberation.
—Resolution, First Methodist Church, Americus, 1963

We have always prided ourselves that what we believe is what we do.
—Roy Parker, Americus resident

Summer Sundays were uncomfortably hot at Americus's First Baptist.
Gathered on the church lawn, ladies dabbed at their foreheads with handkerchiefs while men shook hands. When Rev. Harold Collins flung wide the
double doors of the sanctuary around 10 A.M., the congregation poured into
the familiar pine pews. The service customarily opened with singing. Maybe
that Sunday the churchgoers sang along with the familiar words of hymn
#412—"Onward, Christian soldiers, marching as to war, with the cross of
Jesus going on before. / Christ, the royal Master, leads against the foe; forward into battle see his banners go!"[1] Their ancestors had been singing that
hymn since the Civil War, and though context had shifted, its meaning had
endured. Surely, the congregants of Americus's First Baptist must have believed, Christ would still lead them against their foes in 1963. Hymns were
followed by announcements, and after the announcements, prayer. Rev. Collins delivered a sermon, and the five hundred or so men, women, and children
flowed out of the sanctuary the same way they came in. A few last words and
embraces on the lawn, and the citizens of Americus were off to Sunday lunch.
Just another Sabbath in Americus.[2]

But on Thursday evening there was business to tend to at First Baptist.
Arriving still dressed for the office in suits and bearing briefcases, the church
deacons gathered in a meeting room. The issue at hand was integration. After
a motion was put forth and a brief discussion, the men voted to approve a

statement that would officially define the church's position on race and be "immediately adopted." This policy, henceforth known as the "closed door" policy, declared that "any Negroes who try and enter this church" should be informed that "this is not an integrated church and that they will not be admitted." The resolution went so far as to detail enforcement of the policy, stating, "The ushers will refer the Negroes to a colored Baptist church of their choice and then, should they insist on entering, the ushers should use the necessary means in preventing their so doing."[3] The "necessary means" are left intentionally vague. But, following the *Brown v. Board of Education* decision in 1954 and a growing fear that "those things" could indeed happen in Americus, the First Baptist Church made its institutional and theological position on racial integration clear.[4] The doors were closed.

How did the very same people who sang hymns declaring, "we are not divided, all one body we, one in hope and doctrine, one in charity" vote to keep certain neighbors out of their congregations?[5] Did segregationist Christians subvert their genuine faith for political expediency? Or did their doctrine somehow support such decisions? Could Jesus Christ and Jim Crow coexist?

In an effort to describe the white Protestant churches of Americus in the postwar period, this chapter assesses how white southern Christianity reckoned with race. White southern Protestants in Americus and throughout the South did not consider racial segregation incompatible with Christian belief. If anything, they envisioned themselves and their churches as guardians of traditional orthodoxy against the grain of an increasingly apostate America.

All along Lee Street: Churches in Americus

Lee Street was one of the main thoroughfares in Americus, lined with trees, historic homes, and churches. Lush greenery framed wraparound porches, sunlight dappled through delicate gingerbread detailing, and houses of worship blended in among the magnolias. Turning onto Lee Street from the center of town, the First Baptist Church of Americus sat on the right, a traditional brick building with a tall, proud steeple. Directly across the street loomed the First Methodist Church, a yellow brick building designed to resemble an Athenian temple, with a copper dome, Corinthian columns, and intricate stained glass windows. One block over stood the First Presbyterian Church, a small and elegant white wooden building. A little farther down Lee Street was the Episcopal Church, built in 1927 and boasting a glazed brick exterior and Gothic walnut archways, its more European style providing, as Americus historian William Williford put it, "a charming contrast to some of the more ornate Victorian churches in town."[6] Still farther from downtown was the Catholic Church. Walking down Lee Street was a bit like meandering through church history, as denominations, traditions, and styles congregated together on one avenue in a small Georgia town.

The oldest was the First Baptist Church; its founding predated Americus itself. Originally called Bethel Baptist, the church boasted fourteen members in 1835, seventeen in 1836, and sixty-six by 1839.[7] Americus and First Baptist both grew with the arrival of industry and agricultural business, and by the dawning of the Civil War, the church had approximately 154 white members and 99 black members.[8] Though the black members began their own congregations after the Civil War, First Baptist continued to expand its total membership to 724 members by 1925. By 1957, its members numbered 1,123, all of them white. A member of both the General Baptist Conference (GBC) and Southern Baptist Conference (SBC), the First Baptist Church of Americus possessed a "conservative to moderate philosophy," and prided itself on its evangelistic efforts.[9]

The First Methodist Church also dated its beginnings to the very establishment of the Americus settlement in 1832.[10] Initially, a circuit rider called Dunwoody led meetings in private homes or cabins, but by 1835, when Rev. J. Edwards came, the 200 Methodist worshippers convened in "a simple wooden structure . . . used jointly with a small group of Baptists."[11] In 1905, the parishioners built an independent structure on the corner of Lee and Church Streets.[12] Many of Americus's most prominent citizens were members at First Methodist, making it a mainstay of Americus life and a pillar in the community throughout the twentieth century.

Though smaller than both the First Baptist and First Methodist Churches, the First Presbyterian Church also claimed a long history in Americus.[13] "By 1836," in fact, "there were enough Presbyterians for a small group of that denomination to meet regularly for divine worship."[14] In 1842, the First Presbyterian Church of Americus was formally constituted under the provision of the Flint River Presbytery.[15] In 1884, on the west side of Jackson Street, one block from Lee Street's main stretch, First Presbyterian constructed a house of worship made "entirely of materials from Georgia," with pine and walnut woodwork, a stately steeple, gingerbread latticework, and an interior like "an old sailing vessel," stained glass windows aside.[16] Though a small congregation, First Presbyterian housed some of Americus's most monied citizens, including business magnate Charles Wheatley, whose funds helped construct the church. The Presbyterian Church reflected a more studious, serious tradition than its Baptist and Methodist counterparts. It privileged doctrine and strict scriptural exegesis. When the Presbyterian Church split during the years of the Civil War, First Presbyterian of Americus predictably joined the Southern Presbyterians. Throughout the twentieth century, the First Presbyterian Church, along with First Baptist and First Methodist, contributed significantly to religious life in Americus.[17]

In the late 1940s and 1950s, churches took on added prominence.[18] Nationally, church membership skyrocketed in the 1950s, with the *Yearbook of American Churches* estimating that American churches had 88,673,005 total members in 1951 and 116,109,929 in 1961, an increase of 30.94 percent in a mere decade.[19] In 1957, the pastor of First Baptist in Americus wrote a letter to the congregation declaring his belief that the church was "in the midst of a great revival" with "indications of a real spiritual awakening among us," challenging his congregation to break their attendance record.[20] Ben Easterlin, a child in postwar Americus, captured Protestantism's cultural expansiveness, remembering nostalgically: "You believed in institutions. God, country, politicians, motherhood, Chevrolet, and apple pie."[21]

"God the Original Segregationist": A Theological Interpretation of Race

Behind the shimmering abundance and full church pews of Americus lingered the question of race and the long history of religiously sanctioned inequality. As many white Protestants in Americus worshipped on Lee Street, they simultaneously sanctified segregation, believing that racial separation was God's intended way, or at least permissible in their churches. Though many ordinary white churchgoers did not comprehensively reflect on the relationship between Christianity and segregation, preferring to categorize segregation as "just the way things are," many complex theological influences contributed to segregation's sanctification.[22]

From its beginning, the Southern race question has always been a religious question. Many in the South "took their theology at least as seriously as they took inherited customs or racial mores."[23] It is nearly impossible to discuss race in the South without also discussing religion, and the ways that Christian theology both supported and opposed formal and informal racism. Since, as historian Joseph Crespino remarks, segregation for many across the South was "not just a political but more important, a theological issue," we must examine race with an eye for theology and theology with an eye for race.[24] By considering certain interconnected and intertwined theological tenets present in mainline Southern Protestantism—biblical literalism and Fundamentalism, congregational autonomy, evangelism, and a particular Christology—the theology of postwar segregationism is properly understood as more than sheer ignorance or hate, but as a complex, enduring theological and political position.

Southern Protestantism was not monolithic. Dispensationalism, premillennialism, postmillennialism, amillennialism, pietism, Calvinism, and Arminianism all swirled through the world of Southern Protestant Christianity, each revealing a staggering diversity of belief.[25] Class and geography further divided forms of white Southern Protestantism. Christian belief articulated in Americus differed from positions espoused at Emory University in Atlanta.[26] There was no one Southern theology, white theology, or Protestant theology. Nevertheless, churchgoers' theological positions in part shaped their ideas and behavior on race.

"For the Bible Tells Me So": Biblical Literalism and Fundamentalism in the South

Biblical literalism shaped the interaction of race and religion in white Southern Protestantism more than any other doctrine. While commitment to inerrancy differed among denominations, the notion that the Bible offered instruction was powerful and enduring across traditions. The Methodist *Confession of Faith* states, "The Holy Scripture containeth all things necessary to salvation," while official Southern Baptist doctrine declares the Bible "a perfect treasure of divine instruction . . . totally true and trustworthy."[27] For most Southern Protestants, including those at First Methodist, First Baptist, and First Presbyterian in Americus, the Bible constituted the basis for teaching and rule for living. Preachers in Americus and elsewhere in the South delivered primarily exegetical sermons, expounding chapter and verse to teach parishioners timeless truths. Sunday school classes, too, conducted "pretty literal studies of the Bible," according to one Americus man.[28] While these Southern Protestant churches were, in the words of Paul Harvey, "captive to racism and a dogmatic literalist theology," surely some of them would have been quick to respond that the Good Book itself says one is either a "slave to sin or a slave to righteousness," and they knew which side they wanted to be on.[29]

Since the antebellum era, many Southern Christians had used literalist interpretations of the scriptures to vehemently defend slavery and white supremacy. "The power of the proslavery scriptural position," historian Mark Noll asserts, "lay in its simplicity."[30] As the famed Georgia memoirist Eliza Frances Andrews put it, "Neither the Bible, nor the Apostles, nor Jesus Christ, ever condemned the institution of slavery as sin."[31] These arguments were not, as historian Paul Harvey writes, "merely hypocritical cant intended to void a clear biblical message" but were sincerely held commitments that "sanctified slavery and defined southern theology."[32]

The debate over slavery became, in essence, an argument over interpretations of the Bible. Abolitionists advocated for the "spirit" of the Word while slavery's proponents positioned themselves as guardians of the "letter" of the Word, which, Mark Noll points out, "came to look like a defense of Scripture itself."[33] After Lee's surrender at Appomattox, "the weary, black-garbed" citizens of Americus gathered at First Methodist to pray and weep as "muffled church bells tolled solemnly" overhead.[34] And yet, of course, the theology of white supremacy was not ultimately defeated. Underneath the question of slavery was the deeper question of race, which would not disappear even in the raging fires of the Civil War.[35]

Through Reconstruction and into the twentieth century, racial inequality and separation were enforced violently and defended biblically, as slavery had been. Over time, white supremacy became enshrined as unassailable dogma, part of "an established tradition of American exegesis," according to religious historian Steve Haynes.[36] Although significant scholarly debate exists regarding the consistency and vociferousness of certain theological positions, what is clear is that a biblical argument for racial separation endured.[37] Even more, the defense of segregation came to look like a defense of a conservative, orthodox Christianity; it came to look like a defense of the Bible itself.

One of the passages invoked most frequently was from Genesis. As the so-called Hamitic hypothesis, or Hamitic myth, goes, Noah had three sons, Shem, Ham, and Japheth.[38] Following the Great Flood, these sons "went forth from the ark" and "from these the people of the whole earth were dispersed."[39] But one of the brothers would be not only separated but condemned. After one awkward drunken night, Noah "awoke from his wine" and, ashamed that Ham had seen "the nakedness of his father," issued a hung-over curse: "a servant of servants shall he be to his brothers."[40] This pronouncement cursed not only Ham, but all of his descendants: "Cush, Egypt, Put, and Canaan," and the unknown people that would come from that line.[41] From this Genesis account, an intricate ethnohistory/anthropology was constructed wherein some lineages of peoples emerged as particularly blessed by God whereas others were cursed to perpetual servitude.[42]

The Hamitic hypothesis in Genesis 9 offered a biblical, pseudoscientific justification for slavery and, after emancipation, racial subjugation.[43] It constituted, along with accounts of the Table of Nations (Genesis 10) and the Tower of Babel (Genesis 11), in Steve Haynes's estimation, a "substantive link."[44] "Many people are using it today to justify the present racial pattern," Baptist ethicist T. B. Maston wrote in 1959, "just as their fathers used it to defend slavery."[45] One such apologist was South Carolina Baptist Humphrey K. Ezell, who, that year wrote *The Christian Problem of Racial Segregation*.[46] Another was Rev. Carey Daniel, a Texas Southern Baptist minister, president of the White Citizens' Church Council, and author of a famous published sermon, "God the Original Segregationist." Daniel explained that Genesis revealed that the descendants of Ham were damned to perpetual servitude but also that God had long intended a pattern of racial separation.[47] The Creator, Daniel railed, "separated the black race from the white and lighter skinned races. He did not just put them in different parts of town . . . HE PUT THE BLACK RACE ON A HUGE CONTINENT TO THEMSELVES, SEGREGATED FROM THE OTHER RACES BY OCEANS OF WATER TO THE WEST, SOUTH AND EAST, AND BY THE VAST STRETCHES OF THE ALMOST IMPASSABLE SAHARA DESERT TO THE NORTH."[48] Of course, in America, blacks and whites were not separated by oceans and continents, but were throughout the South, living closely in small towns like Americus. While absolute separation seemed unlikely, legal segregation seemed a theologically appropriate way for whites and blacks to "coexist peacefully" in the South.[49]

Religious elites like Ezell and Daniel certainly made these biblical arguments for segregation, but so did everyday practitioners. Mississippi Governor Ross Barnett, like Rev. Daniel, declared God "the original segregationist," adding, "He made the white man white and the black man black and he did not intend for them to mix."[50] In a letter sent to First Methodist Church in Americus, a Tennessee man specifically invoked Genesis, writing, "Genesis 11 tells us every one was scattered abroad. Black went to their country, white and yellow to their own lands. And so all were sent to their own countries."[51]

Segregationists found theological justification in other Old Testament passages, too, particularly in God's instruction to Israel not to intermarry with pagan peoples. Abraham, Moses, Nehemiah, and Habakkuk were transformed into prophets of segregation and racial purity. In 1954, G. T. Gillespie, a Mississippi Presbyterian, claimed, "the Hebrews, by Divine command, became a segregated people." L. B. McCord, a Presbyterian minister from Clarendon, South Carolina, maintained as late as 1964 that segregation was "morally right and theologically sound," based on God's command for the Israelites to "remain holy," or separate, from other nations. Numerous Old Testament passages showed the dangers of racial mixing, prompting Rev. Daniel to claim, "Anyone familiar with the Biblical history can readily understand why we in the South are determined to maintain segregation." Embedded within these arguments lurked a particular fear of miscegenation. "The argument that God was against sexual integration," historian Jane Dailey has written, "was articulated across a broad spectrum of education and respectability, by senators and Klansmen, by housewives, sorority sisters, and Rotarians, and, not least of all, by mainstream Protestant clergymen."[52]

Biblical arguments for segregation did not derive solely from the Old Testament. Segregationists often cited Acts 17, when the Apostle Paul told the Gentiles at the Athenian Aeropagus that God had ordained "bounds of habitation" for the people of the earth, pilfering from his words a mandate for racial segregation.[53] Even Jesus Christ became an unwitting apologist for racial separation. Presbyterian minister G. T. Gillespie wrote that Jesus "did not ignore or denounce racial distinctions."[54] If Jesus had wanted to overturn the Old Testament law, these segregationists reasoned, he would have; instead, Jesus affirmed the law when he said: "until Heaven and earth pass away, not an iota, not a dot, will pass from the Law until all is accomplished."[55] This amounted to "proof" of the Bible's position on segregation, or at least, as Edward Blum and Paul Harvey put it, an "argument of absence," that if Jesus did not condemn segregation per se, he supported it.[56]

In the postdiluvian Genesis account, the Old Testament prophets, the epistles of St. Paul, and the words of Jesus himself, segregationist Christians found biblical justifications for their racial views. "Having attended my beloved little country church from infancy," Mrs. Jesse West explained in 1954, "I know the fundamentals of the teachings of God's Holy Word," adding, "nowhere can I find anything to convince me that God intended us living together as one big family in schools, churches and other public places."[57] This was not "simply propaganda"; many truly believed the Bible upheld principles of racial separation.[58] Defending segregation then was akin to defending scriptural orthodoxy.

It was about race, of course, but for many, it was also about the sanctity of the Bible. In the mid-twentieth century, many white Southerners fused defenses of racial segregation and conservative theology, both of which seemed threatened. The struggle against integration in the South became part of a larger struggle against liberalism, communism, and heresy, a struggle over the fundamentals of Christianity and for the soul of America. As historian Joseph Crespino has concluded: "Segregation was one issue in a broader ideological divide separating liberals and moderates from conservatives and 'fundamentalist' Christians."[59]

Fundamentalism has a long and important history in American life. Throughout the first two decades of the twentieth century, Fundamentalists sought to reclaim the inerrancy of the scriptures while articulating a brand of evangelical Christianity that would become a mainstay of American and Southern religion.[60] Between 1910 and 1915, a series of works, *The Fundamentals: A Testimony to the Truth*, set out the basic doctrines of Protestant Christianity and established Fundamentalism as both a lasting movement and descriptor.[61] *The Fundamentals* included essays affirming the Virgin Birth, the Deity of Christ, the Incarnation, the Holy Spirit, and the Resurrection; in essence, it was a lengthy, twentieth-century Apostles Creed. Scriptural inerrancy emerged as the "keystone," as Fundamentalists asserted that the Bible was "scientifically and historically reliable."[62]

This stance countered other movements afoot in American life: socialism, Mormonism, German higher criticism, Catholicism, and, most notably, evolution.[63] The case of the *State of Tennessee v. John Thomas Scopes*, popularly known as the Scopes monkey trial, was an early theological contest over Fundamentalism, one especially important for the South because of the trial's location in Dayton, Tennessee. While condescending reports of the South's ignorance and backwardness served to further isolate the region, they also imbued Fundamentalists with the righteous indignation of the martyred. Fundamentalism gained fervor and membership amongst a broad coalition of Southern Protestants. For this reason, historian George Marsden has remarked, "to speak of most Southern Christians as fundamentalists was to indulge in redundancy."[64] These Southern Fundamentalists came to the conclusion that it was the North that had truly lost its way by abandoning Christian principles; the South, possessing in many ways an "identity by contrast," was determined not to mirror this Yankee apostasy.[65] That was certainly true in Americus.

On July 22, 1925, the day following the Scopes verdict, the *Americus Times-Recorder* published excerpts from a sermon given at First Presbyterian Church on "the theory of evolution and the controversy raging over that question." Evolutionists were "objects of pity and not of scorn," Rev. Richard Simpson declared, since "they do not believe in a personal God, and in Jesus Christ, the Son of God, and in salvation." Calling the Scopes trial primarily a "religious controversy," Rev. Simpson explained the "point of view of orthodox Christianity":

I believe that the world and the universe and all things in them were created by Almighty God . . . they are the result of His will. . . . I believe that Jesus Christ is the Son of God. That he was conceived by the Holy

Spirit and born of the Virgin Mary. I believe that He gave His life's blood in atonement for the sins of His people, which atonement is sufficient for all mankind. I believe that He arose from the dead on the third day, that he ascended to heaven and someday will return to the earth with power and glory.... I believe in the personality of the Holy Spirit. I believe in the plenary verbal inspiration of the Scripture in such a way that the Bible is God's Book and not man's. I believe the Bible ... to be literally true and God's one, complete and final revelation of His will to man.[66]

Rev. Simpson's expressed orthodoxy addressed the controversy over evolution and affirmed the supernatural elements of Christianity that he believed the Scopes trial was bringing into question. In a sense, the Americus minister's declaration reflected the stance of the Christian leadership in Americus and of Fundamentalists throughout the South.

Those controversies made many Southern Protestants wary of national (and especially international) ecumenical bodies, which they associated with liberal theology and a rejection of true Christian doctrine. In the postwar period, Southerners even considered national Protestant governing conventions with mistrust and skepticism.[67] The National Council of Churches (NCC) was particularly suspect; the Southern Baptist Convention called it a "sham union." Many believed that the NCC (and other ecumenical organizations like it) had "rejected biblical Christianity in favor of a modern post-Christian apostasy" amounting to an "outright repudiation of the Gospel itself."[68] Not only had the NCC repudiated the true Gospel, but by the mid-century, Southerners were convinced it had replaced it with the teachings of Karl Marx. One Georgia man, Mr. E. E. Bell Smith Towson, wrote to the Methodist Bishop in Atlanta of the "Communist monstrosity known as the National Council of Churches," which, he claimed, was neither American nor Christian.[69]

"The Big Surprise": Congregational Autonomy

The anger directed at the NCC reveals a Cold War–era fear of liberalism as well as a deep mistrust of central organization. Many Southern conservatives privileged the autonomy of individual congregations, which was a political and theological position. In what he dubs "the big surprise" of segregationism, David Chappell has argued that it was not, in fact, the Hamitic hypothesis or racist exegesis that was most prominently invoked, but "rather, anticlericalism."[70] This anticlericalism targeted Roman Catholics, to be sure, but included

Protestant ruling organizations. Individual congregations consistently as-serted their independence from denominational jurisdiction, particularly concerning race.[71]

The Southern Baptist Convention, Rev. Martin Luther King Jr., mused, "is a denomination which has said over and over again that segregation is sinful," yet most of its churches "still practice it."[72] Even as the Southern Baptist Convention and, in particular, the Christian Life Commission, encouraged compliance with federal desegregation rulings in the 1950s, a majority of white Southern Baptists nevertheless practiced segregation.[73] Overarching pronouncements from national denominational mouthpieces seemed to have had very little to do with what Baptist churches actually did. In Americus, as the chapter's opening narrative illustrates, First Baptist consciously crafted a segregationist policy without concern for denominational edicts. While Methodists had a slightly more centralized structure, individual congregations often rejected the decisions of the Methodist General Conference, particularly in reference to segregation. In 1956, the General Conference of the Methodist Church officially published a resolution that declared the immorality of racial segregation. But in Americus, the First Methodist Church defied this pronouncement and adopted a closed-door policy, wherein black visitors were expressly barred. The church passed a resolution of its own that "emphatically oppos[ed] the action of the General Conference of the Methodist Church in approving permissible integration on a voluntary basis."[74] In 1957, Americus's Lee Street Methodist similarly flouted the national denomination. Issuing a "special resolution," the church warned that if the denominational "bombardment" promoting integration did not cease, "a tragic disaffectation will ensue, seriously, if not irreparably imperiling the spiritual future and financial program of the Methodist Church."[75] Americus Methodists felt that it was their church, their town, and their decision. Governed by the ruling elders, the presbytery, and by the Presbyterian Synod, the Presbyterian Church was not as independent as its Baptist and Methodist counterparts, but it could, through movements and gatherings, assert some autonomy. The Presbyterian Church in Americus never adopted an official closed-door policy, but, with its inclusion into the Southern Presbyterian Church (PCUS), maintained a segregationist stance.[76]

The division between national denominations and individual congregations was made possible both by the governing structure of Protestant churches and their doctrine of the priesthood of believers, a theological tradition dating back to the Reformation. Appeals to the sanctity of the local church offered Southerners a theological way to maintain their way of life in the face of national changes. God's will for their churches, many white Southerners concluded, was to preserve a literal interpretation of the Bible, the fundamentals of Christianity, and the racial hierarchy. The rest of the world could capitulate to communism, liberalism, and integrationism, but Southern churches would maintain theological and racial orthodoxy.

"Come on Down!": Evangelism and the Southern Tradition

The principal job of the church, many white Southern Protestants believed, was not to pontificate on world issues or involve itself in global affairs; it was to preach salvation. In their theological liberalism, Northern Protestants and national ecumenical bodies had, in Carolyn Dupont's words, lost their "zeal to save lost souls."[77] The Social Gospel or any similar emphasis on earthly reform, was seen by many as a distraction from the true mission of the church. Regeneration should not be primarily social, but spiritual. As one Americus native recalled, local churches clung to "classic Christian principles," with "no aspect geared toward changing attitudes."[78] Classic Christian principles meant focusing on a theology centered on individual salvation. The spiritual change offered by conversion would trigger the necessary uplift of society and the desired peace—not that that was the primary reason to evangelize. So privileged was the theological emphasis on spiritual salvation that to shy away from evangelism amounted to a denial of Christian orthodoxy.

Refusal to preach a message of hellfire and brimstone, the eternal stakes of belief in Christ, signaled for many Southerners liberalism's capitulation to the world and weak faith. Sweating, red-faced evangelism was real, it was strong, and it was the Southern way. As one minister, "KKK and proud of it," bellowed from his pulpit in Alabama: "If some of these fat, greasy, panty-waist preachers would get intestinal fortitude enough to preach the Gospel and keep their mouths out of things they know absolutely nothing about. . . . The churches would have more people in them."[79] Certainly most Southern preachers lacked the "intestinal fortitude" of this man, but many of them offered a message of evangelism that dismissed the soft worldliness of less stout churches, overlooked social concerns, and allowed racism to be submerged under the preeminence of spiritual salvation.

In the mid-twentieth century, evangelistic revivals were especially central to Southern social and religious life. Americus hosted annual revivals, which were popular among youth and adults alike. One Americus advertisement proclaimed: "Revival Time is Near! / To prepare for Revival / To glorify my God

/ To serve my Day and Generation / To Strengthen my Home Front / To justify God's Abundant Blessings to me."[80] Americus native Ben Easterlin remembered frequent meetings, "tent-revivals almost," though, he noted, most people in Americus "didn't stand or raise their hands or anything."[81] In additional to annual revivals, weekly church bulletins often included prayers for general revival and increased evangelical zeal. A 1962 First Baptist bulletin read, "Lord, send us out, with heart aflame, To win men's souls for Thee . . . Send us out! With heart aflame; Send us out with power to win the lost; Lord, send us out in Thy name."[82] Evangelists like W. H. Rittenhouse, Frank Boggs, Jimmy O'Quinn, and Bishop Arthur Moore frequently visited Americus, bringing with them a certain brand of evangelical fervor and otherworldly excitement.[83] Bishop Moore especially was "highly inspirational," a "forceful, charismatic preacher," one Americus man remembered, who always stressed personal faith in Christ, and "coming down front" to confess Christ and recite the sinner's prayer.[84] At revivals such as Bishop Moore's, people were frequently "born again," a designation that would gain currency in the next twenty years, especially with the election of Jimmy Carter, who, in all likelihood, heard Moore preach as a boy in Sumter County.[85] The primacy placed on evangelicalism and being born again in white Southern Protestantism reveals a preference for the unseen over the seen, the spiritual over the physical, and the divine over the human.

"Fairest Lord Jesus": Sanctified Racial Identities

The emphasis on evangelism followed from a certain vision of Christ. Many Christians, like those Americus residents who went to Bishop Moore's revivals, considered themselves "born again" after coming to terms with the divine Jesus, envisioning themselves like the Apostle Paul on the Road to Damascus, to emerge better than they were before. The change this Jesus offered was spiritual and then behavioral, a view that stemmed from a particular Christology.

While ideas of and interactions with Jesus varied from church to church and even from person to person, white Southern Protestants tended to emphasize his divine nature with descriptors like "radiant," "fair," "holy," and "pure." Jesus was also usually depicted as white.[86] Conflating Christ's spiritual holiness with racial purity created a powerful and pernicious doctrine. Jesus's whiteness was used to convey righteousness, and his righteousness to convey whiteness, creating a theological as well as sociopolitical connection between Christ's whiteness, his deity, and his salvific role. It was, according to theologian J. Kameron Carter, this Christology that most decisively allowed for racism to permeate Christianity.[87] Carter has identified the theological act of supersessionism—divorcing Jesus from his Jewishness— as a direct precursor to privileging whiteness. Robbing Jesus of his identity as the Jewish Messiah, as the fulfillment of God's covenant with his people Israel, served also to rob him of his physical body. It was this heresy, Carter argues, privileging Jesus's divinity over his humanity, that allowed an opening for racism. When Christ's humanity reentered the Christological conversation, it had been profoundly changed by his time in the ethereal wilderness: Jesus was reimagined as white.

Predictably, white Southerners latched onto this image with fervor, using Christ's whiteness to, in Edward Blum and Paul Harvey's phrase, "sanctify racial hierarchies."[88] "Christ looked like a white guy," one Americus man stated, "you didn't think of him as Middle Eastern [or] a Jew. . . . He wasn't considered a man of color."[89] From their earliest Sunday school lessons at First Baptist, First Methodist, and First Presbyterian, children in Americus imagined their Savior in a manner consistent with Warner Sallman's ubiquitous depiction: ethereal, with blue eyes and sandy hair.[90] A program from the First Baptist Church in Americus commemorating their new building campaign had Sallman's Christ on the cover, as did numerous other materials. While this may seem like a simple instance of people envisioning their God in their own image, it had grave ramifications.

Adopting a view that emphasized Christ's divinity and ignored his Jewishness transformed Jesus into a white moral exemplar and allowed for a theologically mandated racial hierarchy. Jesus was at the top, the whitest of the white (he *was* God, after all), followed by white Americans, with Southerners imagining themselves at the peak, since they were the ones preserving America's racial stock and the fundamentals of Christianity. Much of this corresponds with the language of purity: pure Christ, pure doctrine, pure church, pure race. As Sam Bowers of the Mississippi Ku Klux Klan chillingly put it, Jesus had called him "to the priestly task of preserving the purity of his blood and soil."[91] By privileging the spiritual over the physical, representing Jesus as phenotypically Caucasian, and associating Jesus's racial purity with white Southerners' racial purity, this Christology did not subvert racism; it buttressed it. In their adherence to biblical literalism and the fundamentals of the faith, their insistence on congregational autonomy, and their emphasis on evangelism deriving from a particular Christology, white Southern Protestants maintained a comprehensive theology of Christian segregation.

Lived Theology on Lee Street

Theological segregationism kept the churches of Americus lily-white and demanded a certain racial orthodoxy. This proved problematic for one group of theological dissenters: those at Koinonia Farm. Upon arriving in Americus in the fall of 1942, Clarence Jordan and Martin England began attending Rehoboth Baptist Church, a local white Baptist congregation just a few miles down the road from the farm on Dawson Road. As more people came to live at Koinonia, many likewise chose to attend Rehoboth, a church to which they offered faithful attendance and helpful service. Clarence Jordan occasionally preached and often sang in the choir or played his trumpet in worship. Florence Jordan taught an adult Sunday school class. Tensions arose in 1948, as the leadership of Rehoboth realized that the Koinonians held some "radical" views regarding material possessions and war, but these were diffused by the church's decision that the Koinonians would not hold official leadership positions. The Koinonians' racial views, though, proved too much for the country Baptist church.

One Sunday morning in 1950, a group from the farm went to worship at Rehoboth, taking with them a young visitor, an Indian exchange student studying agriculture who "had expressed an interest in attending an American Protestant worship service." As Florence Jordan remembered, "we thought the people would be delighted to meet him. He was not a Christian but he had become interested and he wanted to go to church." As the Koinonians took their seats, all eyes fixed on the dark-skinned visitor. "Obviously," one commentator sarcastically said, "Koinonia had disguised a nigger, called him an Indian, and sneaked him into divine worship." This presumption infuriated the church, which immediately sought to expel the Koinonians from the congregation. Despite Jordan's explanations and biblical appeals, on August 13, 1950, Rehoboth Baptist formally barred the Koinonians for their "unchristian" beliefs.[92]

The radical orthodoxy of Koinonia Farm grated against the racial orthodoxy of many white Southern churches. Following their expulsion from Rehoboth Baptist, the Koinonians sought entry into the Presbyterian church, a Disciples of Christ congregation, several Methodist churches, and the local Episcopal church, but were unable to gain acceptance anywhere. They were "effectively banished" from the white churches of Americus who insisted that segregation was the Christian view.[93]

Segregated congregations like those of Lee Street perceived themselves as protectors of traditional orthodoxy. Religious devotion included racial separation, even into the 1960s. When the men of First Baptist gathered that Thursday in 1963 to keep their church segregated, they believed they were living their theology. So did the First Methodist Church in Americus when it declared that the "desire for maintaining segregation is a sincere Christian viewpoint arrived at after much prayerful thought and deliberation."[94] Another Americus congregation proclaimed, "there is nothing 'unchristian' in the segregation of the races in the church," going so far as to accuse integrationists of "straying from . . . devoted service to Jesus Christ."[95]

These white Southern Protestants felt they were acting out of the same impulses that motivated them to sing hymns, entreat the Almighty, and worship. They were upholding the sanctity of the Bible and the fundamentals of Christianity against Northern liberals. They were promoting the salvation of sinners. They were, above all, maintaining the purity of their Bible, their churches, their Christ, and their race from the corrupting influences of the world. Biblical literalism and Fundamentalism, congregational individualism, and evangelicalism were the bedrocks of white Protestantism in the midcentury South. And when all these aspects are taken together, a complex political position emerges, one with roots in theology.

For this reason, white Southern Christians cannot be easily dismissed as "stupid, vulgar and one-dimensional."[96] Rather, they emerge as people seeking to preserve their faith and their way of life from the outside incursions of Charles Darwin and Karl Marx, the National Council of Churches and the federal government, and, most pressingly, from the coming civil rights movement.

While the view of the First Baptist, First Methodist, and First Presbyterian churches was the pervasive one in the white community and "very, very, very few people felt differently" (and almost all of those lived at Koinonia), there did exist an alternate view in the South and in Americus.[97] As the white Protestants worshipped on Lee Street, the black community, bearing its own traditions and its own theology, gathered in its own churches on the other side of town.

CHAPTER THREE

Jesus, He's My Brother

The Black Church, Black Theology, and the
Black Freedom Struggle in Americus

The basis for good [race] relations is found in the Christian religion, in the
proper understanding of the Christian doctrines of man, Christ, and God, and
in the application of Christian insights and convictions in everyday living.

—Benjamin Mays, *Seeking to Be Christian in Race Relations*, 1957

Blacks do not ask whether Jesus is one with the Father or divine and human,
though the orthodox formulations are implied in their language. They ask
whether Jesus is walking with them, whether they can call him up on the
"telephone of prayer" and tell him all about their troubles. . . . "If [Martin Luther]
had been born a black slave, his first question would not have been whether
Jesus was at the Lord's Table but whether he was really present at the slave's
cabin, whether slaves could expect Jesus to be with them as they tried to
survive the cotton field, the whip, and the pistol.

—James Cone, *God of the Oppressed*, 1975

Unwanted by your kind who let you in,
Contained, alone, you find your grudged spare place,
And turn your thoughts maybe on God's skin,
Hoping that He like you has a black face.

—Alex R. Schmidt, 1948

Robertiena Freeman grew up in church. "I mean every time that church door
opened—even if no one else was there," she remembered, "we were there."
Robertiena's father, the Rev. R. L. Freeman, was the pastor of Bethesda Baptist Church in Americus, Georgia, and he made sure his family was in attendance. At Bethesda, they learned the Bible, heard the gospel, participated in
community, and served others in prayer and deed. But in the early 1960s,
Robertiena went to church not only on Sunday mornings but also on balmy
summer evenings to attend the mass meetings of Americus' nascent civil rights
movement. "We'd meet in the churches," Robertiena recalled, "they were
packed . . . [but] weren't air conditioned. . . . We were sitting all in the windowsills."

At these mass meetings, heavy with heat and hope, people gathered together to listen to speakers, ask God for help, and sing songs of both protest and praise. "We'd be singing," she mused, smiling, "yeah, they could hear us clear all the way to Albany we were singing so loud."[1]

The church was the center of black life in the South. For all the debates over its precise power and role, the primacy of the black church in the lived experiences of many black Americans cannot be denied.[2] "In the South, at least," W. E. B. Du Bois commented and Benjamin Mays and Joseph Nicholson confirmed, "practically every American Negro is a church member."[3] Born and raised in Americus, Eddie Rhea Walker recalled, "My mother took me, every Sunday, every night. . . . Church was very much a part of growing up, it was as much a part of life as school."[4] Robertiena Freeman echoed this—she was at church, on time, "*every* Sunday."[5] As young children, some resented being forced to wear stockings and memorize scripture, but many came to value the church deeply for offering a loving community, and a coherent (if not always satisfactory) context in which to process their life circumstances. The church provided a place where black people could come together, affirm their personhood, remember the gospel, and worship God, as well as socialize, eat, sing, dance, and rejoice. It was a place of moral and theological instruction as well as "amusement and relaxation."[6] Remembering a childhood spent at Campbell Chapel A.M.E., Americus resident Karl Wilson rhapsodized that "it was like heaven," especially in the hell of the Jim Crow South.[7]

The black church protected the autonomy of both the black religious experience and black protest.[8] As the primary space for planning, cohesion, and community in black life, the church naturally became the base for much civil rights activity.[9] Described by Aldon Morris as an "indigenous institution owned and controlled by blacks," the church gave the civil rights movement an organizational center, a core leadership, a financial well upon which to draw, and spaces for meetings.[10] The church's centrality is usually attributed to its sovereignty and privacy, since churches were among the few places black Americans, living under the constant scrutiny of Jim Crow, could be free.

But the black church offered the freedom struggle much more than buildings and resources. "The black church," Morris stated, "supplied the civil rights movement with a collective enthusiasm . . . the songs, testimonies, oratory, and prayers" and preached a message that "oppression is sinful" and God was on the side of freedom.[11] It offered an intellectual and spiritual alternative to racism and segregation, a profound and powerful black theology. The tenets of this black theology—God's creative authority and goodness, segregation as sin, God as the Deliverer, and Jesus as one who suffered—culminated in a vision for love's redemptive possibilities in the American South. Any understanding of the historical, intellectual, and spiritual genealogy of the countertheology that undergirded the freedom struggle in Americus requires an understanding of the black church.

The Black Church in Americus

Prior to the Civil War and Emancipation, blacks and whites typically worshipped together in Americus. Records for the First Baptist Church of Americus, for example, show that on the cusp of the Civil War, in 1858, the church boasted 154 white members and 99 black members.[12] At times black Americans would gather for separate worship among themselves, but not until the war's end did freed blacks formally seek ecclesiastical autonomy. On December 10, 1865, First Baptist received a petition requesting "use of the church house until they could establish a separate house of worship."[13] In February 1866, First Baptist "approved the move of the colored membership to erect a house of worship" and committed to "render them what aid they need and we are able to give." Black Baptists in Americus acquired a plot of land "on the south fringe" of the white First Baptist Church and formally constituted their own church.[14] While the white First Baptist Church remembered this event as one of "granting," "approving," and helping their less fortunate black brothers and sisters, the congregation of Bethesda Baptist remembered things differently. The church's own history claimed that "the colored membership increased so rapidly that a separation was necessary."[15] According to First Baptist's records, at the time of constitution, blacks did outnumber whites in church membership: 150 black members to 130 white.[16] Whether out of a sense of altruism or intimidation, in 1866, Bethesda Baptist was established, "the first Negro Baptist Church in Americus."[17]

In addition to Bethesda Baptist, Americus soon saw the establishment of an African Methodist Episcopal Church (A.M.E.). This small congregation of twenty-five began to meet during Reconstruction, in 1869, "at Hampton and Anshron Streets, under the supervision of the white Methodist church"[18] and was dedicated under Bishop Campbell in 1877.[19] The church increased in membership and prominence and joined the A.M.E. national conferences. In 1922, Campbell A.M.E. moved to a more permanent structure by the "Negro Hospital" and high school. This new building, "a towering cathedral unmatched in its eloquence and beauty by any other African American structure in southwest Georgia," became a landmark in Americus and source of pride for the congregation, especially after the church hosted the annual meeting of the

A.M.E. Conference.[20] Throughout the twentieth century, Campbell Chapel continued to be an important site: hosting conferences, revivals, guest lectures, and even dramatic and musical presentations, as well as contributing significantly to life in Americus.[21]

As the oldest black churches of their respective denominations, Bethesda Baptist and Campbell Chapel A.M.E. typically attracted congregations possessed of a certain amount of money or social respectability. They incubated leadership, economic independence, and social autonomy. But there were other, smaller churches as well. Over time, Bethesda Baptist and Campbell Chapel A.M.E. multiplied congregations. For example, from Bethesda Baptist came Shady Grove Baptist in 1868, Mt. Olive Grove in 1881, Bethel Baptist in 1885, Friendship Baptist in 1895, and Peace (later Union Tabernacle) in 1907. From Campbell Chapel came Allen Chapel A.M.E., St. Paul A.M.E. in 1890, Mt. Creek A.M.E. in 1893, and Mt. Carmel A.M.E. in 1896. Those Americus residents required to work on Sunday mornings founded their own congregations so they could gather together after the work was done for refreshment, worship, and rest.[22] These congregations, which emerged in the late nineteenth and early twentieth centuries, ministered to those in the city of Americus and those living in the surrounding rural areas.[23] Whether the venerable middle-class sanctuaries downtown or the smaller pine churches way out in Sumter County, these churches were a seminal part of black life in Americus.

Black congregations, like those in Americus, proliferated throughout the South in the years after Reconstruction. Through the "nadir of race relations," strong, separate black churches developed independently of their nearby white counterparts.[24] Faced with the brutality of Jim Crow and white supremacist terror, the black church offered not just spatial and social separation, but theological distinctiveness. For one "terribly fulfilling moment," Howard Thurman explained, those living under oppression remembered that they "[were] somebody."[25] In church, black Christians found a haven from racial oppression and a countertheology that provided a powerful spiritual alternative to sanctified racism.

The Theology of the Black Church

Kidnapped Africans encountered Protestant Christianity soon upon their arrival in the American South, though debates swirled over the consequences of Christianizing slaves.[26] Nonetheless, throughout the Colonial era, baptism, catechesis, and ritual instruction of slaves occurred with regularity. During the Great Awakenings, particularly the Second Great Awakening in the early nineteenth century, the frequency, depth, and sincerity of conversions increased, as itinerant Baptist and Methodist evangelists proselytized large swaths of people, black and white, in the South.[27] At one revival in Savannah, Georgia, an estimated 1,500 "among the colored population" were converted and "received by baptism." At another, the famous Methodist orator George Whitefield boasted, "nearly fifty Negroes came to give me thanks for what God had done to their souls."[28]

From the earliest moments of conversion, black Americans recognized the leveling aspects of Christianity. There was great irony in slaveowners' hopes that conversion and selective sermonizing would produce submission, for Christianity actually provided a logic for rebellion, and a power for resistance.[29] Some used the tenets of Christianity to revolt against their oppressors, others to press for abolition, still others to simply resist dehumanization.[30] Unlicensed black lay preachers, such as Harry Hosier, Joseph Willis, John Chavis, and Henry Evans, began exhorting their fellow men and women, acting "as crucial mediators between Christian belief and the experiential world of the slaves." A distinct black theology developed, one forged in the experience of oppression.[31]

Spirituals offer insight into this powerful theology.[32] The "soul-life of the people," spirituals were, in the words of Benjamin Mays, "songs of the soil and songs of the soul."[33] Despite the plethora of studies on spirituals, still too little has been written concerning their theological elements. "Apparently," Jim Cone remarked, "most scholars assume that the value of the black spiritual lies in its artistic expression and not its theological content." "Is it not possible," he continued, "that the thought of the spiritual is as profound as the music is creative?" The thought is indeed profound, revealing a deep theological sensibility applied to the lived experiences of black people.[34]

Consider one spiritual recalled by Anderson Edwards: "My knee bones am aching, / My body's rackin' with pain, / I 'lieve I'm a chile of God, / And this ain't my home, / 'Cause Heaven's my aim."[35] In these simple phrases, oppressed blacks remembered that they were created by God, that they were his children, and that their true citizenship was not of this world but in heaven. When blacks sang "My Lord delivered Daniel / Why can't He deliver me?" they declared that the God of the Bible, of Exodus and the Lion's Den, was a God of deliverance from bondage and death.[36] Another song claimed: "He have been wid us, Jesus, / He still wid us, Jesus, / He will be wid us, Jesus / Be wid us to the end," affirming Jesus's unwavering presence and identification with his people.[37]

Spirituals proliferated in Americus as well. Rev. Pearlie Brown recalled that his grandmother, sold in slavery from Virginia to Americus, spoke of songs that called on her to "pray hard" in this life and look to the day of meeting "on that other shore" where there was "no more auction block."[38] Amidst suffering, the spirituals declared a countertheology to the racist Christianity of Southern slaveholders. As Howard Thurman put it, "By some amazing but vastly creative spiritual insight, the slave undertook the redemption of a religion that had been profaned in his midst."[39]

This redemptive countertheology persisted after Emancipation. Black clergy, intellectuals, and parishioners defied Christian white supremacy. National figures, such as Nannie Burroughs, Virginia Broughton, Ida B. Wells, Henry McNeal Turner, W. E. B. Du Bois, and Daniel Alexander Payne, spoke out forcefully against racial oppression with theological moral imperatives.[40] Local churches and denominations, too, like Bethesda Baptist and Campbell Chapel A.M.E. in Americus, cultivated a black theology of resistant orthodoxy.[41]

Black Americans found in Christianity a stunning theological power. This power was distilled over the centuries, from spirituals of the cotton fields to abolitionist treatises, from the prayers of forgotten grandmothers to the admonitions of Bible-toting uncles. By the twentieth century, the countertheology of the indigenous black church had influenced the academic discourse over race, largely owing to a "cadre of black religious intellectuals" who made an argument against racism in America.[42] In the 1930s and 1940s, these men—Mordecai Johnson, George Kelsey, Benjamin Mays, William Stuart Nelson, and Howard Thurman—took leadership positions in historically black institutions. With the promise of the black church and the power of black institutions, they "theologized . . . direct action techniques."[43] Years before the modern civil rights movement, these figures, who were located primarily in academic institutions, exerted wide influence by preaching regularly in black churches in the North and South, publishing collaborative works, and organizing conferences.[44]

One such conference occurred at Yale University in 1931. "Whither the Negro Church" considered the role of the black church not only to "uplift the Negro race" but also to create "a new social order based on the principles of Jesus."[45] Speakers included A. Philip Randolph, Benjamin Mays, and Jerome Davis, a white Yale professor who, at one point, suggested the group consider adopting Gandhi's philosophy of nonviolent civil disobedience.[46] The group heeded Davis's advice. Following the 1931 conference, several black religious intellectuals embarked on pilgrimages to India to meet with Gandhi and seek a practical application for their theological convictions.[47] Indeed, they found in Gandhian nonviolence what Dennis Dickerson has dubbed a "praxis."[48]

Black religious intellectuals had long preached prophetic Christianity; Gandhi showed them how it might be applied in collective movement. "Theology and tactics," Dickerson writes, were "bound together . . . in ways that made each intrinsic to the other."[49]

This theology and these tactics again came together in the black church, because, as Benjamin Mays explained, the church "has the potentialities to become possibly the greatest spiritual force in the United States."[50] If black ministers were "prepared theologically" to lead, if they "would envisage God as one who required them to battle Jim Crow with a moral methodology consistent with justice and love," Mays continued, they could lead the black faithful in redeeming America and achieving racial parity.[51] Mays's words were prescient. Future leaders of the civil rights movement were sitting in his classroom.[52]

In the meantime, black religious intellectuals continued to develop an application of Christian theology and nonviolence to race relations in the United States. In 1948, Mays and other black thinkers and theologians compiled an edited volume entitled *The Christian Way in Race Relations*.[53] It described major issues in American race relations and asserted "the central role" Christianity "should play in the solution of these problems."[54] For instance, in his essay, "Crucial Issues in America's Race Relations Today," William Stuart Nelson claimed "the gravest loss from which the nation suffers as a result of the unsolved racial problem is spiritual."[55] As such, demanding a confrontation between America's claim to Christian democracy and the reality of racial inequality amounted, in Nelson's view, to a call for "redemption."[56] Following from Nelson, George Kelsey claimed "the soul that is united with God" would necessarily be compelled to "realize the love of God toward all peoples," while James Robinson perhaps put it even more succinctly: "The God of the Christian way desires and seeks to eliminate any social condition which prevents or impedes [abundant life.]"[57] In some ways, this view appears the photo negative of the spiritualism of the white church. While many white Christians conveniently concluded that obedience to Christ would passively, even automatically, result in improved social relations, these black leaders asserted that obedience to Christ demanded active, intentional attention to social relations, namely racism.

Black religious intellectuals deemed the theology of white supremacy heretical. Benjamin Mays stated that segregated churches were decidedly "unchristian."[58] If "man's relationship to God is automatically one of kinship," Howard Thurman reasoned, to deny a fellow man equality based on race was sinful, "unrighteous," a "repudiation" of God and his ways.[59] There would be consequences for such heresy. Richard McKinney concluded *The Christian*

Way in Race Relations with a sobering warning to segregationists: "to live as though we are not our brother's keeper or to disregard the law of human brotherhood" would invite "the judgment of the eternal God . . . misery and suffering."[60] Calling out heresy requires prophets, so the work concluded with a call for bold leadership. And though George Kelsey cautioned that "Jerusalem always stones her prophets," his friend Howard Thurman insisted that leaders could "depend on the God of life to sustain him even in his moment of greatest despair and frustration."[61]

WHILE *The Christian Way in Race Relations* may not have been read thoroughly by every rural pastor in the South, its ideas became part of a national conversation about Christianity and race that inspired a generation of prophetic leaders. Black religious intellectuals were converting centuries of theologizing into the language of social protest. From the 1931 Yale Conference, to voyages to India, to *The Christian Way in Race Relations*, the black religious intellectuals of the 1930s and 1940s articulated a sustainable theology of racial resistance, and they also discovered a practical application for that theology in nonviolence. In doing so, they equipped generations of prophetic leaders and "laid theological foundations for the civil rights movement of the 1950s and 1960s."[62]

Four theological notions in particular bequeathed the civil rights movement a deep religious power: the creative authority of God, segregation's sinfulness, divine deliverance, and an orthodox Christology. These principles fostered by the black church, articulated by black religious intellectuals, and adopted by civil rights leaders culminated in the hope that Christian love, displayed nonviolently, was redemptive and could transform race relations in America.

The Creative Authority and Goodness of God

"In the beginning," the Bible opens, "God created." This simple statement that white Fundamentalists defended from liberal incursions also formed the basis for a theological objection to racism. Harkening back to a pseudoscientific racism long accepted as biology, the idea that blacks were inherently inferior constituted a common justification for oppression of black Americans based on their skin color. But black theology offered an antidote. "Oh, we never believed that," Americus resident Karl Wilson stated, with a hint of mischievousness, "we knew we were created in God's image, we were his children."[63] This "fundamental" theological assertion offered black Christians assurance of their dignity as sons and daughters of the Creator, as bearers of the image of God, as well as a distinctly theological critique of racism.[64]

To simply exist as a human being meant that one was created and was thus bestowed divine dignity as a possessor of the image of God. In his work *Racism and the Christian Understanding of Man*, George D. Kelsey developed this critique.[65] The argument unfolded thusly: according to the biblical account, God created the heavens and the earth. He proclaimed them good. He then "created man in his own image" and proclaimed this "very good."[66] All humans, therefore, were created in the image of God, bore his imprint, and were very good. While this idea may seem rather basic, it nevertheless provided a powerful theological foundation for racial equality. The notion of God as Creator, as a Creator with both authority and goodness, meant that to disparage black people was either to deny God's authority as Creator of all things, or to deny his goodness, implying that he made a mistake in Creation. Not only so, but if God, in his infinite goodness created man in his own image, then to disparage a man would be to deny that image and to dispute the singular fact of God's creative act. As Kelsey explained: "God has created all men in His own image. . . . The decision as to whether or not men are equal cannot be made by looking at men; he who would decide must look at God."[67] "God alone is the source of human dignity," Kelsey emphasized, and "God has bestowed upon all the very same dignity. He has created them all in His own image and herein lays their dignity." Therefore, he concluded, "human dignity is not an achievement nor is it intrinsic quality . . . it is a gift, a bestowal." The gift of dignity could not be taken away without denying the Giver.[68]

The theology of "the image of God," or *imago deo*, contained not only the belief that all people were created by God, but that all people were also children of God. "Men are equal because God has created them in his own image and called them to sonship," Kelsey explained.[69] In the act of creation, God and man forged a familial bond, what Howard Thurman characterized as kinship through "origin."[70] Human beings were not only made in the image of God and therefore given dignity, but human beings were also loved by God, as sons are loved by a Father.[71] In this way, black theologians insisted that people must treat each other with the same sort of love that God gave to them, ever bearing in mind, as George Kelsey reminded, that "equality is an imperative of love."[72]

This notion of *imago deo* undergirded demands for equality. "The conviction that we are made in the image of God is deeply etched in the fiber of our religious tradition," Martin L. King Jr., said in a call for racial justice.[73] Throughout his ministry and mission, he would reiterate this theological point. In a

1961 speech at the Southern Baptist Theological Seminary, he declared, "the Negro came to feel he was somebody. His religion revealed to him that God loves all of his children and that all men are made in his image, and that the basic thing about a man is not his specificity but his fundamentum, not the texture of his hair or the color of his skin but his eternal significance and his worth to God."[74] "Every man is somebody because he is a child of God," King similarly proclaimed in a sermon in 1967, "Every person has . . . the indelible stamp of the Creator."[75] Many other ministers likewise reminded people of their foundational identity as created and loved by God. The Social Creed of Campbell Chapel A.M.E. in Americus proclaimed in 1952 a belief in "the dignity of man and in the sacredness of human personality."[76] This doctrine was both theologically orthodox and racially subversive. Howard Thurman tells a story about the transmutation and implications of *imago deo*: "Once when I was very young, my grandmother, sensing the meaning of the constant threat under which I was living, told me about the message of one of the slave ministers on her plantation . . . the climactic moment came in these exhilarating words: 'You are not slaves; you are not niggers condemned forever to do your master's will—you are God's children.'"[77]

For the unnamed slave minister, for Howard Thurman, for Martin King, and for many others in the black freedom struggle, the theology of God's creative goodness and authority had profound practical consequences. If all people were equally human, equally created, equally given dignity by their Creator, moreover, equally sons of the Father, they were to approach one another out of this essential likeness and equality. The command to justice and love was built upon the authority of God's creative action and his goodness. And, it followed, any inequality existed in denial of these divine attributes. Kelsey called it idolatry.

Racism as Idolatry, Segregation as Sin

The doctrine of *imago deo* and sonship, once embraced, imbued acts of racism with theological significance. "Since racism assumes some segments of humanity to be defective in essential being," Kelsey argued, "and since for Christians all being is from the hand of God, racism alone among the idolatries calls into question the divine creative action."[78] The presupposition was that God must have erred in creating some races. It was, Benjamin Mays asserted, "tantamount to saying to God, 'You made a mistake, God, when you didn't make all races white.'"[79] Therefore, the doctrine followed, when white Christians engaged in racial discrimination, they diminished God's creative authority and elevated themselves as the rulers and interpreters of the created order. Racism was an affront to men and women, certainly, but moreover, it was an affront to God.

In forming a hierarchy based upon pigmentation, racism privileged the creation over the Creator, succumbing, in the theologians' estimation, to the worst sort of idolatry. As George Kelsey wrote, "the true identity of man is the worship and adoration of God. But man, the master, seeks to displace God and to glorify himself."[80] Racism essentially repeated the original sin of Eden: wanting to be God. It was, as Kelsey put it, "complete self-deification"; it was "utter blasphemy."[81] "No group is good enough, wise enough, to restrict the mind, circumscribe the soul, and to limit the physical movement of another group," Benjamin Mays declared, "To do this is blasphemy. It is a usurpation of the role of God."[82] Racism and segregation, for these black religious intellectuals, constituted an expression of godlessness, that man is "by himself and for himself."[83] It was theologically wrong, idolatrous, "the ultimate sin . . . the rejection of life as the gift of the Creator, based on the false assumption that life is self-procured."[84]

Many black Christians adopted this belief, frequently alluding to segregation as sin.[85] In "Paul's Letter to American Christians," Martin King, like his teachers before him, declared notions of God-sanctioned racial difference to be no less than "blasphemy."[86] "Segregation is wrong," he stated, channeling Buber, "because it substitutes an I-It relationship for the I-Thou relationship and relegates persons to the status of things."[87] More than a principle put forth in the *Dred Scott* decision, the notion of persons as things was a theological inversion that heretically vaulted white men to the status of God. Perhaps Eddie Rhea Walker of Americus put it best. Though many whites perpetuating racism "felt God had given them the right," she said, "we knew better."[88]

The God Who Delivers His People

While black Christians may have known they were created in God's image and that segregation was sinful, they still had to deal with the reality of their oppression. From the days of enslavement to the era of Jim Crow, the story of Exodus, of God's deliverance of his people from bondage, served as a powerful motif in the black church and in black theology.[89] Spirituals like "Go Down, Moses," "Didn't Ol' Pharaoh Get Lost?," "Walk Together Children," and "God call Moses!" had long been part of the black theological canon.[90] As one slave recounted, "de preachers would exhort us dat us was de chillen o' Israel in de wilderness and de Lord done sent us to take dis land o' milk and honey."[91] Blacks in the American South took on the mantle of the people of Israel so that the liberation of the Exodus was theirs and so the hope of Canaan, the promised land of freedom.[92] "When I heard of his delivering people from bondage," Polly, a slave woman recounted, "I know it means poor Africans."[93] The exodus narrative did not exhaust its utility after Emancipation; it endured and animated the civil rights struggle. As King famously remarked in a sermon at Dexter Avenue Baptist in Montgomery, "Men cannot be satisfied with Egypt. . . . And eventually they will rise up and begin crying out for Canaan's land."[94] As Rabbi Abraham Joshua Heschel noted, "It was easier for the children of Israel to cross the Red Sea than for a Negro to cross certain university campuses."[95]

Within the Exodus story, black Christians discovered assigned meaning to their oppression, gave a language to their nationhood, and saw a linear, progressive hope for liberation. Exodus provided a "public vocabulary" deeply entrenched in Christian theology that reminded people, even those laboring under oppression, that there was a "transcendent God active in history" and that he acted on behalf of his people.[96] Not that people were without their part to play. Indeed, King warned in 1957, "whenever you break out of Egypt, you better get ready for stiff backs. You better get ready for some homes to be bombed. You better get ready for some churches to be bombed. You better get ready for a lot of nasty things to be said about you, because you're getting out of Egypt, and, whenever you break aloose from Egypt, the initial response of the Egyptian is bitterness."[97] Blacks in America would have to face the bitterness, cross the Red Sea and march through the wilderness, but God, the Deliverer, would go with them. As the spiritual went: "de God dat lived in Moses' time is jus de same today."[98]

Martin Luther King became the Moses of the movement, while Southern segregationists were cast as "pharaohs" keeping blacks in "the Egypt of segregation" rather than freeing them to go to the "Promised Land" of equality.[99] If that was true, black Americans understood their oppressors would face judgment just as the Egyptians had. Exodus theology offered biblical grounding for jeremiads.[100] "I can hear God speaking," King said, in his exposition of Exodus, "I can hear him speaking throughout the universe, saying, 'Be still and know that I am God.' And if you don't stop, if you don't straighten up, if you don't stop exploiting people, I'm going to rise up and break the backbone of your power. And your power will be no more!"[101] The God of Exodus was a God who delivered and who punished.[102] Thus, the appropriation of the Exodus narrative, Eddie Glaude has stated, "not only gave an account for the circumstances of black lives . . . it ensured retribution for the continued suffering of God's people."[103]

The narrative of the children of Israel being led out of slavery in the Old Testament offered hope of freedom for oppressed blacks in the South. It also caused them to envision, as Albert Raboteau has phrased it, "their own sense of peoplehood."[104] In the Exodus account, following their deliverance, the people of Israel were given the law in a covenant with God and constituted as his people. The notion of deliverance and covenant has often been historically constitutive for groups. For example, the American colonists took on the motif of exodus when establishing their new government, as immortalized by John Winthrop's "A Modell of Christian Charity."[105] For the Puritan colonists, England constituted Pharaoh's oppressive Egypt, the code of conduct Winthrop and others established before God and each other was their new covenant, and America was the Promised Land.[106] Of course, blacks in America saw things differently. For them, America was not the Promised Land but Egypt herself, the land of their oppression and exploitation. But they, too, like the Puritans of old, found a collective identification in the delivered Israelite people. This peoplehood was grounded not in ethnicity; it was a spiritual peoplehood, born of oppression and born into hope.[107] While the covenanted people of Israel sought a new place, blacks in America, in the main, did not.[108] The Promised Land for them was not another land, but the America they inhabited, restored and redeemed and fulfilling its promise. As Allen Callahan said: "The Promised Land is not a home. It is a hope."[109] This hope drove the civil rights movement—a political request but also a deeply theological demand for the covenantal promise to be fulfilled.[110] In 1961, King could sense the narrative arc: "We've broken loose from the Egypt of slavery and we've moved through the wilderness of segregation, and now we stand on the border of the promised land of integration."[111] Practitioners of black theology in the United States would continue the struggle out of bondage that the ancient Israelites began.[112] They would live the theology they espoused.

The Black Christ: Son of Man, Son of God

St. Paul's Letter to the Colossians declares that in Jesus Christ "all things hold together."[113] The same might be said of the theology of the black church. The fourth theological notion that animated thousands of chanted sermons and the civil rights movement was a profound, practical Christology. This Christology freed Jesus from the whiteness of the mainstream American imagination and remembered him as both the Jewish Messiah and the Incarnate God-man, the suffering servant ever present with those who suffer.[114] Lest this seem the esoteric murmurings of academic hermeneutics, this theology, rest assured, was intensely practical for black Christians. "If our existence were not at stake," Jim Cone explained, "then the Christological question would be no more than an intellectual exercise for professional theologians." "But," he continued, for black Christians, "for Christians who have experienced the extreme absurdities of life," the "Christological question is not primarily theoretical but practical. It arises from the encounter of Christ in the struggle of freedom."[115] Christ's presence in the freedom struggle was the "essence" of black theology and had long been one of its most assertive doctrines.[116] From stories of slaves searching for letters of Jesus's name in the Bible to calling out for him in the shadows, the Jesus Christ black Christians knew was never far off in the heavenlies, but one intimately acquainted with them and their plight; indeed, one who shared it.[117] When in the black church and later in mass meetings, throngs of black Americans sang "Give me Jesus, / Give me Jesus, / You may have the world, / but Give me Jesus," they were not, as is often blithely asserted, selling out to the otherworldly. They were recognizing the supremacy of the person of Jesus Christ in the practice of Christianity. Christology had special relevance for black Christians. As James Cone put it, Jesus Christ was not only the source but also the "content of the hopes and dreams of black people."[118]

As the previous chapter chronicled, in the twentieth century, mainline white Protestant theologians in Europe and America increasingly envisioned Jesus as an abstract Being with only incidental effect on life on earth. But most black Christians never adopted this "thin Christology," as Charles Marsh has described it. Rather, they maintained an intimate relationship with the God who became man and entered history. King himself, as a graduate student and young theologian, criticized white Protestants (in this case Niebuhr) for their Christ of "pure abstraction," preferring "the Jesus of history who walked in Jerusalem."[119] King rejected the Christological liberalism of Crozer and instead looked to theologians like Howard Thurman and back to the tradition of the black church for a savior real enough to meet the harsh reality of American racism. To be fair, many white evangelicals, too, dismissed theological liberalism and treasured Jesus's immanence, but there were differences. Black theology viewed Jesus as not only incarnately real, but as one who, in his earthly form looked like them and likewise suffered. Refusing to allow neo-Gnosticism to co-opt their savior, black Christians reclaimed Jesus in all his human concreteness.

This began, as Howard Thurman wrote in his seminal 1949 work, *Jesus and the Disinherited*, "with the simple historical fact" that "Jesus was a Jew."[120] The fact of Jesus's Jewishness meant that he existed as a man, and a racialized one at that, with real flesh, most likely brown. Jesus's Jewishness made him not only a man of color, but an exiled one, born into a minority ethnic group within an empire.[121] Naturally, he was poor.[122] Jesus's racial marginalization and economic deprivation linked him, according to Thurman, with "the masses of men on the earth," those who "live with their backs constantly against the wall . . . the poor, the disinherited, the dispossessed," including, certainly, blacks in the American South.[123] These masses understood that when God chose to come to earth, he chose to come like them—racialized, ostracized, and poor.[124]

Emphasizing Jesus's Jewishness not only recaptured him as concretely, pigmentedly human, but also revealed him as a member and savior of God's chosen people.[125] "The particularity of Jesus's person as disclosed in his Jewishness is indispensable for Christological analysis," Jim Cone stated. "On the one hand, Jesus's Jewishness pinpoints the importance of his humanity for faith, and on the other, it connects God's salvation drama in Jesus with the Exodus-Sinai event."[126] The God who sent Jesus Christ, black Christians held, was the same God who covenanted to redeem Israel, with Jesus the Messianic fulfillment of God's covenant and therefore evidence that God keeps his promises and will, in fact, save his people.[127] Just as the black church tenaciously clung to the Exodus story, Jesus's incarnation as the Jewish Messiah was yet another confirmation of both God's covenantal love and the liberation from bondage for God's people.[128]

But how would this liberation come? Looking to Jesus, many black religious leaders wondered if it would be through redemptive suffering. After all, Jesus had been persecuted and killed. He knew the disgrace of marginalization and understood the degradation of poverty, he had felt the sting of the lash, and had, moreover, tasted the bitter cup of God's wrath. He had died an ignominious death, like so many blacks in the South, which was why they could, in the very same breath, speak of "the cross and the lynching tree."[129] Black Christians saw that they were not alone in suffering, or even in death; Jesus understood it. He knew, like them, what was meant when it was written "cursed is everyone who is hanged on a tree."[130] The cross was the best proof of Jesus's immanence in black theology: he suffered *with* them and he also suffered *for* them. If Jesus's terrible suffering and death were part of God's redemptive plan, it was possible, many black Christians believed, that their the plight could be as well.[131]

But the crucifixion itself could not bring hope, cosmic companionship notwithstanding. Hope would come with the morning, as, according to orthodox Christianity, Jesus rose from the dead. The resurrected Jesus emerged as not only a fellow sufferer but as the One who brought full liberation, even from death. Though crucified as a poor Jew, "he was resurrected as Lord," Cone remarked, "thereby making good God's promise to bring freedom to all who are weak and helpless."[132] For many black Christians, the resurrection of Jesus was the ultimate symbol of hope, a guarantee that their struggles would end in victory and in liberation. The resurrection meant freedom from death, sin, and oppression. It meant that Jim Crow would be defeated.

Living Black Theology: Redemption and the Love Ethic

These principles, long guarded and molded by generations of black Christians, offered a powerful countertheology to white supremacist religion. But how could it be lived? In the twentieth century, the "love ethic" and the praxis of Christian nonviolence gave the struggle concrete expression. Men like Martin Luther King Jr. and James Lawson, both ministers nurtured in the black church, fused their theological training with the ideas of Bayard Rustin, A. Philip Randolph, and Gandhi to create a protest movement designed for black Christians in the South. The way to live theology, they declared, was to demonstrate it in love and nonviolence, as Christ himself did.[133] "Although crucified by hate," King taught, Jesus "responded with aggressive love."[134]

"Love," King unequivocally proclaimed, "is the key."[135] The love that King and his fellows referred to, though, was "not to be confused with some sentimental outpouring." No, King clarified, "love is something much deeper than emotional bosh."[136] Certainly weepy emotionalism was no match for police dogs, billy clubs, and mocking mobs. More than mere feeling or sentimentalism, love constituted the conscious decision of religious conviction. This love meant consistently deciding to put off bitterness and hatred even for the most rabid racist, following the example of Jesus, who instructed his followers to "love your enemies and pray for those who persecute you."[137] Love like this required, in Howard Thurman's words, "painstaking discipline."[138] For blacks in the struggle, the love ethic required the discipline of both nonviolence and forgiveness, since in America, to love one's white neighbor meant almost necessarily to love one's antagonist. Here again, it was the life and message of Jesus, to "forgive seventy times seven" and to "turn the other cheek," that offered the theological motivation for nonviolence and reconciliation. Transformed

by the love and forgiveness of Christ, many hoped they could likewise transform their oppressors. In a famous sermon, King explained:

> To our most bitter opponents we say: "We shall match your capacity to
> inflict suffering by our capacity to endure suffering. We shall meet your
> physical force with soul force. Do to us what you will, and we shall con-
> tinue to love you. . . . Throw us in jail, and we shall still love you. Send
> your hooded perpetrators of violence into our community at the mid-
> night hour and beat us and we shall still love you. But be ye assured that
> we will wear you down by our capacity to suffer. One day we shall win
> freedom, but not only for ourselves. We shall so appeal to your heart and
> conscience that we shall win you in the process, and our victory will be
> a double victory."[139]

In nonviolence, in redemptive suffering merged with the love ethic, black activists believed they could not only bring down segregation and Jim Crow but
convert America to brotherhood and goodwill. In Jesus's teachings, in the crucifixion and resurrection, many black Christians found proof that love was
more powerful than hate, that justice would prevail over injustice, that life
would conquer death. For these, nonviolent resistance was the flesh and blood
incarnation of their theological heritage.

The God who created them in love, who delivered from bondage in Egypt,
who, in Jesus, was like them and with them, would be present in their struggle
in the twentieth-century South against the sin of segregation. As Americus
minister J. R. Campbell put it, "the same God that was with us before was with
us [now], 'cause he had to be with us," so "[we] woke up and found out [we]
could be defiant, could assert [our] rights."[140]

Lived Theology Takes to the Street

This theology mattered not just to trained intellectuals but to less formally educated, more rural populations of black churchgoers as well. Too often, scholars assume everyday church folk were only marginally theologically engaged.
And if theology means studying Tillich in a gleaming library, then that is surely
true. But this narrow definition pretentiously and wrongly limits the profun-
dity possessed by the ordinary faithful who were, in Jonathan Walton's phrase,
"theologically trained within seminaries of suffering."[141] Theological principles formally espoused from the lectern and in treatises echoed in quotidian
life, in whispered bedtime prayers and sweaty "amens" in plain pine churches.
Black theology pervaded everyday life and addressed the harsh realities of

everyday living.[142] As Benjamin Mays stated, blacks were "not interested in any fine theological or philosophical discussions about God," choosing to emphasize *lived* theology, the God "who is able to help him bridge the chasm that exists between the actual and the ideal."[143]

The civil rights movement embodied this lived theology and gave it real expression. John Lewis, the famous activist who at one time worked in Americus, tells an illustrative story: there was a minister picketing at a county courthouse when a white observer chided, "'You shouldn't be doing that, you should be preaching the gospel!' To this, a SNCC worker standing alongside the minister replied, 'He is preaching the gospel!'"[144] "What is remarkable about the civil rights movement," David Chappell claims, "and what makes it like one of the great historical [religious] revivals is that the enthusiasm moved out of the church and into the streets."[145] Lee Street in Americus would be no exception.

In Americus, the theological civil rights movement was led primarily by two ministers: Rev. J. R. Campbell and Rev. R. L. Freeman. Since the church occupied such a pivotal place in black life, ministers were often regarded as leaders in the community, offering religious instruction and serving as pillars of education and respectability. This proved true in Americus. Campbell and Freeman used their positions as ministers to provide resources for and to apply doctrines to the nascent civil rights struggle. The lives and work of these two men offer meaningful insight into black theology and how it was indeed lived in the civil rights movement in Americus.

Born in 1925 in Newport News, Virginia, and reared in South Carolina, J. R. Campbell possessed a deep familiarity with the rhythms and strictures of the Deep South. After being abandoned as an infant, J. R. lived with four different families before settling with the Campbells, whose surname he adopted. His surrogate father then died when J. R. was twelve, leaving him largely on his own, as he worked in the Carolina Lowcountry "pulling turnips, picking peas, cleaning fish, catching crabs." Even in these difficult circumstances, Campbell claimed he was "an ordinary black boy in the slum part of town," who, of course, "grew up going to church." After enlisting in the army and serving in World War II, J. R. Campbell returned to South Carolina. He initially worked in a restaurant as "the best cook in the state of South Carolina," but soon felt a pull into Christian ministry. "I was called to preach," he stated, "I ran as long as I could but the Lord pushed me forth to preach, I couldn't run no further." Campbell accepted his call and began to preach in the A.M.E church, pastoring several congregations in Georgia, including Allen Chapel A.M.E in Americus.[146]

When J. R. and his new bride, Mamie, of Savannah, arrived in Americus in 1963, they encountered a place where blacks faced severe racial discrimination. Only seventy-nine black Americans were registered to vote. But a struggle was stirring, and though Campbell set out solely to preach God's Word and minister to his flock, he soon found himself swept up in the movement. "When I came to Allen Chapel," he remembered, "the Sumter County Movement, the [local civil rights] movement was getting people registered to vote. The boys [Don Harris, Ralph Allen, John Perdew, and Bobby Mathis of SNCC] came before I got here and told me all the preachers was in the movement. I said, 'Oh, that's marvelous. That's wonderful. If all the preachers in it, sure I'll join.' I joined." But when Campbell arrived at the small mass meeting out at a little community church, he noticed "there weren't no preachers." In rural areas like Americus, preachers feared repercussions from the white community. They also, Campbell explained, sought to maintain their elevated status and influence in the community; they "didn't want to lose fifteen minutes of air time for 'rescue hour' on Sundays."[147] Despite the deception and the lack of ministerial presence at the mass meeting, Campbell stayed. He was taken with the students' enthusiasm and committed himself to the local movement, eventually becoming its leader and hosting mass meetings at Allen Chapel.[148]

Buttressed both by his newcomer status and his theological convictions, Campbell was able to eschew the trappings of worldly prominence and lead a movement of passionate young people. Initially, the local movement lacked organization, but with outside support from the NAACP, SNCC, and other groups, it began to hold mass meetings, marches, voter registration drives, pickets, and boycotts. Churches were the most common venues, as "pastors opened the door for the children to meet." Eventually, too, even once-hesitant ministers joined in, lending a theological foundation and strong leadership for the young students who made up the majority of the movement. Black religious leaders fused social activism with religious devotion, claiming, like Campbell, "We just got to pray every meeting." "The leadership of the movement," Charles Sherrod recalled, "was populated in all these [rural Georgia] counties by and with deacons, deaconesses, ushers, people who had leadership in the church . . . all the churches in the community."[149] Nevertheless, as support mounted, activist ministers faced the retribution they had once feared. "White people told me they was going to kill me," Campbell reported, "my phone rang off the hook . . . just rang, rang, rang night and day." Even so, Campbell claimed he "didn't fear nothing," gaining strength and courage from his theological convictions. "I knew there was a God upstairs," he insisted, "and I was doing the right thing. I know God had no respect for persons."[150]

One of the black ministers that joined J. R. Campbell in the movement was R. L. Freeman. Freeman had been born one of nine boys in a prominent Atlanta family. The Freemans were well connected within black Atlanta. R. L. attended Morehouse College and was mentored by "Daddy" King himself.[151] After college, Freeman heard the call to the ministry and became a Baptist preacher, serving parishes in Toccoa, Georgia, and South Carolina before arriving in Americus. Rev. Freeman initially visited Bethesda Baptist to fill the pulpit in September 1946, at a time when the church was looking for a pastor. He preached "a gospel sermon with so much power that it was deeply felt by all present," prompting the church to ask him to accept the position of pastor "before leaving that day." Rev. Freeman accepted and began his tenure at Bethesda in October 1946. Almost immediately, he began a series of improvements at the church, including renovating the church building and parsonage and reinvigorating the youth programs. Following his arrival, Bethesda Baptist prayed over Rev. Freeman that "God would bless his life and [that he] would live long to render loving-hearted service for the Master."[152] Not only would Freeman rend service to God, but to the civil rights movement.

Despite an initial reticence, possibly owing to his other position as assistant principal at Staley High School, Freeman was drawn into the civil rights struggle by his daughter Robertiena. A high school student during the early 1960s, Robertiena had been "long vigorous and conspicuous" in the Sumter County movement.[153] In addition to her active participation in organizing, Robertiena was also one of the first black students to integrate Americus High School, making her a target for white authorities. She was arrested on petty morality charges and, though they were soon dropped, and Robertiena released, the incident awoke a sleeping giant in Rev. Freeman. At the moment of his daughter's arrest, Freeman's remaining hesitancies evaporated in hot anger, and he devoted himself fully to the civil rights struggle in Americus. He registered his parishioners to vote, talked about the movement in late-night living room conversations, took all the black newspapers he could that reported on civil rights happenings, and constantly bailed young people out of jail. "Whenever something would happen in town," one Americus resident remembered, "everyone would always come talk to Rev. Freeman."[154]

Both Rev. Campbell and Rev. Freeman found themselves in positions of influence theologically and socially in Americus. The organizational and institutional tools afforded by the black church uniquely equipped them to be leaders while their moral status allowed them to engage the struggle for civil rights theologically. "In the act of faith," Martin King, Sr., stated, "every minister became an advocate for justice. In the South, this meant an active involvement in changing the social order all around us."[155] This involvement demanded practicing forgiveness and compassion in the push for change. As Robertiena Freeman recalled, her father "taught us to look at the world and see it as it is, but not to see race, not to see color . . . to be forgiving. God gave us His son, Jesus, He forgave us from our sins. We are forgiven, when we accept Christ, you know, we are forgiven, then we should also show compassion for other people and situations."[156] As the civil rights struggle manifested in Southern towns like Americus, the animating power was both institutional, bequeathed by the rich tradition of the black church, but more significantly, the power was theological, sparked and sustained by deep convictions.

Arguably, the power of the civil rights movement *had* to be theological. "It is hard to imagine masses of people lining up for years of excruciating risk against southern sheriffs, fire hoses, and attack dogs," David Chappell has argued, convincingly, "without some transcendent or millennial faith to sustain them."[157] The risks defied a worldly calculus. "How can black people account for the power and courage to struggle against . . . the Ku Klux Klan and police? What keeps the community together when there are so many scares and hurts? What gives them the will and courage to struggle in hope?" Jim Cone posits, "I think the only 'reasonable' and 'objective' explanation is to say that the people are right when they proclaim the presence of divine power, wholly different from themselves."[158]

From Yale University to Friendship Baptist, from Morehouse College to the streets of Americus, certain theological beliefs born in oppression and nursed in the black church allowed practitioners of black Christianity the strength and power to stave off racism's mendacity and affirm both their temporal and eternal dignity, in a countertheology to white Protestantism. In investigating this theology, the actions and words of the foot soldiers of the civil rights struggle are properly understood within their black theological heritage and imbued with compelling theological power.

Dressed in sundresses with hair fixed nicely in defiance of the heat, Robertiena Freeman and her friends sat close in the smooth wooden pews. As they had done so many days in their lives, the girls clapped and sang in the church, fanning themselves occasionally and exchanging excited glances. But this was not a regular Sunday worship service; it was a mass meeting. And on this hot

July night, after the meeting ended, Robertiena and the others in the packed church did not go home to supper. Instead, enlivened by the hymns, the sermon, and by each other, they marched two by two out of the church and onto the dark, unpaved road leading to the Sumter County courthouse. The time had come in Americus: the black church and black theology were taking to the streets.

Part II

CHAPTER FOUR

Marching to Eternity

Theology Takes to the Streets of Americus

Will we march only to the music of time, or will we, risking criticism
and abuse, march to the soul-saving music of eternity?

—Martin Luther King Jr., "Transformed Nonconformist," 1963

What were these new ideas? That all men and women were created equal.
That there is a place in the Sun for us all. Where did these ideas come from?
From God of course. So they were not new ideas, nor were they old, they
were eternal, and folks were coming upon them and incorporating them
in consciousness and living them.

—Peter deLissovoy, *The Great Pool Jump*, 2010

Willie Bolden had been in Americus all summer. And all summer, he had been
waiting for this moment. The organizing, the leaflets, the threats of violence,
the mass meetings—they had all led him to this speech. "People may say we
are agitators," he shouted to the swaying crowd around him. "They may say
we are extremists. But let me ask you something," he intoned, with the cadence
of a preacher. "Okay, alright, yeah man," the crowd murmured in anticipation
as Bolden dramatically paused. "Was Jesus Christ an extremist when he died
for you and me?"[1]

On the sweltering July night that Bolden delivered these words, protestors
in Americus like Robertiena Freeman were marching to the courthouse to protest the unjust imprisonment of four local women. But the women's release
was not their only goal. They were also, in their nonviolent protest and "ex-
tremism," seeking to embody Jesus Christ.

The civil rights movement was certainly a social and a political protest,
but this part of the story centers on the theological components of that dissent, both in Americus and more broadly. In marching down the streets of
Americus, protestors claimed they were children of God. In waiting in voting registration lines, they fashioned themselves as the children of Israel
wandering in the desert before entering the Promised Land. In enduring
beatings and humiliations, they took on the mantle of Christ at Golgotha. In
languishing in fetid jail cells, they imagined the sufferings of Paul and Silas in

a Roman prison centuries earlier. This chapter lays out the general theological origins of the civil rights movement and then traces it through SNCC, into Albany, and finally to Americus, where beliefs incarnated in the lives of local men and women.

Since the first Africans landed on Virginia's soil, the centuries have brought new trials—enslavement, Black Codes, *Plessy*, lynching—and new opportunities for resistance—revolt, emancipation, uplift, the NAACP Legal Defense Fund. Much of the freedom struggle, from Nat Turner to David Walker, from Jarena Lee to Nannie Burroughs, was theologically motivated. But all along, black Americans insisted on the rights promised in the U.S. Constitution and by God. In the 1950s and 1960s, though, owing to a great conflation of international, national, and local events, activists throughout the South collectively asserted their demands to bring down Jim Crow in an unprecedented way. This story is well documented, well known, and extremely important. Yet as the familiar political battle raged, another, quieter phenomenon was taking place. This was a spiritual revolution in which many people asserted the primacy of their religious beliefs over and against the confines of a racist culture. As the movement gained momentum, political hopes merged with Christian theology, speaking truth to power.

The movement had lofty goals. It sought to "redeem the soul of the nation" by bringing the Christian principles of nonviolence and redemptive love into the public fight for civil rights.[2] For instance, the Southern Christian Leadership Conference (SCLC) assembled, in the words of its founders, "because we have no moral choice, before God, but to delve deeper into the struggle—and to do so with greater reliance on non-violence and with greater unity, coordination, sharing and Christian understanding."[3] These ministers brought Christian theology into direct conflict with segregation in the South, involving local communities and tapping into the wellspring of religious power within the black church. With the *Brown* decision in 1954, the effectiveness of the Montgomery Bus Boycott in 1955, and the formation of a major national organization in the SCLC in 1957, black Americans felt change coming.[4] Students especially, with the impatience of youth, began to organize in grassroots movements and make demands.[5]

A Theology for Radicals: SNCC

This grassroots stirring, "initiated, fed and sustained by students," was steeped in the practical strategies of direct action and expounded a philosophy of redemptive nonviolence.[6] Much of this ideological foundation came from the

Rev. James Lawson, sometimes referred to as the "teacher of the movement," who had given lectures and held workshops in Nashville for years.[7]

The son and grandson of Methodist ministers, Lawson was highly educated, devout, and had long had a commitment to nonviolence, one that landed him in prison as a conscientious objector in 1951. Upon his release, Lawson traveled, like the cadre of black religious intellectuals before him, to India. There he learned techniques in satyagraha from Gandhi, which he fused with his Christian faith.[8] When he returned to the United States in 1955, he enrolled in the Graduate School of Theology at Oberlin College, where one of his professors, Rev. A. J. Muste, introduced him to another young activist preacher, Martin Luther King Jr. Lawson had been impressed by King's ability to mobilize the masses in the Montgomery Bus Boycott, and King was taken with Lawson's philosophical and theological depth. As the story goes, King told Lawson, "Come now. Come immediately. We don't have anyone with your background in the South."[9] So Lawson transferred from Oberlin to Vanderbilt Divinity School, where he conducted workshops in Christian nonviolent action with local students.

"Teaching nonviolence in the '50s was a major challenge because it was like teaching in a foreign language," Lawson recalled, "though it was a language deeply rooted in the spirituality of Jesus, deeply rooted in the spirituality of many of the prophetic stories of the Hebrew Bible." Lawson's task, then, was to refamiliarize the students with the power contained in black theology in the context of protest. It was a "magnificent story," a glorious "secret"; "nonviolence was rooted in their own history and religion." Martin Luther King, Lawson explained, "was not a man from Mars, but a man out of the black church and out of the black Scriptures."[10] His power was their power. The fusion of black Christianity with Gandhian nonviolent resistance, Lawson asserted, could sustain a movement for revolutionary change in the South. It was "God's promise," he declared, "that if radically Christian methods are adopted the rate of change can be vastly increased."[11]

In this spirit of God's promise, and inspired by sit-ins in Greensboro and Nashville, Lawson, Ella Baker, Charles Sherrod, John Lewis, Diane Nash, and others convened at the Southwide Student Leadership Conference on Nonviolent Resistance to Segregation at Shaw University in Raleigh, North Carolina. Out of this Easter 1960 meeting, they founded the Student Nonviolent Coordinating Committee (SNCC). "It was touching, important," Charles Sherrod said of that initial gathering, "Some of the smartest guys I've ever known, and they were speaking for me. I was feeling the same way that they were feeling. Camaraderie was the name of the game."[12] As the conference title suggests, much of this unity stemmed from a shared belief in Christian nonviolence. "Down in Carolina there's a great wind," Jane Stembridge wrote, "It is the wind of the word of God. . . . People are always asking about God and always waiting for Him to act. Well now, it seems, He is. What a glorious, marvelous, unutterable April day!"[13] SNCC's Statement of Purpose, drafted by Lawson, read: "We affirm the philosophical or religious ideal of nonviolence as the foundation of our purpose, the pre-supposition of our faith, and the manner of our action. Nonviolence as it grows from a Judaeo-Christian tradition seeks a social order of justice permeated by love."[14] This nonviolence was possible, even in a violent society, because of the hope of redemption and transformation. The statement continued, "Through nonviolence, courage displaces fear; love transforms hate. Acceptance displaces prejudice; hope ends despair. Peace dominates war; faith reconciles doubt. Mutual regard cancels enmity. Justice for all overthrows injustice. The redemptive community supersedes systems of gross social immorality . . . by appealing to conscience and standing on the moral nature of human existence, nonviolence nurtures the atmosphere in which reconciliation and justice become actual possibilities."[15]

SNCC harnessed a creative religious power to foster racial change.[16] It was theology made practical; it was theology lived. Not all its members were religious, of course, nor was theological adherence a requirement for participation; nevertheless, theological principles gave SNCC its foundational identity. Believers and nonbelievers alike recognized the functional, confrontational power of Christian nonviolence as well as the discipline and cohesion it offered their movement. As Charles Marsh has noted, SNCC was "initially anchored in the language, imagery, and energies of the church, in search of a 'circle of trust,' a band of sisters and brothers gathered around the possibilities of agapeic, the beloved community."[17]

This concept of the beloved community motivated much of the struggle. From the first direct action in Montgomery, King reminded people that the boycott and even integration were not the main aims. Rather, he stated, "The end is reconciliation, the end is redemption, the end is the creation of the beloved community."[18] SNCC, too, described its ultimate goal not as political or economic power, nor even democracy, but as the creation of the beloved community.[19] The beloved community signified a society that was bound not only by laws of justice but relationships of love. It was not, as some have misrepresented it, a pie-in-the-sky, heavenly vision for someday but an urgent longing for shalom, "the passion to make human life and social existence a parable of God's love for the world," and an attempt to usher in the Kingdom of God on earth.[20]

It is worth mentioning that in Americus there was already a small place where the beloved community existed as a parable of God's love: Koinonia. Koinonia presented a real vision for civil rights activists. Some have suggested that it was, in fact, Koinonia Farm that Martin Luther King Jr., had in mind later when he infamously intoned, "I have a dream that one day on the red hills of Georgia, the sons of former slaves and the sons of former slave owners will be able to sit down together at the table of brotherhood."[21] Sitting down at the table of brotherhood happened daily at Koinonia Farm, a living picture of beloved community in the Deep South and an inspiration to the theological civil rights movement.[22]

As the example of Koinonia reveals, the beloved community was not merely a vision of legal rights and political access, though it certainly included that. It was a vision of a redeemed America, an America that resembled the Kingdom of God. Sounding like Benjamin Mays and George Kelsey, Jim Lawson asserted, "The Christian favors the breaking down of racial barriers because the redeemed community of which he is already a citizen recognizes no barriers dividing humanity. The kingdom of God, as in heaven so on earth, is the distant goal of the Christian. The kingdom is far more than the immediate need for integration."[23]

Both the aim and the "essential message" of the movement were, to quote Lawson, "theologically specific."[24] Segregation was sin. It corrupted creation, dehumanized God's children, and violated God's divine authority. Integration, then, had to be more (but certainly not less) than demanding political personhood. Integration meant rectifying damaging exclusion, participating in the restoration of godly human relationships, and worshipping God through honoring one another.[25] "We who are related to the movement," Lawson wrote in a 1966 article, "are trying to raise the 'moral issue'" by "pointing to the viciousness of racial segregation and prejudice and calling it evil or sin." In framing segregation as sin, "the matter" became, in Lawson's words, "not legal, sociological, or racial; it is moral and spiritual."[26] In sum, as Charles Marsh has contended, "the theological language could not have been more unapologetic in its specificity and scope, or more subversive of the racial status quo."[27]

Though theologically specific, SNCC's ideology was adaptable to quite different circumstances. While teaching its volunteers religious tenets and rooting its activism in Christianity, SNCC also allowed for a certain degree of ecumenicalism. A nonbeliever could embody Christ, if he or she chose to act like him. SNCC's sturdy and capacious theological foundation drew in the energies of young volunteers both secular and devout and made them participants in the struggle toward the beloved community.[28] As Albany Freedom

Rider and SNCC activist Casey Hayden remarked, nothing mattered "except the willingness to act out your beliefs."[29] The beliefs were in place, and young people throughout the nation were ready to act.[30]

Charles Sherrod and the Movement Next Door

Almost immediately upon its founding, SNCC determined to send leaders out to galvanize local movements. Charles Sherrod volunteered. "First I told Ms. [Ella] Baker that I'd be willing to be placed anywhere," Sherrod remembered. "I told her, the only thing that's holding me back is [$500 owed in] the student loan. So she raised the $500 immediately." He added, "I don't know where she got it." The organization set its sights on Southwest Georgia, in Terrell County, since the Justice Department had recently issued an injunction there because of the county's discrimination in voting.[31] Southwest Georgia was the belly of the beast. Though the Southwest Georgia Freedom Project, as it came to be known, initially targeted rural Terrell County, Sherrod had taken the train in to Albany, where SNCC's contacts were, and decided to stay for a bit. He "found it good to have a place to stay and food to eat," though in time he discovered that Albany was "the stomach of the monster" of racism, too.[32]

Deep in the black belt of the South, Albany, at least in SNCC's materials, "sits (or sleeps) amidst the largest pecan and peanut growing area in the U.S."[33] Sherrod would later call Albany the "Rome of Southwest Georgia," since "all roads lead to it, the most urban city in the whole area."[34] Still a "backwater" city of about 60,000 inhabitants in the "typically 'rural South,'" Albany possessed a mostly calm history of deeply unequal race relations.[35] Only in the early 1960s did people in Albany begin to persistently agitate for massive and comprehensive desegregation, the likes of which had not yet been attempted in the South.[36] The story of the Albany Movement is well known: the Freedom Singers, the cunning obduracy of Mayor Asa Kelley and Police Chief Laurie Pritchett, and, not least, the "failure" of Martin Luther King Jr., to secure lasting change in the city.[37] Yet its theological elements have been less acknowledged. Under the leadership of Charles Sherrod and in conjunction with local clergy, the Albany Movement possessed a deep theological power, one that would influence the civil rights movement in the surrounding rural areas, including Americus.

Charles Sherrod was born in 1937 outside of Petersburg, Virginia, a "speck" in Surry County.[38] His mother was fourteen at the time of his birth, so Sherrod and later his seven younger siblings lived in Petersburg with their extended family.[39] The family was close, though desperately poor. Even as a young child,

Sherrod recalled "carrying junk and shining shoes" to bring in money for the family.[40] Growing up in Virginia, Sherrod was exposed to the reality of Southern racism from a young age. His family lived in a tenement on the black side of town, with twelve people occupying two small, adjacent apartments. His aunts, uncle, and mother worked in a tobacco factory, while his grandmother "washed clothes for white people." His grandfather worked as a carpenter, until he was forced to flee after publicly asking, in the wake of a lynching, "why was he lynched last night?" Threatened with death if he remained, Sherrod's grandfather chose exile. Racism was choking in Petersburg, a reality for Sherrod from an early age. As he remembers, when he was two years old, he boarded a bus, and his mother yanked him from a front seat in the white section to the very back. The incident emblazoned on a young Sherrod the inequality of racial space in the South; he learned fear, which "creeped in."[41]

Yet even in suffocating poverty and violence, Christianity offered a respite and a counternarrative. His grandmother taught him "that as a Christian, if he acted humbly and in step with the teachings of Jesus, he need not fear any man."[42] With her encouragement and instruction, Sherrod developed a deep spiritual devotion. "I was preaching when I was about six years old," Sherrod said, "I was born a preacher." He and his boyhood friends would even "play church," preaching from a makeshift fort of sorts. At the real church his family attended, Mt. Olive Baptist Church, Sherrod served as the assistant superintendent of Sunday school and sang in the youth choir.[43] Mt. Olive offered the young Charles Sherrod a powerful black Christian theology, one centered on Jesus. The preacher "put the Lord on the cross every Sunday and took him off and rose him again," he recalled. "Every Sunday morning the life of Christ was told." Sherrod's first foray into activism came through the church. "Billie Lee and a bunch of boys came to me to integrate churches in 1954," Sherrod said. "I saw the [lynching] rope in my mind," he confessed, but he also "had these boys coming to me, asking me for leadership to go into these white churches." They went, visiting about ten churches in Petersburg. "There was always trouble," Sherrod recalled, "they seated us in the front, they seated us in the back, they seated us upstairs. . . . They didn't welcome us, it was always a pressured place." One Sunday, a church called the police. "After that we stopped going," plus, Sherrod added, "it was about time for me to go to college."[44]

Sherrod threw himself into his studies, working "as hard as two men to get through school."[45] At the same time, Sherrod's theological beliefs and prior activism led him to seek possibilities for the practical application of the gospel in protest.[46] After graduating with a degree in sociology from Virginia Union University, Sherrod stayed on to study theology. During this time, he began attending meetings of the Human Rights Commission, an integrated group in Richmond. Along with his friend Frank Pinkston, Sherrod also helped lead student protests and marches.[47]

It was that activism that led to Sherrod's presence at the founding of SNCC in the spring of 1960. Meanwhile, indigenous student movements were emerging across the South. In Rock Hill, South Carolina, nine students at Friendship College had gone to jail. SNCC encouraged them to stay, pioneering a strategy of "jail, no bail." But the word went out: "If you're serious, you need to join them." Sherrod, Charles Jones, Diane Nash, and Ruby Smith did, traveling to South Carolina, where they, too, were jailed almost immediately. Sherrod and Jones worked on the chain gang while "armed guards with shotguns on horseback surrounded them," reporting that they could be "whipped or even shot for looking these deputies in the eye." At one point, they were put in "the hole," a terrifying experience but one that provided "one of the most important times we spent together," according to Sherrod. The imprisonment, hard work, and constant threat of violence actually nurtured their activism. Diane Nash recalled reading the Acts of the Apostles during her time in jail, discovering "a surprising spiritual side to her time there."[48] "You learn the truth in prison," Sherrod asserted, "You learn wholeness. You find out the difference between being dead and alive."[49] Having looked straight into the "ever present threat of death," Sherrod claimed his time in Rock Hill "transformed" him. "I was already in progress of praying to take away fear," which "became very meaningful on the chain gang." He looked the specter of racism in the eye, he looked squarely at death, and concluded, "there's nothing that anybody can do to me."[50] This theological realization offered Sherrod peace even in horrific imprisonment. The eighth chapter of Romans offered "particular comfort:": "For I am sure that neither death nor life, nor angels nor rulers, nor things present nor things to come, nor powers, nor height nor depth, nor anything else in all creation, will be able to separate us from the love of God in Christ Jesus our Lord."[51] "Those verses have led me through my life and led me into the slashing of fear," Sherrod said, claiming he could stand before the worst racist "without fear, without one shaking finger . . . knowing that the Lord was with me."[52]

The time in jail not only allowed movement leaders opportunities for theological introspection, it also allowed them to refine their tactics. They committed to serving jail sentences rather than posting bond immediately; this, they believed, would highlight injustice, allow them to remain nonviolent, and put pressure on the criminal justice systems in small towns. They saw that imprisonment could bond students to one another and refine the spiritual

Charles Sherrod and Randy Battle canvassing in Southwest Georgia, 1963.
(Photographer: Danny Lyon/Magnum Photos)

nature of their struggle, as they themselves had experienced. "Our best selling point," Sherrod explained, "is that we are students with nothing but our bodies and our minds. . . . Yet we stand with Love."[53]

Following the Rock Hill incident and his graduation from Virginia Union in the spring of 1961, Sherrod set out for Albany as the field secretary for the Southwest Georgia Freedom Project, taking his theological activism to the most recalcitrant corner of the state. Joined soon by Cordell Reagon and Charles Jones, Sherrod envisioned doing very much the same things that Jim Lawson had done in Nashville: organizing young people, teaching workshops on Christian nonviolence, and taking direct action. He and Jones were twenty-two years old; Reagon, at eighteen, was even younger.[54] The men arrived in Southwest Georgia "full of zeal and empty of almost everything else."[55]

The first thing they had to do was meet people. One way "to be out there" was to "play three man basketball with everybody." Another was to go to the churches. Sherrod introduced himself to local pastors, identifying himself as a fellow minister of the gospel. There was some initial hesitation to be associated with SNCC on the part of Albany's religious institutions. These black ministers had to be "fearless," one movement activist recalled, because if "they opened the doors of their churches for mass meetings," they were "defying authority, risking the loss of church mortgages, the loss of members and, for some, the loss of jobs."[56] The president of the local NAACP chapter pastored a small church, C. K. Smith Presbyterian, and let the group meet there. Shiloh Baptist Church, under the direction of Rev. H. C. Boyd, also allowed Sherrod to use its church facilities for meetings with the high schoolers in the earliest days.[57] Over time, many churches opened their doors and "[gave] their support."[58] By 1962, a SNCC report stated: "The ministers are a great help. Their churches are the meeting halls."[59] "People would be going to these church meetings, union meetings, associations. The set up was already there just waiting," Sherrod reported. So when they got in the churches, "that was the ballgame." With the support of the religious community in hand, SNCC, the local Baptist Ministerial Alliance, and the local Interdenominational Alliance all united under the moniker of the Albany Movement.[60]

A 1961 handbill from the Albany Movement captured the intellectual and theological engagement that accompanied their action. "Those who love the Lord and Freedom" were invited to a mass meeting at Macedonia Baptist Church to "Come; Listen; Learn; Love!" The Albany Movement asserted, "We believe in the Fatherhood of God and the brotherhood of man . . . we believe that God made of one blood all nations for to dwell on all the face of the earth," before making its critical declaration: "Our beliefs have consequences." The Albany Movement proclaimed, "If there is the seed of God in every man, then every man has, by reason of that fact alone, worth and dignity," and concluded, "it follows that no man may, with impunity, discriminate against or exploit another."[61] Theological beliefs animated their struggle for freedom. With a faith at once "incurably optimistic and unyieldingly realistic," the students and clergy of the Albany Movement clung to "the power of Love and Nonviolence," which "is creative and redeems." Creative redemption grounded in orthodox Christian theology was the intellectual foundation and practical power of the civil rights movement, both in Albany and elsewhere.[62]

Mass meetings like the one advertised in the handbill occurred in churches throughout Albany as the movement began to spread. Charles Sherrod remembered: "The night of the first Mass Meeting came! The church was packed before eight o'clock. People were everywhere, in the aisles, sitting and standing in the choir stands, hanging over the railing of the balcony upstairs, sitting in trees outside near windows." The meeting began, Sherrod recalled, with freedom songs and then "petitions were laid before Almighty God by one of the ministers." Singing together with determination and hope, the people intoned "the Lord will see us through . . . we are not afraid . . . we shall live in peace . . . God is on our side."[63] By the end of that first meeting, Sherrod reported, "tears filled the eyes of hard, grown men who had known personally and seen with their own eyes merciless atrocities." Those present not only wept over oppression but looked ahead to the hope of victory. "When I momentarily opened my eyes," Sherrod recalled, "something good happened to me. I saw standing beside a dentist of the city, a man of the streets singing and smiling with joyful tears in his eyes and beside him a mailman with whom I had become acquainted along with people from all walks of life. It was then that I felt deep down within where it really counts, a warm feeling and all I could do was laugh out loud in the swelling of the singing." He continued, "when we rose to sing 'We Shall Overcome,' nobody could imagine what kept the top of the church on four corners. It was as if everyone had been lifted up on high and had been granted voices to sing with the celestial chorus in another time and in another place." Sherrod himself was deeply affected. "I threw my head back and closed my eyes as I sang with my whole body," he remembered.[64]

SNCC volunteer Prathia Hall recounted that "the mass meeting itself was just pure power. . . . You could hear the rhythm of the feet, and the clapping of the hands from the old prayer meeting tradition . . . people singing the old prayer songs." "There was something about hearing those songs, and hearing that singing in Albany in the midst of a struggle for life against death," she remembered, "that was just the most powerful thing I'd ever experienced."[65] The power of the community singing and praying together "amazed" even SNCC workers like Sherrod and Reagon, who were stunned to see "people who had inched tentatively into the church take up the verse in full voice." Mass meetings displayed both the courage of ordinary black Southerners and the deep theological power they harnessed in their struggle for equality and freedom.[66] The "spiritual leadership" of the people in Albany and Southwest Georgia convinced Sherrod that "we had a religious meeting—just as much religious as political." The two were inextricable, in the mystery of lived theology. As Sherrod said, "I couldn't tell, didn't want to tell, the difference."[67]

Soon after the first mass meeting, the Albany Movement conducted a direct-action protest at a Trailways bus station on November 22, 1961.[68] As Sherrod recalled, perhaps with the romanticism of hindsight, "The idea had been delivered. In the hearts of the young and of the old, from that moment on, Segregation was dead—the funeral was to come later."[69] It was not quite as simple as that, though. As the Albany community mobilized, they faced staunch opposition from municipal leaders. Though activists sang songs like "A'int Gonna Let Chief Pritchett Turn Me Round," they nonetheless faced arrest.[70] In the late fall of 1961, somewhere between 500 and 700 black citizens and SNCC workers, including Sherrod, Jones, and Reagon, were arrested for their protests.[71] This put intense pressure on the community, and many faced retribution from employers.

Nevertheless, in the face of opposition, the civil rights movement found strength in faith. "I realized that the multitude, most of the people who were action minded and showed that by going to jails, were raised up in the same Sunday school lessons that I went to," Sherrod stated. He went on to say, "the power of love, the power of Christ, the power of God. . . . His hands are our hands, our hands are his hands. And so it all locked together. The strength of the movement was powered by the strength of God." "When I realized that," he continued, "I just kept on keeping on . . . firing up the love of God in Christ Jesus."[72] The Albany Movement continued to do what it had done from the beginning: its followers prayed and asked God for help, and they frequently conducted prayer meetings on the steps of the Albany courthouse and in local churches. As one Albany man intoned, "We pray, oh Lord, that oppression will end, that domination will end, that prejudice will cease. Thou, who overruled the Pharaohs, overruled the Babylonians, overruled the Greeks and Romans, You alone is God, always have been God . . . may our suffering help us. For the Lord is my shepherd, I shall not want . . ."[73] At that point in the prayer, those assembled joined in, repeating the words of the twenty-third psalm. The beleaguered movement looked again to God, and then to each other, sustaining its activism with biblical logic.[74]

But it still needed help. With much of the leadership in jail and the community growing weary under the weeks of protests, Albany Movement President William G. Anderson called on an old friend from his days in Atlanta: Dr. Martin Luther King Jr.[75] Sherrod, who was then himself imprisoned, laughed, "they called in the big guns."[76] On December 15, 1961, King arrived in Albany, bringing eloquence and prominence to Southwest Georgia. Walking from porch to porch and pool hall to pool hall encouraging the tired citizens of Albany, King had an electrifying effect on the city. One night, he addressed the movement at a mass meeting at Shiloh Baptist Church. As William Anderson recalled, the church "was filled to the rafters. People were sitting in the aisles. They were hanging out of the windows. The choir stands were filled."[77] People from local counties "had come from hundreds of miles around because they had heard that King was coming."[78] When he walked up to the pulpit that night, King's steps were accompanied by "roaring cheers, clapping, a booming of the movement chorus."[79] The handkerchiefs waving aloft from the pews "made the church look like a cotton field in cross cutting breezes," one observer noted.[80] And though he began with an erudite message, it was indeed the theology of the cotton field that King channeled that night. "You are saying you don't like segregation," he thundered, "You are saying . . . that you are willing to struggle, to suffer, to sacrifice, and even to die if necessary in order to be free in this day and in this age."[81] "It may look dark now, maybe we don't know what tomorrow and the next day will bring," King would later tell the people of Albany, "but if you will move on out of the taxi lane of your own despair, move out of the taxi lane of your worries and fears, and get out in the take off lane and move out on the wings of faith, we will be able to move up through the clouds of disappointment."[82] The suffering was sure, but, with faith in God, so was the victory. Although Laurie Pritchett, imprisonment, and beatings surely waited for the churchgoers, that night it was as though they had lifted "from all the daily oppressive gravities of the earth and on up into the quiet evening sky into eternity with Abraham and Moses and the prophets and Jesus himself . . ."[83]

The next day, the movement marched again, ready to embody the notions of redemptive suffering that King had preached. Over 250 people, holding hands and clutching Bibles, filed out of church into the cold December light to go "pray at the City Hall."[84] They were quickly arrested, but over the panic and din, the voice of one marcher could be heard. "The blessed Son of God was born about this time of the year two thousand years ago to bring peace to the world," he yelled out, "and here we stand two thousand years later."[85] Connecting the protest in Albany directly to the incarnation of Jesus, the movement found a deep theological power not only to endure, but to hope for peace.

Marching in Americus

Along with many others at the City Hall, Martin Luther King Jr., was jailed. And with the Albany jails filled to capacity, he was taken to a small town called Americus.[86] Sherriff Fred Chappell was waiting for him. Chappell, a "surly fellow with a splenetically bulb-eyed face," possessed decidedly less tact than his Albany counterpart, Laurie Pritchett. Chappell was "like a bulldog" one civil rights activist remembered, "red in the face, already . . . even when he wasn't mad he was always red in the face . . . red in the face, and white hair, and big, heavy jowls . . . thick as an oak tree." In addition to being known for his imposing physical presence, Chappell prided himself on being a "tough," "independent" man who "said 'nigger' to and about any person of color . . . with a half smile of defiant assurance, as though to emphasize his absolute disregard for polite convention." King himself famously designated Fred Chappell "the meanest man on earth." True to form, Chappell swiftly threw King and those with him, Ralph Abernathy and William Anderson, in the small cells of the Americus jail.[87]

Upon release the following day, King spoke to those gathered in Americus's downtown square, encouraging his listeners to protest nonviolently and join the struggle for freedom. Teresa Mansfield, then thirteen years old, remembers King's arrest and speech as the catalyst for her desire to see racial change. "We got tired," she said, of the black community in Americus, "we got fed up." Mansfield and others started chanting, as they had heard in Albany, "Ain't going to let Fred Chappell turn us round." King soon left Americus to go on to Atlanta and to Birmingham and to Selma and to Memphis. But his short visit to Americus served to further ignite the movement in this corner of Southwest Georgia, to inspire a generation of young people and students, and to encourage the ministers and adults who would lead them.[88]

Sherriff Pritchett's decision to regionalize the Albany struggle propelled SNCC to do the same, and they began to expand into the rural counties, which had been their intention from the beginning. In April 1962, at their third general conference, SNCC staff acknowledged the challenges posed by these "hard-core," deeply racist, and, as one worker described, "very, very hostile" areas of Southwest Georgia.[89] Given nicknames by activists to match their reputations, these rural counties—"Terrible" Terrell, "Bad" Baker—were strongholds of Southern segregationism. One SNCC research report dubbed the region a "tragic area, the stepchild of the New South."[90] It was here that civil rights activists like Clarence Jordan twenty years before them had decided to root their project in justice.

"The way we organized in Americus was the way we organized every other county we worked in," Sherrod explained; this involved assigning young people to a place and "working with the truth . . . developing trust in one another." To Americus, Charles Sherrod assigned four young field workers: Bob Mants, John Perdew, Ralph Allen, and Don Harris. Bob Mants was an Atlanta native who got interested in SNCC while a student at Morehouse College. Though he would later go on to work in Lowndes County, Alabama, Mants got his start in Southwest Georgia. "The one thing I remember most," Mants recalled, "was a conversation with [Charles] Sherrod nagging me to come." No one from Atlanta went down there in those days. Mants explained: "Here I was, a young student, first generation to be college educated . . . [and] here's ol' Sherrod talking to me about coming to Southwest Georgia, dropping out of school." He did—and he wasn't alone. John Perdew also dropped out of school to get involved in the movement, leaving Harvard in his junior year. The son of a Harvard professor, the white twenty-three-year-old recalled volunteering to come to Southwest Georgia because "he wanted to do something adventurous and different." As a white man living and working with blacks in the Deep South, Perdew could not have imagined what he was in for. He recalled that he "had no idea at all of [the] kind of violence and daily oppression" blacks endured, "but then I got my ass kicked," he laughed.[91] Another white college student who joined the movement in Americus was Ralph Allen.[92] Allen, a Massachusetts native, had been enrolled at Trinity College in Hartford, Connecticut, when he decided to join the movement. Classmates described the New Englander as having "everything that [college] could give; he was in a fraternity, he was popular, he had good marks, and he seemed destined to become a typical turtleneck sweater Big Man on Campus."[93] But Allen left his collegial pedigree behind to serve as an SNCC field secretary. The final activist tapped for Americus was Don Harris. A "charismatic," black, twenty-two-year-old, Harris had been a student at Rutgers University when he decided to head to Georgia.[94] He had already been involved in local civil rights efforts up North and made a conscious decision to participate with SNCC. He was "unusually gifted" at community organizing and "developed a tremendous fellowship" within SNCC, with one fellow worker calling him "a quasi-saint."[95] Mants, Perdew, Allen, and Harris, an integrated group from different backgrounds, began work in Americus.

They were joined by female volunteers as well. Joan Browning, a young, white Methodist woman who grew up on a farm in South Georgia, worked in the region with SNCC from 1961 to 1965. Noting her "deeply religious perspective," Browning believed that "the courage and moral clarity to be part of SNCC" came from her "religious convictions." For Browning, participating in the movement was a way for her to live theology; it was "practicing [her] religion."[96] Penny Patch was another white woman who worked with SNCC in Southwest Georgia. In a letter to a friend in Atlanta in December 1962, Patch recounted that she and a group of other SNCC volunteers had recently moved into Southwest Georgia "as an integrated group," though she admitted, they had not been fully aware of "the magnitude of this move or its full implications." "The significance [of SNCC's interracialism]," she continued, "creeps up on me more and more every day," as "Southerners are able to see Negroes and whites working side by side as equals and friends." "Rather than talking about black and white together," Patch boldly asserted, "we are showing here and now . . . that a dream can be a reality. . . . There are few things that are designated as totally, absolutely, and completely right. Integration is one of those things." She concluded: "This is why the integrated group is an essential part of our entire philosophy."[97]

Unlike other projects that hesitated to fully include whites, the Southwest Georgia Freedom Project considered an integrated SNCC essential to incarnating the beloved community.[98] Sherrod explained that racial change would come only "if [the South] see[s] white and black working together, side by side, the white man no more and no less than his black brother, but human beings together."[99] Of course, this was radical in the 1960s Deep South. As Anne Braden, another white activist who worked with Sherrod, wrote in 1962, "Anyone who would go into an area like this [South Georgia] with interracial teams of registration workers has to be a little bit wacky; either that, or he has to be gripped by a vision of a whole new world."[100] Sherrod may have been a little wacky, but he certainly had a vision for a new world—the beloved community—in which blacks and whites took on a common identity as children of God and a common purpose for justice and shalom.

SNCC's vision, again, recalled that of Koinonia Farm. By the 1960s, Koinonia Farm had been hurt by persecution, but the farm still did much to further the movement in Southwest Georgia. "Much of the spade work [for civil rights]," Sherrod noted, has "been done by the Koinonia Farm people. . . . This is a good start even if it is emblazoned with bullet fringes."[101] Not only did Koinonia offer an early embodiment of the beloved community, it also supported SNCC in important ways.

The Koinonians never envisioned themselves participating in the civil rights movement and insisted that, while they, too, hoped for racial justice to be realized in the South, their project was not a political one. For one thing, Clarence Jordan disagreed with some of the tactics of the civil rights movement. In the late 1950s, Jordan and Martin Luther King Jr., exchanged a series of letters on that point. King had heard of Koinonia when news of its violent persecution rippled through the South, and he had written a letter of encouragement to Jordan. "You and the Koinonia community have been in my prayers continually the last several months," King wrote in February 1957. Even in "these trying moments," he continued, "I hope . . . you will gain consolation from the fact that in your struggle for freedom and a true Christian community you have cosmic companionship."[102] King and Jordan shared a faith in God and a vision for the possibilities of integrated Christian community. They differed sharply, however, both in approach and method. King, having experienced success with the bus boycott in Montgomery, began to adopt boycotts and mass demonstrations as useful tactics in the nonviolent protest movement. Jordan, on the other hand, opposed boycotting in all forms (having been the victim of such a suffocating boycott himself) and shied from direct provocation, a view that he expressed to King.[103] Although the Baptist ministers had much in common, their disagreements prevented them from forging a close bond. The farm never associated itself directly with the civil rights movement, preferring instead to identify with, in Jordan's words, "the God Movement." In 1960, Clarence Jordan was asked if Koinonia Farm believed in racial integration. He replied: "I wouldn't put it in those terms. Being followers of Jesus, we accept as our brother anyone who is a son of God whether he is black or white or what." But "we do not call that integration," he clarified, "we simply call it a practice of our Christian beliefs."[104] For the Koinonians, integration was just lived theology. Yet, despite the Koinonians' reticence to march and to boycott, they supported the cause and the work being done by local black and white civil rights activists.

Then in the early 1960s, a "remarkable thing" happened at Koinonia.[105] The farm began to welcome scores of young activists, who were offered a home-cooked meal, a soft bed, a welcoming community, abundant prayers, and peace and quiet. Frequently, exhausted volunteers and leaders would come out to Koinonia for an afternoon simply to rest in the pecan grove. "They have acres and acres of beautiful land, valleys and hills, creeks, fields, and pastures," one SNCC worker reported in a letter, "I EVEN WENT HORSEBACK RIDING."[106] At one point, Julian Bond asked the SNCC office in Atlanta: "How many people—at the most crowded—can Kiona (you know what I mean) hold?"[107] It could hold quite a few. Some estimate that in the early 1960s up to a thousand people visited the farm in search of respite and community.[108] They would pray with Clarence Jordan, play with the farm kids, and get a break from the stress of canvassing. In 1962, Koinonia hosted a retreat for SNCC workers from nearby Albany for several days, and Jordan allowed Charles Sherrod to conduct SNCC training and orientation at Koinonia in June 1963.[109] "Last week was spent orienting summer staffers at Koinonia," Faith Holsaert wrote, "we have fifteen kids."[110] In 1963, a friend of Koinonia wrote that he was "pleased" that the farm had chosen to "aid and abet the SNCC people."[111] And it did.

For these young protestors, Koinonia, or "that farm," as it was referred to, was "like a retreat" during the years of the movement, as the Koinonians "opened their arms" to them.[112] Frances Pauley, a young white activist, recalled, "Koinonia was my haven. . . . And I would always leave there like I could keep on, always."[113] One CORE activist, Zev Aelony, actually spent a prolonged season living at Koinonia. In fact, he was so attached to the place that, in a will he drafted from prison, he requested that his body be buried at the farm.[114] Aelony remarked that Clarence Jordan "knows the civil rights movement well, and helps it by keeping a kind of place of refuge on the farm for battle-fatigued workers who need to rest up and get a grip on themselves."[115] Sherrod echoed Aelony's words. He remembered: "On Sundays I used to go out there and talk to Clarence and meditate. . . . It was nice just to be on a farm and be quiet."[116] In those silent moments at Koinonia Farm, with the warm breeze rustling through the fields, activists like Pauley, Aelony, Sherrod, and many others found the strength they needed to continue on in the difficult struggle. Collins McGee, the young black man who lived at the farm, provided an important link, as he became increasingly involved in the movement over the early 1960s. Quite simply, as Sam Mahone put it, "The supportive relationship and shared experienced between the Koinonia community and the Americus movement cannot be overstated."[117] Koinonia was a stream in the desert.

With the support of Koinonia and experience gained in Albany, the SNCC activists set out to create a theological protest movement in Americus. SNCC's stated goal in Sumter County was organization and voter registration, but first the activists had to acquaint themselves with the local people. In the beginning, days were spent mostly in the fields, talking to people. A few people, mostly young, showed up to the weekly public meetings.[118] These gatherings, like the ones in Albany, occurred in churches. Rev. J. R. Campbell remembered that soon after he and his family arrived in Americus in 1963, he received a visit from Mants, Perdew, Allen, and Harris, who "informed me that they wanted me to join the Movement." Although he was "thirty-eight, a family man," Campbell agreed and became the Americus Movement's official local leader.[119] Of course, activists also sought out Rev. R. L. Freeman of Bethesda Baptist, who, too, lent his support.[120] While some ministers required prodding, SNCC had no trouble recruiting students. Since King's imprisonment the previous December, young people were especially eager to join the struggle. Students, some as young as ten, got involved. As James Brown, the youth secretary for the NAACP in Georgia, noted, students simply "could not see the struggle for freedom without participating themselves."[121] Sandra Mansfield was just eleven years old in 1962 when she was drawn into civil rights activism, despite warnings from her parents. She attended "regular mass meetings" at Allen Chapel and other churches and was even arrested the following year.[122] "I remember we started planning, going to mass meetings every day, picketing," Carolyn Melinda Mary recalled, adding, "it was exciting for me because I was young."[123]

The mass meetings described by Mansfield and Mary were held mainly outside of town and out of the reach of the Americus authorities. For the first gathering, twenty-three brave citizens ventured out to the small, country Pleasant Grove Baptist Church, where they were led by the "instructing and exhorting" Charles Sherrod.[124] He was the field secretary, but he was, foremost, a minister. "That's where most of my sermons were preached," he reflected, "about seven o'clock in the night of the day. . . . My church [was] whatever church we was meeting in that night." He "preached at every meeting," and the people responded— call and response. "Most of the people in the movement," Sherrod stated, "were religious people. And I realized that." So as he "preached the whole progression of the Christian gospel," he also taught about nonviolence and the "love approach" to racial change.[125]

These Americus mass meetings combined the new excitement over civil rights change with the familiar tenets of Christianity. Take, for instance, a mass meeting at Mt. Olive Baptist Church in rural Terrell County in July 1962. On this particular night, Charles Sherrod had invited visiting reporters Claude Sitton of the *New York Times* and Bill Shipp of the *Atlanta Constitution*. Sitton and Shipp joined people from all over rural Southwest Georgia who gathered in a small pine church "with Jesus and the American Presidents on the walls." Local leader Lucius Holloway began the meeting with a summary of the preceding week's events. Then it was Sherrod's turn to speak. He issued a spiritual admonishment to his listeners, one rooted in the deep theological tradition of the black church. "Do you believe in God?" Sherrod began, to murmurs of affirmation. "If you believe in God," he continued, "do you also believe that God said 'Thou shalt have no other God before me?' Are you not making the white man a god, if you afraid of this white man?" By establishing the relationship between man and God, Sherrod was able to challenge, theologically, unequal human relationships. Sherrod insisted that for black Christians, God's existence and holiness meant that both racial discrimination and capitulation to it were sinful—an affront against God and a transgression against the first commandment. But by employing the same Christian theology, he offered a way out of this fearful bondage—faith. "What do you believe?" Sherrod asked, his voice filling the small pine church. "Do you really believe you are going to heaven? Do you really believe that nothing can separate you from the love of God?" Even death was less powerful than God's love for them, Sherrod explained, concluding with his favorite passage from Romans: "If God be for us, who can be against us?"[126]

By this point, the local sheriff, Z. T. Matthews had had just about enough of Sherrod's preaching. He stormed into the meeting, shouting that he was "fed up." But the presence of the white reporters alarmed him. "Hey there, boy," he reared around, directing his words at Sitton, "put that pencil and paper away. Who you anyway?" "I'm Claude Sitton from the *New York Times*," the frightened reporter replied, "and I'm a native Georgian, just like yourself." Matthews left in a huff, but two weeks later, Mt. Olive Baptist Church was burned to the ground.

As the movement gained momentum, opposition increased. Another civil rights worker in Georgia reported receiving threatening phone calls within hours of the first mass meeting held in Sumter County. "The night following the meeting," Faith Holsaert recorded, "we received two phone calls" threatening to "blow the sons of bitches integrationists up."[127] As the ashes of Mount Olive and the shards of Koinonia's roadside stand attested, these calls were more than empty threats. Many white Southerners would stop at little to prevent the social, political, and theological revolution that was occurring throughout Southwest Georgia. They were willing to use intimidation, violence, and even arson.

One of the most infuriating things to white locals was SNCC's interracial living. Most of the volunteers in Americus lived in the local SNCC house, "an old three room house" at 406 Jefferson Street, that sometimes saw visits from the local Klan and others who wanted to scare off the activists.[128] Don Harris recalled that the house was "shot into a number of times" and that, predictably, "there was no protection at all offered by any officials." "As a matter of fact," Harris noted, "officials were the ones carrying out most of the intimidation."[129] Willie Turner also described intimidation from local law enforcement, saying at one point that the "police stopped us and said if they saw us in a car with the white girls [SNCC activists] they would kill us." One night after a mass meeting, Turner remembered, some of the SNCC students "decided after to go down to the Dairy Queen to get some ice cream. And we rode in the same car." "Little did we know," he continued, "the police was watching the car that we was in. So we guys who was black had to get down in the seat and hide underneath the seat. . . . That was one of the most frightening experiences that I've ever had in my life."[130] The specter of violence was omnipresent. Ralph Allen, for example, sustained serious injuries when he was beaten up while attempting to register an elderly black woman to vote.[131] Despite these threats and instances of violence, the Americus activists, emboldened by the courage of the local people and their own theological commitments, persisted.

Often, the only way to combat the obstacles in South Georgia was to call on the power of the Almighty for help. SNCC members in Americus did so daily. "Anyone who went down there and worked with Sherrod in Southwest Georgia remembers the Prayer Breakfast," Bob Mants recalled. "Every morning, over a glass of orange juice and a cinnamon roll. . . . We would sing and pray."[132] SNCC recruit John O'Neal remembered that the first time he rode with Sherrod, "he pulled the car off the highway . . . and said, 'let's pray.'" Sherrod proceeded to bow his head and pray for "what seemed like three hours. And then after a while he took his handkerchief and wiped the tears from his eyes and said, 'Amen.'" When O'Neal inquired about this, Sherrod responded that "he always prayed before he got on the highway because he didn't know [whether] he was going to get where he was going."[133] Sherrod and others found that the only way to live and work in Southwest Georgia was to seek God's divine guidance and protection in prayer. As Rev. Campbell echoed, "we just got to pray."[134] Prayer was a major part of every movement meeting. These were "very meaningful experience[s]," Bob Mants remarked; they provided "a sense of reverence for what we were all about, a sense of commitment to what we were about."[135] Prayer also comprised a component of protest. As King demonstrated in Albany, praying in public created a striking image of segregation's moral dilemma, one that Americus activists used to great effect. In this way, both believers and nonbelievers contributed to the power of lived theology. Many of those involved in the Americus Movement believed in the invisible efficacy of prayer—that God heard them, cared for them, and acted on their behalf; yet, even those who did not believe still participated in the outward action of prayer. Although certainly not the same—the believer was an individual embodiment and the unbeliever a collective participant—both were examples of lived theology. Prayer was "vital" to the theological civil rights movement in Americus.[136]

But the Americus Movement did "more than just pray."[137] From meetings in small churches on the outskirts of town, long conversations in pecan fields, and mounting excitement among Sumter County's students, the grassroots movement was drawing momentum, culminating in the formal establishment of the Americus and Sumter County Movement in January 1963. Prominent citizens, such as Lonnie Evans, Leland Cooper, and Hope Merritt Sr., as well as, of course, Rev. Campbell and Rev. Freeman, offered their support, as did scores of students, many of whom came against the wishes of their fearful parents. Deacon Evans was named president of the movement and John Barnum, whose family provided all the bail money, was named treasurer.[138] Under the auspices of the Americus and Sumter County Movement, SNCC activists, students and others continued to meet throughout the winter and spring of 1963. Then, on the night of July 17, 1963, after leaving a 350-person mass meeting at Peace Baptist Church, some inspired students decided to engage in the city's first direct action protest.[139]

Direct Action, the Leesburg Stockade, and the Americus Four: 1963–1964

Eleven young blacks sought to buy tickets at the "white" entrance of the Martin Theater on Forsyth Street in downtown Americus.[140] The Martin Theater was segregated, Sammy Mahone recounted, and blacks had to walk "around the side of the theater down a dark alley about a hundred or a hundred fifty feet, then walk up three flights of stairs, and sit in the balcony to look at the theater." On this night, though, the group of students "decided we were going to go to the front entrance and try to purchase tickets" instead. They were arrested and formally charged with "disorderly conduct" and "failure to obey an officer."[141] "I remember the Martin Theater," Bob Mants mused, that was "before the Civil Rights Act was passed."[142] Attorney C. B. King of Albany defended the students who were released on probated sentences.

The incident sparked a desire for action. Three days later, eighteen blacks, "eleven juveniles and seven adults" were arrested again at the Martin Theater.[143] The theater's attempts to quell the demonstrations by closing the "colored balcony" were unsuccessful. The following week, on July 24, the Americus Movement conducted a nighttime demonstration, resulting in another wave of arrests.[144] Students Sammy Mahone, Lena Turner, Lorene Sanders, and Bobby Lee Jones received a sentence of sixty days in the Americus City Prison, unable to post bail since they were "under a probated sentence" from their arrests the previous week. The jailers ordered the students to work, but they refused, "going limp." Incensed, city authorities assigned Jones and Mahone to an isolation cell, a four-foot by six-foot concrete box dubbed "the Hole." The young men responded with a hunger strike. When the young men "passed out" four days later, they were taken to the hospital. Following this episode, the Americus authorities again put Jones and Mahone on prison work detail. They had to "get up at six o'clock in the morning, get on these trucks, and go out and cut grass on the side of the road, pick up garbage on the weekends." "The most horrendous job they gave us to do," Mahone recalled, "was to clean up the city sewage." But, as had been true for Sherrod in Rock Hill, Mahone's time in prison strengthened his resolve. Upon release, he determined to become a SNCC staff member.[145]

Mahone's experience was not uncommon. Many civil rights activists found prison a fortifying experience. "We would demonstrate all night at the jailhouse and we would sing our songs," Jake Dowdell, another student, remembered. They would sing, "Fred Chappell, you know you can't turn us around."[146] Exasperated, authorities ordered "no singing and praying" in jail, claiming that "when you come here you lose all your rights." Charles Sherrod and others re-sponded, "We may be in jail, but we're still human beings," adding defiantly, "and still Christians."[147] Christianity changed the experience of imprisonment. Activists frequently invoked the biblical story of Paul and Silas, imagining that, with God's help, they, too, might be supernaturally freed or able to convert their jailers.[148] By singing and praying, many found deep comfort and power in their beliefs. Joann Christian exemplified this spiritual succor. A fourteen-year-old girl from Albany, Christian was placed in a "pitch black" jail cell in Terrell County, Georgia. When her attorney, Dennis Roberts, went to visit her and asked about the lack of light, Christian told him that the Sherriff had taken out the light bulb from her cell as punishment for leading the other prisoners in freedom songs. "But," she quickly noted, "I don't need a light, 'cause Jesus is my light."[149] Jesus's presence brought light; it consoled her and empowered her. For Jo Ann Christian and many civil rights activists, Christian theology brought comfort in imprisonment and transformed it into a liberating experience.

Nevertheless, imprisonment in Americus could be a harrowing experience, a reality illustrated by an episode that has become known as the Leesburg Stockade. In July 1963, the Americus and Sumter County Movement organized another demonstration. "The plan," recalled James A. Westbrooks, then a nineteen-year-old student and SNCC secretary, "was for half of the demon-strators to head to the segregated Martin Theater, while the rest were to veer right toward the White waiting room of the Trailways bus station."[150] The group met at a church on Cotton Avenue. Dressed in starched short sleeve shirts and sundresses, they began to walk towards downtown Americus sing-ing, "before I'll be a slave, I'll be buried in my grave and go home to my Lord to be free."[151] As they approached the downtown square, though, the demon-strators saw "a large white mob" waiting for them, including "law-enforcement officers, known Ku Klux Klan members and self-deputized citizens who had apparently heard about the protests."[152] When Sherriff Fred Chappell yelled for them to disperse, the marchers "dropped to their knees and began to pray." The infuriated white mob descended. Thirteen-year-old LuLu Westbrooks was hit with water from a fire hose, which "felt scalding" and the force of which "blew off [her] shoes."[153] At that moment, two policemen, "one 6′4″, the other 6′5″," slammed Lulu in the head with clubs. Her brother James remem-bered seeing blood "pouring" down the face of his little sister.[154] In the din, the Americus authorities began arresting the demonstrators, including around thirty girls.[155] "We were in the paddy wagon," one of the girls remembered, and "we had no idea where we were going."[156] At first neither did their im-prisoners. But eventually, after being transferred to a couple of different facilities, the girls were placed in the Lee County Public Works Facility, located twenty-six miles south of Americus on a deserted stretch of the Leslie Highway, where they remained for forty-five days. Almost completely isolated, the facility had not been used since the Civil War. Sandra Mansfield described the terror that the girls, some as young as ten, felt being away from their parents, who had no knowledge of their location. "We were hoping to go home," she said, "but we were told we were going to be taken out one by one and killed. So everyday we lived in fear."[157]

The girls were kept in a single, large concrete cell, measuring approximately twenty feet by twenty feet. They slept on the floor, until they were given three old mattresses, "dirty and full of cigarette burns." "Because the toilets were stopped up to the top," remembered Robertiena Freeman, "we used the mattresses" instead. The cramped cell was so putrid that one girl declared she would "never forget the stench." On top of this, the summer heat was unrelenting, as were the mosquitoes that came in through the cell's barred, screenless window. For sustenance, the girls were given four, reportedly raw, hamburgers, though many said they were too repulsed to eat them. Their only water came from a broken, dripping shower. "Sleeping on the floor, with no mattresses, no blankets, no sheets, no nothing," the girls nevertheless kept on "singing and praying."[158]

The guards often taunted the girls. "They called us pickanninnies and stupid niggers," one girl recounted, noting that there was no escape from their mocking. When Dr. King was imprisoned that summer, the guards jeered, "Who's going to be your Savior now?" But the girls knew King was not their Savior. They kept singing and praying, and they refused to allow the guard's words to penetrate their souls. LuLu Westbrooks thought about the hymns her mother used to sing, especially the lyrics, "How sweet the name of Jesus sounds / In a believer's ear! / It soothes his sorrows, heals his wounds / and drives away his fear." Singing hymns like that one and praying with the other girls, Westbrooks claimed, "strengthen[ed] my faith and sustain[ed] me . . . during the stockade ordeal." The girls' defiant spiritual expressions further antagonized their oppressors. At one point, a guard even "opened, cracked," the door and tossed a rattlesnake in their cell. "This is to teach you a lesson," he said, "and to stop you singing and praying." The snake remained in the cell the entire night—"we could hear his rattle," one girl explained—until finally a guard removed it as his compatriots laughed.[159]

The conditions and cruelty at the Leesburg Stockade would most likely have remained unknown if not for the efforts of Danny Lyon. The first SNCC field photographer, Lyon had been born in Brooklyn, New York, and was en-

Danny Lyon snapped this photograph through the bars of the Leesburg Stockade, outside of Americus, Georgia, 1963. (Photographer: Danny Lyon/Magnum Photos)

rolled at the University of Chicago when he hitchhiked down to Southwest Georgia.[160] One day in September, the girls in the Leesburg Stockade heard Danny Lyon whisper through the barred window. "Shhh, be quiet," he said, "Some of you girls go distract the guard. I'm taking pictures and hopefully they'll get you released."[161] His hands trembled as the shutter clicked, some of the photos slightly blurry as a result. Danny Lyon knew that, to many in Georgia, the life of a Jewish, Yankee activist was worth no more than the lives of these brutalized black children.[162] Lyon sent his photos to the SNCC headquarters in Atlanta, which promptly sent them to a number of national figures. Senator Harrison Williams of New Jersey was so appalled that he spoke on the Senate floor of the "disgraceful" conditions of the Leesburg Stockade. "Mr. President," Senator Williams thundered, "I wish the RECORD could show the jail facilities in use in Americus. But I have with me some pictures that were secretly taken and smuggled out. They really make you wonder whether they could have been taken in the United States of America at this point in the twentieth century. I invite any Senators who may be interested to examine them."[163] Lyon's photos also found their way to Attorney General Robert Kennedy, who, furious and disgusted, passed them on to his brother. President

Kennedy sent the National Guard to Georgia on September 6, 1963, to release the girls from the Leesburg Stockade.[164]

Demonstrations continued in Americus, now drawing the attention of the national press. A little over a month before the Leesburg girls' release, Don Harris, Ralph Allen, and John Perdew led a nighttime march from Friendship Baptist to the downtown square. A confrontation erupted between the demonstrators and the Americus authorities, who used electric cattle prods and other violent means to disperse the crowd. Police arrested Sallie Mae Durham and Thomas Daniel, who were charged with unlawful assembly, rioting, and assault. Harris, Allen, and Perdew were similarly charged with inciting a riot, resisting arrest, and assault, but they were also charged with insurrection. In the state of Georgia, insurrection was a capital offense. Dating back to 1871, Georgia's Anti-Treason Act, also known as the Sedition Act of 1871, stipulated that anyone arrested for attempting to incite rebellion against the state could be put to death.[165] A week later, at a prayer demonstration at the police station, a fourth protestor, Zev Aelony, was arrested on the same charge. Together, they became known as the Americus Four.

After about a month in the Sumter County Jail, Ralph Allen smuggled out a letter containing a jarring description of the circumstances surrounding his arrest. A city marshal "charged me from across the street and hit me . . . hit me twice on the head with a billy club," Allen wrote, "then, he said, 'When I say run, you'd better run, you nigger-lovin' son-of-a-bitch.'"[166] This encounter had brought the charge of insurrection. Zev Aelony also smuggled out a letter, written on brown wrapping paper. Tellingly, it was his last will and testament, addressed to Koinonia Farm. Though Aelony thought he might die, he reiterated that he would not "hit back under any circumstance," continuing, "I want so badly to live and get out of here, but if I am killed, perhaps I can still dry some tears and bring some joy." In similar fashion, Aelony then requested that if he were to die that he be buried at Koinonia, saying, "just please plant a tree, a plum or fig or peach or a pecan, something that bears sweet fruit and has a long life, so that it may use what remains of my body to make pleasures for children of my brothers in Sumter County."[167]

The imprisonment of the Americus Four and the intensification of repression did not deter the Americus Movement. Movement treasurer John Barnum stated that people should gather "to pray and protest the arrests and brutal beatings." And so they did. "They left the church," according to Claude Sitton's report, "and walked four blocks in orderly columns" to the courthouse. Armed troopers and deputized citizens, led by the City Marshal and Police Chief Ross Chambliss, attacked protestors with billy clubs, cattle prods, and baseball bats;

some present insisted shots were fired.[168] Many were injured and arrested.[169] Violence and intimidation had become regular features of life in Americus. James Williams, a young man active in the Americus Movement, described in a sworn statement that, while he was walking along the street near a demonstration, troopers and policemen had halted him. One officer clubbed him while another "jumped on his leg and had broken it." A state trooper then burned him with an electric cattle prod, "a hot shot," as Williams called it. Americus whites maintained that Williams's leg broke when "he fell in a ditch."[170] In another incident several weeks later, James Brown, a black Korean War veteran, was allegedly shot in the back and killed by an Americus police officer following a protest.[171] Eventually, the Americus and Sumter County Movement filed a petition with the U.S. Justice Department to investigate police brutality. Nine days later, Attorney General Kennedy announced that the Justice Department and the FBI found no evidence of police brutality in Americus.

While police violence against protestors in Americus went largely unacknowledged, the fate of the Americus Four eventually garnered national attention, because of both the severity of the charges and the backgrounds of the victims.[172] Prompted by Don Harris's enrollment at Rutgers University, New Jersey senator Harrison A. Williams took an interest in the Georgia case and brought it to the attention of his senate colleagues.[173] In September, Williams gave a speech protesting the charges leveled at the Americus Four as well as the conditions of the Leesburg Stockade girls' imprisonment. He stated that Harris's arrest "passes all understanding," and declared that the boy's only "crime" was "making the mistake of believing that people have a right to vote in Americus."[174] The senator highlighted "what seems to be a growing trend in the South": "leveling [severe] charges . . . as a way of cutting the heart out of the civil rights movement." While most revere America as the land of the free and home of the brave, Senator Williams continued, "there are some areas and towns in the United States where this is not so. . . . One of them, I am sorry to say is a small town of Americus, Georgia. For in Americus, most of those who are brave are not free." By focusing national attention on the case of the Americus Four, Senator Williams hoped to help the men receive a fair trial, noting that he would have more peace of mind if "the eyes of the world were focused on Americus."[175]

The ears of the world nearly had been. Several weeks earlier at the March on Washington for Jobs and Freedom, John Lewis (in the original transcript of his famously edited speech) demanded to know, "What about the three young men in Americus, Georgia, who face the death penalty for engaging in peaceful protest?" The young men he referred to, of course, were his three SNCC fellows—Don Harris, John Perdew, and Ralph Allen.[176]

National attention continued to mount during the fall of 1963. Don Harris's hometown of Riverdale, New Jersey, erupted with protests in early October after a local paper ran the headline "Death Sentence Hangs Over Youth's Head."[177] The *Harvard Crimson* took an interest in the case because John Perdew was a former Harvard student.[178] Likewise, lawmakers from Connecticut organized in support of Trinity College student Ralph Allen. The *Hartford Times* reported on October 11 that over 350 individuals, including Senators Thomas J. Dodd and Abraham A. Ribicoff, gathered at the Connecticut State Capitol to protest Allen's imprisonment. At the protest, the Trinity College president spoke, declaring that he was "proud of Ralph," as did Senator Dodd, who called the arrest of the Americus Four a "glaring" example of "the way the law has been manipulated by local authorities to halt the drive for equal rights." Senator Dodd also claimed he had confronted President Kennedy with these issues and asked that "all the influence and power within the purview of the federal government be brought to bear" in releasing the students and overruling Georgia's outdated statute.[179]

Many white Georgians vehemently disagreed with Senator Dodd; they maintained that race fell under the jurisdiction of the states and abhorred the idea that President Kennedy or any federal body would meddle with Georgia's affairs. Americus Solicitor General Stephen Pace even boasted that the insurrection charge was "the most serious charge" ever meted out in the entire nation.[180] According to SNCC, Pace consistently evidenced a "remarkable disregard for legal ethics, justice, and good public relations." The organization decried Pace's decision "to use the insurrection charge by claiming that the Four were responsible for all the racial tension in the city." Pace's only reason for choosing the capital charge, SNCC asserted, was to jail the protestors "indefinitely."[181] While the movement condemned it, many Americus citizens were pleased with the harsh sentencing. One man asserted his hope that the authorities "get any outsider for anything they can get them for until they find out they are not wanted here."[182] Harsh sentencing became part of what *New York Times* journalist Claude Sitton referred to as "legal terror."[183]

Finally, on October 31, 1963, the Americus Four case went to trial.[184] Attorneys D. L. Hollowell of Atlanta and C. B. King of Albany represented Harris, Allen, and Perdew, while Aelony had different counsel provided by CORE.[185] On November 1, 1963, the federal court ruled 2–1 that the Georgia state law was unconstitutional, and the men were released.[186] According to the *New York Times*, the federal intervention in the proceedings "marked the first time that the federal judiciary had halted a state court proceeding in a civil rights case."[187] With the verdict, it seemed as though a major victory had been won for the cause of civil rights in Americus and throughout the South. The ruling "may become a far-reaching precedent in the civil rights field," the *Atlanta Journal-Constitution* reported, as it could allow "civil rights demonstrators to go directly to federal court with complaints of excessive bond, or other violations of constitutional rights."[188] In the short term, however, what the verdict offered the beleaguered SNCC workers of Americus was too little too late.

The harsh indictment succeeded in impeding the movement by taking away its leaders and instilling fear. By the fall of 1963, SNCC fieldworkers conceded that "the many big and little pieces of the movement drifted apart and a lot was lost in the immediate effect of the August demonstrations and in the long-range strength of the movement in Americus."[189] Sherriff Chappell and other law enforcement officials, emboldened by being cleared of the charges of police brutality, continued their work of intimidating and harassing those who defied their wishes. In November 1964, one year after his release from prison, Don Harris was again arrested by the Americus police and charged with "assault with intent to murder" a police officer. The falsified charge was eventually dropped, but the threat of arrest continued to haunt Harris and others working for civil rights in Southwest Georgia. Not only did "legal terror" plague the Americus Movement but so did actual acts of terror. From 1961 to 1963, eight black churches were either bombed or set on fire. Individuals, too, became targets. In one incident, Deacon Trim Porter's home was burned to the ground.

Despite the recurring violence, the Americus and Sumter County Movement reorganized and regained momentum over the next year. On May 3, 1964, local students issued their first newsletter: the *Voice of Americus.* Sammy Mahone served as editor. Collins McGee, Jan Jordan, Jim Jordan, Zev Aelony, Gloria Wise, and Jewel Wise all contributed articles; Bill Wittkamper drew cartoons. "Perhaps you have noticed that little material, if any, is carried [in the *Times-Recorder*] when civil rights issues are involved," Mahone wrote. "This is to keep people from knowing the truth and the truth is the people here are no longer satisfied with the evil system of segregation." "We have to show everyone," he urged in the newsletter's first issue, "that we are dissatisfied. . . . This means that every citizen, Black and White, needs to get together and help in this fight for equality and human dignity (nonviolently, of course) and with God's will, we shall overcome."[190] Thus encouraged, the students continued to demonstrate. Three days after the Civil Rights Act was signed into law in the summer of 1964, activists in Americus set out to test it by seeking to integrate a local restaurant, the Hasty House. For their efforts, they were beaten.[191]

While the movement still faced opposition, there were signs of change. Georgia Governor Carl E. Sanders, elected in 1962, was a self-proclaimed "progressive" who liked to boast that he was "Georgia's first modern Governor."[192] Sanders sought to avoid any situation where federal authorities might intervene. This meant obeying national laws and promoting "law and order" throughout the state. It also meant following the federal mandate to integrate public schools. Much to the chagrin of Americus's white residents, in August 1964, four black students integrated Americus High School.[193] Despite these changes, the late months of 1964 were relatively calm. By the summer of 1965, though, Americus exploded again.

The Hot Summer of 1965

In June 1965 the Americus and Sumter County Movement enacted a boycott of three local grocery stores to push for integration in hiring. Locals and SNCC volunteers picketed in front of the Piggly Wiggly, Kwik-Chek, and Colonial supermarkets, which were transformed from spaces of domestic provision to daily reminders of the changes coming in America. Tensions gripped Americus as temperatures rose. White patrons mocked, spit on, and beat the integrated demonstrators. An Atlanta journalist, Walter Lundy, sent to cover the protests, recalled that one day, "all of a sudden" a pickup truck screeched up in front of one of the grocery stores, jumping "up on the sidewalk." A white man got out of the truck and "without any warning, turn[ed] and shove[d] [a white demonstrator] as hard as he [could], in sort of an upward direction." The man went "flying at an angle in the air and dropp[ed] into the street . . . land[ed] in a crash, his glasses [went] flying." Journalists and FBI agents looked on, but "no one did anything." The episode, though relatively inconsequential in the larger scope of the civil rights movement in Americus, was, for the young reporter, "symbolic of the whole fight." "At the ripe old age of 22, it was the evilest thing I'd ever seen," Lundy recalled, "it was [so] shocking to me [that] almost 50 years later, I can describe it."[194]

Journalists like Walter Lundy were not the only newcomers gracing the sidewalks of Americus in the summer of 1965. In late June, SCLC sent twenty additional workers as part of its Summer Community Organization and Political Education Project, meant to register blacks to vote in six Southern states.[195] SCOPE Director Hosea Williams, as well as Ben Clarke, Julian Bond, and Willie Bolden were among the new arrivals. In a town as small as Americus, the presence of nonlocals was easily discerned and usually not appreciated. A few days after the new volunteers arrived, white night riders welcomed them by driving through the city, tossing homemade explosives, and firing guns. The threat of violence remained ever present despite the heightened attention. Organizational meetings and demonstrations continued through June and July, as did regular marches. Opponents also mobilized. It was "the Ku Klux Klan on one side, and [us] on the other," Rev. J. R. Campbell said.

Then, on July 20, 1965, the city erupted. Four women, Mary Kate Fishe, Lena Turner, Mamie Campbell, and Gloria Wise, were arrested for attempting to vote in a local election. Strangely enough, Fishe was actually one of the candidates; she was running against "avowed racist" J. W. Southwell, a former Georgia Bureau of Investigations officer. Mamie Campbell described the events leading up to the arrests: she was at home, "getting ready for a meeting at the church," when she heard a knock at the parsonage door. It was Lena Turner, asking after her husband, Rev. Campbell. When Mamie informed her that the Reverend was not home, Ms. Turner said she was going down to vote and asked Mamie to come along too. "Come on with us" she said, "you'll be home before [Rev. Campbell] even gets here." Impulsively, Mamie agreed, without even "thinking to weigh it. . . . I just jumped in with some of the girls." She would not be back by the time her husband got home; in fact, she would not return home for over a week. When the women arrived at the courthouse, there were three voting lines: "white men, white women, and colored."[196] They got in the line for white women. While debate swirled over whether some of the women were intentionally testing the Civil Rights Act by standing in the white line, Mamie Campbell, for her part, maintained that she was an accidental activist. "I walked straight," she recalled, "I just got in the line and it was a long line." When the women waiting their turn approached the courthouse door, Sheriff Chappell greeted them. "You're standing in the women's line," he informed them, to which Campbell bluntly replied, "I don't know what you call me, I have five children." "I guess that was too smart for him," she laughed. The women were arrested and taken across the street to jail.[197]

Rev. J. R. Campbell remembered hearing the news that his wife Mamie had been arrested. "Lo and behold," he recalled, "one of the young men came to me where we used to have our hair cut then and told me, 'Rev. Campbell, you in here watching the TV and Mrs. Campbell, and Lena, and Miss Fishe and Gloria Wise have gone to jail!'" The Reverend shrugged it off, chiding, "Don't tease me like that." But the man "prevailed" upon Rev. Campbell, who decided to go downtown and see what was going on. Sure enough, when he got to the courthouse, a crowd had gathered, upset over the arrests of the women, one of whom was indeed his wife. Campbell rushed back to the parsonage and promptly "called Martin Luther King's office in Atlanta."[198]

Six days later, on July 26, Rev. Campbell, Hosea Williams, and John Lewis held a press conference in Atlanta to discuss the situation in Americus. "Ladies and Gentlemen of the press," Williams read from a scripted statement, "the Negroes of Sumter County Georgia, the Student Nonviolent Coordinating Committee, [and] the Southern Christian Leadership Committee have united their forces" and are committed to "do whatever it takes to bring justice here and now, even in the deepest Black Belt of Georgia." Williams declared that there would be a "massive, united invasion on segregation in Georgia" taking the form of "massive nonviolent street protests, demonstrations." The current "mild" marches and protests would be "stepped up to our maximum potential," Williams warned, "unless there can be an immediate meeting of the minds and an acceptable settlement of Sumter County's racial problems."

They provided a list of demands. These included a recall of the justice-of-the-peace election, the immediate release of the four women with all charges dropped, police protection for blacks in Americus, open and fair voter registration, the appointment of one black registrar, and finally, the formation of a biracial committee to discuss race relations in Sumter County. If these demands were met, Williams stated, "demonstrations would be halted for a time," but if they were not, marches would continue and even be escalated. John Lewis described it as "an all-out effort" to demand justice.[199]

Immediately upon the women's arrest, "all the churches got opened" for mass meetings to organize people and coordinate activities. Activists from Atlanta descended on Americus to help demonstrate, march, and hold rallies demonstrating for the women's release. Inspired and bound together "like cement," hundreds of people marched daily from Allen Chapel A.M.E. to the county courthouse and back again, "a good little jump."[200] "We could see the people [marching] outside from in the jail," Mamie Campbell remembered, to which Rev. Campbell added, "We marched until you got out." The Campbell children even marched, yelling, "Fred Chappell, I want my mama out of jail and I want her out now!" Even as events escalated, the movement in Americus never strayed far from its theological origins; in fact, those origins became more pressing than ever. "Oh Lordy, oh Lord, we need you right now, Jesus," a woman prayed at an Americus mass meeting, "Don't leave us right now, Father. You know what we're going up against Jesus . . . oh Lordy, oh Lord. Don't leave us Father. You know nonviolence has got some who are willing to come . . . oh Lordy, oh Lord. I know, I know, I know you Jesus. Done tried you, my Father. Tried You a long time ago. Don't doubt you

Rev. J. R. Campbell and Rev. R. L. Freeman leading a march in Americus, Georgia, 1965. (Photographer unknown; courtesy of Americus and Sumter County Movement Remembered, Inc.)

nowhere, Jesus. I'm going on in this movement in your name."[201] And they all said amen.

The constant demonstrations terrified and incensed much of the white community. For Mark Pace, who was a child that summer, the marches made an indelible impression. "I can remember standing on the streets," he recalled, "watching the blacks march down."[202] Disbelieving that "their Negroes" could possibly be so riotous, many Americus whites blamed the racial situation on the presence of nonlocals. Americus Mayor T. Griffin Walker claimed, "If [outside groups] were not here, the situation would not be what it is today."[203] At the same time though, segregationists hosted some guests of their own. Over the previous decade, many white citizens in Americus had joined conservative organizations such as the Citizen's Council and John Birch Society, which occasionally welcomed speakers. In May 1964, for instance, Alabama Governor George Wallace came to Americus to pay a visit to the local chapter of the John Birch Society. At a standing-room-only affair held at the Americus Country Club, just down Lee Street from the First Methodist and First Baptist Churches, Governor Wallace gave a "race-baiting" speech and applauded the community for its opposition to civil rights.[204] During the summer of 1965, the frequency and intensity of these meetings increased.

Lester Maddox speaking at the Sumter County Courthouse, 1965. (AP Photo)

On July 26, in the midst of the marches for the four women, the Americus Country Club welcomed Lester Maddox, a rabid Georgia segregationist, a man once characterized as "a cracker Don Quixote," and the future governor of the state. Maddox had been passing through from Valdosta when he decided to accept an invitation to speak in Americus. He laughed at the media's suggestion that they had "imported Lester Maddox to Americus," joking, "no one imported me! I belong here in Georgia!" Submitting that he was "proud to be a segregationist" but was in town on a "mission of peace," Maddox, in his "high tinny hectic" voice, addressed the eager crowd packing the room. He commended his listeners on "what you've done this far" in resisting integration, adding, "We're going to restore states rights. . . . We are going to get them like George Wallace in the state capitol . . . in the White House, and save this great land." Maddox concluded his speech with the assertion that integration was "against the Constitution" as well as "ungodly," "sinful," and "unchristian." As we have seen, white supremacists possessed their own claims to theological and racial orthodoxy. Maddox's address was met with enthusiastic applause and heartened cheers.[205]

A few weeks later, Maddox returned, leading a march of 600 Ku Klux Klan members and sympathizers through downtown Americus.[206] A week later, the Klan held rallies at the Sumter County Fairground and in front of the Americus courthouse, the same spot where civil rights demonstrators had been gathering in previous weeks. Led by Imperial Wizard Robert Shelton of Tuscaloosa, these rallies garnered support from Atlanta Grand Wizard Calvin Craig and the conservative organization "Americans for States Rights."[207] At one of the rallies, Lester Maddox again gave the evening's keynote address to hundreds of angry citizens. Some claimed that, despite his public admonitions, Mayor Walker was actually in attendance. When Tom Brokaw later asked Walker about it, he replied that he "would welcome any patriotic group," noting that it was "a fine meeting," with "the gist" to "abide by the law."[208]

With activists both for and against civil rights pouring into Americus, pressure continued to mount. Rev. Campbell remembered, "We had our rallies and they had theirs. We had our march and they had theirs."[209] Frank Myers, a young man who would go on to be mayor of Americus, recalled those tumultuous weeks. He reported being amazed by the courage of Americus's black citizens, commenting that their marches were his "real conversion."[210] At the same time, Myers understood the determination of whites to preserve the social structure. "I saw the KKK march in downtown Americus. I saw that."[211]

Facing more danger than ever, the movement clung to its theological foundations. God had given them "a right just like white people." "I didn't fear nothing," Rev. Campbell insisted, "I knew there was a God upstairs, and I was doing the right thing. I knew God had no respect for persons." Since God did not privilege some people over others, Campbell believed, those in the civil rights movement were justified in agitating for their rights. And with God on their side, they could endure even the worst violence. "Those people," Campbell told his listeners at a mass meeting, referring to white segregationists in town, "said there was going to be red blood running down Lee Street if we come out one more day." The minister continued, "All y'all who want to march, to go to your bloody grave, stand up."[212] That night almost two hundred black citizens marched, singing and praying as they went.[213] These marches were an exercise in community cohesion and organized discontent, but they were also an expression of theological principles. God made them, God would help them and strengthen them, God would protect them, God would deliver them out of bondage and into freedom as he had the Israelites of old. And even if they did face their bloody graves, God would raise them up, like Jesus.

A few days later, Judge Frank Hooper released the four imprisoned women, officials promised a biracial committee and desegregated elections, and the city agreed to appoint two black registrars.[214] Marches abated, national civil rights leaders and the media went on to other destinations, and students returned to school. Despite the harassment and threats, despite Sherriff Chappell and the Leesburg Stockade, despite the insurrection law and the Klan rallies, it seemed as though the movement had been victorious in Americus in the early 1960s. And not simply in the legal concessions that had been eked out. In the streets of Americus, it appeared the appeal to freedom, to human dignity, and to God-given rights had prevailed.

FROM SNCC'S FOUNDING, to Charles Sherrod's vision for Southwest Georgia, to Rev. Campbell's religious leadership in Americus, Christian theology was central to the freedom struggle. Nonviolent workshops taught students to take on the mantle of Christ. Freedom songs, hymns, and spirituals channeled the tradition of the black church, as prayers called upon the divine power of the Holy Spirit. The community of activists mirrored the early church as those imprisoned reflected the joy of Paul and Silas. It was performed belief; it was practiced faith; it was lived theology. Though certainly helped by national-media exposure and a national zeitgeist of change, the movement possessed an undeniable theological power. "We didn't have anything—no money, no decent places to live, no schools," Americus resident Karl Wilson put it, "but when you've got God, you overcome. We just believed in the higher power." Teresa Mansfield agreed. There was an "Almighty Being looking out for us." "It was a spiritual movement," Wilson concluded, "And that's why it was victorious—it was the will of God, not our will."[215]

But victory would not come easily, as opponents, who also claimed to stand for the will of God, mobilized. The theological conflict over civil rights was not over.

CHAPTER FIVE

The Devil Won, Hands Down

Opposition in Americus

Well, the Devil has just made Jesus look bad in Americus. . . .
The Devil won hands down.
—*Daytona Beach Morning Journal*, 1965

We weren't so upset about integration. . . . It was the government
running schools and having no prayer.
—Harry Entrekin, Americus resident, 2012

Around midnight it began to rain, and warm droplets anointed the peaceful demonstrators camped out in front of the Sumter County courthouse. On the night of July 28, 1965, clergy, students, and activist leaders had conducted a mass meeting at Allen Chapel and marched down to the courthouse, where they sang, prayed, and planned to spend the night on the lawn in protest. Suddenly, cutting through the chorus of cicadas and drizzle, a shot rang out in the dark. "Between twelve and one in the morning," Rev. J. R. Campbell recounted, "the news media came to me and said, 'Rev. Campbell, I don't want to get you all upset, but we got trouble.' I said, 'what trouble?'" When the informants told Campbell the news, he replied, "Oh my, it gonna be the Devil. Oh my God."[1]

About two blocks from the courthouse, there had been a murder. A twenty-one-year-old man, Andrew Whatley, on his way home from work at the local drive-in movie theater, had been gunned down at the corner gas station by two black males, Charlie Lee Hopkins and Willie Lamar, as they drove by. Most believed that Whatley, shot in the head by a .38 caliber pistol, had been mistaken for some "white youths" who had been throwing rocks and bottles at passing cars.[2] Andrew, or Andy, Whatley was an "energetic, quiet, friendly youth" from a working-class family. He had attended school in Americus, was a member of the First Baptist Church, and worked two jobs, one at the Manhattan Shirt Factory and one at the Sunset Movie Theater.[3] The industrious Whatley had also recently enlisted as a marine. Some suspected he suffered from developmental disorders of some kind, making his work ethic all the more remarkable.[4] In an interview with Tom Brokaw, then a young TV correspondent already in

Americus to cover the protests, Mrs. Whatley meekly answered questions about her son's murder from her front porch.[5] By all accounts, Andy Whatley was a good kid who worked hard and mostly kept to himself. He was also white.

Neither Whatley nor his murderers were directly associated with the civil rights movement; nevertheless Whatley's tragic death became a turning point for race relations and the development of civil rights activity in Americus. The tensions that had increased throughout the summer combusted with that .38 caliber weapon. Although a random act of violence, the murder of Andy Whatley gave opponents of the movement an opening. The opposition now found its footing, invoking arguments that would become the hallmark of conservative racial politics for years to come. By subverting the moral legitimacy of the movement, ostracizing dissenters, forming Christian private schools, and redoubling their theological position, the white opposition to civil rights in the South and in Americus, Georgia, not only weakened the civil rights movement's power but created a powerful political and theological movement of its own.

"It's Gonna Be the Devil": The Murder of Andy Whatley

The death of a white citizen both petrified and enraged the white community. Mothers forbade their children from going downtown, while fathers readied their weapons. One *Americus Times-Recorder* headline that week simply stated: "Americus is Armed."[6] Whatley's funeral was held at the First Baptist Church, where the altar was adorned with flowers, some sent by Lester Maddox himself. The self-proclaimed proud segregationist, recognizing the political opportunity presented by an innocent white victim, made several trips to Americus in the weeks following Whatley's death to hold rallies where he condemned the movement.[7] Even the minister at First Baptist, Harold Collins, felt compelled to speak out about the incident, remarking that Whatley's death was "the sheer product of hate, indifference and pressures on mind and heart—such as distrust and greed."[8] Although Rev. Collins did not specify the individuals or groups to which he was referring, he seemed to imply that the murder had resulted from the mass protests and their demands.

The Americus Movement remained undeterred. "We regret very seriously the death of Mr. Andy Whatley," Benjamin Clarke of the SCLC stated, but he also announced that after a twenty-four-hour moratorium, marches would continue.[9] Respect for one deceased person, they argued, could not be traded for respect for thousands of the living. The following day, 150 black citizens marched again, singing and praying.[10] But the tides had turned.

Police in front of the Sumter County Courthouse, 1965. (Photographer unknown; courtesy of Americus and Sumter County Movement Remembered, Inc.)

In the days following Whatley's murder, leaders in Americus began to speak out more forcefully against the civil rights movement. Calling on the black leadership to cease demonstrations, Americus Mayor T. Griffin Walker remarked, "one death is enough."[11] For his part, Georgia Governor Carl Sanders blamed the tragedy on individuals seeking justice in the streets and not through the legal system of Georgia. "The proper way to implement the law," Sanders claimed, "is through the courts and not through a brawl in the streets."[12] Though Sanders commended the movement's moratorium, he remarked that the action was "a little late," clearly linking Whatley's death with direct action.[13] At the city's request, Governor Sanders ordered over 100 state troopers down to Sumter County.[14] These state troopers posted up in front of the courthouse, policed the streets and, as Rev. J. R. Campbell remembered, "[rode] through town."[15] The heightened police presence intimidated marchers and stifled the spirit of nonviolent protest.

The opposition's rhetoric also escalated. In a statement regarding the "present racial situation," Mayor Walker called the continued protests "completely unwarranted and irresponsible." "For two weeks now," he stated, "this community has been subjected to uncalled for actions that would have tried the patience of a Job."[16] With this, the mayor not only dismissed the demands of the movement, but he characterized the white citizens of Americus as innocent and afflicted victims. Commenting on the ongoing grocery store pickets, he said,

"It is sad that in Americus, Ga., today . . . peace-loving citizens may be kept from performing such routine chores as shopping because of a feeling of fear."[17] The nonviolent movement had been recast as disrespectful and fearsome.

It did not matter that Andy Whatley's murderers were not even tangentially involved in movement; it did not matter that the violence had been just as surprising and frightening to the black community as it had been to the white community in Americus. The murder had nothing to do with the movement; it had everything to do with it. The *Americus Times-Recorder* gave Whatley's death such "great and extensive coverage" that it became "inseparably related" to the Americus and Sumter County Movement.[18] A murder was something civil rights opponents could work with. They could peddle the notion of black people as inherently threatening, they could accuse protestors of being uncontrolled, and most significantly, they could assert that the movement was not really nonviolent nor was it Christian.

By 1965, the movement itself had splintered between those who upheld the transformative moral power of nonviolence and those who asserted that nonviolence meant a bloodbath for blacks in the South. The latter voices had always existed within the conversation over rights and revolution, but they spoke louder in 1965 than before. Stokely Carmichael, wearied by SNCC's nonviolence, skeptical of integrationism, and frustrated holding out for the beloved community, was organizing a new black political movement in Lowndes County, Alabama.[19] The accompanying rise of Black Power and its declaration that it would fight whites with arms, if necessary, renewed fear among whites. Perceptions of black violence and criminality especially took hold of the American imagination as the freedom struggle, in some places, eschewed the movement's theological roots. "The leaders of civil rights are always crying out against prejudice and hate," one prominent evangelical declared. "They are always talking about love," he continued, but "I am fearful that all of the rioting and demonstrating has produced a great amount of hate as evidenced through recent murders and other forms of violence."[20] A week or so after Whatley's murder, the Watts Riots broke out in Los Angeles.[21]

Displays of violence allowed white citizens to frame the movement as dangerous, chaotic, and immoral and justified a new fervor for "law and order." The phrase was invoked constantly in Americus, as police presence dramatically increased. "Law and order," Americus Police Chief Ross Chambliss assured, will be "maintained in the city under all circumstances."[22] Arrests, even in nonviolent demonstrations, continued, accompanied by punitive sentences. Andy Whatley's alleged killers were quickly found, arrested, and charged.[23] And with Los Angeles still burning in the minds of the public, it was unlikely, the defendants' attorney, C. B. King, argued, that the proceedings would be objective. "In the minds of the public," King stated, there existed "a merger of identity of the defendant with the Movement . . . [which] inflamed the prejudices and passions of the white community of Sumter County to the extent that the defendant is virtually foreclosed from the possibility of receiving a fair and impartial trial."[24]

Charlie Lee Hopkins and Willie Lamar were both black men in their early twenties with criminal records. Though there exists some debate on the details of the case, evidence suggests that Hopkins and Lamar were, in fact, responsible for Whatley's death. But it is likely they did not intend to kill anyone, and certainly not Whatley. Hopkins, the shooter, appeared before a special grand jury consisting of twenty-three Sumter County residents and chaired by avowed racist W. D. White.[25] Hopkins pled not guilty to the charge of murder "with malice aforethought."[26] On March 3, 1966, however, a jury of twelve pronounced Hopkins guilty, though they requested that the court "have mercy."[27] He was sentenced to be "confined at labor" for "the rest of his natural life."[28] Lamar, already out on bond for possession and manufacturing of illegal whiskey, plead guilty to voluntary manslaughter and was sentenced to five years in prison.[29]

Defense attorneys did challenge the sentences, though most of their case centered on the impossibility of receiving a fair trial in Sumter County, not around proving innocence. Attorneys filed a "motion to quash the indictment" on that grounds that the Sumter County Grand Jury was not representative of the community. Attorney C. B. King noted that "the defendant herein is a member of the Negro race" while "all of [the grand jury's] 22 members were of the white or Caucasian race, except one." Furthermore, King protested, "the jury commissioners of Sumter County are now, and in the past, have always been members of the Caucasian race" and "select a disproportionately small number of Negroes . . . to comprise the jury list from which grand jurors are selected." Black residents "have been and are now deliberately, systematically, arbitrarily and expressly discriminated against."[30] Such discrimination violated the Fourteenth Amendment and thus, the defense argued, nullified the ruling. King's defense also requested a "change of venue," claiming that Hopkins and Lamar could not "obtain a fair and impartial trial in this county because of the prejudice against Negroes." Attorney King noted "that Sumter County has been the site of demonstration by the Ku Klux Klan, following the alleged murder," appealing to the court that "the Ku Klux Klan is an organization of considerable influence in said County."[31] Hopkins especially could not receive a fair trial "in the County aforesaid" since "the act for which he was indicted involves the alleged death of a white person at the hands of a non-white person; a crime for which white jurors . . . have historically permitted emotion to interfere." In Sumter County, a black person accused of killing a white person simply would not receive a fair trial. Despite the defense's protestations, the trial proceeded, and both men were convicted and imprisoned. Indeed, beginning in the 1960s, the constant invocation of law and order and draconian punishments meted out disproportionately to black Americans contributed to a new system of legal oppression.[32]

As they invoked law and order to suppress protest, Americus officials and white citizens condemned outsiders in their midst. Mayor Walker cited the "irresponsible statements" and "vulgar language" of "outside agitators" in explaining the racial tensions in town. Their words, Mayor Walker claimed, "are calculated for one purpose . . . the creating of ill will and violence in this good city."[33] Governor Sanders estimated that 75 percent of civil rights demonstrators did not live in Americus; his belief was that these outsiders sought to "stir up emotions and perhaps cause more violence."[34] "It would be a tragedy if there is a further loss of life because of outsiders coming to our state," the governor intoned, "I would like to see those outsiders leave so our differences can be resolved by responsible Georgians and not by outsiders."[35] Sanders implied that the movement was disingenuous, imposed by nonlocals, and claimed Christian morality while fostering hatred. As he put it, "An invitation for continued violence is being sponsored by so-called apostles of goodwill."[36]

This notion that unrest and violence had been incited by outsiders perpetuated the myth that local black residents were content in the unequal system of Jim Crow. A few days after Whatley's murder, a series of curious and revealing editorials to this effect appeared in the local newspaper, the *Americus Times-Recorder*.[37]

On August 2, the newspaper printed a rather unusual piece attributed simply and obliquely to "A Negro Citizen." Calling it "an unsolicited letter received by *The Times-Recorder*," the newspaper noted that although it "ordinarily requires that names be listed with letters printed from the public, it is not doing so in this instance because of the writer's fears." "His identity is known to the newspaper, however," the editor assured readers. The anonymous columnist insisted that he was an Americus native who had lived there "for many years in peace and harmony with my own race and the white people." He claimed, "Our town has been a good town," one that had "always treated negroes fairly." Americus, the man wrote, had "abided by the laws of the United States and has let those of us who wanted to enter public eating places, picture shows, and schools and to vote." While first absolving the city, the author then pivoted to make an argument for continued segregation. "Most of us do not want to mix with the white people," he explained. "We are proud of our color and of our race. We feel that God made us black and the white man white and He made the segregation [*sic*]. . . . We do not want to go with our white friends, to their churches and schools, we have our own, we are happier with our own race as God intended us to be." Since God had sanctioned racial difference, the editorialist reasoned, the movement could be characterized as "a force of evil."

"White people who we never saw before," the column continued, "come into our streets begging us to march and always we find letters begging us to march and not to buy anything from the white people." This hampered progress, the author claimed, noting, "We colored people have had less freedom the past two weeks in Americus than we ever has [*sic*] in our lives. We do not know why these outside white people and negroes come into our town to cause us trouble. We do not like it. We feel like it is an outside force, maybe this Communism we hear about. Whatever it is, it is not good and the average Americus negro does not want it." Not only did local blacks not benefit from the movement, they suffered for it. Though the author admitted he was "not smart enough to know why" these events were occurring, he nevertheless called for an end to civil rights activities, stating, "We are scared to go on the streets of a town where we have been happy, we are scared for our wives and children." He concluded the piece with a plea for help from the white community and a return to the halcyon days of segregation, saying, "I have been thinking and I would like to know if the good white people could back us the good negroes and all stick together to fight the devil that is among'st us."[38]

The authenticity of this column is doubtful. Though such a "negro citizen" may have existed, the arguments invoked suggest the projected hopes of white Southerners, while the condescending, occasional grammatical errors (appearing disproportionately toward the end of the letter) look more like calculated counterfeit than earnest ignorance. If this letter was written by whites, as seems likely, it shows the intellectual, moral, and theological chasm separating white Southerners' perception of their black neighbors from the reality of most black Americans' feelings and beliefs.

The notion that "Americus has always treated negroes fairly" seems less a reflection of actual labor conditions and social arrangements (especially considering the recent Kwik-Chek grocery and Manhattan Shirt Company protests over discriminatory hiring) and more a tired argument that Jim Crow was a system built on a fair system of separate but equal. Certainly, the argument that Americus had been always integrated is false; so, too, is the claim that strides toward integration of public facilities resulted from white benevolence. Moreover, it seems highly unlikely that blacks would characterize the movement as "a force of evil" in which black citizens were harassed on their porches and "begged to march" by outsiders. It is even more unlikely that they would characterize local protestors as "the devil amongst us." The assertion that "we do not want to go with our white friends, to their churches and schools, we have our own, we are happier with our own race as God intended us to be" sounds like a fantastical formulation of segregationists since civil rights proponents rarely spoke of joining white institutions for the sake of joining them; they spoke much more of integration as ending the evil of segregation and providing equal access to American life. The editorial's religious arguments are particularly interesting as they reveal the continued resonance of white supremacist theology imagined as universal orthodoxy. The statement that "God made us black and the white man white and He made the segregation" may have been dogma in the white community, but it had no purchase among blacks.

Two days later, a response to the column appeared in the *Americus Times-Recorder*, this one proudly authored by a prominent white citizen, Wm. Harry Moore. Writing "TO THE FRIGHTENED COLORED PEOPLE OF AMERICUS, GEORGIA," Moore assured his "friends" that they were "not alone in these troublesome days," but were joined by "a vast host of white persons who are interested in your welfare, safety and security." Moore agreed with the "Negro citizen" that much trouble was being caused by outsiders, reiterating, "these outsiders who have invaded our City are not your friends, they have only one interest and that is the furthering of their selfish ambitions and the money that they can collect." "When all of this is over," Moore claimed, "they will be hundreds of thousands of dollars the richer," but "guilty of taking little children and marching them through the streets for their own selfish ambitions." He continued, "if these outsiders threaten you in any way do not hesitate to call the Police Department and they will see that you have every protection." Moore entreated the black community of Americus to trust the city authorities and not these outside influences. "I know the Mayor and the Members of the City Council and the other elected officials of Sumter County," he testified, "They want to be your friends," and have at their heart "the welfare of all the City of Americus." So, too, did the business community, which "appreciate[s] your patronage. . . . You are welcome in their stores and on the streets and in any of the public places of this city." "Americus is made up of people of good will," Moore assured his readers, "if this had not been so, there would have been violence." Instead, "We have all tried to keep cool, calm, and level headed in these days." He pledged, "when the outsiders, the renegades, and the paid tools of violence and ill will have gone home, you may rest assured that the white people of goodwill will sit down with responsible people of your race and find a solution for any problems that may exist," noting however, that "no right thinking person . . . can sit down and council together as long as there is a gun leveled at [their] heads." But, Moore declared, with God's help and provision, there was hope for a peaceful future for Americus. "Like the Hebrew children of old," he wrote, "Americus is walking through the fiery furnace, but by the Grace of God, we shall come out safely on the other side." Moore concluded his editorial with a benediction: "May our Heavenly Father protect you, comfort your hearts and drive fear from your lives."[39]

This editorial reveals much about the thoughts and feelings of the white community of Americus: that the "vast host" of white people was basically good, and that civil rights activists were not. Americus, they thought, would return to its normal equanimity as soon as the outside agitators left, since the native black community was content and race relations mostly peaceful. Moore's editorial not only captures the white community's perceptions of outsiders and hope for resolution, but it also reveals a significant theological reconstitution. Moore recast the whites of Americus rather than black Americans as the Israelites yearning for freedom. Imperial minions were no longer enslavers and oppressors but opportunist agitators. The concluding benediction, "May our Heavenly Father protect you, comfort your hearts and drive fear from your lives," patronizingly positioned Moore and those he represented as protectors; this was sealed with the salutation "Yours in Christ."

Opponents of civil rights insisted on law and order and sought to undercut the movement's moral and theological claims. With the murder of Andy Whatley, the opposition in Americus found its footing and began to regain its theological high ground. Anyone who hesitated or expressed contrary viewpoints was quickly hushed and ostracized.

Warren Fortson: A Southern Heretic

Warren Fortson took one last look at his beautiful new home on Taylor Street before pulling out of the driveway. Earlier in the day, he had wandered through the nineteen rooms of his home, sadly imagining the life that could have— should have—been. This was where he was going to raise his family, where he was going to build his law practice, where he was going to live his days in peace. Those dreams now seemed forever lost, lost somewhere between justice and the law, between doing the right thing and saying all the wrong ones. All he knew was that he had to leave Americus. In addition to subverting the moral position of the movement, opponents of civil rights also maintained power and influence by ostracizing dissenters and alienating those who possessed different views. As in issues of religion, issues of race became dogmatic, and those who held heretical notions were ousted from the fellowship of believers.

Fortson was a Georgian. Born in 1928 in Washington, Georgia, he was the youngest of eight children.[40] After attending Oxford College of Emory University and two stints in the Marine Corps, Warren Fortson read the law and began to set up a practice in Georgia, first in Hawkinsville and then in Americus, where he moved with his wife and young family in 1958. At first, everything was wonderful for the Fortsons. The family thrived, with Betty Fortson happily occupied at the Americus Country Club, the Junior League, and the Americus Garden Club, and the children engaged in school and other social activities. Warren's law practice prospered, and he was soon named the Sumter County attorney.[41] Additionally, he served on the school board, taught Sunday school at First Methodist, and held numerous other leadership positions in the community, including president of the Rotary Club. Fortson humbly insisted his community involvement was "what all young lawyers do."[42] He was happy to be in a town where he possessed both influence and friends.

But in 1963, the happy life the Fortsons had built in Americus came under fire. The students who had fought for the integration of the Martin Theater that summer had been arrested and placed in an abandoned building in downtown Americus, a building near Warren Fortson's law office. "I came to work, saw all those children," Fortson recalled, and "I made it my point to get to know those kids who were down there." In time, most of the students were released on bond and given probationary status. Vulnerable under the law, they were "snatched up for anything." Forston took on their cases, working closely with Albany attorney C. B. King. This legal work soon brought Fortson into conflict with the white power structure. For example, in 1964, Robertiena Freeman was arrested under charges of "fornication." Freeman, the daughter of Rev. R. L. Freeman and "a straight A student," had recently integrated Americus High School, and some in Americus wanted her gone. When Fortson heard the news of her arrest, he "knew damn well that the next morning her father was going to be in my office." Fortson negotiated a deal in which Robertiena avoided jail time in exchange for an extended stint at a camp in California, a deal that was actually arranged through connections with Koinonia Farm.[43] A few years earlier, Fortson had interacted with Clarence Jordan and the Koinonia children when they were banned from attending Americus High, even testifying that he didn't think they were dangerous.[44] This action had already made him "a trifle gamy" to his white neighbors, and his involvement with the Freeman case solidified their suspicions. Fortson insisted that his primary allegiance as an attorney was to uphold the law; his defense of the students stemmed not from activism or radicalism, but from devotion to the American legal system. But in addition to having a lawyer's mind, Fortson did have something of an activist's heart. Around this same time, Fortson began to "work behind the scenes" on racial issues, urging the schools to integrate voluntarily, "quietly integrating the library," and building business relationships in the black community. Then, in the contentious summer of 1965, Fortson unknowingly committed his "final heresy."[45] At the request of black protestors, Fortson advocated for the organization of a biracial committee to discuss the racial situation in Americus. Although the committee never truly came to fruition, Fortson had taken a step too far, emerging unquestionably as a civil rights sympathizer, a Southern heretic, and a target for the segregationist orthodox.[46]

For his part, Fortson insisted that he simply hoped that fair agreements would "quiet all this down."[47] Of the South's struggle to accept racial equality, he mused, "It was like watching a child trying to master a puzzle. And you get frustrated and you want to say 'Just pick it up and put it over here!'"[48] In Fortson's estimation, change was undeniably coming to the South, and pragmatic Southerners would work to ensure that that change came about peacefully and justly. Fortson assumed that people would ultimately act in accordance with their economic interests. Americus defied his prediction.[49]

Whereas leaders in most Georgia cities sought to mollify protestors at the very least, the president of Americus's Chamber of Commerce took no such stance; instead, he met calls for the biracial committee with a bemused "What the hell for?"[50] In Americus, as Frances Pauley, then the director of the Georgia Council on Human Relations, concluded, "They would rather have had their banks and businesses fail than to desegregate their town."[51] Or, as Fortson himself said: "The voice of reason is very weak in our community."[52] Pauley and Fortson's comments reveal how deeply segregation was entrenched in white Americus—so much so that maintaining it was worth sacrificing economic solvency. At one summer dinner party, a local business leader approached Fortson and, in slurry speech, informed him that "what's wrong with you, Warren, is that you're trying to be the conscience of this town." Tired, Fortson replied that no, in fact, "what's wrong with me is I just want this town to find its conscience."[53]

Fortson's activities and opinions earned him the ire of much of the white community—his friends, neighbors, and even his fellow church members.

To them, his racial pragmatism amounted to a "heretical streak."[54] There were "threatening phone calls and charges of Communism."[55] According to then-Georgia State Senator Jimmy Carter, Fortson became the "victim of a whisper campaign in which he has been accused of being a member of the Communist Party and a supporter of the NAACP."[56] The campaign against Fortson culminated in a petition demanding he be ousted as the county attorney. The petition garnered over 2,000 signatures, and he was summarily removed from his position.[57] "By this time," Fortson remembered, "I had publicly become the centerpiece of it all, and there was a growing antagonism toward me. . . . They pretty much turned against us." He and his family soon found themselves cast out socially and even in physical danger. Upon arriving at her regular Junior League meeting, Betty discovered that she had become "invisible." Warren's once-flourishing law practice shriveled. The family received harassing phone calls and threats around the clock. Their son was nearly shot and killed by a playmate who called him a "nigger lover." Thankfully, someone walked by and took the rifle out of the youngster's hands.[58]

The church, too, turned on the family, even exerting a "discreet hand in the ostracism of Fortson."[59] In the South, racial inclusion could easily lead to religious exclusion, as Clarence Jordan and the Koinonians had learned years before. But even those who stood within the community of the church could be ousted for refusal to comply with theologically reinforced segregationism. Though he had been the superintendent of Sunday school at First Methodist for years, Warren was relieved of his Sunday school responsibilities. When asked, the church's pastor, Vernard Robertson, "declined comment."[60] In time, the Fortsons stopped attending church altogether because of the mounting hostility.

One man from Athens, Georgia, blasted the church for dismissing Fortson, saying he was "sickened" by their actions. "When I read of the failure of your church to renew [Fortson's] capacity as a Sunday School teacher," the Athens man wrote, "I could easily have thrown up." "You are a pitiful spectacle before decent mankind," he declared, "you and your church, along with your sick community . . . will hardly see the incompatibility of your professed belief in Christ, history's chief rabble rouser and agitator, and your nauseating silence when one of the few Christians in Americus takes a stand on the side of Christianity. How will you face your congregation? As if nothing has happened?" The man concluded by condemning the church and Rev. Vernard Robertson: "You are merely another manifestation of the failure of modern Christianity to serve its founder who according to my memory and recollection of the Scriptures never avoided an issue because of its being unpopular in the community."[61] Ralph McGill, the famous Atlanta journalist, also expressed contempt over Fortson's removal at First Methodist. "The firing of a Sunday School teacher for practicing Christianity," McGill exclaimed, "is so grotesque and preposterous a thing that one can only break into a loud, mocking laughter." He concluded that if the church represented Christianity in the South "perhaps it is just as well that there is in this country a recession in religion."[62] The church's action toward Warren Fortson, at least for some, exemplified those who "preach the gospel or profess the church in hypocritical fashion."[63] Fortson could defensibly be kicked out of the Rotary Club for his racial politics, but not the church. The shunning of racial dissenters was certainly political and social, but like so many things caught in the nexus of race and religion in the South, it also contained a theological component.

After weeks of terror and loneliness, Warren Fortson decided that it was time to leave Americus behind. He had already sent his wife and children out of town, and the house on Taylor Street was quiet. Fortson sat in his beautiful living room that was once the setting for dinner parties and children playing, and where he now sat alone "with [his] rifle across [his] lap." Right then, he recalled, "I realized it was over in Americus." He soon left for Atlanta. The experience scarred the young attorney. As he put it, "to have your people turn against you is an experience you shall never forget." He hadn't meant to disrupt anything, he hadn't intended to lose his job, and he certainly hadn't planned on souring his friendships and being run out of town. It just happened. "It was just like getting into a canoe in the Colorado River," he remarked, "once you're committed to the rapids, there's nothing you can do but ride them out."[64]

Warren Fortson was not the first person to be ostracized for daring to question the Southern racial hierarchy. Before him, Clarence Jordan had faced comparable treatment, with similar threats to his life and the lives of his children. After him, Lloyd Moll, the progressive president of the local college, Georgia Southwestern, encountered similar social isolation because of his moderate racial views. While Southern segregationists sought to control the legal and political systems, they also sought to control the less formal, but no less significant, realm of social relationships. Of course, these social relationships included the church. Ostracizing dissenters was both a subtle and strong part of the opposition to the civil rights movement and to racial change, as these Southern dissenters were treated as heretics and expelled from the fellowship of believers.

"God and the Devil on an Equal Plane": School Desegregation, Private Education, and *Engel v. Vitale*

In August 1964, four black students integrated the previously all-white Americus High School. When they arrived on the first day, angry mobs awaited them. People stood "as far as you could see," one of the students recalled, "I'd never seen so many white people in all my days." As they pulled close to the school's entrance, "bricks started hitting the car." One student remembered, "I prayed, 'Lord . . .' then boom!"[65] Once inside the building, the students were predictably harassed and harangued, both by their classmates and occasionally by their teachers. Scenes like these replayed in hundreds of Southern schools during the 1960s. And while resistance was certainly part of the story of white opposition to the civil rights movement in Americus, it was not the whole story, nor even the most significant part. Instead of engaging in a prolonged campaign of massive resistance to school integration, many whites in Americus quietly abandoned the integrated public schools for private schools of their own. While the impetus for the flight from public schools was almost certainly racial, the move involved both racial and religious logic. Since the early 1960s, many conservatives had been suspicious of government intervention in public education for theological reasons.[66] The reality of integration following the 1964 Civil Rights Act served only to deepen existing resentment. Citing theological and racial justifications, many Southern whites, including many in Americus, fled integrated public schools for all-white private Christian academies. Racial anger merged with theological mandate.

When Ernest Vandiver ran for governor of Georgia in 1958, he ran under the campaign motto "No, Not One!"[67] Not one black child would enter a Georgia school on his watch, he railed, a promise that got him elected but that would prove difficult to keep. In the case of *Calhoun v. Latimer* in 1959, U.S. District Judge Frank Hooper ruled that Atlanta's segregated school system was unconstitutional, giving the state one year to either implement the *Brown* decision and integrate the schools or face penalties levied by the federal government. Governor Vandiver had a crisis on his hands. He could defy the court, which would halt funding to Atlanta's schools and effectively shut down the public school system in the state—fulfilling his campaign promise. Or, he could comply with the federal ruling and allow for the integration of Atlanta's schools, which would preserve public education but incur the sure ire of his white electorate. Throughout Atlanta, the tension was palpable. Organizations such as Help Our Public Education (HOPE) pushed for integration of the city schools, while the Metropolitan Association for Segregated Education

(MASE) and Georgians Unwilling to Surrender (GUTS) countered.[68] The governor was torn.

After convening with political leaders in the state, Vandiver established the General Assembly Committee on Schools, better known as the Sibley Commission, named for its chair, Atlanta attorney John Sibley.[69] The brainchild of Vandiver's chief of staff, Griffin Bell, the Sibley Commission set out to gauge the "sentiment" in Georgia over school desegregation and make a recommendation to the state General Assembly about what to do before *Calhoun's* deadline. In Georgia, the vast majority of those who advocated compliance *and* those who advocated resistance were segregationists. That segregation was preferable was never really in question. As Atlanta journalist Ralph McGill explained, it "was never a question of being for integration or against it. It was, and is, a question of public schools or no schools."[70] Ten meetings were held across the state to listen to residents, and, as Griffin Bell stated, to elect "whether to close the schools or integrate them."[71] The first meeting was held on March 3, 1960, in Bell's hometown—Americus.

On an unusually icy day, the first meeting of the Sibley Commission rang into order.[72] People filed into the Americus County Courthouse. Some were clad in coveralls and others in suits, and many had prepared notes and speeches tucked into their pockets. The group assembled represented the twenty counties of the Georgia's Third District, an area colloquially known as the Black Belt. As predicted, these counties proved to be the most dedicated to complete segregation in schools, since all but six of them had a black student majority. After clarifying the state's options, John Sibley called upon witnesses, who included W. C. Mundy, the superintendent of Americus schools, Charles Crisp, a prominent local businessman, Louise Hines of the Manhattan Shirt Company, George L. Mathews, chairman of the County Commissioners, and Marvin McNeill, a businessman and farmer. These witnesses all insisted that the best tactic for the state was "segregation now, segregation forever, by any means necessary, and at all costs," as did forty-two of the additional fifty-one people who testified at the hearing.[73]

As the Sibley Commission continued its meetings throughout the state, from the mountain lakes of Appalachia to the Spanish moss-covered oaks of the Lowcountry, the message was largely the same as it had been in Americus. Attentive Georgians listened to the hearings on the radio and read reports in the morning news, with many joking that they were keeping score.[74] Sibley himself, although a segregationist, was surprised by the consistent willingness of most Georgians to sacrifice the public school systems rather than allow for even token integration. Altogether, an estimated 60 percent of Georgia residents reported that they favored closing the schools rather than integrating them.[75] In the end, searching for some way to stay on the right side of the law and placate the people, the Sibley Commission recommended complying with Judge Hooper's desegregation ruling nominally, while coming up with alternative measures to keep schools practically segregated. It was a compromise. Georgia's leaders certainly wanted to maintain white supremacy, but they also desperately sought to avoid the racist spectacles of the surrounding states.[76] In the months following the commission hearings, Sibley, Bell, and others traversed the state to drum up support for their plan before the Georgia General Assembly's slated vote in January 1961. But before the day of reckoning arrived, a crisis occurred that forced Governor Vandiver, unilaterally, to choose between integrating Georgia's schools or closing them.[77]

On January 6, 1961, Federal Judge W. A. Bootle ruled that the University of Georgia must admit two black students, Hamilton Holmes and Charlayne Hunter.[78] In a move that provoked controversy and defined his tenure, Vandiver decided that he would not defy the court. Compliance with federal regulations in matters of desegregation became the state's position. Because of Judge Bootle's rulings, the Sibley Commission's better judgment, and Governor Vandiver's prudence, Georgia, unlike its neighbors, did not undertake a campaign of massive resistance. In time, schools throughout the state integrated, while resistant Georgians were forced to find other ways to subvert federal rulings and preserve segregation in education.

In Americus, school desegregation became an inevitability after the 1964 Civil Rights Act. Part of the landmark 1964 legislation, Title VI provided the federal government the authority to withhold funding from any institution, school, or organization that it deemed to be racially discriminatory. Congress then sweetened the deal with the 1965 Elementary and Secondary Education Act, which added $590 million to Southern states for the 1966 fiscal year.[79] Ten years after *Brown*, the federal government was putting its money where its mouth was, and it seemed like an offer public education in the South could hardly refuse. While a paltry 1 percent of black schoolchildren enrolled in previously all-white public schools in the ten years following the initial *Brown* ruling, that number spiked to a respectable 46 percent in the second decade after *Brown*.[80] Much of this implementation came under the so-called freedom of choice plans, which, ostensibly, gave schoolchildren the ability to decide which school they wanted to attend, thus complying with *Brown* and protecting federal funding.[81] Under these freedom of choice plans, any child in a given school district could decide to attend any school in that district, with the provision that they could be rejected due to "overcrowding or some other extraordinary circumstance."[82] The U.S. Commission on Civil Rights noted that freedom of choice plans were "favored overwhelmingly" by the 1,787 Southern school districts that had chosen to desegregate voluntarily, including 83 percent of such districts in Georgia.[83] By giving families a decision over where their children would go to school, Southern schools could comply with the Civil Rights Act, receive federal funding, and yet, by "choice," remain largely segregated. Employing some "mystifying" logic, Southern lawmakers, educators, and courts concluded that while *Brown* outlawed segregation, it did not require integration.[84] As Joe Crespino has written, freedom of choice plans, despite the moniker, "had little do to with freedom or choice."[85]

The Americus School Board decided to implement a freedom of choice policy for the 1964–65 school year.[86] Though the integration effort was more symbolic than substantive, the adoption of a freedom of choice plan nevertheless indicated a sharp turn.[87] Just four years prior, in 1960, the school board had barred white Koinonia children from attending Americus High School just for possessing integrationist views.[88] It was again Judge Bootle who ruled in their favor, claiming, somewhat ironically given later political battles, that the students were being unjustly persecuted for their religious beliefs.[89] So wary were Americus residents of integration in the early 1960s that even three Koinonia children posed a grave threat. In September 1962, the "citizens of Americus, GA" sent a telegram of support to Mississippi Governor Ross Barnett and Lieutenant Governor Johnson in their effort to stave off integration at Ole Miss. "We stand four square behind you in your magnificent handling of the integration efforts at the University of Mississippi," they wrote, "would that all state officials and citizens everywhere have the courage, as you have shown, to fight against this despicable movement which can only result in the downfall of the white race. God be with you."[90] These citizens were not pleased when, only two years later, the "despicable movement" for school integration came to Americus High School. The decision to implement a freedom of choice plan produced such anger that some decided they would rather see the school reduced to ashes than integrated, setting it ablaze in January 1964.[91]

Nonetheless, despite the hostility from the local white community, four black students—David Bell, Robertiena Freeman, Dobbs Wiggins, and Minnie Wise—opted to attend the previously all-white Americus High School under the freedom of choice provision.[92] "I wanted to go," Freeman recalled, "I thought white kids will be my friends. . . . I thought it was going to be wonderful . . . one big, rosy happy thing. I told Daddy, 'I want to go.'" The reality must have shocked her. Tensions were so high that the school's principal arranged for the black students to enter each classroom five minutes before or after the other students to avoid a hallway confrontation, and he had them released from school an hour early. Although these details were ostensibly arranged for safety, they also served to keep the four black students separate from the other students. In keeping with Georgia's acquiescence in state desegregation, any integration would be token integration. Technically the students were enrolled, but they were not included in school life in any meaningful way.

Yet even these precautionary measures were not enough to protect the students from ridicule and harassment, which they took in stride. "I got pushed up against the wall, just slammed, people just spit on you," Freeman said, shrugging, "what are you going to do? I was 96 pounds at the time." Dobbs Wiggins recalled that on one occasion, "three coke bottles hit me simultaneously."[93] Taunts and threats abounded. "We were called all kinds of names," Wiggins remembered, "all of which we ignored."[94] Jewel Wise described how they were "met with all kinds of atrocities, met with rocks," remarking, simply, "we went into the school and we tried to survive."[95] Greg Wittkamper, who lived at Koinonia, sympathized. He had experienced similar harassment and violence over the previous years and offered his support and friendship.[96] Still, only one of the black students, Robertiena Freeman, made it through the entire school year. Integration would not come easily in Americus.[97]

But school hall skirmishes were not the primary obstacle to integrated education. Realizing that integration of public schools was becoming inevitable, white segregationists throughout the South began to focus their energies on the establishment of separate schools, dubbed "segregation academies" by many.[98] Like other civil rights conflicts, the battle over school integration had theological as well as social, cultural, and political elements. As white conservatives fled the public schools, they often did so with racial and religious justifications, evidenced by the fact that many of these new schools were not only privately funded but also explicitly Christian. These schools would resist integration rulings and promote a particular theological vision for education.

Almost immediately following the 1964 integration of Americus High School, white citizens in Americus began to research and discuss options for private education. In May 1966, a public meeting announced the establishment of a new, private school in Sumter County and solicited support. "If you are interested enough," one founder announced to the hundred people gathered in the Americus County Courthouse, "we are prepared to start the school."[99] The private school, to be called Southland Academy, would be organized as a nonprofit.[100] Its stated mission was "to offer an education equal to, and preferably superior to [,] that offered in public schools . . . composed of local individuals with the belief that we are better qualified to know what is best for our own children than anyone else."[101] Organizers also emphasized the school's religious component. The mission statement continued that Southland Academy "will be influenced by belief in God and that daily worship is desirable in the lives of our children."[102] Headmaster McManus likewise noted that "commitment to the Christian faith" was an objective of the school, elaborating that Southland's founders began the school out of a desire to "provide a Christian environment."[103]

Private schools, like Southland Academy, were usually labeled as either segregationist or Christian.[104] But, race and religion cannot be so easily untangled; the schools were segregationist *and* Christian. The theological element is often dismissed as outright subterfuge. But this is a mistake. Indeed, as one commentator cautioned, to "reduce" the impetus behind Christian private schools to sheer racism is "to ignore two decades of social and cultural upheaval."[105] In the 1960s, changes in American life had produced deep divisions. These divisions were, in large part, theological. Many private schools, even those without official religious affiliations, possessed a values system rooted in Christian theology. These underlying theological tenets included, according to a 1970 study, a "strict and literal reading of the Bible" as well as "aggressive preaching of the gospel" aimed to encourage students to "come forward and be saved by accepting Christ."[106] This pattern holds in Americus. Southland Academy not only promoted its identity as a Christian school but required "daily . . . Scripture and prayer" with "special programs at Christmas and Easter."[107] Oversimplifying the rise of private Christian schools as merely segregationist academies obscures the profound religious elements that intermingled so perplexingly with the more obvious racial politics.

Whether for racial or religious reasons, support for a private school mounted in Americus, and in July 1966, Southland Academy's Board of Trustees announced that it would begin accepting applications.[108] A year later, the school boasted an enrollment of 150 incoming students, in addition to a headmaster, seven teachers, and a newly purchased school building. It was all set to open its doors in August 1967.[109] But there was a problem. Southland had not yet received its nonprofit status. School officials alleged that the U.S. Internal Revenue Service had "apparently engaged in a massive scheme to thwart the efforts of the local school group and other private school groups in the South" in their efforts to have private schools recognized as tax-exempt nonprofits.[110] Southland Board Chairman Harry Entrekin claimed that the school made its initial application for the nonprofit status through the Atlanta IRS office on August 26, 1966, and, two years later, had still not received "what should have been routine approval."[111] Southland's leaders initially expressed concern in the spring of 1967, over six months after they submitted their application. "Various correspondence and telephone conversations," Entrekin claimed, "have led to the conclusion that the IRS, in cooperation with the Justice Dept., has willfully declined to make a ruling on this tax exemption application for the purpose of harassing the local group and bringing about an embarrassing financial situation." The school contacted Georgia Senators Richard B. Russell and Herman Talmadge, Third District Representative Jack Brinkley, and other "personnel in the offices of our elected representatives in Washington" who confirmed that "high-placed officials in the IRS and the Justice Dept. have declared their intention to do everything possible to prevent the granting of the exemption." The Georgia officials went on to say they could find nothing wrong with the application and predicted that the IRS would "have to grant the exemption eventually."[112] Finally, on August 4, 1967, it did, and Southland received its tax exemption.[113]

After getting the news, school officials released a statement explaining what they saw as the reason for the delay in tax-exempt status, a statement that offers insight into the vexing relationship between race and religion in the formation of private education. The granting of tax-exempt status should have been simple; "the laws are specific," they claimed, "either you qualify, or you don't." What should have been rote, however, the government made arduous. But, why? According to Harry Entrekin and the Board of Southland Academy, the government's interest in undercutting white religious schools in the South stemmed from "a desire on the part of the Justice Department and the Internal Revenue Service to impose their desires . . . rather than to administer the law as it is written . . . arbitrary government at its worst." In concluding their statement, the representatives of Southland Academy expressed their "concern over the loss of local control over public schools, over the Supreme Court decision concerning prayer in schools, and over the use of schools as tools to bring about social revolution, rather than the purpose for which they were created—education." In contrast, Southland would be private: out of the reach of the encroaching federal government, explicitly religious, and safe from the American racial revolution.[114]

When Harry and Ann Entrekin decided to send their sons to Southland Academy, they cited a recent Supreme Court decision as justification. But it was not *Brown v. Board*. It was *Engel v. Vitale*, or, as it is more commonly known, the "school prayer decision." The *Engel* decision, according to one legal scholar, was "greeted with more shock and criticism than *Dred Scott v. Sanford*, affected more school districts than *Brown v. Board of Education*, and brought together conservative Roman Catholics and fundamentalist Protestants in a common cause a decade before *Roe v. Wade*."[115] Historiographically, and even in the American popular imagination, *Engel v. Vitale* is more commonly associated with *Roe v. Wade* and the culture wars than the discussions of civil rights and school desegregation. But that association is somewhat anachronistic, and furthermore, it obscures the significant link between racial prejudice and religious liberty in the construction of white religious private schools.

In 1962, five families from Nassau County, New York, challenged the constitutionality of the brief, voluntary, nondenominational recitation of prayer in their children's school before the Supreme Court.[116] The Court ruled in their favor 6–1, with two justices abstaining. The morning prayer, the ruling stated, "officially establishes . . . religious beliefs," and was thus in violation of the establishment clause prohibiting the government from sanctioning a state religion. "It is neither sacrilegious nor anti-religious," Justice Hugo Black wrote, "to say that each separate government in this country should stay out of the business of writing or sanctioning official prayers and leave that purely religious function to the people themselves."[117]

Reactions were immediate and vehement.[118] Schools that had been founded to instruct citizens in Christianity, many lamented, had now been expressly barred from doing so. To many Americans, including many in Americus, this seemed to portend utter disaster for students, teachers, communities, and the nation. Georgia Senator Herman Talmadge lambasted the decision as "outrageous," commenting that it would "do incalculable damage to the fundamental faith in Almighty God which is the foundation upon which our civilization, our freedom and our form of government rest."[119] Another Georgian, gubernatorial candidate (and later Governor) Carl Sanders, felt so strongly about the ruling that he pronounced that he would "not only go to jail but give up [his] life" to protect the right of Georgia students to pray in school.[120] Of course, arguments about the constitutionality of prayer are not only political disputes but theological ones. And with the *Engel* decision, the Supreme Court, many Southern Christians believed, found itself on the side of heresy. "The Court," Talmadge continued, "put God and the Devil on an equal plane."[121]

When, only two years later, it was announced that enforcement of the *Brown* decision would begin, segregationists felt they had ample grounds to object: not only had the overreaching federal government forcefully integrated schools, but it had banned Christianity.[122] It amounted to, in the words of Mississippi Governor James Eastland, "judicial tyranny." Alabama Congressman George Andrews stated succinctly the views of many Southerners: "they put the Negroes in the schools; now they put God out of the schools."[123] Many felt they were left with no option but to start their own schools. And rather than having to do so solely on the basis of race, they could do so on the basis of religion. "We weren't so upset about integration," Harry Entrekin later said, "it was the government running schools and having no prayer."[124] No doubt it was both. But Entrekin's words conveyed something powerful stirring in America. Soon, a new generation of leaders, like the segregationists of the 1960s, would submerge racial preference under appeals to religious freedom. Senator Trent Lott put it bluntly: the establishment of tax-exempt private schools was "not a racial question, but a religious question."[125] Jerry Falwell himself started a school that, according to his wife, was not founded "in response to desegregation" but "because God and prayer had been kicked out of the public school."[126] In founding private Christian schools, white conservatives not only resisted integration but also found theological justifications for doing so, ensuring that the conflict over race would continue to be one over religion.

Old Theology, New Conservatism

By the mid-1960s, many white Southern Protestants had reclaimed their theological footing. They recaptured the old tenets—biblical literalism, evangelism, congregational autonomy—and refitted them. Instead of attacking German higher criticism and the National Council of Churches, these conservatives attacked the civil rights movement and the federal government. In doing so, racial and theological conservatives laid the foundation for the powerful political and theological coalition that emerged in the 1980s as the Religious Right.

On March 21, 1965, a man whose name would eventually become synonymous with the Religious Right delivered a sermon, "Minister and Marches," that captured the theological position of many Southern Christians regarding the civil rights movement.[127] The Rev. Jerry Falwell's sermon that day was largely what one would expect from a conservative Southern Baptist at this time. It proclaimed traditional theological tenets and used them to denigrate the civil rights movement, particularly its faith claims, which, Falwell asserted, stemmed from "making the Bible say what you want it to say." He claimed to have the true orthodox interpretation. In addition to misinterpreting the Bible, Falwell criticized the civil rights movement for becoming entrenched in politics and, therefore, having forsaken traditional Christianity. "Believing the Bible as I do," Falwell said, it would be "impossible to stop preaching the pure saving gospel of Jesus Christ and begin doing anything else—including fighting communism, or participating in civil rights reforms."[128]

For Falwell and other conservatives, the real problem in the American church, and in American society, was not racism, it was not inequality, and it was not irrelevance; it was forsaking orthodox Christian principles for a "liberal gospel." In this way, Falwell's critique in the mid-1960s sounds much like that of the Fundamentalists of the early twentieth century. Instead of holding the Bible as the inerrant Word of God, American Christians had twisted it to meet their own political ends; instead of preaching salvation through Christ, people were preaching civil rights and voting. This amounted to heresy.

In crafting a theological response to the civil rights movement, conservative white Protestants ensured America would remain bitterly divided over issues of religion and of race. Rather than hearing the prophetic calls of the movement or the reasoned appeals of moderates, they refused to listen and retreated into familiar, albeit powerful, arguments. These arguments—about the Bible and the gospel, about religious freedom and racial justice—would continue to be politically and theologically meaningful. While the movement vociferously and audibly invoked God's sanction in its quest for freedom, its opposition tended to be quieter. Most white citizens of Americus were not marching down Lee Street. They weren't making signs and picketing at the supermarket. They weren't singing, that's for sure. Instead, they largely ignored questions of racial justice. They asked for the preservation of law and order. They stayed home. They whispered among themselves about what should be done. They also criminalized activists and challenged the morality of the movement, ostracized white dissenters, and formed private Christian schools. In this way, the opposition to the civil rights movement coalesced, not only as a political reaction but also as a theological statement.

In 1965, when Jerry Falwell preached "Ministers and Marches," he mostly exhorted his listeners to stay home, read their Bibles, pray, go to church, and avoid the civil rights movement. But the movement was approaching the church. And as it did, white Southern Christians faced a direct theological reckoning.

CHAPTER SIX

Kneeling-In
The Theological Struggle Comes to Church

I am told that you must live in the South to understand the race question and it is true to a degree. But must I live in the South to understand the love of Jesus Christ?

—Helen Thoburn McCafferty, Letter to First Methodist Americus, 1965

This distortion of the faith aids and abets the sinfulness of man and society. This is the theological key to our dilemma. The really tragic thing about the un-Christian Christian is that he has really convinced himself that he is right in his sin and heresy.

—Martin Luther King Jr., "The Un-Christian Christian," 1965

I would tremble for the Christian cause if 50 Negroes were to enter an average local church in this country on a Sunday morning and ask to become members. Fundamentally, we are afraid . . . to practice the Christian religion.

—Benjamin Mays, *Time Magazine*, 1946

As soon as he opened the side door, hot air hit Kellete Heys in the face. The nice shirt he had to wear on Sundays (that he could not seem to keep tucked in, much to the annoyance of his mother) instantly felt damp as he stepped outside. Kellete could tell something unusual was going on from the nervous whispers and panicked glances his Sunday school teachers exchanged, but when he asked, the adults kept shushing him. So Kellete and his friends decided to sneak out and find out for themselves what was happening. They slid around the Greek-style church building, breathing shallowly and concealing themselves behind the massive columns. Kellete closed his eyes. He could hear the thumping of his heart, indeterminate shouting, the murmur of women talking, the click of cameras, a mosquito chorus. He drew a deep breath and then peered around the column.

He could see the deacons of the church, clad in their dark suits and aviator sunglasses, standing a few feet in front of him on the church steps, their arms crossed. Even from the back of their heads, he recognized them as men he knew. Below the formidable line of deacons, a large crowd had gathered.

People stood around on the church lawn, watching and waiting and whispering. Among them, Kellete was especially impressed to see reporters, wielding big news cameras and holding microphones. In the middle of it all, a huddled group of young people, some black and some white, knelt on the ground below the steps, almost at the deacons' feet. It looked to young Kellete Heys like they were praying—something, he thought to himself, people usually did *inside* the church.[1]

The weeks prior had been contentious. Boycotts, marches, rallies, press conferences, visits by national figures, and even a murder filled those long days of summer. The civil rights struggle had come to Americus. And on Sunday, it went to church. The scene Kellete Heys witnessed on the steps of the First Methodist Church was not the product of a random desire on the part of civil rights activists to attend a white church, nor was it merely an opportunistic ploy for sympathetic media attention. Rather, kneel-ins comprised an important facet of the larger freedom struggle. These deliberate demonstrations intended to reveal the hypocrisy of Christian segregationism and frame the movement in moral and theological terms. In the same way, the refusal of the church to admit integrated worshippers that morning was not an isolated instance of hatred by a rogue group acting according to their individual prejudices. No, this was the stated policy of First Methodist. In 1963, the church board expressly voted to bar blacks from attending—to "close the doors," as many Southern Protestant churches did in the 1950s and 1960s.

That morning represented years of struggle—over race, over the church, over Christian orthodoxy. How should Christians approach the race question? Who could come to church? Did they owe their allegiance to the laws of their state, to their denomination, or to God? Were they with God? Was He with them? Exploring the kneel-in movement and its opposition, as well as the specific 1965 kneel-in in Americus and the reaction it provoked, reveals a compelling story of theological conflict.

The Kneel-In Movement

As religious scholar Steve Haynes defines them, kneel-ins constituted "attempts by blacks or integrated groups to occupy segregated ecclesiastical space."[2] Essentially, groups of men and women, black and white, would seek entrance to Southern churches. If admitted, they would go in to worship; if denied, they would kneel in prayer as protest. The kneelers remained largely silent, respecting the Sabbath solemnity. Indeed, no signs, slogans, or chants were necessary, as the presence of these visitors to the churches was statement enough.

In the charged atmosphere of the 1960s, as Carolyn Dupont has put it, even "the ordinarily unremarkable act of going to church acquired new meaning."[3] Some estimate that kneel-ins occurred hundreds of times in the 1960s, in small towns and major cities, and at churches affiliated with every major Christian denomination.[4] They tended to play out similarly. One Southern journalist described the familiar scene: "a dozen or so funereal-faced deacons standing shoulder to shoulder . . . mouths clamped tightly shut, arms unanimously folded . . . their black gazes fixed just an inch or two over the heads of a small delegation . . . clustered on the sidewalk below them."[5] Kneel-ins were, in his estimation, "one of the more curious spectacles produced by *the most profound domestic moral crisis of our time.*"[6] As moral spectacles, kneel-ins produced stark spiritual confrontations in the most sacred and most separate of Southern spaces. A compelling theological drama, the kneel-in movement vividly embodied the difficulty of reconciling Christianity and Jim Crow in the South.

Despite its importance, the kneel-in movement receives too little treatment in accounts of the civil rights struggle.[7] While sit-ins are as familiar to schoolchildren as they are to scholars, the mention of a kneel-in usually draws raised eyebrows and quizzical shrugs. The movement was for the streets and lunch counters, the shrugs imply, not for church pews. As Stephen Haynes states, "Church desegregation campaigns have received very short shrift in the historiography of the American civil rights movement."[8] They have "fallen through the sifting bowl of history" and have been, in his estimation, "all but ignored."[9] Forgetting kneel-ins conceals the spiritual intentions of the movement and the intensely theological elements of the struggle. Indeed, there exists a "striking discrepancy" between the ways in which early civil rights activists envisaged church desegregation campaigns and the way those efforts are usually treated in historical accounts.[10]

Activists began to conduct kneel-ins at almost the very inception of the student movement. A few months after SNCC's initial convening, a group decided again to test segregation— this time not in public facilities but in religious spaces. Demonstrations at white churches began "as a variation on the sit-in theme," like the wade-ins, lie-ins, or stand-ins, but the kneel-ins soon became a distinctive protest form in their own right.

In 1960, the *Student Voice* dubbed kneel-ins "one of the next important phases of the student movement." SNCC secretary Jane Stembridge called kneel-ins "the start of a new movement in the South," while James Laue reported likewise that whenever he was asked about the direction of the movement, his response was "invariably . . . kneel-ins."[11] Moreover, activists considered kneel-ins essential to the moral thrust of the movement. "Throughout the years," SNCC students asserted, "the white Southerner has failed to realize the moral wrongness of segregation" because the racial struggle "had not been presented . . . as a moral problem." But SNCC developed the notion of a kneel-in out of the need not only to demonstrate that "segregation is morally wrong," but also "because the church is the house of God, to be attended by all people, regardless of race, who wish to worship there."[12] As Ruby Doris Smith claimed, "Segregation is basically a moral problem and for this reason I feel that Church is the one institution where the problem can be 'thrashed out.'" "The kneel-in movement," she continued, "is an appeal to the consciences of Christians."[13] By August 1960, the students felt "that the time [had] come to awaken the dozing consciences of white Southerners"; the time had come for kneel-ins.[14] Martin Luther King Jr., echoed the students in September of that year, when he proclaimed, "Our students will stand-in, sit-in, and kneel-in until they awaken the conscience of the white man in the South."[15]

The conscience of the church most desperately needed awakening. "The stigma of racial segregation," a 1960 article in *Christian Century* stated, "will not be removed until it disappears from white Christian churches, where it began."[16] "The sit-ins and the wade-ins [may] succeed," the author declared, "but the will of Christ for the races will not be accomplished until the Negro Christians and white Christians break bread together on their knees."[17] Token integration, or "merely juxtaposing whites and Negroes in the same church," the article claimed, "may be enough to satisfy the elemental demands of justice [but]. . . . It is not enough to meet Christ's claim that his disciples are one." In other words, "bread served at a lunch counter is one thing; bread shared in church is another."[18] For many Christians, both black and white, partaking of Christ in true fellowship was the ultimate hope of the movement, and the true test of brotherhood, justice, and love. Kneel-ins, SNCC, King, and others believed, would illustrate, perhaps more than any other form of civil disobedience, the moral and theological elements inherent in the contest between segregation and true Christian community.[19]

Although the formal notion of a kneel-in began in the summer of 1960, the idea of integrated worship as a means to confront white Southern Christians was much older.[20] Charles Sherrod had tried to attend white churches in Virginia as early as 1954. Even before, black religious intellectuals developed philosophies and tactics that would support kneel-ins. "It must be exceedingly embarrassing to Southern ministers," Benjamin Mays wrote, "whose congregations deny fellowship to members of the Negro race while they preach about the Righteous and Holy God who is the Father of mankind."[21] White and black Christians' shared theological heritage in Christ offered possibilities for inclusion and redemption unique to spiritual institutions. Though those opportunities were often forsaken, they nonetheless existed. Edler Hawkins, a black Presbyterian minister, asserted that the church must employ "its own distinctive language to stress . . . the moral dimension of this issue."[22] Martin Luther King Jr., wrote that "no one can deal with the ideational roots of racism and prejudice as the church can," calling for religious leaders of both races to preach "the truth of the biblical teaching on the brotherhood of man with courage and conviction."[23] Yet, King acknowledged that "Sunday morning segregation is the biggest obstacle to the fulfillment of the goal . . . of the redemptive Christian community."[24] The church could be the most significant agent for change or a major source of opposition to the real hope of the movement, the pursuit not of mere token integration but true interracial communion. For this reason, activists knew they had to confront the church.

With these theological foundations and spiritual hopes, the kneel-in movement began in Georgia. In March 1960, students in Atlanta met and drafted a document, "An Appeal for Human Rights," which stated: "Our churches, which are ordained by God and claim to be the houses of all people, foster segregation to the point of making Sunday the most segregated day of the week."[25] "As I grew up here in Atlanta," John Gibson wrote, "I heard constantly in Sunday School at Wheat Street Baptist Church and later at the Catholic schools I attended of the Fatherhood of God and the Brotherhood of Man. Unfortunately," he continued, "I saw little of this as a reality in the relationships between white Christians and Negro Christians. And, like many of my fellow students, I was forced to agree with the truth of the statement that the most segregated hour in America was eleven o'clock on Sunday morning."[26] It was that bastion of separation that Gibson and other activists sought to challenge through kneel-ins.

A few months later, the students met again to plan their confrontation of this social and ecclesiastical evil. "For the greater part of this year," one student leader described, "we have been concerned with the refusal of human dignity in the political, economic, and social spheres. During this summer," he continued, "most of us in the Atlanta student movement have increasingly felt the need to place this problem squarely on the hearts and the moral consciences of the white Christians in our community . . . feeling that every church, if it is truly Christian, by its very presence extends in the Savior's name the unspoken invitation: 'whoever will, let him come.'"[27] Thus, they decided to test the "truly Christian" nature of Atlanta's churches.

On August 7, 1960, an integrated group of over twenty trained and determined Atlanta students divided up and visited six Atlanta churches, keeping in mind their theological purpose.[28] "I approached Grace Methodist Church," one of the students claimed, "not as a demonstrator, but as a believer in an eternal, common Cause."[29] For the most part that first morning, they were admitted and seated, though sometimes in another area of the sanctuary.[30] To many, this seemed a rousing success.[31] Dr. Harry A. Fifield, minister at First Presbyterian, told his wife that he was "so proud of my people" he didn't "even know what to do."[32] Black leaders, too, initially expressed hope, even of the tepid sort, regarding the kneel-ins' successes. An Atlanta headline the day following read, "Negro Leader Hails Churches for Courtesy During Visits."[33] The students were even more enthusiastic. Gwendolyn Harris, who had sought entry to St. Mark's Methodist, called the kneel-in attempt a "rewarding experience," saying she was "deeply inspired" having experienced "far beyond the realm of mere physical integration" but "true spiritual integration." John Gibson jubilantly reported, "This experience showed me that once people of seemingly different backgrounds, and ancestral origin find a common denominator, they can live in loving peace as men and women and not merely representatives of various races." Even when they had been rebuffed, the temper of the students was optimistic. "Even if we were not admitted to worship, as was true in my case," Ruby Doris Smith said, "I think that the attempt in itself was a success, because the minds and hearts of those who turned us away were undoubtedly stirred. I'm quite sure they had to do quite some 'soul-searching' when they realized that they had turned Christians away from the House of God." To almost everyone, the initial Atlanta kneel-in seemed to indicate a hopeful future for the theological movement.[34]

But soon, opposition from white churches increased. A week later, on August 14, half of the ten churches visited denied kneelers entrance, including Grace Methodist, in an about-face from its decision to admit black worshippers just seven days prior. The following Sunday, August 21, the students were barred from all the churches they attempted to integrate.[35]

In October 1960, several young women from Spelman College decided to venture into the crisp fall air and seek entry to several West End Atlanta churches "to go to worship the God of ALL mankind." Refused entry at several white churches, the women reported interesting dialogues with these church leaders. At one, they were stopped in the driveway of the church by a deacon who told them he "hoped they hadn't anticipated worshipping there," directing them over to Wheat Street Baptist, a black church nearby. The women then sought entry at another white church, finding the doors locked and guarded by several waiting men, to which one woman asked, "What power do [you] have to hold the doors of the church closed to anyone?" Another student chimed in, asking one man "if he would be holding the doors of the Kingdom of God." Flummoxed, the man curtly responded, "Yes, I'll be there and a host of others, and you won't get in there either." The women left, "with tears falling silently from their eyes."[36] Despite (or maybe even because of) these signs of mounting resistance, the kneel-in movement emerged as a theologically and morally confrontational direct-action protest. From Atlanta, kneel-ins fanned out across the region, occurring at churches in Rock Hill, Augusta, Tallahassee, Durham, Savannah, Memphis, Jackson, Birmingham, Albany, and many other smaller towns, including, eventually, Americus.

The theological components of kneel-ins couldn't have been more explicit. As a distributed leaflet in Georgia pronounced: "Only in open fellowship and love can the real presence of God, the Lord and Father of us all, be shared. As believers in the fatherhood of God and brotherhood of man, we humbly seek to worship with you in fulfillment of Christ's commandment that his children may be one in him, even as he is one in God."[37] For those who participated in kneel-ins, theological orthodoxy—the belief in the Fatherhood of God, the brotherhood of man, and the truth of Christ's teaching—led them directly to integrated worship.

Of course, this interpretation was not accepted by many white Southern Christians.[38] A real theological crisis was emerging. "A tense situation exists within the heart and soul of our people," one Georgia minister explained, "as the white Southerner within us tangles with the Christian within us." This theological entanglement, he claimed, "is of much more ultimate importance than any of the pushings and shovings at Woolworth's lunch counter."[39] Many Southern segregationists, though, refused to engage with the theological issue being presented, preferring invective over introspection. For these, Carolyn Dupont writes, kneel-ins simply "confirmed the crass opportunism of the freedom struggle and the apostate character of their denominations." Therefore "the moral theater played out on these church steps worked no conversion on their racial attitudes."[40] Herein lies the central tension of the story: for some, the kneel-ins constituted the most stark, embodied confrontation between the Christianity of Christ and the segregated church of religious hypocrisy; for others, the kneel-ins represented the defilement of sacred space and the exploitation of pure religion for politically and theologically suspect ends.

But kneel-ins not only provoked conflict between the movement and the old church guard, they also exposed deep divisions within established ecclesiastical bodies over issues of race and theology. One of the deacons in Atlanta admitted when turning away the Spelman women, that the church had "trouble enough holding the congregation together without Negroes coming to Church."[41] "During the kneel-ins," one historian has stated, "churches themselves became the actual arenas of conflict."[42] These conflicts did not begin with the kneel-ins of the 1960s; in many ways, they represented their culmination.

"To Hell with Christian Principles, We've Got to Save This Church!"

Since the Civil War, the national Baptist, Methodist, and Presbyterian churches had been divided between North and South over the issue of slavery.[43] These splits endured through the late nineteenth and early twentieth centuries, resulting not only in divergent views on race, but also, as chapter 2 delineated, in different views on theology.[44] Southern Protestants adopted a system of strict segregation, positioning themselves as defenders of biblical inerrancy, while Northern Protestants tended to advocate policies of racial inclusion, which earned them designation as liberals.[45] Following the 1954 *Brown* decision, intra-denominational tensions spiked. The Southern Baptist Convention, the Council of Methodist Bishops, and the Southern Presbyterian General Assembly immediately came out in favor of the *Brown* ruling, to the shocked horror of many local Southern congregations.[46] These congregations, including those in Americus, simply defied these denominational pronouncements on race, asserting their congregational autonomy and preserving their sense of theological and racial orthodoxy.[47] Deep theological and ecclesiastical rifts had long existed within white Protestantism, rifts exacerbated by *Brown* and exposed by the kneel-in movement of the 1960s.

In a 1960 *Atlanta Constitution* editorial, journalist Ralph McGill made the comment that "to bar the doors of churches may not be explained away as anything but an affront to Christian principles."[48] A few hundred miles west on I-20, an Alabama segregationist responded, "to hell with Christian principles, we've got to save this church!"[49]

To him, and many like him, the church needed to be saved both from encroaching liberalism and the kneel-in movement. Some historians have missed the complexity of the religious opposition to civil rights, concluding that segregationists were "unwilling, or unable, to mount a robust theological defense of Jim Crow Christianity."[50] Yet, a robust theological defense was mounted in opposition to the kneel-in movement, a defense based on notions of orthodoxy and the sanctity of the church—quite resilient arguments that remained powerful throughout the twentieth century.

Familiar arguments about congregational autonomy persisted in the theological conflict over kneel-ins. In the fall of 1960, only weeks after the first Atlanta kneel-in, a lawsuit was brought to the DeKalb County court against
Dr. King for his "direction and orders" in organizing a kneel-in. The prosecu-
tion accused King of disturbing "the worshipping of God according to the tenets of the congregation."[51] The charges were eventually dropped, but the
case against kneel-ins would endure. In 1963, Atlanta Judge Durwood Pye ruled
that churchgoers could "worship a segregated God in a segregated church if
they please," adding, "men have died on a thousand fields of battle for that precious right."[52] While some segregationists may not have thought of enforcing
congregational policy as necessarily theological, the closed doors themselves
represented a considered theological stance developed over time, as we have
seen. Opponents of the kneel-in movement not only asserted a theological position regarding the *autonomy* of the church, they also claimed a theological
position regarding the *holiness* of the church. "Jesus had run money-changers
out of the Temple, just as we had good reasons to keep those [civil rights] agitators out of our Church," one Americus woman proclaimed. By invoking the
New Testament story of Jesus's righteous outrage at the temple being defamed
by commerce, many segregationists identified a biblical justification for turning visitors away.[53] If God was holy, they believed, then His house was to be
as well.

The church was no place for politics. As the woman declared in the conclusion of her letter to the Georgia bishop: "Those people were at our church
for a far worse purpose than money changing."[54] Even worse than the ancient
capitalists who defiled God's temple with business, civil rights activists, many
reasoned, were sullying sacred space with political posturing.[55] Though some
white Southern Christians in the 1960s felt increasingly uncomfortable defending racial segregation biblically, they refocused their arguments to emphasize
ecclesiastical propriety, a no less theological position of exclusion. Since kneel-
ins represented, in the words of one historian, "a sacrilegious incursion of
politics into a pristine space of worship," Southern Christians could justifiably
bar activists.[56] They were simply defending the church's purity. This theology
of ecclesiastical holiness extended from the spatial to the internal.[57]

In locating an argument for ecclesiastical propriety, white opponents to
kneel-ins usually turned to what Stephen Haynes has called the "question of
motives."[58] They determined kneeling activists were not truly seeking entry
for worship; rather, they were mounting "political stunts" that mocked sincere
devotion to God.[59] Kneelers were, in the oft-repeated adage, "agitators," a
label often modified by "outside" or even "Communist." In Americus, some

alleged that those kneeling in represented "insincerity and manipulation of civil rights."[60] Even at the first kneel-in in Atlanta in 1960, the accusation of insincerity was leveled against the students. "They were just a bunch of agitators," an usher at First Baptist reported, while some at Grace Methodist characterized the students as "agitators not interested in truly worshipping as Christians."[61] In short, defenders of segregated churches "turned racial equality into a question of religious sincerity."[62] This pattern continued as the kneel-ins expanded throughout the South. By ascribing "unholy motives," segregationist Southern Christians "discovered that the Bible could indeed inform a Christian response to interlopers."[63] If the kneelers could be characterized as mere agitators, then the church's refusal to admit them shed its problematic moral and theological ramifications. If their prayer huddles could be reframed as window dressing for pernicious politics, or, even more, the mockery of God's holy church, then the moral, scriptural, and theological basis for their actions could be, in good conscience, dismissed.

But even if the kneel-ins could be disregarded as political ploys in the minds of Southern segregationists, they nevertheless created a very external confrontation, one that was visibly theological. As one Georgian put it, "Whatever the motives of the kneel-ins, they have placed the Southern Christian Church in a position of choosing."[64] In Americus, Georgia, they had made their choice.

Kneeling Down on Lee Street

On August 1, 1965, integrated activists targeted two Americus churches, First Baptist and First Methodist.[65] The plan was relatively simple: neatly dressed for the service, the group would politely seek entrance at the churches, and, when predictably rebuffed, they would kneel down in front and pray together.[66] That morning, Carolyn DeLoatch, Lena Turner, David Bell, John Lewis, and others met early at the Barnum Funeral Home.[67] They prayed together and then filed into a car that dropped them off at the intersection of the downtown district and Lee Street.[68] Some approached First Baptist.[69]

Before they reached the entrance, twelve or so ushers, including Americus Fire Chief H. K. Henderson, intercepted them in front of the stately brick edifice. Marion Hicks, a member of the "welcoming committee" for the 500-member church, recalled that he "met [the integrated group] on the sidewalk" and told them that "the church agreed not to accept black people."[70] Although the Baptist ushers prohibited the group from entering the church, they did permit them to kneel and pray where they were out on the sidewalk.[71]

But the threat of violent confrontation lingered like the humidity on that stifling morning. One report claimed that Fire Chief Henderson made the threat explicit, telling the kneelers, "I can tell you seriously, if you come down here looking for violence, you're going to get it; if you come down here for bloodshed, you're going to get it."[72] Another man later boasted, "We had what it took to keep them out."[73] An Americus onlooker snickered to the press, "I bet it was mighty uncomfortable, coming inside after they got those niggers to leave and having to sit down in the pews with those hard [guns] in their hip pockets—and having to go down real slow so there wouldn't be a clunk."[74] It is clear from the swagger of the statement that keeping demonstrators out of white congregations was a duty of which many were proud. What had occurred in more liberal congregations in Atlanta was not going to happen in Americus, if local churchgoers had anything to say about it, which, as Baptists, they did. It was their church as much as the Lord's church, and as Chief Henderson put it, "No black foot should cross in."[75] Inside the church, the oblivious minister, Harold Collins, was purportedly preaching a sermon on grace and the need "for God's love to come into the hearts of all men."[76]

As this was happening, another group walked across the street to the First Methodist Church, where they found a crowd already gathering on the lawn. Unlike the quieter integration attempt at First Baptist, the kneel-in at First Methodist caused quite a stir. Methodist church members—including Mayor Walker—onlookers, and even members of the national press who had come to Americus during the previous week of protests, were all milling about, waiting and watching. "It was one of the few times I was concerned about my welfare," movement veteran and kneeler David Bell remembered, "I had never seen that many people." Twelve church representatives were "standing shoulder to shoulder" like "a militia in suit and tie," and behind them stood several lines of younger men on the tall stone steps of the church. Bell recognized "they were going to do whatever they needed to do to keep us out."[77] With some trepidation, the spokesman for the kneel-in group addressed the line of suited gatekeepers: "We just want to worship." That was not to be. "We don't have room for you," an unidentified Methodist usher responded.[78] "But I'm a Methodist," the spokesman protested, before being quickly interrupted by a booming voice that said, "I don't care what your religion is."[79] Segregationists at First Methodist intensely opposed ecclesiastical integration. "They felt like it was their church," a later minister of the church, Rev. Bill Dupree said, "and they had the authority to decide who was going to attend and who wasn't. If they didn't want blacks to go they had the right to tell them they couldn't attend." "They literally looked on blacks as being inferior," he concluded. "It's just a fact of life."[80]

The small group knelt in prayer, still and silent in the midst of the surrounding chaos. As their heads bowed in a display of reverence and humility, the white anti-apostles with stern faces, clenched jaws, and crossed arms blocked the church doors.[81] After the prayer, Police Chief Ross Chambliss arrived on the scene and arrested the kneelers for disturbing the peace, for "disturbing divine worship." They were taken to the Sumter County Prison, where Charlie Lee Hopkins and Willie Lamar, under arrest for the previous day's murder of Andy Whatley, were also being held.[82]

As had been the case at First Baptist, the pastor of First Methodist, Vernard Robertson, was nowhere to be seen during the kneel-in. Presumably, he was inside preparing for the morning's service. Vernard Robertson was born in 1914 in Guyton, Georgia. He attended Young Harris College and Emory University's Candler School of Theology, pastoring several other Georgia congregations before eventually making his way to Americus in 1962.[83] Robertson almost certainly possessed more moderate racial views than the majority of his parishioners, but as one woman in the church put it, he "rode the rail" and was "caught in the middle."[84] Since the congregation exerted tremendous pressure to have their way, it seems Robertson decided that compliance was the best path. "Vernard tried to keep peace in the church and do the right thing at the same time," a subsequent minister of the church explained, "which was a real difficult position to be in." "You might have said he should have taken a stronger stand," he acceded.[85] Another (admittedly lapsed) congregant had a harsher take, calling Rev. Robertson "the weakest sonofabitch I ever saw."[86] These views notwithstanding, Robertson knew he would almost certainly lose his job if he spoke out for Christian inclusion, and so "what he tried to do was keep peace through a difficult season."[87] Keeping the peace would prove difficult, as the pastor found himself the subject of reams of critical responses in the press and from letter writers around the world.

In the midst of that chaotic morning at First Methodist and First Baptist, a reporter took a photograph that would become emblematic of the entire theological struggle.[88] The camera's flash captured integrated activists kneeling on the concrete in prayer, while the church's scowling white defenders towered above them on the church steps with arms crossed in defiance. For many this photo represented the hypocrisy of Southern Christianity and race relations; for others, it represented a courageous stand against a "heretical culture"; and for us, it represents the theological stakes of the civil rights struggle.

An integrated group conducts a kneel-in at First Methodist Church in
Americus, Georgia, 1965. (AP Photo)

"A Picture to the World": Responses to the Kneel-In

Accompanying both Associated Press and United Press articles, the photograph of the Americus kneel-in found its way to the front page of morning newspapers in Portland, Spokane, and Seattle, in Los Angeles, New York, and Philadelphia, and, even more remarkably, in Vancouver, Christchurch, Edinburgh, and La Paz.[89] The kneel-in in Americus was also reported on the NBC Nightly News in a compelling scene akin to the fire hoses of Birmingham and the charred buses of Anniston.[90] The bent knees and bowed heads, the set jaws and folded arms were now on display not only for the people of Americus but for all of America. Over 300 letters of response poured into the First Methodist Church. Some praised the Americus church, others chastised it, some offered sympathy, and some commented with emotional or comical asides. Some sent scathing political cartoons that appeared in various newspapers, while one man sent one he had drawn by hand. Postmarked from cities around the nation, including East Longmeadow, Massachusetts; Port Angeles, Washington; St. Paul, Minnesota; Fort Collins, Colorado; and Elizabethtown, Tennessee, the letters provide riveting insight into national beliefs regarding religion and civil rights.[91] Retired veterans, hopeful college students, concerned housewives, and members of the clergy all made their voices heard, mailing their opinions and questions down to Americus. First Methodist preserved them all.

The majority of the letters chastised the church. The incident amounted to "a shame," "a travesty," a "disgrace"; it was "regrettable," "upsetting," and "deeply disturbing."[92] Many berated the congregants in Americus for not being Christians at all. Of the letters received, around two-thirds condemned the church's actions.

Many of these writers were concerned Methodists who criticized the church either for its outright denominational rebellion or for forsaking the mission of the church universal. "I respectfully call your attention to Paragraph 1820 of the 1964 *Discipline* of the Methodist Church which you, as a minister, took a vow to uphold and enforce," thundered Mr. Elmer Hill of Sherman Oaks, California, "your action and those of members of your church is in violation of the church discipline and is a disgrace." He then noted that he would be contacting the bishop regarding the matter to "take whatever action may be necessary."[93] Another concerned Methodist also confronted the congregation about its position with respect to national denominational edicts. From Christchurch, New Zealand, Mr. Armstrong wrote, "I understand that every official pronouncement of the American Methodist Church is against segregation" and "that the Negro 'central jurisdiction,' or segregated organization of Negro

Methodist churches, has been abolished." He claimed, "There is no vestige of support for segregation in any ecumenical body."[94] One Methodist minister, outraged that the church was flaunting the national guidelines, wrote that First Methodist of Americus should "please, please, please do Methodism a favor and lead your people out of the Methodist Church!" "Since there is obviously no intention of following the *Discipline* either in letter or in spirit," he concluded, "this is surely the most honest thing to do."[95] From San Diego, a self-identified "appalled Methodist" requested that the church "either change your policies or please discontinue your relationship with the Methodist church as you fail to live up to the Spirit which formed our church or even to the ideas of Christ."[96]

Another line of argument was that First Methodist was not only in violation of denominational rule, but that it had forsaken its core identity as a church. "The building which houses those of the First Methodist Church, Americus, Georgia," a Massachusetts man proclaimed, "should no longer be referred to as a house of worship, but a house or a club."[97] From Longview, Washington, a Mrs. Pritchard remarked, "I am shocked that you publicly denied these brethren entrance to your building declaring it to be private property. May I ask to what extent is a house dedicated to the worship of God considered private?"[98] For her, the church was the house of God, open to all his children of whatever race. The same proved true for Mrs. Upshaw who added, "Even if these people are not sincere, which I doubt, is it not your duty to permit them to enter? This church of yours is not an earthly possession, but the house of God. He must be heartily displeased." One California woman intoned succinctly, "A church of God? Don't you realize that a church is 'God's House,' *not yours*?"[99] Even a "Methodist teenager" understood this. From St. Paul, Minnesota, he wrote, "A place belonging to God shall be for *all* people, no matter what kind, they are still his creation."[100] Mr. Loury also challenged First Methodist's actions based on his view of the church. Commenting from Lake Placid, New York, he conceded that "we cannot force anyone to be friends with us or accept us into their homes or clubs or social groups," but then he reminded his readers that "the Church is not a social club, is it?" The church, if it was to be the Church, had to be different. These letters claim that the First Methodist Church in Americus defied both denominational guidelines and its very ecclesiastical identity.

Other responses fixated less on church issues and more on explicitly theological ones. Many quoted scripture.[101] "I can't help but wonder," one Indiana man mused, "what doctrine your church is built upon. Surely not the doctrine of brotherhood and love as taught by Jesus Christ—Saviour of all mankind!"

Segregationist doctrine, for many outraged and befuddled observers, seemed incompatible with the message of Jesus and the meaning of the scriptures. From Los Angeles, one man exclaimed, "Shame on all ministers who follow the patterns of segregation which [is] unchristian and *unbiblical*."[102] As one perplexed woman wrote, "Why don't you people down there read your Bible? And why don't you learn your Commandments? Is that what your Bible teaches you? I'm glad mine doesn't."[103] The Bible itself offered evidence for racial inclusion, many asserted. After listing half a dozen bible verses from the New Testament, Robert Morris, himself a pastor from Endicott, New York, claimed that the Bible "seem[s] to speak to us so clearly that we are all saved only by the grace of God through faith and that we are all brethren in His Spirit." The church's actions, though, led him to believe that his fellow Methodists in Americus "differ[ed] in [their] interpretations."[104] Some declared outright that the white Southern interpretation was heretical. "Baptists and Methodists of the South," one California man warned, "better . . . cease giving a false interpretation of the Bible." In his estimation, "The Bible [did] not teach segregation anywhere regardless what text you may parrot"; to insist on segregation was to practice "a decadent and false Protestantism."[105]

Mr. Dennis, of Tucson, Arizona, centered his critique on the spiritual nature of God and his creative authority. He wrote, "Have you forgotten that all peoples, all colors, from all lands are products of God's hand or did you ever consider this fact? . . . God made man in his own image, if we are to believe the bible, and I hope you do. Then, by your actions Sunday, do you consider yourself an image of God? Would He have done the same?"[106] "I raise my voice in protest," one Missouri Methodist wrote, "that any church bearing the name Methodist would refuse admittance to anyone [sic] of God's children." He explained his position theologically, averring, "The price was paid nearly 2,000 years ago to break down the wall of partition that separated God's people. Let's not hold that account open any longer."[107] If God, in Christ, had demolished the divisions between people, he believed, a church in Christ's name should not reconstruct it. "It hurts me," one such letter opined, "that although Paul found that in Christ there is neither Jew nor Greek, so many of us have created false barriers of race or creed between the children of God."[108]

Many of the theological opinions voiced centered on the person and work of Jesus. Eugene Tomlin, the chairman for the Commission for Social Concerns at the First Methodist Church in Champaign, Illinois, wrote, "One can only think 'What would Jesus have done?'" Mr. Tomlin went on to say, "[Jesus] accepted all people as they were, and caused them to want to change *their* lives through exposure to his presence. He was sorely tried, many times, yet he preached and practiced forgiveness, not once, but 'seventy time seven' if necessary. Can we call ourselves Christians and do less?"[109] "I hope," another man wrote, that you have "meditated long and deeply on what Jesus would have done when confronted with this situation." He continued, "Would He who sought the outcast, taught love and forgiveness, asked us to pray for our enemies and those who wrongly use us, have turned anyone aside?"[110] A letter from Mexico, New York, declared, "In the days of Jesus' ministry, *all* people were allowed to come to Him for healing, not only physical ills but spiritual ills as well. He did not say only a few can come in My temple. . . . He said *all* must come, be baptized in faith and accept Me as their Savior and Redeemer."[111] Mrs. King of Los Angeles put it even more bluntly. She prodded, "Sincerely— and reverently—do those look like the real CHRISTian faces on the top step? *Are they acting like Jesus?*" After quoting some of Christ's words from the New Testament, Mrs. King asked the congregants to "*Search your HEARTS . . . compare these faces to the face of your Master, Jesus.*"[112] The comparison certainly would not reflect well on the church's actions. One fellow minister illustrated this, asking, "Can you imagine Christ standing with his arms folded, denying the comfort and challenge of the Gospel, saying 'I don't care what your religion is?'"[113] The answer, of course, was no. The First Methodist Church had sacrificed the teachings and identity of Jesus on the altar of its own racial views, these responses insisted.

Many replies implicitly incorporated a critique of divine whiteness. Dripping with disdain and sarcasm, one letter declared: "Perhaps your bible gives an account concerning the color of God's skin. Unfortunately mine does not." "May God have mercy on your soul," the author continued, "should, on that Great Day, you find your Judge does not have the same color skin as you."[114] A Lutheran man from McLean, Virginia, echoed this criticism. He wrote, "Do these members think that God is white?" Such a claim, he purported, would deny "the very foundation of our Judaic-Christian religion which is the universal brotherhood of all mankind under the Fatherhood of God." For emphasis, he added, "It is very possible that Christ Himself would not qualify for this Lily-White League."[115] Not only did the Bible not identify God as white, these citizens pointed out, but when, in Christian belief, God became man, he chose to inhabit nonwhite flesh. As Bessie Wilson, of Des Moines, simply but bitingly inquired, "Just what proof do you or any of us have that Jesus had white skin?"[116] One Georgia woman explained, "When I visited the Holy Land in 1960, most of the People who walked in the streets of Jerusalem were very dark skinned." "Is it possible," she prodded, that "Jesus and his parents were also?"[117] A Clayton, New Jersey, resident provided an answer, writing, "Christ, too, was colored, a Sumerian of Africa, also a Jew."[118] The irony of a segregated church existing in this Jesus's name was not lost on the letter-writers. A Plymouth, Massachusetts, woman observed that if Jesus should "come again to earth as a Hebrew or with colored skin, the chances are that He would not be recognized or allowed in many of our churches."[119] Or, as Ms. Fairchild mused, "the thought keeps returning to me—what would they have done had Jesus, if His skin was a different color, walked up just then seeking a place to worship?"[120] The theological question loomed large for many observers: How could segregated congregations claim to worship one to whom they likely would deny entry?

Numerous responses opposing First Methodists' actions employed theological arguments for racial inclusion that invoked views of ecclesiastical orthodoxy and biblical Christology in the same letter. For instance, Alfred Achert of Yeadon, Pennsylvania, "a white Methodist laymen [*sic*]," wrote that he was "distressed" over the kneel-in. "As a member of a church that has been integrated for about fifteen years," Achert explained, "I know that white and Negro Methodists can effectively work together in the same local church to serve the Kingdom of God." He then urged the Americus congregation to seek the same integrationist spirit, employing first theological and then ecclesiastical arguments. He pressed the church "to accept and support the teachings and example of Christ concerning brotherhood." As he reasoned, Jesus's "association with the Samaritan people and His parables concerning them" revealed "that Christ believed these despised people to be acceptable to God and therefore to Him and all men." Jesus's involvement with the Samaritans led Achert to believe that Christians likewise should associate with the outcasts in society—in this case, their black neighbors. After establishing this biblical line of argument, Achert turned to an ecclesiastical one, writing, "The General Conference has made it clear that all men should be permitted to attend any Methodist Church." Thus, Rev. Robertson should have been able, he declared, to "bring about compliance with the requirement of church law."[121] Others, too, combined the theological and ecclesiastical. Richard Hurley of Mamasqua, New Jersey, wrote to remind the Americus Methodists not only of "Paragraph 106.1, *The Discipline*," but also "that Christ said 'Inasmuch as ye did it to one of the least of these, ye did it to me.'"[122] For many, what the First Methodist Church of Americus had done was wrong both for its violation of church law and of Christ's law.

While most critiques were circumspect and reasoned, some were less inclined toward gentle theological prodding and more inclined toward enraged exposition. "You UnAmerican Vultures," one began, "you have about as much

Los Angeles Times cartoon clipping sent to First Methodist Church following the 1965 kneel-in. (First United Methodist Church Archive)

of Christ's love in your heart as had Adolph Hitler, a fanged rattlesnake or a head hunter! . . . To think that human beings, in the name of Jesus, could stand on their church steps and deny entrance to any other human on earth is unbelievable! I hold you to be criminals of the lowest type as does [*sic*] most Americans know you to be, low, ignorant, prejudiced and as unholy as serpents." The writer benedicted, "May an Omnipotent Power dawn upon you and offer you Light," but confessed his doubt that "there be any sort of intelligence or love within you to receive such Light."[123] Similarly, a fellow Methodist railed: "You people call yourselves Christian? You are the rottenest hypocrites this side of hell, and way down deep in your heart you must know it." He added, "I'll bet you and the boys are real heroes to the rest of the Klan for the splendid stand you made against 'them niggers.' . . . As you put on your pointed hood and sheet and burn your next cross on somebody's lawn, you might think about whether that would be Christ's way!" He concluded his condemnation with a chilling malediction: "May God have mercy on your filthy souls! I certainly wouldn't."[124] A news reporter from Milwaukee voiced his opinion that "even the Almighty must be disgusted with your ignorance and prejudice and your hate filled actions against your fellow man." "How can you dare even open your church doors," he wanted to know, "when you are such narrow-minded hypocrites????" He concluded, searingly, that "God must be disgusted with you people."[125] Another letter writer claimed: "You have retreated into the devil's midst," clarifying further, "You do NOT have God's approval."[126] Mrs. Ruby D. of Massachusetts likewise excoriated the church, calling their actions "sickening" and expressing her hope for poetic justice, that "some day God will turn white skin into brown."[127]

A few concerned citizens, usually from regions a great distance from the South, asked simply for clarification as to how something like this could occur. For example, John Soltman, from Tacoma, Washington, wrote, "I need your help in understanding why the visitors were turned away. As you realize we are too far away to know—or even imagine—the true dynamics of the situation there." He continued to say that, as a fellow Methodist, "the refusal is difficult to understand in relation to the Methodist *Discipline*." For those unfamiliar with the folk theology and custom of the South, the refusal of Southern congregations to comply with the national denominational edicts was truly baffling.[128] Mr. Eagle asked, "with all due sympathy for the extreme difficulty of changing the customs of your city entrenched there many years," why the church maintained a policy of racial segregation. "Would it not be better strategy," he offered, "to admit those seeking to worship so long as they enter quietly and conduct themselves with decorum?"[129] A Methodist from South Bend, Indiana, wrote in a "sincere desire to learn another's understanding of one of the problems of our time." He expressed his belief that "your people love the same God and with as much sincerity as we do," and simply asked that they explain to him why they acted in such a manner.[130] The most haunting of these inquisitive notes came from Worthington, Minnesota. Mrs. D. M. Johnson asked, "How do you explain to your youth the action you recently took in turning away colored people from your church? My husband, I, and our four boys would like to know. The boys have colored friends they play with and cannot understand why."[131]

While the majority of the letters received criticized the church in anger or disbelief, a number praised the minister and deacons of the church, commending their stand for their Christian righteousness. One Americus resident penned a letter to the minister of his own congregation in the wake of the incidents, sending a copy as well to the Georgia bishop, John Owen Smith. "I joined the Methodist Episcopal Church-South in 1903," he wrote, "I have been a Methodist for over 62 years, and I can state without fear of truthful contradiction that the rank and file of Methodists in Georgia are opposed to mixed congregations at worship services." He claimed that the kneelers were "paid troublemakers," "the scum of the earth," and that their integration attempt was designed simply "to drive a wedge between our people." The church, he insisted, had "rightly" turned them away.[132] Other sympathetic responses came from outside of Americus. A man from Columbia, South Carolina, wrote "to congratulate your members for standing up and defending their rights."[133] While "it seems that we have reached the point that whatever we do is wrong," wrote a Waycross, Georgia, man, "I feel that God is still on his throne and a day of judgment will come to those who desecrate the Sabbath and certainly to those who disturb the worship of Almighty God."[134] A North Carolina individual also affirmed segregation in the church. "I believe the same way you fellow Christins [*sic*] believe about the mixing of the races," he said, "God's approval is [not] upon it." This man then stated, "We as you believe there is a dividing point in races; had it not been, all of us would have been the same color, and I do not believe 'God' made a mistake when he made all races and all colors." He concluded, "may God bless you all, and when you have done all 'Stand,' and stand fast, and 'God himself shall take care of the rest.'"[135]

A Tallahassee man expressed his bafflement at the civil rights movement, demanding to know "why some Washington officials condone or overlook the offense of sending our boys to risk their lives fighting COMMUNISTS in the hellish jungles of Viet Nam, while at the same time some Washington officials seem to support or neglect completely evidenced COMMUNIST-inspired gimmicks in Selma, Alabama; Americus, Georgia; Bogalusa, Louisiana; Chicago, Illinois; Newark, New Jersey; St. Augustine, Florida; and other places in the good ole U.S.A."[137] Laudatory notes came from outside the South as well. From Rockford, Illinois, Mable wrote, "Dear Pastor, Hooray for you. I don't believe demonstrators should force themselves in. We are getting so tired of reading of civil rights."[136] From Washington state, one man ridiculed the kneelers as looking more like they were "shooting dice" than praying. "Our sympathies are surely with the South in this phony and communistic 'Civil Rights' deal," he declared.[138] An Ohioan wrote, "As a fifty-four year old person, who has been a Methodist all of his life, I cannot compliment your church and its members highly enough." Though a lifelong Northerner, he described himself as "more and more a Southern sympathizer," whose "heart goes out to the white people and the good colored people of your city."[139] An important figure in the Los Angeles Citizen's Council declared what "a wonderful feeling [it is] to know that there are other people in America that are standing up for the rights of the white race and the right to gather without being mixed with the Savages of Africa." Calling integration a force of the "AntiChrist," he bestowed this benediction: "God Bless all of you people down there." He signed his letter, "For God, Country, and Freedom of choice."[140] A Pennsylvania Baptist declared that segregation was "God's command." "We believe in segregation here at my church, but many churches here do not," he stated, promising, "We shall be praying for you."[141]

Many moderate responses simply offered sympathy to Vernard Robertson, acknowledging the "trying times" and urging patience and prayer. "Brother Robertson," one fellow Methodist wrote, "I know that you are a man of deep convictions. I know you want the spirit of Christ to prevail regardless of the conditions."[142] Other ministers especially expressed sympathy, like the Macon preacher who claimed, "My heart goes out to you and your members in this very trying time. . . . I am praying for you each day."[143] Rev. Thomas M. Lee wanted to let the reverend know that "I am thinking of you and the ugly situation in Americus. . . . I know there is hate on the part of many of our white Methodists toward negroes and I assume there is also bitterness on the part of many colored people toward us white folk. But if ever we needed the spirit of the Christ to be manifested fully it is in critical situations such as you are facing."[144] A Savannah minister reiterated this sentiment, noting that "at times like these the Christian minister finds himself too much alone." Ministering "to all people is not an easy thing," he wrote, assuring his brother that "you and all the people of Americus have our prayers in these days."[145]

This cache of letters—at turns arresting and alarming, heartwarming and heinous—provides extraordinary insight into the impact of the kneel-in movement on the church and illustrates the variegated ways in which Americans processed issues of race theologically. And, of course, it demonstrates that Christian Americans *did* interpret issues of race theologically.

Repercussions in the Denomination and in Americus

Two weeks after the incident, John O. Smith, a bishop in the Methodist Church, sent a letter from his office at Candler Seminary in Atlanta to Rev. Robertson in Americus.[146] The bishop's office, he noted, had been "deluged" with correspondence. He reported that though some of it was "as foolish as the signs of the times," other parts of it represented "intelligent, concerned, long-suffering people" who were asking "if something can't be done to protect the image of the Church of Christ." Smith agreed; it had been very bad publicity for the church. As many laypeople had, Smith cited the *Discipline*'s stance on the matter. He was not "pulling the *Discipline* on the congregation," he insisted, but simply hoped to "remind" them of the church's official position. Qualifying that he was "not an outsider pushing in" and had "no desire to apply pressure from the Bishop's office," Smith nevertheless suggested that Robertson's "good" church "decide to seat all well-behaved people who come their way at the time of worship" and avoid anything that could "be considered un-Christian." The bishop, who had served in both South Carolina and Georgia, claimed he was "as well versed in the problems we face as any person who wears shoes." He was familiar with "all the arguments against seating people" and conceded that in many cases protestors did possess insincere motives coming "for publicity rather than the purpose of worship." Still, Smith counseled, it would "be unfortunate for us if God judged our motivations every time we turned to Him for guidance and help," urging the congregation to reflect Jesus in his statement, "whosoever will, let him come."[147]

Smith also felt compelled to issue a formal statement on the Americus kneel-in.[148] This statement, "A Reminder Concerning the Open Door Policy of the Methodist Church," declared that it had "always" been the Methodist stance to welcome "all who come in a sober and dignified manner, regardless of race, color, or creed." Claiming that any "departure" from this policy was the result of "sectional custom" not "rule or principle," the bishop sought to distance official Methodism from unofficial Methodist segregationism.[149] In his "Bishop's Column" in the *Wesleyan Advocate*, Smith articulated this position even more forcefully: "Dear friends of Georgia Methodism, I earnestly implore, as I have repeatedly done before, all of our Churches to admit those who come to worship. You can't afford to do otherwise. You will regret not having done so. We do not question motives for coming to the Father's house."[150] Smith's statement was printed in publications around the country, including the *Americus Times-Recorder*.[151]

White Americus residents responded with a mix of dismissiveness and defensiveness. While their congregations were undoubtedly acting out of "sectional custom," they were also, many believed, acting in accordance with "rule or principle," since they possessed official closed-door policies. As previously noted, for many Methodists, congregational authority was equal to, even superior to, denominational authority. They had been ignoring the national denomination's racial position for years, at least since 1954. Moreover, many reasoned, a bishop in Atlanta could not possibly understand the local situation in Americus.

"First of all let me say that you have a perfect right to your opinion," Americus resident Harry Moore wrote to Bishop Smith, "and you have the right to issue any statements you may desire to issue." But, he continued, "the issuing of this statement at this time has not helped our situation here in Americus but rather it has tended to alienate a vast host of Methodists." The kneel-ins were staged "for only one purpose," Moore informed the bishop: "to disrupt public worship." Methodists in Americus, Moore claimed, already felt misrepresented by the "biased press" and exploited by "a vast community of outsiders . . . who came to Americus to make trouble." These outsiders, "beatniks, prostitutes, [and] derelicts, all of whom were paid to come to Americus," were led by known civil rights agitators who, Moore dubiously charged, had "made the statement that 'they would take Americus apart and that when they went to the churches they would break them up.'"[152] They "are not welcomed in our community," he wrote, "nor will they be welcomed in any of the churches of Americus." Smith's response was also unwelcome. Another letter writer, a "member of the Methodist Church since 1921, a steward since 1936, and a[n] Associate Lay Leader of the Atlanta-Emory district for the past several years," wrote, "You have disturbed the membership of the Methodist Church. . . . You have disturbed the peace of mind of many of its members. . . . You are lending aid and comfort to the paid agitators and law violating paid demonstrators. . . . You are inciting more difficulties for the days that lie ahead to the utter disgust of loyal and faithful members of the Methodist Church."[153]

Despite having made public pronouncements that so enraged the Methodists of Americus, privately, Bishop Smith was, in fact, quite sympathetic to them. Claiming he had been "involved in that problem about as deeply as the citizens of the town itself," he wrote a letter to a friend in San Jose describing "the extreme emotional setting that [had] prevailed in Americus," the "terrific demonstrations of all sorts." He even referenced the shooting of Andy Whatley.[154] Not only did he understand the local tension, Smith himself had doubts about the nature of kneel-ins themselves. Though he had publicly pronounced that that church could not "question motives for coming to the Father's house," the bishop suspected the kneel-ins were exploitative and insincere. He wrote to a friend that he possessed an "inherent tendency against" the demonstrations, against "large groups of outsiders who come from a distance to settle all local affairs." "The expert camera man with telecast facilities for publicity purposes," Smith opined, did not belong at church, and furthermore "impresses a group of ushers rather unfavorably." The bishop questioned "if there is any relationship between [kneel-ins] and worship," and he pinpointed activism, not racism, as "basically the problem."[155]

Missing the fundamental theological message of the kneel-in movement, Smith took a pragmatic approach to church integration. He encouraged

Vernard Robertson to acquiesce and let a few people integrate the Americus church for symbolic value. Black Christians did not actually want to attend white churches, he assured, the kneel-ins were merely publicity stunts. If the church treated them accordingly, Smith advised, it would find a way to be left alone and to continue to worship in segregated churches. "Negro representatives will stalk your shadow," until they are allowed in, Smith told Robertson, but "once they are seated, they do not return."[156] In a lost opportunity for theological correction or pastoral propheticism, Smith denigrated kneel-ins and took a cynical approach to church integration. Although symbolic integration may have temporarily solved the public crisis within Southern Protestant Christianity, it did nothing to address serious theological issues, much less allow the church to speak boldly on issues of race. The lukewarm position of the bishop, and of the national Methodist Church, did not mollify divisions; it intensified them.

The kneel-in movement caused a crisis over and within the church, what Stephen Haynes has called "institutional trauma."[157] As a result, in the years following the movement, many Protestant congregations (and at least one denomination) split over issues of race and orthodoxy. In Americus, despite the tension and bad publicity, the leadership of First Methodist still voted for closed doors several times after the 1965 kneel-in. As a result, the church ruptured, with a faction forming a new, more racially progressive congregation. Vernard Robertson left the congregation in 1968. The church did not officially adopt an "open-door" policy until the late 1970s. Like First Methodist, the First Baptist Church in Americus also split in the wake of the 1965 kneel-in. On March 16, 1972, the Board of Deacons reopened the issue of racial integration. Rev. Harold Collins added that on this point he was "NOT neutral," that he felt strongly "that Christ would not have us bar anyone from our fellowship." Nevertheless, just as it had been nine years earlier, the motion to open the church doors was defeated, by a vote of 130–270. Collins's wife called it a "dirty policy." The Collinses soon left Americus; the vote was the "final blow."[158] Finally fed up, 130 more progressive members left First Baptist and formed a new congregation, Fellowship Baptist Church.[159] The same pressure divided Presbyterians in Americus, even though they had avoided direct-action protest during the years of the kneel-in movement. In the shadow of a national denominational schism in 1973, First Presbyterian Church also split, with some choosing to remain at the downtown First Presbyterian Church (PCUSA) and others fleeing to the newly formed St. Andrew's Presbyterian (PCA). Americus residents remembered this era with bitterness and sadness, if they let it creep into their memories at all. "They say time heals," one Americus man mused, "but it was an unpleasant time in the church, and in the city."[160]

LOCAL CHURCH SCHISMS represented not only racial but also theological drama. In fact, most congregations blamed church fractures on theological differences. Those defending racial separation maintained that they also defended biblical orthodoxy and theological conservatism. "This assertion," Haynes declared, "though accurate in the broadest sense, veils the church's racist origins in the myth of a noble quest to defend Christian orthodoxy."[161] Certainly, justifications subsumed under the orthodox apologetic often contained racial elements. But again, religion and race are not easily disentangled. These issues would continue to split congregations and denominations throughout the twentieth century and beyond.

The struggle over kneel-ins was really a struggle over orthodoxy, over correct interpretation of the Christian faith, over no less than God's favor. What was at stake for civil rights activists was not just participation in American democracy but participation in the kingdom of God, not just political equality but Christian love. Their opponents, too, fancied themselves defenders of the divine. For many white Southern Protestants, kneel-ins threatened their beliefs about religious liberty and the sanctity of the church as well as their segregationist sensibilities. And because the kneel-ins were so public, these theological contestations extended from the church steps into all Americans' homes. Everyone who opened the morning newspaper witnessed the theological drama.

The kneel-in movement of the 1960s, as envisioned by the Atlanta students, produced a theological confrontation, one that forced Americans to reckon with the bewitching relationship between race and religion, between color and the church. Many segregationist white Southerners, who may have begun the decade with vigorous defenses of their way of life, ended it with a quiet acquiescence that times had changed. Sometimes their own hearts had. Though "some hardliners maintained their views throughout the 1970s," as evidenced by church splits, most were forced to accede that the Bible did not in fact support racial segregation, and that it was, in fact, "unchristian."[162] In this sense, the kneel-in movement was successful. Yet, in other ways it failed. Churches largely remained segregated in practice, if not in theory. Even ministers like Vernard Robertson, Harold Collins, and Bishop John Smith were unable to bridge the theological chasm as the rifts between Christians—black and white, liberal and conservative—widened. With kneel-ins, civil rights activists had hoped to ignite a movement within the church for Christian love and brotherhood. But "it was," one Southerner said, "like trying to strike a match on a wet windowpane."[163]

Conclusion

The white people of the South are truly religious people. You start talking to
the average man on the street about Jesus and he'll get teary eyed. But if you
can get it through a man's head that what he's been doing is wrong, he will
either scrap his faith or he'll change.

—Millard Fuller, *Look* magazine, 1970

Doctor Jordan, when you get up to heaven and you are walking down the
pearly streets and the Lord comes along and meets you and stops you and says
"Clarence, old buddy. It's good to see you up here. I wonder if you could tell
me in the next 5 minutes what you did down on earth. You know, how did
things go?" What would you tell the Lord?

    "I'd tell him to come back when he had more time."

—Clarence Jordan to Phil Gailey, 1969

On the evening of the Americus kneel-ins, the August air still dense with heat
and fear, the deacons at Plains Baptist Church called an emergency meeting.
At their church, just seven miles from where integrated worshippers had been
denied entrance that morning, the deaconate dashed off a resolution. In unflinching language, it proclaimed that Plains Baptist would officially and expressly "bar Negroes and outside agitators."[1] The church's most famous deacon
was not in attendance, as he also served as a state senator in Atlanta. And although he voted against it a couple of weeks later at the congregational meeting, the resolution barring black worshippers passed overwhelmingly. Eleven
years later, that deacon from Plains Baptist would be president of the United
States.

    How did Jimmy Carter, a man from Sumter County whose church incu-
bated a segregationist theology, go on to champion human rights around the
world? How did a boy from Plains become the nation's most famous evangelical? And how did this old-time Baptist get left behind as the South turned to
the New Religious Right? Moreover, what does this mean for race relations?
For lived theology? For the shifting terrain of American politics and religion?
From the summer of 1965 to November 1976, much changed in Americus, in
Plains, and in the nation. And yet, vexing issues of race and religion remained,

reconfigured and reconfiguring in a new era in American life. The theological drama thickens.

IN 1971, *Life* magazine ran a piece on Americus. And this time it was not about violence, murder, hatred, or agitation. It was about football. But of course, it was about race too. The author, Marshall Frady, had covered Americus during the crisis summer of 1965, and now he was back on a crisp November Friday night. In describing the "immemorial pageant" that is high school football in the South, Frady noted what he called a "surreal change." The same men and women who had cheered Lester Maddox's promise of segregation were now cheering for Calvin Prince, the all-star black halfback. United on the field and in the bleachers on behalf of the Americus High Panthers (the mascot's political symbolism "not only does not seem to have disconcerted anyone, but even to have occurred to anyone"), Frady mused over "how ephemeral all human furies and irreconcilabilities might actually be." If the comment now seems hopelessly naïve, it stands as an indication of how hopeful many Southerners, including Frady, were in 1971.[2]

Despite the formation of Southland Academy and the long resistance against complying fully with federal desegregation orders, by the early 1970s, school integration was thoroughly completed and, according to onlookers, "startlingly serene."[3] Frady reported that of 3,105 students enrolled at Americus High, 1,850 were black. They seemed to be fully, if yet imperfectly, included in the life of the school, enjoying a curriculum that included James Baldwin as well as Mark Twain. Teresa Mansfield, the student who had once heard King preach upon his release from jail, had gone on to Georgia Southwestern College in Americus and now taught American history, sociology, and world affairs at Americus High. She made sure that the courses reflected a measure of diversity.[4] In 1968, the Americus School Board, once a bastion of segregationism, welcomed two black members, Thomas Blount and Eddie J. McGrady. Four years later, Willie Paschal became the first black principal of a formerly all-white school when he took the helm at Furlow Grammar School. As Thelma Barnum affirmed, "Americus has come a long way."[5]

Much of this progress occurred during the mayoral tenure of J. Frank Myers, a racial moderate elected in 1971. Upon assuming office, Myers successfully established a biracial committee, the sin for which Warren Fortson had been excommunicated half a decade earlier.[6] He appointed two local blacks, J. W. Jones and Henry L. Williams, to the police force and began to integrate the city leadership.[7] By 1975, Lewis Lowe was elected to the Americus City

Teresa Mansfield teaching at the newly integrated Americus High School, 1971. (Photographer unknown; *Life*)

Council, becoming the first black resident to serve in such a capacity.[8] Mary Myers, the longhaired, earnest, bright, seventeen-year-old daughter of the Americus mayor, commented of the vast change, "It's so different now it can't be described." She remembered the tension in Americus when she was a child, saying "everyone was so scared," but by the early 1970s, she could dismiss all of it with a shrug, saying, "Who wants that again?" Even Warren Fortson, from exile in Atlanta, claimed "a lot of progress has been made."[9] For Frady, the progress in Americus was "giddying."

Not everyone was quite so optimistic. Even as black Americans in Americus took their rightful places in the voting booths and on school boards, full equality eluded them. Black students were still punished harshly in altercations with whites. The Americus School Board included several prominent members whose children attended Southland Academy, prompting a massive boycott in May 1971. The Americus Public Safety Department was "notorious for its brutal treatment" of black Americus citizens.[10] Black neighborhoods remained poor; black populations underserved. In nearby Baker County, children were segregated on the playground by their teachers in September 1965.[11] Privately, black Southerners began to express misgivings that the mandates of the federal government in the Civil Rights Act of 1964 and Voting Rights Act of 1965 would make much difference in rural Georgia. Racism still lurked. Even the beloved Calvin Prince had his doubts. "The whites are going to love you as long as you playing football," he astutely observed, "but I don't trust them after that."[12]

And so the work of racial justice continued, weighed down by death, by defections, by violence and prison. While many activists abandoned the Deep South, a few stayed. After a "movement sabbatical" spent earning a master's degree in sacred theology from Union Seminary in New York, Charles Sherrod, remarkably, returned to South Georgia.[13] In 1966, he married Shirley Miller, a native of Baker County whose sisters had been involved with the movement. Before she met him, it was "Charles Sherrod everything," Shirley joked. One of her family members had actually saved Sherrod's life during one particularly brutal beating from the local sheriff, "Gator" Johnson. At one point, Sherrod had gathered a group to go down to the Baker County Courthouse to register to vote. This, predictably, provoked the rage of the sheriff, who began pummeling him with all the fury of one who feels his power fleeting. Seeing that Sherrod lay unconscious and bleeding, close to death, Josie Miller flung herself onto him, absorbing the violent blows until the sheriff tired. Later, Josie introduced "Sherrod" to Shirley, who had been away at school. Though she didn't think much of him at first, he won her over when she saw "how he had pulled people off plantations . . . how he had helped them to stand up and be strong." Charles and Shirley Sherrod would live and work, pray and worship, and continue the nonviolent struggle for justice and freedom in Southwest Georgia for the rest of their lives.[14]

The Southwest Georgia Project also continued its work in the region, developing programs for education, community engagement, agricultural development, and Christian community. But as the national political focus increasingly turned outside the South, Southern projects, like those in Southwest Georgia, struggled. "There is hell in the South," one SNCC report stated, "there must be some type of response to our desperate cries for help."[15] SNCC workers were frequently pulled over by law enforcement and subjected to harassment and acts of violence. On several occasions, Sherrod called on the federal government but "failed to obtain protection."[16] Without much help from the national SNCC office or the government, activists in Southwest Georgia continued to rely on God for protection and provision.

Largely because of the influence of Charles Sherrod, the Southwest Georgia Project maintained its theological vision for the beloved community throughout the 1960s. When SNCC opted to expel white members in 1967, Sherrod resigned, saying sadly, "I did not leave SNCC, it left me."[17] Even when other groups abandoned Christian nonviolence or forsook an integrationist approach, Sherrod's did not.

Even before, in 1965, the Southwest Georgia Project embraced a partnership with the Student Interracial Ministry (SIM), an explicitly interracial, religious group. SIM emerged from the same meeting at Shaw University in 1960 that SNCC had. While undergraduate students devised a plan for direct-action protests across the South, a group of seminary students came up with a plan of their own. They, too, desired to see interracial social change in the nation, but they "also felt called to act within the church itself."[18] In the months after the Shaw meeting, then, SIM was formed. It was essentially a cross-racial pastoral exchange program, anchored by Union Theological Seminary in New York and Gammon Seminary in Atlanta, in which white seminarians spent summers in black churches and black seminarians in white. The hope was that these exchanges would foster understanding and forge reconciliation among Christians. By the time Charles Sherrod matriculated at Union in the fall of 1964, SIM had been operative for five years, and it was looking to expand both in scope and in geography. Sherrod had an idea where willing seminarians could go to seek racial justice.

When he arrived on campus, his presence was immediately felt. "The charisma of Sherrod is incredible!" one SIM seminarian remarked while another marveled at him as he sang freedom songs through the Union hallways. His fellow students wanted to learn more about the freedom struggle, so Sherrod formed a civil rights discussion group. Interest mounted. By 1965, Sherrod had developed a proposal for a partnership between SIM and the Southwest Georgia Project.[19]

The proposal bore his theological stamp. "I bring many sears," he confessed, "I am a victim as well as a product of this [segregated] church and this society." But he nonetheless affirmed, "We are . . . Christians desiring to see a revolution within the body of Christ, the church, wherever it is found; we seek to find where and how it can most effectively witness; we will work with it whenever it is found." After laying out the theological foundation for the project, Sherrod proposed: "a group of seminary persons, male and female, black and white, Jew and Gentile, locate in a specific southern area—Southwest Georgia—seeking an active witness and worship, in and with the world, to understand our 'call' in Christ and in such a time as this and from there to take another step." The proposal showed Sherrod's typical humility. The group would not be referred to as SIM nor "as a group of 'preachers' or seminarians" but would "be announced as 'some more students' who have come to live and work and suffer and have joy among the people of Southwest Georgia." It also had his determined interracialism. Though he suggested "attempts to get as many Negroes as possible" in the group, he said "an all-white group wouldn't sabotage the project because we do not work alone." The SIM project, like SNCC, would embody the beloved community. "The important fact," he stated, "is we are God's Workers and show it in love and serious work."[20]

Sherrod concluded his proposal with an impassioned plea for the church—for its resonance, and for its power, even in 1965. He wrote, "Let me bear witness before you that I have seen the church, moving, surging and falling, struggling to breathe, eager to learn the truth; I have seen it in stinking jail cells packed with people, singing and sweating people, brought before the Pilates of this day; I have seen the church under the stars praying and singing in the ashes of a burned down church building." He had seen the church in Southwest Georgia. And he wanted that church to testify to the seminarians, to get them out of, as one volunteer phrased it, "their intellectual ivory tower theological security," as they served. SIM in Southwest Georgia would be "an experiment in truth to find truth."[21]

The proposal was accepted, and Sherrod took over as project director. Throughout that school year, he planned, even as volatile divisions and violent confrontations wracked the nation. Perhaps the South needed his vision for lived theology and racial justice more than ever. He called for volunteers. Paul Menzel was quick to sign up. "You can definitely count me in on the SIM-SNCC group going to Southwest Georgia under your leadership," he wrote to Sherrod in March 1965, "I'm rearin' to go!"[22]

That summer, Sherrod returned to Southwest Georgia, bringing five seminarians with him.[23] They lived with black families, "fully accepting their hospitality," and worked in the community, often going to jail and suffering persecution.[24] They helped register people to vote, they participated in canvassing, they organized black farmers, they prayed and preached, but mostly, they blended in to SNCC and the local movements. The SIM volunteers were "nearly invisible" as such.[25] But over the next several years, from 1965 to 1968, forty-four SIM volunteers worked in the Southwest Georgia Project.[26] The relationship between locals and SNCC volunteers and the SIM seminarians wasn't perfect; issues of race and autonomy and money and tactic simmered, but it was an exercise in loving community. As Shirley Sherrod put it: "we needed each other in order to bring about the change that needed to happen here."[27]

Whites predictably detested the work being done by SIM and the Southwest Georgia Project, and they responded with arrests, harassment, and burglaries. In 1967, the Albany SIM office was burned by six white men; "all papers, records, correspondence and typewriters were destroyed. No one was hurt," the SIM headquarters recorded.[28] But someone almost was later that year, when the SIM students were shot at in Crisp County. As SIM volunteer Larry Mamiya said, "It was brutal and bloody."[29] This hostility of course, extended to the church, which remained obstinately opposed to change, even when proposed by white seminary students. The students, shaken but undeterred, sympathized with their assailants. "I can understand their hostility toward someone who is telling them they must examine what they have stood for all of their lives," SIM volunteer Edward Weaver wrote. "In a sense" he explained, "I was saying that your whole life has been a sin."[30] That was something they would not hear, especially not from a liberal seminarian. As one SIM report simply put it: "The white church refused to take any meaningful step in the direction of integration."[31] In Americus, First Baptist and First Methodist maintained official segregationist policies on the books until the late 1970s.[32] Though the partnership between SIM and the Southwest Georgia Project was effective under Charles Sherrod's leadership, and some SIM volunteers stayed for a decade longer, the results of the "experiment in truth" were "modest."[33]

For the most part, in the late 1960s and early 1970s, Americus residents were eager to leave the turbulence of the 1960s behind. They got back to their lives, their teams, their farms, their businesses, and their still mostly segregated church pews.[34] They also closely watched the political career of one of their own.

JIMMY CARTER WAS BORN on October 1, 1924, in Plains, Georgia, the eldest son of Earl Carter and Lillian Gordy Carter. The family had deep roots in South Georgia on both sides.[35] Jimmy was born in Plains but, in 1928, shortly before he turned four years old, the family relocated to the community of Archery, two and half miles south.[36] In Archery, the Carters occupied a white clapboard, six-bedroom house on a big piece of land, though the spacious home lacked electricity or running water. Earl Carter had invested wisely in his youth, and by the time of Jimmy's birth, he was a successful farmer, employing over 200 mostly black workers. These workers lived on the Carter property in primitive wooden shacks and worked from before the sun rose until it dipped low in the west for pitifully low wages.[37] While Earl Carter rarely toiled in the fields, young Jimmy was expected to earn his keep. He labored in the fields—mopping cotton, plowing and stacking peanuts, milking cows, plucking geese, hauling sugarcane, and minding the small store. From a young age, Jimmy was serious, dutiful, conscientious, and eager to please his father, his mother, and God.

Like so many Southerners, Jimmy Carter grew up steeped in religion. "The churches," he said, were at "the center of our spiritual, educational and social lives."[38] While his mother was Methodist, Earl Carter was a Baptist and, as he was the more active, the family attended Plains Baptist. Throughout his childhood, Jimmy fully participated in church, where he was consistent in attendance and attentive in study. But Carter understood that presence in the church was not sufficient for salvation, but that he must ask the Holy Spirit to be present within his heart. In fundamentalist parlance, he must be born again. And so following a revival in the summer of 1935, he was. At the age of eleven, Jimmy "proudly declared himself to be a Christian" and received the sacrament of baptism.[39] By the time he was twelve, Jimmy was proclaimed old enough to drive the dusty roads of South Georgia, so he used to drive with his sisters back to church on Sunday evenings for Baptist Young People's Union.[40] The Plains Baptist Church provided the foundation of his religious community and instruction, though not all of it. His black friends and neighbors also exerted a strong influence.

As has been well documented, Jimmy's mother, Lillian Carter, or "Miss Lillian," as she was known in Plains, possessed racially liberal views, views that influenced her eldest son even as they isolated her in her community. Lillian made a point to serve black patients in the hospital where she worked as a nurse, and she visited black neighbors in their homes and welcomed them into hers, even through the front door. Lillian Carter championed racial parity. In fact, Lillian and Earl attended the Dodgers game when Jackie Robinson first took the field. "I was the only one standing up and applauding," Lillian beamed.[41] A lifelong Democrat, she campaigned for Lyndon Johnson in Sumter County in 1964, a move that, because of the president's unpopular civil rights legislation, earned her the epithet "nigger lover" and meant that her car was frequently vandalized. Lillian remained unfazed.[42] Earl Carter, though generous, if paternalistic, to blacks, did not possess the same racial views as his wife. A segregationist, Earl was a Eugene Talmadge supporter, so much so that he used to load up his one-ton farm truck and take his neighbors to Talmadge campaign rallies. A young Jimmy loved these rallies and barbeques. He even named his pet goat "Old Gene Talmadge."[43] Herman Talmadge, son of the long-serving racist Georgia governor, even stayed at the Carters' home when he visited Southwest Georgia during *his* time as governor.[44] Carter later described the younger Governor Talmadge and his father as "personal friends."[45] Despite his admiration for Gene Talmadge, Jimmy did not seem to adopt the man's racist views. How could he, surrounded as he was by black neighbors, workers, playmates, teachers, and friends?

Archery was a mostly black community, composed of twenty-five to thirty sharecropping families. There was only one other white family, the Watsons, and so most of Jimmy's early socialization, education, and community came from his black neighbors.[46] The most prominent resident of Archery was black: A.M.E. Bishop William Decker Johnson, a man who commanded great respect and possessed great influence. "Everyone looked [up] on Bishop Johnson," one neighbor remembered.[47] In addition to preaching, Johnson also ran a school in Archery. "A master of the English language," Johnson, in his sermons at St. Mark's A.M.E, "dominated the consciousness of everyone in the church . . . the sense of being brothers and sisters in Christ wiped away any thoughts of racial differences."[48] For Carter, the black Bishop Johnson appeared "the epitome of success and power."[49]

Even less prominent black neighbors exerted a profound influence. Annie Mae Jones and AnnieLee Lester, both black women, served as nannies to the Carters. "The black women who cared for Jimmy," one historian remarked, "were as intimate a part of his young life as were his parents and sisters."[50] Jimmy's closest boyhood friend, Alonzo Davis, nicknamed A. D. or "Knock," was black, and the two boys hunted, fished, boxed, swam, and even ate together. Almost every day, Jimmy worked alongside black laborers on the family farm, developing deep relationships of familiarity and affection even as old racial mores and power structures remained.

One family to whom Jimmy became particularly attached was the Clarks. Jack and Rachel Clark lived on the Carter farm in a neat, comfortable cabin. As a boy, Jimmy often spent the night with the Clarks, sleeping on a pallet on the floor. Their home "would be filled with a natural exuberance, loud talk and arguments, and subtle jokes," and it was the place, Carter claimed, where he "felt most at home."[51] Jack taught Jimmy about farm work and hunting while Rachel fished with him and became his beloved friend and confidante.[52] Years later, Rachel recalled of the young Jimmy, "He just liked to follow me, that's all. He just liked to be where I was at."[53] He later described her as "aristocratic"; to him, she possessed "the aura of a queen."[54] Later, Jimmy Carter would claim Rachel as one of the four most influential people in his life, behind only his parents and Rosalynn.[55]

Rachel also taught Jimmy the theology of the black church. In Rachel, Carter saw a powerful affirmation of Christianity in the face of poverty and disenfranchisement. They would talk about Jesus. "He was a religious boy," she recalled, the faith "got in him."[56] Years later, when Carter was beginning his political life, Rachel told Jimmy, "I want you to do right, ask the Lord to help you. If you put your trust in Him, He'll lead you right. . . . The Lord will take care of you, and he will, he will. He'll take care of you. Trust him."[57] Carter biographer E. Stanly Godbold claimed that through his black neighbors and friends Jimmy "witnessed poverty and frustration" but "absorbed some of their good qualities of character and spiritual richness."[58]

Carter later reminisced that he "grew up" in black culture and even "saw the devastating effects of racial discrimination."[59] If he did, he nevertheless also absorbed the strict racial etiquette of the Deep South. Carter later attributed the separation he felt to "social custom," to the "unchallenged law of the land as mandated by the United States Supreme Court," and presciently, to "misinterpretation of Holy Scriptures."[60] Though the lives of whites and blacks were "almost totally intertwined," Carter explained, "the political and social dominance of whites was an accepted fact."[61] For a boy in Southwest Georgia, even a generally kind one, that was just the way it was. He did not really question legal or theological segregation until after he left.

Following his graduation from Plains High School in 1941, Jimmy Carter first attended Georgia Southwestern College in Americus (where he was awaiting a recommendation from local congressman Stephen Pace), then Georgia Tech in Atlanta, and finally, the Naval Academy in Annapolis.[62] With World War II ramping up, he expected to be deployed, but never was.[63] Following his graduation, Jimmy, who by this time had married Rosalynn Smith, was stationed on the USS *Wyoming* in Norfolk, Virginia.[64] After several years, Jimmy applied for submarine service and was accepted, beginning a time in New London, Connecticut; Honolulu, Hawaii; and San Diego, California. Jimmy and Rosalynn enjoyed the life the navy offered—making interesting friends, traveling, honing new skills, and raising their children. At the Naval Academy and then in his time in the navy, Carter continued the practice of his faith, attending chapel services and teaching Sunday school to the young daughters of his fellow enlisted men. But if his Christian devotion was not waning, his zeal was. Carter later admitted, "The seven years I spent in the navy were a relatively dormant phase in my religious life."[65]

Then, in 1953, while stationed on the *Sea Wolf* in Schenectady, New York, Carter received news that would alter the course of his life. His father had fallen ill. The Carters rushed home to Plains to Earl's bedside. As his father lay dying, a twenty-nine-year-old Jimmy Carter spent hours sitting with him, listening, discovering a deep admiration and affection for a father with whom he had felt some emotional distance in his childhood. Though his father's views on certain matters, particularly on race, were unyielding, Jimmy also discovered a kindness and compassion that he had not previously known. Earl Carter, much to his eldest son's surprise, had been an extremely generous member of the community. For years, he had been offering money and gifts to his needier neighbors in secret. He was beloved in Plains, and when he finally died, his funeral was packed. A troubling question loomed large in Jimmy's mind: "Whose life is more important in the eyes of God—mine or his?"[66]

His father's death marked a spiritual and personal awakening for Jimmy Carter, or, as he called it, a "turning point."[67] After being tremendously moved by the theological and communal power displayed at his father's funeral, and perhaps, a son's awe for his father, Carter made the fateful decision to leave the navy and its life of adventure and come home to Georgia.[68] He also began a serious intellectual reckoning with his Christian faith. Like so many in Southwest Georgia, Carter had consistently practiced the Protestantism of his youth throughout his life, as the comfort he felt in its rhythms was enough to stem the rising tide of doubts. But losing his father forced Carter to finally confront the tensions and questions inherent in sincere belief. It was a "tortuous time of searching." In his recollection, he poured over the theological works of Dietrich Bonhoeffer, Karl Barth, Martin Buber, Paul Tillich, and Reinhold Niebuhr, the same giants of Western theology that captivated Clarence Jordan and Martin King.[69] This theological journey would radically affect Jimmy Carter's intellectual and spiritual positioning, though it would take some years to fully come to fruition.

Upon his return to Plains, Carter began to distance himself from the more reactionary and racist elements of society, even as he upheld its segregationist mores. He adamantly refused to join the White Citizen's Council, earning him the frustration of his fellow citizens and, in true Southwest Georgia form, a short-term economic boycott of his farm warehouse. In an effort to get Carter on board, the council, led by the Plains police chief and railroad depot agent (also a Baptist minister), paid Carter a visit in which, he remembered, their spokesman "outlined the segregationist principles with which I was, of course, thoroughly familiar, including the supposed biblical foundation for the separation of races, potential damage to the quality of our schools . . . and eventual destruction of the white race through the intermarriages that would inevitably occur." The council spokesman informed Jimmy that "only a few radicals, mostly outsiders, wanted to make any change," an all-too-familiar charge in Southwest Georgia, as we have seen.

"A line was being drawn among white citizens concerning the civil rights movement," Carter understood. But in the 1950s and early 1960s, though quick to offer charity and sympathy, he was reticent to ostracize his white peers and colleagues. As Peter Bourne commented, "How one felt and what one could do on a personal basis was very different from what one could afford to do publicly."[70]

In November 1955, the Sumter County Grand Jury appointed Carter to the Sumter County School Board to replace his father, who had served since 1936. Only months after the *Brown* decision, a position on the school board offered an almost unparalleled opportunity to determine the course of integration in Americus and Sumter County. It was an opportunity that Carter did not fully take. He largely acquiesced to the segregationist resistance, though he petitioned "to improve education for African Americans within a segregated framework." Although he advocated for the black school to be relocated "more conveniently" for black students, requested running water for black schools, and gave the black schools the old typewriters when the white schools got new ones, he made few efforts to comply with federal mandates to ensure real equality in education.[71] He recalled, on a tour of black schools (most of them actually held in churches or homes), seeing "large teenage boys trying to sit in chairs designed for children of kindergarten age," and, though he expressed distress at the sight, no direct change corresponded.[72] When the Koinonia children petitioned to attend Americus High School in 1960, the school board refused their request. Carter did not intervene.[73]

Similarly, on the most pressing issue of the day—integration—Carter "remained silent."[74] When the Sibley Commission held its first meeting in Americus in 1960, he did not speak at all during the hearing. Three months later, he was named chairman of the Sumter County School Board. The minutes of the Sumter County School Board are likewise tellingly silent on the subject of racial integration.[75] Though Carter had left Sumter County by the time the school battles really began raging in the mid-1960s, he did not advocate for racial equality strongly in the years he served. To be fair, whites in Americus desired to remain segregated so overwhelmingly that to dissent in any way was politically prohibited.

One issue that Carter did tackle during his years on the Sumter County School Board was that of school consolidation. While the Sumter County School was underattended, lacking in funding, in teachers, and in classes, the Americus City School was overwhelmed and overpopulated. The school board began hearings to consider combining the schools. Carter largely viewed the consolidation issue as, at its core, about funding and providing excellent education for white students. But the timing of the move—concurrent with the integration of Atlanta's public schools per federal order—turned the discussions acrimonious. Though Carter assured residents that the consolidated school would be for white students only, suspicion continued, and the opposition deepened. His cousin, Hugh Carter, led a group called Sumter County Citizens Opposed to School Consolidation. Jimmy dug in his heels. Feeling certain that consolidation would offer the best education for Americus and Sumter County students, he painstakingly explained the merger in a series of newspaper articles in the *Americus Times-Recorder*. Days later, Sumter County Citizens Opposed to School Consolidation ran an editorial of its own. In the end, the proposed school consolidation was defeated. While Carter thought it a loss for efficiency and excellence in education, many of his fellow residents found it a victory, albeit a temporary one, for white supremacy.[76] The racial element was made brutally clear to Carter when, the night after the vote, he and Rosalynn found their peanut warehouse vandalized, inscribed "Carters and Coons go together."[77] Ignoring this, Carter remained on the school board, and remained its chairman for several more years. Nonetheless, the fight was so bitter that Carter later said of his decision to run for state senate, "I decided I would rather be in Atlanta serving in whatever way I could, than to remain here on the school board in Sumter County."[78] Whether the issue was school desegregation or consolidation, Carter's primary concern remained his own stature in the community, the economic success of his family's farm, and increasingly, his political ambitions.

By 1961, Carter had set his sights on political office outside of Sumter County. As the anecdote goes, on October 1, 1962, his thirty-eighth birthday, Jimmy Carter put on his Sunday slacks and, without consulting Rosalynn, made his way down to the Sumter County Courthouse to register his candidacy for the Georgia State Senate. If Rosalynn Carter didn't know what he was doing, truth be told, neither did Jimmy. Carter was, according to his own admission, a "naïve thirty-eight-year-old farmer and small town businessman," albeit one with some big ideas for his state and himself.[79] The *Americus Times-Recorder* ran Carter's announcement in that afternoon's paper, although the news was overshadowed by coverage of the violent confrontations over James Meredith's enrollment at Ole Miss. Carter had likely long harbored broader political ambitions, but his decision to run in 1962 indeed seemed unplanned, spontaneous, and thus, somewhat ordained.[80] His campaign displayed what would become characteristic folksiness, a sort of good-natured everyman quality, as well as a shrewd vagueness on specific issues. Rosalynn also proved herself an able political partner to Jimmy. "I tried to call everyone on the voters list in Sumter County," Rosalynn remembered, "I went door to door, to every house in Plains, to tell people that Jimmy was going to run for Senate, asking them to vote for him."[81] She also made his campaign signs and showed undeniable political instincts.

With the integration of schools looming ever larger, some joked that Jimmy was running for state senate to escape the Sumter County School Board.[82] But 1962 was not only a contentious period in Southern life; it was also an interesting moment in Georgia politics. With the racial revolution under way on a grassroots level, Georgia electoral politics was undergoing a significant shift due to the 1962 *Baker v. Carr* and *Sanders v. Gray* decisions, which dismantled the county unit system, giving urban Georgians more influence and rural Georgians less.[83] It was a major decision to be "discussed at our peanut warehouse, at church, at Lions Club meetings and in the small county newspapers," Carter recalled.[84] The people were less concerned with the political ramifications (Sumter was a medium-sized county whose influence would not be greatly affected), but they were highly agitated over possible racial ramifications. "Many people believed," Carter said, that the decision would bring "the disruption of religious worship, the end of public education for white students, and numerous interracial marriages."[85] But the decision would also provide a political opening for Jimmy Carter.

The overturning of the county unit system caused a reconfiguration of Georgia's districts. Americus and Sumter County would be part of Georgia's Fourteenth District, which additionally included Webster, Terrell, Stewart, Randolph, Chattahoochee, and Quitman Counties. The Fourteenth District spanned 2,000 square miles, "two dozen little communities," and seven county seats. The Carters were personally known in at least half, and recognizable in the others because of Jimmy's involvement in the Lions Club, though his push for school consolidation and the family's reputation as moderates made him suspect to some. Despite Carter's integrity, the change in districts, and the efforts of the family, the Carter campaign encountered trouble.

Carter's opponent for the Democratic nomination was Homer Moore, a man who in addition to having already won under the county unit system also possessed the support of local political boss Joe Hurst. Hurst cut the classic figure of a Southern political boss: a large man dragging on a cigar, a hat pulled low over his eyes. Hailing from Alabama originally, Hurst had moved across the state line to Quitman County, Georgia, in the 1920s, selling moonshine and beer and eventually becoming county commissioner and then a member of the Georgia House of Representatives. Quitman County became his "personal fiefdom."[86] His role in hand-delivering welfare checks and making deals to bring certain projects to his home county, plus his powers of sheer intimidation, made him the unassailable determinant of the electoral process. This meant, of course, that under his watch Homer Moore would be state senator.[87]

On election day, about mid-morning, Rosalynn Carter got a phone call from her cousin Ralph Balkcom claiming that something was up in Quitman County. Jimmy hurriedly asked a reporter and his friend John Pope to go check it out, which they did. They found massive fraud: Carter's name had been crossed off the ballot; the ballot box was stuffed with ballots from the imprisoned and deceased; there was an absence of voting booths; and voters had been intimidated when casting ballots. When confronted, Hurst replied, coolly, "I have been running my county my way for twenty years and no one from Sumter County, or any other county, is going to come in here and tell me how to run my county," adding that he had killed men for less of an affront than the Carter friend had already committed.[88] When the results for the district came in, Quitman County had narrowly delivered the election for Moore. Out of the 333 ballot stubs cast, the final tally had Moore receiving 360 votes to Carter's 136, a highly irregular victory indeed.

Deeply distraught by both the loss and the injustice, Carter decided to challenge the decision, revealing, as historian Dan Carter put it, "an extraordinary kind of doggedness."[89] In challenging the outcome, he turned to an excellent attorney and one of his closest friends, Warren Fortson. In 1962, Warren Fortson had not yet been kicked out of Americus for defending black students, had not yet been fired as county attorney for doing his job, and had not yet lost his home and community for advocating a biracial committee. No, in 1962, he was simply an attorney helping his friend fight fraud. He also happened to be the brother of Ben Fortson, Georgia's secretary of state.[90]

This was significant since, to successfully overturn the election, the campaign would need to solicit attention outside the Fourteenth District, at the regional and state level. Carter and Fortson contacted John Pennington, a sharp young journalist at the *Atlanta Journal* from Sumter County.[91] He came to Americus the next morning and launched an investigation. With time running out before the general election, Carter and Fortson frantically filed the necessary paperwork (which was difficult, because of the procedure and the fact that much of it necessitated cooperation from Homer Moore) while Pennington penned a series of articles detailing the contested election, which comprised in sum a scathing expose of rural Georgia politics. For instance, Pennington explained, 117 people who cast their votes for Moore did so, curiously, "in alphabetical order, even down to the second and third letter of name."[92] These *Journal* articles piqued the interest of Atlanta's elite, including Charles Kirbo, a thoughtful attorney with Atlanta's prestigious King & Spalding law firm. When Jimmy Carter and Warren Fortson called Kirbo then, he took the case.[93] Finally, due to excellent lawyering and a surprising victory for common sense and fairness in Georgia, Judge Carl Crow invalidated the fraudulent votes and delivered the Fourteenth State Senate District to Jimmy Carter.[94] That night, Fortson and Carter imbibed deeply from a bottle of bourbon—one of them intoxicated with political victory; the other, with the triumph of fairness and friendship.

This victory launched Carter's long political career and ushered in a new (if transitional) era in Georgia politics. Carter performed well in the state senate, proving himself an industrious, meticulous, if somewhat reserved figure. He championed fair, honest governance and low taxes, emphasized education and economic issues, and scrupulously avoided more divisive issues. Although a racial moderate, Carter understood, as his friend Warren Fortson still did not, the potential professional cost for moral courage on race.

As Carter worked in Atlanta, Americus seemed to lose its mind. The years that Carter spent in Atlanta were, as we have seen, among the most tumultuous in Americus's history. While marches, violence, riots, and corruption roiled his hometown, the senator from the Fourteenth District largely stayed out of it. Carter's primary role in the theological and political conflict in Americus was that of informed spectator. He privately lamented the treatment of white racial moderates (with little concern articulated for the oppressed black citizens) and publicly demurred.[95] "Nobody can remember him having much to say, publicly at least, one way or another in those troubled times," one reporter claimed.[96] "People tend to forget how mean things were in those times," Warren Fortson offered in a meek defense of Carter's silence, adding, "it wouldn't have done him any good to go round screaming for integration as a State Senator." Of course, Fortson spoke from experience. Similarly, Carter's friend and biographer Peter Bourne has argued that "feelings were so inflamed, the pressure on politicians to make ill-conceived, pro-segregationist statements so strong" that Carter's silent refusal to comment was "itself a measure of courage." But some disagreed. "He was right here," Rev. J. R. Campbell, the 1960s activist minister said, "and when we had our struggle, I don't remember [him] saying anything."[97]

Perhaps Carter's strongest stand for racial equality was a theological one. The state senate election was not the only one Carter won in 1962. That same year, Plains Baptist elected him to the office of deacon. Deacons served the congregation as esteemed leaders, men who "meet the qualifications of 1 Timothy 3:8–13."[98] Carter had been approved as one who was, according to the scriptural description, "dignified, not double-tongued, not addicted to much wine, not greedy for dishonest gain," one who "[held] the mystery of the faith with a clear conscience," one who was "blameless . . . the husband of one wife, managing their children and their own households well."[99] He may well have fit that description of orthodoxy, but Carter would also fit a description less desirable to the deaconate: racial moderate. Plains Baptist, like First Baptist, First Methodist, and First Presbyterian in Americus, largely supported a theological segregationism in the 1950s. Carter remembered, "Most of our church leaders nodded approvingly" as individuals "'proved' that segregation was condoned or even mandated by God." He claimed most Christians in Plains found the legal, constitutional, and theological arguments for racial division "reassuring."[100] But, because of the influence of his mother, his "second mother," Rachel Clark, and his time outside of the South, Carter had come to find those claims to theological orthodoxy neither consoling nor convincing.

In August 1965, when the deacons at Plains Baptist officially barred black worshippers from their sanctuary, Carter dissented. Though he missed the initial meeting where the resolution was drafted, he would not miss the vote. While the segregationist view of the church's leadership was unquestioned, according to Baptist polity, the congregation had to approve the measure.[101] Few doubted that that it would pass when the vote was scheduled two weeks later. Rosalynn insisted it was a losing fight, that they should not make the trip back down to Plains just to incur ire and a political liability. "I was tired of confrontation," Rosalynn confessed, "I was not very courageous and didn't want to take the risk, but Jimmy insisted on being there."[102] Hustling to Plains after a wedding in Atlanta, the Carters made it just in time for the vote. Two hundred people waited anxiously as the resolution was read aloud. When the floor was opened for comments, Jimmy Carter spoke plainly but forcefully against the resolution. Eyebrows raised, lips pursed, and the vote was taken. Though many abstained, in the final tally, fifty-four voted for the resolution and only six against: Jimmy, Rosalynn, Chip, Jeff, Lillian Carter, and Homer Harris, a deaf farmer who had not a clue what the vote was even for. It was Carter's worst electoral defeat but perhaps his greatest theological victory.

Disappointed but not surprised, Carter left Plains and went back to Atlanta for his final term in the state senate. After a successful four years as a state senator, having cultivated a reputation for being hardworking, fair, and thorough, Carter set his sights on the governorship. The *Atlanta Constitution* captured his baffling ambition with the slightly teasing headline, "Jimmy Carter Thinks He Could Be Elected Governor."[103] But Jimmy Carter did. Carter hoped that he could reason with his fellow Georgians, that they would opt for good governance and fairness to all over racist theatrics. He was mistaken.

The 1966 gubernatorial race was a circus. It also marked a sea change in Georgia politics, offering the first proof of a deepening fissure within the Democratic Party, a fissure significant enough to give the GOP a fighting chance. While Howard "Bo" Callaway, the first Republican to seek the governorship since Reconstruction, easily secured his party's nomination for the GOP, the Democratic nomination would be hotly contested.[104] Ellis Arnall, the former governor of Georgia and prominent Atlanta attorney, Lester Maddox, the outlandish segregationist who had wowed the crowds gathered at the White Citizens Council meetings in Americus with his inflammatory rhetoric and wild stories of chasing blacks from his Atlanta restaurant with an axe handle, and Jimmy Carter, the naïve peanut farmer-turned-diligent state senator, each laid claim to the Democratic nomination. When the September 13, 1966, primary results came in, Arnall had earned 29.4 percent, Maddox 23.6 percent, and Carter 20.9 percent.[105] Since the primary votes were so scattered, there was a runoff between Arnall and Maddox, neither of whom could claim a majority. In the end, the Georgia legislators gave the race to Maddox. Carter was headed home to Plains. Although he had campaigned hard, deployed his family across the state, and run a clean race, he had lost.

Jimmy Carter returned to Plains. Bitterly upset, disappointed in his loss, stinging with exhaustion and debt, Carter did some soul searching. After long, meandering conversations with Rosalynn, with his sister, with his friends and advisors, and with God, he committed himself to another run. He also recommitted himself to Christ, describing this new phase of his spiritual life with a phrase that would define him: "born again." It was the rebirth of Jimmy Carter. Many accounts suggest that he fully relinquished his life to Christ, recommitting himself to the quiet practice of his faith, and to church attendance, Bible reading, and prayer. If that was the case, though, his theological reckoning had not yet translated into coherent politics; his professed theology was still lived imperfectly, even manipulatively. He did not tell voters that his faith in Christ had increasingly led him away from the well-trod path of Plains Baptist, First Baptist Americus, First Methodist Americus, and the rest of the segregationist evangelicals; it had instead led him down the less trod path of Reinhold Niebuhr, Martin King, Benjamin Mays, and Clarence Jordan, the path of Southerners committed to justice and mercy for all. The path Carter would try to walk first, though, was to the governor's mansion.

He brought in Jody Powell and Hamilton Jordan, both from Southwest Georgia, to prepare for a 1970 run at the governorship. Joseph "Jody" Powell, a native of Cordele, Georgia (located in Crisp County, Sumter County's southwesterly neighbor), was a sandy-haired young man, thorough and deft. He quickly assumed control of Carter's communications. Working alongside Powell was Hamilton Jordan, Carter's executive secretary, who essentially ran the campaign. For his part, Carter insisted that "no other human being has affected my career more profoundly or beneficially than Hamilton Jordan."[106] Both Powell and Jordan possessed formidable political skill and would advise Carter for the duration of his career.[107] But in addition to offering political acumen, Hamilton Jordan would provide yet another link between Jimmy Carter and Americus, Georgia, and Koinonia Farm.

William "Hamilton" Jordan was the son of Richard Lawton Jordan and, in the sort of wonderful, baffling twists of Georgia genealogy, the nephew of Clarence Jordan.[108] In his early years, Hamilton knew little of his uncle, who was disdained as "the black sheep of the family," the one excluded from the Talbotton family reunions.[109] While his "unusual" uncle may have supported integration, Hamilton's immediate family did not. Jordan rode in Confederate parades as a boy, was looked after by black nannies, and enjoyed all the privileges of his status. But in 1961, when Jordan was seventeen, he witnessed the civil rights struggle in his hometown of Albany. "My father surprised me by inviting me to go downtown with him one Saturday morning to witness King's first march," Jordan remembered, though he added, he was "fairly certain that we were going in the spirit of curiosity—not support."[110] Jordan and his father were shocked as they watched the dignified procession to spot Hattie, their housekeeper for over fifteen years—"'Our' Hattie in a protest march?"[111] Despite feeling confusion and shame on seeing her in the march, Hattie's action had a profound effect on Hamilton Jordan. The day following the march, a serene and impeccably dressed Hattie slipped into the Jordan home, as she always did. Yet on that morning, Hamilton recalled, Hattie hugged him. She did that often, but on this particular day, the young man wondered "if that hug was a way of forgiving us all"; maybe it was even Hattie's way of "bringing King's message into our home: I love you even though you have mistreated me and my people." The lived theology of the civil rights struggle had won the notice of the future advisor to Jimmy Carter. As he put it, "It was through Hattie's quiet commitment that I slowly began to appreciate the civil rights struggle."[112] After this, Jordan began to sneak out to Koinonia to see his Uncle Clarence. He began to admire him.

The last time Hamilton Jordan saw his Uncle Clarence was in the spring of 1969. On that afternoon, when the air was turning warm, Clarence's mood was cool, reflective. "We have made progress, but not much," Uncle Clarence confessed, "every inch, every centimeter has been so hard and at such a great price. But we have survived." His voice trailed off: it was "a tiny light in a vast sea of hate." Hamilton listened to his uncle, but his own life was in a different place—full of youth and optimism and energy and excitement. Hamilton had just returned home from Vietnam, and he was about to begin a new job working for Jimmy Carter's gubernatorial campaign. Hamilton asked his uncle about his long-time neighbor. Clarence replied, in his typical fashion, "He's a nice fella, Hamilton, but he is just a politician." Jimmy Carter may have been just a politician, but he was a politician on the rise.[113]

On April 3, 1970, Carter announced his candidacy. His platform pledged clean governance and championed individual responsibility, conservationism, improved education, and progress for Georgia. His old political views were joined by his newly fervent faith. He told his neighbors in Plains, "We are deeply religious. Most of our lives are centered around our belief in God."[114] Carter had clearly developed strong theological and racial beliefs by this point; but in order to further his political career, he was willing to mislead people regarding those beliefs and the beliefs of others. He understood that running on a campaign of racial fairness and God-ordained equality would not result in a victory. And so, he campaigned as an everyman, a devout, rural candidate with concerns just like the rest of rural Georgia.

Carter's opponent for the Democratic ticket in the 1970 gubernatorial race was Carl Sanders, a moderate former Georgia governor with an excellent reputation, high approval ratings, and a comfortable double-digit lead in the polls. Following his term as governor, Sanders had proved himself to be a successful businessman in Atlanta, and he established a reputable law practice. By all accounts, he was a competent leader, one who opposed vitriol and segregation and prized pragmatism and efficiency. He was a formidable opponent, and the Carter campaign strained to attack the preeminently respectable Sanders.[115] The primary tactic was to attack Sanders on class, with Carter positioning himself as the champion for the rural everyman and Sanders as a city slicker lining the pockets of the Atlanta business elite and himself. The campaign resorted to calling Sanders "Cufflinks Carl," mocking the attorney for his suits, while Carter consistently appeared in overalls and denim in ads. When these class-based assaults proved only partly successful, Carter went after Sanders on race.

Although Sanders was personally comfortable with segregation, he believed primarily in good governance and was opposed to the sort of suicidal segregationism other Deep South states had chosen for themselves. This left an opening for Carter. He knew that many segregationists, including those in Southwest Georgia, were left dumbfounded that their state representatives so passively and peaceably accepted the Civil Rights Act and Voting Rights Act.

They shook their heads in dismay when Sanders not only eschewed massive resistance but also refused to invite Alabama Governor George Wallace to Georgia. Jimmy Carter promised to let him come. "Jimmy Carter campaigned as a George Wallace supporter, which was contrary to what his real beliefs were," Sanders recalled, years later, he ran as a "cousin to George Wallace."[116] Sanders added, "It got to be a pretty vicious campaign; it was just filled with sly innuendoes and I might say deceit."[117] "Carter himself was not a segregationist," biographer Stanly Godbold argued, "but he did say things that segregationists wanted to hear." Political Scientist Betty Glad put it more bluntly: "he courted the racist vote."[118]

Sometimes this courting of the racist vote included more than declarations of free speech and sly innuendoes. "They used a lot of dirty tactics," Sanders recounted. The most egregious occurred in the form of a flyer distributed by the Carter campaign showing Sanders standing between two large black men holding bottles of champagne. Sanders explained: "I had owned a part of the Hawks basketball team and at one point they won the western division, I was in the dressing room and they were celebrating, pouring champagne." The campaign got a copy of the photo and, in Sanders's memory, "sent it out to ministers all over South Georgia, and they sent it out to militants, people who still believed very strongly in segregation, as if I was crossing the line and advocating integration." The strategy worked. Though the September race was close enough to force a runoff, Carter soundly defeated Sanders in the runoff election, 59 percent to 40 percent. Jimmy "lied," Sanders recalled, with some understandable acrimony. "He ran under false pretense."[119] But he won.

Jimmy Carter was officially governor of Georgia. The boy from Archery who learned theology in the segregationist Plains Baptist Church and countertheology from Rachel Clark, the boy who had grown up in the cradle of the Old Confederacy a few miles from Andersonville prison and seen the civil rights struggle firsthand would bring that knowledge with him. It was a new era in Georgia racial politics. As Carter himself admitted, "It's a long way from Plains to Atlanta."[120] Once Carter won the office, his theological and moral stand for racial equality was clear. In his inaugural address, he proclaimed words not usually heard in such a Southern drawl: "The time for racial discrimination is over."[121] Had he heard it, Clarence Jordan would have likely been pleased. But Clarence Jordan didn't hear Carter's speech. He had died three months prior.

FAR AWAY FROM THE governor's office, Clarence Jordan was buried in a pine box in an unmarked grave at Koinonia Farm. He had died on October 29, 1969, after suffering a heart attack while writing in his humble shack on the Koinonia property.[122] With a cool wind blowing across the barren autumn fields, a small number gathered graveside to honor the "Prophet in Blue Jeans." The music that day was a child's rendition of "Happy Birthday," purportedly the only song the little girl knew.

The girl was Faith Fuller. In the previous months, Millard and Linda Fuller had moved with their young family to join Koinonia. Worn low by persecution, internal strife, and financial duress, Koinonia Farm welcomed the new family into their community. The Fullers had first visited Koinonia in December 1965. On the way back to Montgomery, Alabama, from a vacation in Florida, Millard remembered that he had a friend somewhere in Southwest Georgia living at a Christian community. "When we stopped in Albany for breakfast," Linda recalled, "he decided to call up his friend Al Henry." Of course, Al Henry lived at Koinonia. Soon the Fullers were taking their station wagon on a little detour. "We were just going to stay a couple of hours," Linda remembered, "but then we met Clarence."[123] They decided to stay for a month.

Millard Fuller, a millionaire then thirty years old, was searching for meaning and redemption. A native of Lanett, Alabama, Fuller was an intelligent and driven man with natural entrepreneurial instincts. He began his business career while still in elementary school, selling pigs, chickens, rabbits, and then cows. He and a friend committed to make a million dollars before the age of thirty. Millard did it. He attended Auburn University and then the University of Alabama Law School. While in Tuscaloosa, Fuller met Linda Caldwell and the couple married. In addition to practicing law, Fuller also went into business with a friend, forming a marketing company that quickly made, in his words, "significant money." He was a lawyer, businessman, and self-made millionaire, but he was facing an increasing sense of emptiness as well as a crumbling marriage. Linda, widowed by Fuller's single-minded pursuit of mammon, had left him. This marital crisis precipitated a spiritual reckoning. Following an emotional reunion, Millard, Linda, and their two young children set out to repair their family, spending two weeks in Florida and a fateful afternoon in Americus, Georgia.

Millard Fuller and Clarence became fast friends, sharing ideas, fellowship, and a vision for the farm. "I had never met anyone," Fuller recalled, "who was so completely in touch and in tune with Jesus."[124] Jordan's theological and racial orthodoxy intrigued the young businessman, who wondered that Jordan "took God's word so seriously and so literally."[125] For a month, the two "talked a lot about theology and practical Christian discipleship . . . about God, racism, greed, discipleship to Christ [and] the meaning of life."[126] Millard was "captivated," as his wife put it, "by the whole idea of putting Jesus' teaching into action."[127] The Fullers left a month later, changed. That last-minute phone call in Albany, Georgia, had changed the course of their lives, the life of the farm, and indeed, it would change the world. "God led us to Sumter County," Linda Fuller simply stated. The family gave away their wealth, Fuller left his law practice, and he began volunteering with international missions projects before accepting a position fund-raising at Tougaloo College in Jackson, Mississippi. After a few years, though, the Fullers were looking for a change. Millard wrote to Clarence: "I resigned from Tougaloo and wondering what you've got up your sleeve." Clarence replied, characteristically: "I don't have anything up my sleeve but maybe God has something up His sleeve for the both of us."[128]

It was an important moment for the farm. Ironically, in the mid-1960s, when the changes the Koinonians so longed for began, the experiment in Christian interracialism seemed to falter. The population had dwindled to four, and violence had isolated Koinonia from its black neighbors. Not to mention, the farm had been struggling financially since the economic boycott in the late 1950s. Koinonia hadn't planted crops in years and was wholly dependent on the mail-order pecan business. They would have gone under had it not been for, in Clarence Jordan's words, an "avalanche" of charitable gifts. As early as 1962, Jordan was soliciting financial help from an outside consultant who remarked that the "burdensome" financial circumstances were "clearly affecting the effectiveness of your spiritual ministry."[129] The communal model broke down—the farm's income simply couldn't cover costs. Under this financial strain, some Koinonia members were forced to leave the fellowship in 1963. Since Clarence and Florence Jordan were foundational to Koinonia and Will Wittkamper was too old to relocate, Con and Ora Brown would "have to go."[130] They were devastated. Con wrote, "Our parting from Koinonia during the time that it was most difficult to keep the community alive, was one of the most wrenching experiences we have known."[131] While visitors continued to come to Koinonia, the core of the community was struggling, and the future of the farm seemed uncertain.

By the late 1960s, Clarence was increasingly devoted to writing his *Cotton-patch Translations* and considering leaving the farm entirely for Atlanta. Though he opted to stay, he began to imagine changes for the farm. It was during this transition period, in July 1968, the Fullers moved to Koinonia, bringing new energy and inspiration to the community. Linda typed up Clarence's *Cotton-patch Translations* while Clarence and Millard dreamed about the future of Koinonia.[132]

Clarence Jordan and Millard Fuller at Koinonia, 1968.
(Courtesy of Fuller Center for Housing)

In October 1968, Clarence Jordan mailed a letter to the some 12,000 people on Koinonia's list of friends and supporters announcing the establishment of Koinonia Partners. Koinonia Partners committed itself to the continued mission of incarnating the gospel in Sumter County through the farm's interracial community but looked to expand by incarnating the gospel outside of the community as well. "We can be, by God's grace, partners with Him," Clarence explained, but humanity, he said, still suffered from "alienation and isolation and loneliness and anonymity of man, his competitiveness, his wars, his racial pride." The key idea for Jordan was "this word 'partners'" which, he claimed, "speaks of an upward reach and an outward reach."[133] The new vision for Koinonia Partners continued the spiritual component of the farm— spreading the gospel and coordinating what they called "discipleship schools" for bible study, prayer, and fellowship. But it added a new "application": Partnership Farming, Partnership Industries, and Partnership Housing. In addition to regular farming, Koinonia Partners contained an industrial component consisting of a pecan-shelling plant, a fruitcake bakery, and a candy operation.

This would all be made possible through a financial package known as the Fund for Humanity.[134] Jordan had incubated the idea for the Fund for Humanity since his Louisville days. It was, in essence, a contained economy of charity. Donations would be solicited from "people who want to incarnate their Christian religion in the form of helping their neighbors whom they have seen in need," or, as Jordan put it, helping those who "need a wise, honorable and just way of divesting themselves of their overabundance."[135] The money would, in turn, be used to buy land. The poor and dispossessed could then live and work on the land, providing for one another financially.[136] Any excess money would be given back to the fund for more land. While this seems like classic economic redistribution, there is, of course, a theological component to it. For Fuller and Jordan, Koinonia Partners emerged less from Marx and more from Moses as they sought to obey Exodus 22:25: "If you lend money to any of my people who are poor, do not act like a moneylender and require him to pay interest."[137] In the theological economy of Koinonia Partners there would be no profit, no interest, only jubilee. The first step for Koinonia Partners was "to beg." "We are boldly going to become monumental beggars," Jordan quipped, with his characteristic impudence and humility.[138] The begging worked. Donations began pouring in immediately, as hundreds of people sent in cash donations. Koinonia Partners was under way. The goal, Jordan said, was a "million acres"; the goal was to build the Kingdom of God.[139] "Something's been set in motion here," he said, "something that is eternal. I'm beginning to see that I'm in this koinonia thing for life."[140]

When Clarence suddenly died in October 1969, it was the young Millard who would find himself at the helm of Koinonia Partners. The two men could hardly have been more different. While Jordan was contemplative and folksy, easy with a joke, Millard was always moving, direct, and dogged. Jordan could be languid; Fuller had energy like "Niagara Falls."[141] He was, as one companion described him, "dark and brooding and preoccupied, always plunging to and fro in an angular, hurried stride, elbows flying, his mind focused on what counted the most—money."[142] Yet Jordan and Fuller shared a theological mission for Koinonia. Sounding remarkably like Jordan, Fuller told a journalist in 1970, "You know, the South, while it's the Bible Belt of the nation, at the same time is the most militaristic section, the most materialistic, most racist. . . . It's just that tradition and custom have gotten between them and Christianity, and they can't see clearly what the real message is all about."[143] Fuller continued his mentor's vision for a Christian community that embodied racial justice, but he brought to that goal a business acumen and organizational flair that the farm had never previously known.

Koinonia Partners expanded its operations to building homes. It was lived theology expressed as, to borrow Fuller's phrase, "the theology of the hammer." "The theology of the hammer," Fuller explained, "is that our Christian faith . . .

must be incarnated; that is to say, it must become more than a verbal proclamation or intellectual assent. True faith must be acted out."[144] The housing
project began with a plan for forty-two homes, to be constructed near Koinonia for dispossessed farm families. The aim was not only to provide housing
out of a sense of charity, though that was a part, but also to connect people
with the Christian mission of Koinonia. Millard Fuller expressed his hope that
those receiving homes "will join the rest us here in the spirit of community,
the spirit of sharing and Christian cooperation."[145]

Soon after Jordan's death in 1969, Koinonia Partners completed its first
home, built for Bo and Emma Johnson. "The day they moved in," their daughter
Queenie remembered, "was a day full of the purest joy." "My mama, daddy,
brother and sister were running all over the house talking about who wanted
which bedroom, who was going to be where," she said, adding, "it was so
happy."[146] The Johnsons had been longtime friends and neighbors of Koinonia. Bo Johnson had even been at Clarence Jordan's side when he died.[147] "This
house is something we prayed for," Emma Johnson said, "I think it was God's
will that we have it."[148] Many other black families like the Johnsons began to
openly develop relationships with Koinonia. A Koinonia newsletter reported,
"Much of the fear that has gripped Southern blacks for decades is slowly wear-
ing away. Black families are readily responding to Koinonia's housing village
and are moving into their new homes without fear."[149]

One such family was the Dunnings. Ethel and Tom Dunning were from
Sumter County, where they had been subjected to the crushing poverty experienced by blacks in rural Southwest Georgia. They had worked as sharecroppers into the 1970s. Ethel dreamed of a house of her own, a new life. She prayed.
A friend suggested Koinonia. Koinonia Partners began building the Dunnings
a home. When the white woman who employed her at the "plantation" found
out the Dunnings were moving to Koinonia, she had the water in their shack
turned off. "For four months," Ethel recalled, "I hauled water four miles and
hitchhiked to Americus every Friday to do laundry, until our house was
done."[150] Another family was kicked out of their home when the landowner
found out they were planning to move to a Koinonia house. They spent the
construction months living in a guesthouse at Koinonia. One farmer, so incensed that one of his sharecropper families was moving to a Koinonia house,
went straight to their shack and killed their dogs.[151] Despite these horrific incidents and the still-regular indignities and oppression faced by black Americus residents, the program thrived. In 1975, Florence Jordan wrote to Harry and
Ailene Atkinson that Koinonia's new building program was "a very gratifying
thing," adding, "Americus has changed radically and while we can still find

animosity without much trouble, there have been changes."[152] In fact, the lived theology of Koinonia was the one thing that had not much changed. At Koinonia, Ethel Dunning declared, "I have met some of the best folks God has chosen." She continued, "There is no dividing line in heaven, and God doesn't want us to be divided here. We are one big family, black and white."[153]

It is interesting to note that in the late 1960s and early 1970s, young people flocked to Koinonia. Many were drawn by Jordan's theological vision, but many more were drawn by the countercultural lifestyle that young people found so attractive in those years. Norman Race, who moved to Koinonia in 1976, recalled that many came in protest against the Vietnam War.[154] New programs in bread baking and ceramics appeared alongside traditional agriculture as young visitors came, staying for various amounts of time. In a humorous example of the changing times, the farm began "creative tie-dying of t-shirts" to sell along with the pecans.[155] Yet even as the farm expanded its operations and hosted less devout visitors, the original theological vision remained. Ted Swisher, who in the 1970s coordinated many activities at Koinonia, noted Koinonia Partners' enduring "theological rootedness."[156]

Koinonia Partners built over thirty houses before the Fullers went to Zaire in 1973.[157] In Africa, Millard Fuller honed his vision for affordable housing and began connecting his theological vision with an ambitious plan to eliminate poverty housing (shacks) back in the American South.[158] Upon their return in 1976, the Fullers moved back to Americus. Their house on West Church Street became not only the center for Millard's law office but the new headquarters for Koinonia Partners' "mom and pop" affordable housing organization.[159] The housing project and its "theology of the hammer" were a natural expansion of Koinonia's humble vision for incarnational Christian community. The Fullers decided to call this partner organization "Habitat for Humanity."[160]

Of course, 1976 was a big year for Sumter County for reasons that had little to do with affordable housing. Jimmy Carter, a nearly unknown governor from Georgia, had decided to run for president of the United States.

To quell the cries of "Jimmy Who?" Carter's friends from Sumter County helped campaign. Though at first simply called "Georgians for Carter," the group was soon dubbed the "Peanut Brigade" by a reporter.[161] "Here's somebody suddenly in one of the New England states or wherever from Americus or Plains, Georgia," one brigadier recalled, "going on their own, providing their own expenses and time, just going out and campaigning for him. . . . It made a very real impression." Voters seemed impressed by the down-home campaign and the kindness of the Southerners they met. Weary with corruption and disillusioned with Washington, Americans responded to Carter's outsiderness, what Marshall Frady called his "innocent remoteness." They also responded to his lived theology.

Americus Times-Recorder reporter Rudy Hayes claimed the question he was "invariably" asked on the trail was: "Is this guy for real; is he really a goody two-shoes or Christian?" Hayes would respond, "Well, he's not a goody two-shoes, but he's a Christian and he's dedicated and he's not going into the church just because he thinks it might sound good and make good copy."[162] The wholesome peanut farmer from Georgia with a strong faith appealed to an electorate disillusioned by Watergate, an electorate that at least wanted to believe him when he promised never to lie to them. Religious Americans in particular delighted in hearing a candidate express his theological beliefs in the public square. "Carter's unabashed declaration of faith," historian Randall Balmer has argued, "lured many hitherto apolitical evangelicals into the political arena."[163] Carter's declarations of faith and the groundswell of evangelical voters famously prompted *Newsweek* to declare 1976 the Year of the Evangelical.[164] Even those who remained skeptical soon realized Carter's religion was for real. As Rudy Hayes put it, they realized "they had been wrong and that he really was dedicated and loved the Lord and followed him."[165] With his folksy rhetoric, the support of the Peanut Brigade, and his sincere faith, Jimmy Carter, however improbably, won the Democratic nomination for the presidency.[166]

Nonetheless, a president from Southwest Georgia was almost unbelievable. Mark Pace, son of Solicitor General Stephen Pace declared, he never thought Carter had "a snowball's chance in hell, but he won!" "I wanted him to win," Eloise Paschal recalled, "but I never thought he would. I thought Plains and Sumter County would be the thing that would kill him. I was as shocked as anyone . . . a glad shock."[167] As election day approached, though, and the numbers stayed up, a "soft euphoria" overtook Sumter County. "The people of Americus," the *New York Times* reported, "are waiting eagerly, hopefully, for whatever changes may come with [Carter's] election, which almost to a person they assume is foreordained." Even Baptists believed in electoral predestination in 1976, it seemed. Rachel Clark had read in the scriptures that God "changeth the times and the seasons: he removeth kings, and setteth up kings." She knew God had put the boy she had helped raise where he was. "If the Lord didn't have him in His hands he wouldn't be where he is," she explained, "he wouldn't go like he goes."[168] But before the nation's most famous evangelical could be elected, the nation's most famous Georgian would have to deal with the South's most pressing theological conflict.

ELEVEN YEARS AFTER the deacons slapped down their resolution barring black worshippers and days before the election, Clennon King approached Plains Baptist Church. It was a crisp October morning as King and his three friends walked up the brick steps to the white clapboard church, the golden sun causing the church's stained glass windows to glow shades of purple and blue, mingling with the falling yellow leaves.[169] Perhaps imagining himself a racial activist, perhaps hoping to be a political influence, perhaps being subject to the unpredictable whims of his internal voices, Clennon King sought to open the door of the church. But it was locked.

Having been notified that King planned to attend, the deacons of Plains Baptist met and decided, against the will of Rev. Bruce Edwards, to enforce the 1965 resolution barring civil rights agitators.[170] Knowing that this decision would draw a media frenzy in the days before the general election and not wanting to embarrass Carter, the deacons had opted to simply cancel Sunday Services. There would be no theological reckoning on that fall Sunday.

King's detractors claimed it was an elaborate publicity stunt designed to embarrass the Democratic nominee. "It seems obvious to me," Rev. Edwards told the press, "that this is an attempt by the enemies of Governor Carter to sabotage his campaign."[171] Indeed, the timing seems more opportunistic than redemptive. When asked about this, King replied, "God times things. I don't know why God timed it this way."[172] For his part, Carter tried to sidestep the controversy. From the campaign trail in Texas, he stated, "The only thing I know is that our church for many years has accepted any worshiper who came there," adding, "my own belief is that anyone who lives in our vicinity who wants to be a member of the church, regardless of race ought to be admitted."[173]

Not only did the timing appear suspect, King's application actually did smack of insincerity. He was the pastor of (the non-Baptist) Divine Mission Church in Albany, for one thing. He was something of a career activist with a penchant for the flamboyant and, some argued, the insane. He had run for president in 1960 on the Afro-American ticket and called for an African exodus of sorts for black Americans. King himself had sought asylum in Jamaica for what he called "insidious persecution in the United States," but which was actually legal trouble for failing to pay child support, charges for which he would serve four years in a California prison. He was a far cry from the nonviolent student activists who championed theological protest. Even Miss

Lillian, who had courageously voted against the closed-door measure in 1965, said she was "glad" Plains Baptist had rejected King, though she added, "I'd be very happy if we had some black members of the church." As for King, she commented, "He is an activist and he is a man who screams on the street corner and he is against everything."[174]

Whereas the 1965 kneel-ins constituted theological drama, their 1976 counterparts were more like political theater. The old segregationist theology may have buttressed the church's claims, but it lacked the old conviction. The racial orthodoxy of Plains Baptist repelled many congregants, led to the firing of its young pastor, and eventually wrenched the congregation in two.[175] As for Clennon King, his visit did not stem from a thoughtful desire for the beloved community as much as for a moment in the spotlight. From that sweltering August morning in 1965 to that chilly fall one in October 1976, the time for real theological reckoning seemed to have passed.

Despite Clennon King's visit and the media melee that followed, Jimmy Carter won the presidency. In his inaugural address, Carter prominently quoted Micah 6:8: "He hath showed thee, O man, what is good; and what doth the Lord require of thee, but to do justly, and to love mercy, and to walk humbly with thy God." By all accounts Carter tried to do this in his years in office. While Carter's racial and political record has been criticized, his faith has not. Even the less religiously inclined, those who mocked the "born-again" Jimmy, could not deny his utter sincerity.

And yet, Carter lost the election of 1980 at the hands of evangelicals. Historian Randall Balmer, who endeavors to "take Jimmy Carter's religious commitments seriously," has claimed that "during the four years of Jimmy Carter's presidency the political ground shifted seismically beneath him."[176] So did the theological ground. In 1976, the televangelist Pat Robertson said that he "had great hopes" for a Carter presidency and claimed he was "our champion."[177] But Robertson supported Ronald Reagan in 1980. Evangelicals, Southern Baptists even, abandoned the devout Carter for Reagan, an apostle of optimism and a new conservatism.[178] Of course, even as a new evangelicalism spread through the nation, old racial issues grew up with it, intermingled like Southern kudzu.

Bitterly disappointed, the Carters left Washington, D.C., and returned to Sumter County. There, they became actively involved with Habitat for Humanity. They fundraised for the organization, regularly volunteered in local builds, and traveled each year on an international Habitat trip.[179] Millard and Linda Fuller became some of Jimmy and Rosalynn's closest friends. By 1996, former President Jimmy Carter, who as young man and aspiring politician never visited or mentioned Koinonia, publicly praised the farm's efforts.[180]

"Too often we think about evangelicalism as only preaching the Gospel," he stated, "but there is also powerful ministry in the alleviation of suffering, reaching out in harmony, respect, and partnership to other, and sharing life." He had adopted Koinonia's incarnational theology, after all. "Christ was a doer," Carter explained, "one who faith took the form of action, not merely words."[181]

WHILE THEOLOGY CERTAINLY still compels individuals like Jimmy Carter, it seems to have lost its wider cultural relevance. In his 2012 work, *Bad Religion*, Ross Douthat argues that America has morphed into "a nation of heretics." "The United States remains a deeply Christian county," Douthat writes, "but a growing number are inventing their own version of what Christianity means, *abandoning the nuances of traditional theology* in favor of religions that stroke their egos and indulge or even celebrate their worst impulses."[182] According to a 2016 poll, only 45 percent of Americans strongly agree with the bodily resurrection of Jesus, while less than half agree that "the Bible alone is the word of God."[183] Without theologizing, religion can become mere justification for selfishness and self-righteousness. Indeed, in the tumult of the post–civil rights era and the culture wars, theology was the big loser.

It is a familiar story. America was secularizing, and the South, which still retained the veneer of Christianity, had mostly exchanged deep theological commitments for either political posturing or saccharine substitutes. In the late 1970s and 1980s, the Religious Right, though quick to invoke the Bible and boast God's favor, took the fundamentalist beliefs of many, especially Southerners, and turned them toward contemporary conflicts. Conservative leaders produced a powerful voting coalition but not a particularly theologically reflective one. The black church, too, ceded some of its theological power. Many churches shelved their more subversive theological tenets and embraced the easier prosperity gospel, trading Charles Sherrod for Creflo Dollar, Ella Baker for Eddie Long.[184] Indeed, the prosperity gospel and the rise of the megachurch have captivated Southerners, black and white, many of whom remain undereducated and desperately poor.[185] These shifts have limited the opportunities for redemptive community and resulted in a theological watering down. Lived theology is in crisis.

But some still hope. Koinonia Farm still exists out on Dawson Road in Americus, Georgia. Jimmy Carter still teaches Sunday school each week in Plains. Charles and Shirley Sherrod still press for justice in Southwest Georgia. In 2018, First Methodist and First Baptist in Americus will host a symposium to honor Clarence Jordan, a man they once shunned. There is a remnant of radical orthodoxy, what theologian Hans Frei and more recently journalist

Malcolm Gladwell have called "generous orthodoxy."[186] There are still communities, families, and individuals who desire to put belief into action in ways that are sensible, biblical, communal, and powerful. Throughout Americus, throughout the South and the nation, people of all races still meet in churches. They still sing. They still march for justice. They still kneel and pray. They still ask God to be with them.

In a time when issues of race and religion continue to polarize Americans, the lessons of the theological civil rights struggle of the 1960s are more pressing than ever. While theology may have lost then, its emancipatory and conciliatory possibilities remain. In late 1965, after Collins McGee and Carol Henry and Clarence Jordan had been dragged out of the church at Christmastime, someone wrote a poem set in Americus called "A Christmas Dream."[187] This anonymous work presents a theological vision, religiously specific and yet astoundingly capacious.

This Christmas, I am dreaming
About a place I'll never forget—Americus.
I am dreaming that it is Christmas Sunday;
It is the most beautiful Sunday in all the South.
The whole town is gathered in Friendship Baptist Church!

After the main part of the service is over,
Rev. Thomas leads us in singing,
"Amazing Grace, How Sweet it Sounds."
Because it is our movement church, and we are rejoiced,
Willie Mae leads us in "We Shall Overcome."
There is an electric feeling of ecstatic joy in the air . . .

Old wealthy Charles Wheatley slowly rises,
"I've come here today, y'all, this Christmas, 1965,
'Cause I just can't go on living the way I have;
I've tried to rule little Americus,
From the mayor to the moonshine maker.
I want to confess that the summer past
I did way too much
To keep the merchants from hiring y'all
And a Bi-racial Committee from forming at all!
All generations of Wheatleys tried to rule this town,
But justice has been coming, it's nearly 1966.
And I've too few years left to hate."

"Amen, yes brother," responds the congregation.

Before the surprised faces of the town,
Sheriff Fred Chappell rises to respond.
His huge form shakes, his face, as usual, is very red.
"I'll never beat another in yonder courthouse,
The drinking fountains will stay on, the door unlocked,
We'll all meet together in the old courthouse!
I was the one this summer who kept
The Negro women voters under arrest.
I was damn proud to let white folks think
I'd be the first to give I to voting integration."

"Amen, yes brother."

Then, puffing, rises Police Chief Ross Chambliss.
"We on the police force just felt we HAD to win,
I confess we committed a terrible sin.
On August 28, when y'all were marching up Lee Street,
We broke in and arrested y'all
For marching without a permit for parades and ordinances.
We knew, uh, you were on the sidewalk, not the street,
And the constitution supports your right to protest.
But the wicked thing called 'hate' broke loose,
And we threw y'all in Lee County prisons." . . .

Suddenly, a tall blond youth breaks in,
"Let me speak for all us white folks,
I guess I'm the worst of all.
I know that hate killed my brother, Andy Whatley,
Possibly the Negro youths last August . . .
This same hate made all of us beat and chase you in the last march
So you'd never march again
I'm still young and I want to start a new life.
I've expressed as much hate as I possibly can, and
I have nothing left but to love my black brother,
For we all are in poverty and without decent jobs."

Then, Mayor Walker rises:
"I have some news to greet y'all,
For Warren Fortson and Lloyd Moll shall return!

We must prove to them that we can accept them
As the best and most honest folks in town,
And hope they can forgive us
For excluding them from the human race;
We need Fortson for our lawyer;
Dr. Moll can unite us all
To revive the now dormant anti-poverty council
Most of all, we need the guidance of these humanitarians."

"Amen, yes brother," responds the congregation.

Minnie Jewel Wise rises, her dark eyes flashing,
"I truly believe now what I hear,
For you are not merely coming to us with promises,
But asking forgiveness for your sins.
I've done hard things:
I've survived the blows, frustrations and humiliations
With those that dare to attend white schools.
I now speak for my mother, worn out from scrubbing kitchens,
For teacher and Rev. Freeman, who did not, after all,
Get fired for standing up for his rights;
For Reverend Campbell, who led the past eventful summer,
For Sammy Mahone, of SNCC, who said, 'Never Turn Back,'
And never did.
If this love will truly exist, as you now say,
Then let Americus citizens ask forgiveness,
If they EVER think ill of one just 'cause he's black or white
Most of all we'll show the world what trust and love can bring."

In the congregation, there was a moment of grateful silence.
Then all stood to sing a glorious hymn,
"JOY TO THE WORLD, THE LORD HAS COME!"

Within the church, because of the power of theology, Charles Wheatley, Ross Chambliss, Mayor Walker, and even Fred Chappell can sit with Warren Fortson and Minnie Jewel Wise. People can tell the truth about racism and hatred, receive forgiveness, and be reconciled. They can sit in grateful silence. They can unite their voices together up to God who has come to dwell with them. This Christmas vision, of God with us, with all of us, remains as radically hopeful now as it was then.

Notes

Introduction

1. Esther Mohler Ho to Clarence Jordan, MS 756 13:7, Clarence L. Jordan Papers, Hargrett Rare Book and Manuscript Library, University of Georgia Libraries [hereafter Clarence L. Jordan Papers]; Ho, "Koinonia Farm," *Christian Advocate*, Feb. 1967, 5–7, 11, AR 39 1.4, Clarence Jordan Collection, Southern Baptist Historical Library and Archives, Nashville, Tennessee [hereafter Clarence Jordan Collection]; Millard Fuller, Speech Given to the Atlanta Christian Council, Dec. 4, 1969; Jim Auchmutey, "Christmas 1965," Dec. 4, 2015, http://jimauchmutey.com/blog/2015/12/24/christmas-1965.

2. Hedgepeth, "The American South," 19.

3. See Lawson, "Freedom Then, Freedom Now"; Branch, *Parting the Waters*; Branch, *Pillar of Fire*; Branch, *At Canaan's Edge*; Gardner, *Andrew Young*; Garrow, *Bearing the Cross*; Lawson, *Black Ballots*; Lewis, *King*; Lincoln, *Martin Luther King, Jr.*; Manis, *A Fire You Can't Put Out*; Oates, *Let the Trumpet Sound*; Reddick, *Crusader without Violence*; Whalen and Whalen, *Longest Debate*.

4. This move toward viewing civil rights as part of a larger struggle for racial equality has allowed for an expanded chronology, scope, and geography. See Borstelmann, *Cold War and the Color Line*; Carson, "Civil Rights Reform"; Carson, *In Struggle*; Chafe, *Civilities and Civil Rights*; Dittmer, *Local People*; Dudziak, *Cold War Civil Rights*; Dyson, *Making Malcolm*; Fairclough, *Race and Democracy*; Greene, *Praying for Sheetrock*; Hahn, *A Nation under Our Feet*; Hall, "The Long Civil Rights Movement"; Hogan, *Many Minds, One Heart*; Joseph, *Black Power Movement*; Kelley, *Race Rebels*; Lee, *For Freedom's Sake*; Marable, *Race, Reform, Rebellion*; Marable and Mullings, eds., *Let Nobody Turn Us Around*; Kelley, *Hammer and Hoe*; Ogbar, *Black Power*; Patterson, *Brown v. Board of Education*; Payne, *I've Got the Light of Freedom*; Ransby, *Ella Baker and the Black Freedom Movement*; Savage, *Broadcasting Freedom*; Schultz, *Going South*; Sitkoff, *Struggle for Black Equality*; Sugrue, *Origins of the Urban Crisis*; Sugrue, *Sweet Land of Liberty*; Sullivan, *Lift Every Voice*; Tuck, *Beyond Atlanta*; Tyson, *Radio Free Dixie*; von Eschen, *Race against Empire*.

5. Marsh, *Beloved Community*, 4.

6. On King, see Ansbro, *Martin Luther King, Jr*; Baldwin, *There Is a Balm in Gilead*; Baldwin, *To Make the Wounded Whole*; Baldwin, *Never to Leave Us Alone*; Lischer, *Preacher King*. In general, see Morris, *Origins of the Civil Rights Movement*; Raboteau, *Fire in the Bones*; Washington, *Black Religion*; Zepp, *Search for the Beloved Community*.

7. Chappell, *Stone of Hope*, 3, 83, 87. See also Harris, *Something Within*; Harvey, *Through the Storm*; Marsh, *God's Long Summer*; Ownby, *The Role of Ideas in the Civil Rights South*; Williams, *African American Religion*.

8. See Grem, *The Blessings of Business*; Kruse, *One Nation under God*; Kruse, *White Flight*; Lassiter, *Silent Majority*; MacLean, *Behind the Mask of Chivalry*; McGirr, *Suburban*

Warriors; Schulman, *From Cotton Belt to Sunbelt*; Schulman, *Seventies*; Schulman and Zelizer, eds., *Rightward Bound*; Sokol, *There Goes My Everything*; Webb, *Rabble Rousers*. Many historians differentiate between the Sunbelt and the Deep South, between political conservatism and racial/evangelical conservatism. Too often, Joe Crespino writes, these historians "make facile distinctions between Sunbelt conservatives, who are figured as modern, principled and broadly ideological, and Southern conservatives, who are figured chiefly as backward and racist," which creates a "flattened portrait" of the South, and also a portrait of "Sunbelt conservatives as racially innocent, free from any taint of racial politics" (Crespino, *Strom Thurmond's America*, 8–9). It also masks the significance of evangelicalism in creating racial supremacy outside the South, a topic that beckons.

9. The exceptions have typically been denominational histories. See Alvis, *Religion and Race*; Goodwin, *Down by the Riverside*; Lucas, *For a Continuing Church*; Murray, *Methodists and the Crucible of Race*; Newman, *Getting Right with God*; Sledge, *Hands on the Ark*.

10. Harvey, "God and Negroes," 285.

11. Dailey, "Sex, Segregation, and the Sacred after *Brown*," 144.

12. Genovese, "Christian Tradition," 285.

13. Dailey, "Theology of Massive Resistance," 151–80. Dailey argues that this historical misinterpretation amounts to a veiled orthodoxy of its own.

14. Newman, *Getting Right with God*, 48; Crespino, *In Search of Another Country*; Dailey, "Sex, Segregation, and the Sacred After *Brown*," 119–44; Dailey, "Theology of Massive Resistance"; Haynes, "Distinction and Dispersal"; Harvey, *Bounds of Their Habitation*; Harvey, *Christianity and Race*; Harvey, *Redeeming the South*; Harvey, *Freedom's Coming*; Leonard, "A Theology for Racism."

15. Crespino, *In Search of Another Country*; Dupont, *Mississippi Praying*.

16. Marsh, Review of Chappell, *A Stone of Hope*, 266–271; Chappell, "Religious Ideas of the Segregationists"; Chappell, "Disunity and Religious Institutions."

17. Newman, *Getting Right with God*; Lyon, "Doing a Little Something to Pave the Way for Others"; Lyon, "Lifting the Color Bar"; Lyon, *Sanctuaries of Segregation*; Kosek, "'Just a Bunch of Agitators'"; Haynes, *Last Segregated Hour*.

18. Dailey, "Theology of Massive Resistance," 153.

19. Questions of religious belief are often dismissed as unimportant or unanswerable by contemporary scholars. Historian John McGreevy commented that "historians of modern America give matters of faith and belief only fleeting attention" while Jon Butler asserted, "Religion has not fared well in the historiography of modern America" (McGreevy, *Parish Boundaries*; Butler, "Jack-in-the-Box Faith").

20. *A Midsummer Night's Dream* 5.113–18, quoted in Dark, "Insert Soul Here," in Marsh, Slade, Azaransky eds., *Lived Theology*, ,159.

21. Marsh, through his own scholarship and through the founding of the Project for Lived Theology at the University of Virginia, has coined the term "lived theology" and established it as a field of study for academics. See also Marsh, Slade, and Azaransky, eds., *Lived Theology*.

22. Augustine, *City of God*, Part VIII, I; Marsh, "Editor's Preface," in Marsh, Slade, Azaransky eds., *Lived Theology*, viii. Classic articulations of theology represent an attempt by mankind to find, interpret, and understand God, usually through a combination of reason and revelation.

23. Warnock, *The Divided Mind of the Black Church*, 188.

24. Marsh, "Conference on Lived Theology and Civil Courage: A Collection of Essays," 4.

25. Marsh, "Introduction," in Marsh, Slade, Azaransky, *Lived Theology*, 6; Meeks, *First Urban Christians*.

26. Marsh, "Introduction," in Marsh, Slade, Azaransky, *Lived Theology*, 15–16.

27. Hall, *Lived Religion in America*, viii.

28. Orsi, "Everyday Miracles," 8–9.

29. The first definition belongs to Marsh (Marsh, Slade, Azaransky eds., *Lived Theology*, 7); the second is my own.

30. Marsh, *God's Long Summer*, 4.

31. Sayers, "The Greatest Drama Ever Staged," 1.

32. Merton, *Faith and Violence*, 131.

33. Marsh's *God's Long Summer*, as the most notable example, includes the lived theology of several prominent individuals in the struggle.

34. Community studies are one of the most fruitful approaches to the civil rights movement. "Each community now has its own story to tell" historian Steven Tuck has written, "and only when more of these stories are told will the Southern civil rights movement be understood" (Tuck, *Beyond Atlanta*, 109).

35. Tuck, 176. As Marshall Frady, a prominent Southern journalist recalled, Americus "had the appearance of having been abruptly dropped down intact, out of nowhere, into the negligibly inhabited spaces of South Georgia" (Frady, *Southerners*). In the 1940s, 1950s, and 1960s, the 13,000 residents were almost exactly 50 percent black/50 percent white. According to the 2000 Census Record, Americus has 17,013 residents, or 1,623 residents per square mile, with a population that is 39 percent white, 58 percent black, 2.49 percent Hispanic, .86 percent Asian, and .23 percent Native American. The median income is $26,808 with 27.7 percent of those living below the poverty line.

36. A few historians have considered Koinonia Farm (Chancey, "Race, Religion, and Reform"; K'Meyer, *Interracialism and Christian Community*; Lee, *Cotton Patch Evidence*); others have examined the civil rights movement in Georgia (Tuck, *Beyond Atlanta*); and accounts of SNCC and Martin Luther King Jr., sometimes contain passing references to this little city. Nevertheless, no comprehensive study of this community exists. In 2015, journalist Jim Auchmutey wrote *Class of '65*, an account of four classmates from Americus High School bound together by the tumult of the 1960s and their process of reflection and reconciliation over the next fifty years. His compelling story adds much to the Americus narrative, though it is limited in scope (Auchmutey, *Class of '65*).

37. O'Connor, *A Prayer Journal*, 4.

38. Marsh, *God's Long Summer*, 3.

Chapter One

1. Lee, *Cotton Patch Evidence*, 33. Dallas Lee was a close personal friend of Clarence Jordan and actually lived at Koinonia for a time. Although these sorts of hagiographies (especially those with Lee's lack of citation) can be historically problematic, his work is the most detailed and colorful account of the farm and is mostly corroborated by scholars.

2. Koinonia is pronounced Coy-No-NEE-Ah and means *fellowship* or *communion* in Greek. See Acts 2:24–27.

3. Lee, *Cotton Patch Evidence*, 5.

4. Martin England to Mack Goss, July 15, 1942, MS 2340, Clarence L. Jordan Papers.

5. Lee, *Cotton Patch Evidence*, 81; Koinonia newsletter 1954, Koinonia newsletter 1955, MS 756 3:1, Clarence L. Jordan Papers. .

6. Jordan was "was no student of community." Rather, "he was moved solely by his immersion in the Scriptures" (Lee, *Cotton Patch Evidence*, 88). Nonetheless, Koinonia had connections with other radical and utopian communities, like Highlander Folk School in Tennessee; Providence Farm, the Penn School, and the Ruskin Community in Ware County, Georgia; the Bruderhof in Germany, North Dakota, and New York; and the Hutterian Brethren. See Bestor, *Backwoods Utopias*; Boyer, "Joyful Noyes"; Chancey, "Restructuring Southern Society"; Guarneri, *Utopian Alternative*; Manuel, ed., *Utopias and Utopian Thought*; Pitzer, *America's Communal Utopias*.

7. Lee, *Cotton Patch Evidence*, 1.

8. Barnette, "Clarence Jordan"; von Hoffman, "Clarence Jordan," MS 2341 3:6, Clarence L. Jordan Papers.

9. Letter from Frank Jordan, 1928, MS 756 1:2, Clarence L. Jordan Papers; Letter from sister, Sep 28, 1928, MS 756 1:2, Clarence L. Jordan Papers; Letter from Mother, May 31, 1929, MS 756 1:3, Clarence L. Jordan Papers; Lee, *Cotton Patch Evidence*, 6–7.

10. Lee, *Cotton Patch Evidence*, 5, 5, 7, 12.

11. This refrain is actually the chorus of a hymn penned by the Chicago preacher C. Herbert Woolston (1856–1927).

12. Quoted in Lee, *Cotton Patch Evidence*, 7–8.

13. The stretcher was a structure that bound one's feet to the ground while lifting the hands that were tied by a rope too, thus painfully stretching the body when extended.

14. Lee, *Cotton Patch Evidence*, 8.

15. Howard, "Legacy of Clarence Jordan," *Faith at Work*, April 1970, 16, AR 39:1.13, Clarence Jordan Collection.

16. Lee, *Cotton Patch Evidence*, 9.

17. Lee, 8–9.

18. Letter to mother, 1933, MS 756 1:6, Clarence Jordan Papers; Letter from George Jordan to mother, July 1932, MS 756 1:6, Clarence Jordan Papers.

19. Letter from mother, Sep. 16, 1933, MS 756 1:7, Clarence L. Jordan Papers; Jordan, "My Call to the Ministry"; MS 756 1:7, Clarence L. Jordan Papers; Lee, *Cotton Patch Evidence*, 11

20. MS 756 1:7, Clarence L. Jordan Papers; Lee, *Cotton Patch Evidence*, 15–17.

21. One of Jordan's seminary classmates recalled years later: "I along with every other single man, possibly some married ones too, were envious of [Jordan] in dating the lovely creature who became his wife!" (Letter from J. Winston Peace, MS 2341 3:8, Clarence L. Jordan Papers).

22. Letter from father, May 19, 1936, MS 756 1:10, Clarence L. Jordan Papers.

23. *Louisville Journal Courier*, July 26, 1936; MS 756 28:5, Clarence L. Jordan Papers.

24. This intense study of Greek was the most profound influence on Jordan's life and theology. His wife, Florence, later commented, "In his study of the Greek, he did much research into the roots, derivation, and nuances of words. He also studied the papyri for the

common usages of phrases and meanings. A single passage could take hours of study and meditation." She also mentioned some influential teachers, among them were Dr. A. T. Robertson, Dr. Wm. Hersey Davis, Dr. E. A. McDowell, and Dr. J. B. Weatherspoon (Letter from Florence Jordan to Ken Corson, Aug. 10, 1976, MS 2341 2:8, Clarence L. Jordan Papers; He also corresponded with Liston Pope of Yale University about Koinonia (Letters from Pope, MS 756 2:3, Clarence L. Jordan Papers).

25. Howard, "Legacy of Clarence Jordan," 16, AR 39:1.13, Clarence Jordan Collection.

26. Lee, *Cotton Patch Evidence*, 17.

27. Various correspondence, 1940, MS 756 1:11, Clarence L. Jordan Papers; Letter from Bob Herdon, MS 2341 3:8, Clarence L. Jordan Papers.

28. Letters from Foreign Missions Board, Letter from Mrs. Hoffman, MS 756 1:11, Clarence L. Jordan Papers.

29. He made sure that the mission's board was interracial and pressed for black leadership to stem paternalism. Jordan's accounts of the Fellowship Center are quite colorful, due not least of all to the fact that the building was formerly a brothel (Letter from Bob Herdon, MS 2341 3:8, Clarence L. Jordan Papers; Letter to Brother Arthur Dailey, April 3, 1939, MS 756 1:11, Clarence L. Jordan Papers; Letter to Marg, MS 756 2:2, Clarence L. Jordan Papers).

30. Letter to Brother Arthur Dailey, April 3, 1939, MS 756 1:11, Clarence L. Jordan Papers.

31. K'Meyer, *Interracialism and Christian Community*, 32. Jordan himself attended a conservative seminary and did not consider himself an advocate of the Social Gospel. In a letter written after his death, his wife, Florence, said that any connection with Walter Rauschenbusch was "entirely unfounded." She continued, "I do not recall any references or even approval of Rauschenbusch and his writings." Though Florence is correct that Jordan probably did not consider himself a student of Rauschenbusch, he was undoubtedly influenced by the Social Gospel to some degree. Koinonia, even unwittingly, can be seen as an exercise of that tradition. For the Social Gospel, see Handy, ed., *Social Gospel in America*; Hopkins, *Rise of the Social Gospel*; Luker, *Social Gospel in Black and White*; White, *Liberty and Justice for All*.

32. Lee, *Cotton Patch Evidence*, 22.

33. Correspondence, MS 756 1:11, Clarence L. Jordan Papers.

34. Letter from Duke McCall, March 3, 1982, MS 2341 3:8, Clarence L. Jordan Papers; Letter from Edward Byrd, MS 2341 3:8, Clarence L. Jordan Papers.

35. For the Great Migration, see Arnesen, *Black Protest and the Great Migration*; Grossman, *Land of Hope*; Hahn, *Nation under Our Feet*; Sernett, *Bound for the Promised Land*; Wilkerson, *Warmth of Other Suns*.

36. Howard, "Legacy of Clarence Jordan," 1–13, Clarence Jordan Collection.

37. Acts 2:44, 45, Acts 4:32–33 [all English Standard Version (ESV), unless noted]; K'Meyer, *Interracialism and Christian Community*, 34.

38. Jordan, "Christian Community in the South," 27–36.

39. "Cotton Patch Translation," Bible Collector, April–June 1965, Koinonia Scrapbook, quoted in Chancey, "Restructuring Southern Society," 79.

40. Walker L. Knight, "A Prophet Moves On," 1969, 3, AR 39 1.2, Clarence Jordan Collection.

41. Hollyday, ed., *Clarence Jordan: Essential Writings*, 33.

42. Letter from Sammie, Nov. 9, 1969, MS 2341 1:11, Clarence L. Jordan Papers.

43. Martin England, letter to Walt N. Johnson, MS 2341 3:8, Clarence L. Jordan Papers; Martin England to Henlee Barnette, MS 2341 3:8, Clarence L. Jordan Papers; Williams, *By Faith and by Love*, 55.

44. The criteria for an ideal place included factors such as population, racial demographics, income levels, soil types, tenancy, and typical climate.

45. Jordan joked in a letter that it was next to hell since it was "right across the river from Alabama" (Lee, *Cotton Patch Evidence*, 32–33); Letter from Albert Jordan, 1943, MS 756 2:4, Clarence L. Jordan Papers.

46. Some other organizations that labored specifically in rural areas include Delta Farms, Providence Farms, the Christian Service Foundation of Florida, Fellowship of Southern Churchmen and its Rural Reconstruction Committee and Brush Arbor Institutes, the Christian Rural Fellowship, American Country Life Association, the Rural Life division of the Fellowship of Reconciliation, the Commission for Interracial Cooperation, and the Southern Regional Council.

47. K'Meyer, *Interracialism and Christian Community*, 48.

48. Fellowship of International Communities newsletter 2:1, Oct. 1952, MS 756 22:4, Clarence L. Jordan Papers.

49. Genesis 3:17–19.

50. Jordan, "Christian Community in the South," *Journal of Religious Thought*, AR 39: 1.10, Clarence Jordan Collection.

51. Howard, "The Legacy of Clarence Jordan," AR 39 1.13, Clarence Jordan Collection.

52. "The Spirit himself bears witness with our spirit that we are children of God, and if children, then heirs—heirs of God and fellow heirs with Christ" (Romans 8:16–17).

53. Jordan, "Christian Community in the South," *Journal of Religious Thought*, AR 39:1.10, Clarence Jordan Collection

54. Lee, *Cotton Patch Evidence*, 88. Clarence Jordan, "Christian Community in the South," "What Is the Kingdom of God?," "Thy Kingdom Come—On Earth," Sunday school lessons published in *High Call*, Summer 1950, 29–32, MS 756:15, Clarence L. Jordan Papers; K'Meyer, *Interracialism and Christian Community*, 31.

55. Jordan, "Christian Community in the South," *Journal of Religious Thought*, AR 39: 1.10, Clarence Jordan Collection

56. Morgan, ABC News Report, April 5, 1957, MS 2341 5:1, Clarence L. Jordan Papers.

57. Telegram from Coretta Scott King, Oct. 30, 1969, MS 2341 2:5, Clarence L. Jordan Papers.

58. Hollyday, ed., *Clarence Jordan: Essential Writings*, 15.

59. K'Meyer, *Interracialism and Christian Community*, 33; Jordan, "Christian Community in the South," *Journal of Religious Thought*, AR 39 1.10, Clarence Jordan Collection; Parham, "Reconciler from 'Dixie': Clarence Jordan," *Baptist Peacemaker* July 1983, 6, AR 39, 1.1, Clarence Jordan Collection.. It is worth noting that while the Koinonians' primary understanding of racial equality was theological, Jordan sharply disagreed, even from a secular perspective, with notions of racial difference. He wrote to the *Baptist Student* in 1941, "The penetrating eye of science has been unable to see anything in the human race to justify placing a blue ribbon upon any branch of it. . . . From the purely scientific standpoint, then, we might well suspect that Southern tradition has been guilty of error"(MS 756 1:13, Clarence L. Jordan Papers).

60. "Koinonia Farm," promotional brochure, MS 2341 4:9, Clarence L. Jordan Papers.

61. Koinonia Newsletter, Koinonia Farm Archive.

62. Williams, *By Faith and by Love*, 67; Various Correspondence, MS 756 2:6, MS 756 2:7, Clarence L. Jordan Papers;

63. Auchmutey, *Class of '65*, 15.

64. Koinonia Commitment and Creed, MS 2341 4:11, Clarence L. Jordan Papers. The Koinonia Commitment reads: "We desire to make known our total unconditional commitment to seek, express, and expand the kingdom of God as revealed in Jesus Christ. Being convinced that the community of believers who make a like commitment is the continuing body of Jesus on earth, I joyfully enter into a love union with the Koinonia and gladly submit myself to it, looking to it to guide me in the knowledge of God's will and to strengthen me in pursuit of it."

65. Auchmutey, *Class of '65*, 11.

66. Koinonia Meeting minutes, MS 2341 4: 16, Clarence L. Jordan Papers. In 1949, the group had a prolonged and vigorous discussion of whether to purchase insurance. Some felt it was "a matter of whether you have to fall on the world to support you, or whether you can depend on God to meet your every need." Others, though, "felt other responsibilities." Even issues as mundane as insurance proved difficult when seeking "a common mind," but the Koinonians tried and often succeeded.

67. "Field Work—Howard, Cattle—Jack, Poultry—Clarence, Building and Maintenance—Harry," "household work" fell to the women. Koinonia Schedule 1949, MS.2341 4:16, Clarence L. Jordan Papers.

68. Koinonia Schedule 1949, MS 2341 4:16, Clarence L. Jordan Papers.

69. Conflict in the community could be either interpersonal or institutional. Much of it centered around the Jordans' role. Although these tensions were not unusual for communal living, they produced difficult moments at the farm (Various correspondence, MS 756 3:1, Clarence L. Jordan Papers).

70. Bonhoeffer, *Life Together*.

71. Clarence was a popular speaker from his seminary days, and he continued to have speaking engagements throughout the country at churches, college campuses, and Baptist meetings. Often, people were moved by these presentations and decided to move to Koinonia; this included members Henry Dunn, Howard Johnson, Willie Pugh, Harry Atkinson, Con Browne, Jack Singletary, and Millard Hunt.

72. Nelson, "Why We Are Withdrawing from the World," 12, AR 39 1.4.

73. Jordan, AR 39 1:1; Auchmutey, *Class of '65*, 16.

74. Angry, *My Life Changing and Growing*, 11; Koinonia Farm Archive.

75. K'Meyer, *Interracialism and Christian Community*, 50.

76. Letter from Ethel Miller to Con Browne, July 19, 1955, MS 756 3:3, Clarence L. Jordan Papers; Letter from Ethel Miller to Con Browne March 8, 1956, MS 756 3:3, Clarence L. Jordan Papers.

77. Lee, *Cotton Patch Evidence*, 42.

78. Interview with Martin England, Baylor Institute for Oral History, July–Sept. 1984, 43.

79. Lee, *Cotton Patch Evidence*; Auchmutey, *Class of '65*, 16.

80. *Chicago Daily News*, Aug. 7, 1965, MS 2341 3:6, Clarence L. Jordan Papers.

81. See Patterson, *Brown vs. Board of Education*; Bartley, *Rise of Massive Resistance*. In Americus, a States' Rights Chapter was formed in February 1956 (*Americus Times-Recorder*, Feb. 4, 1956).

82. Author's interview with Teresa Mansfield.

83. MS 756 3:6, Clarence L. Jordan Papers. Jim Weldon, the pastor of the Oak Grove Methodist Church in Atlanta, was the other sponsor. "They had not been put up by the NAACP, nor were their motives to test any laws. They simply wanted the courses," Jordan said. "Their plan," he continued, "was to assume that they were American citizens like everyone else . . . to get in line with everyone else and register for the courses they wanted."

84. Oddly enough, the Board of Regents ruled that Clarence was ineligible as a signatory because he had technically graduated from a different school in the UGA system, the College of Arts and Sciences. In the end, Clarence was unable to serve as an alumni sponsor, but the incident reveals the difficulty, even after the Supreme Court ruling, many black students had in obtaining alumni sponsors and enrolling.

85. *Americus Times-Recorder*, March 24, 1956.

86. Lee, *Cotton Patch Evidence*, 112. Conservative organizations, like the States' Rights Council Burgamy addressed, gained momentum throughout the South, promising "a social boycott of 'the scalawags and carpetbaggers of the modern era' who fail or refuse to join in the fight to preserve segregation" ("White Citizens Council Rally Attacks," *Americus Times-Recorder*, June 23, 1955).

87. *Chicago Daily News*, Aug. 7, 1965, MS 2341 3:6, Clarence L. Jordan Papers.

88. *Atlanta Constitution*, Jan. 29, 1958, quoted in Koinonia Farm Newsletter, 1958, Koinonia Archive.

89. K'Meyer, *Interracialism and Christian Community*, 85.

90. *Chicago Daily News*, Aug. 7, 1965, MS 2341 3:6, Clarence L. Jordan Papers.

91. Lee, *Cotton Patch Evidence*, 106.

92. See Fried, *Nightmare in Red*; Kutler, *American Inquisition*; Schrecker, *Age of McCarthyism*; Whitfield, *Culture of the Cold War*.

93. The investigation, of course, found no evidence of any of this. *Americus Times-Recorder*, Feb. 1957.

94. Letter from Jordan to Howard and Marion, March 29, 1957, MS 756 4:5, Clarence L. Jordan Papers; "Griffin Changes Mind and Signs Koinonia Bill," *Americus Times-Recorder*, March 27, 1958; K'Meyer, *Interracialism and Christian Community*, 90.

95. Letter from Con Browne to Ashton and Marie, July 10, 1956, MS 756 3:7, Clarence L. Jordan Papers.

96. Lee, *Cotton Patch Evidence*, 131; interview with Jordan, Jan. 16, 1967, in Deatrick, "Koinonia," 61.

97. Lee, *Cotton Patch Evidence*, 110–30; Byron, "Courage in Action: Koinonia Revisited," *The Nation*, 84, March 16, 1957, 226–28; AR 39:1.4; "Statement of Koinonia Farm: In response to Sumter County Grand Jury Presentments," 1–7, AR 39:1.24; Lee, *Cotton Patch Evidence*, 136. Koinonia sent a full statement of defense to the *Americus Times Recorder*. When the paper refused to publish it, the Koinonians printed the document and mailed it to every address in the Americus-Sumter County phonebook (*Americus Times-Recorder*, 1957, Koinonia Farm Archive).

98. Nicholas von Hoffman, "Clarence Jordan: A Rights Hero in Faded Blue Denim," *Chicago Daily News*, August 7, 1965, MS 2341 1:1; Clarence L. Jordan Papers. See also: Correspondence, MS 756 4:3, Clarence L. Jordan Papers; Koinonia Newsletters; "Local Ministers Attack Koinonia Farm Violence," *Americus-Times Recorder*, Jan. 17, 1957; "State Church Council Backs Americus Group," *Americus Times-Recorder*, Feb. 2, 1957; MS 2340, Clarence L. Jordan Papers; "Churches to Back Anti-Bias Groups," *New York Times*, March 1, 1957; "Violence Has No Place in Sumter's Problem," *Atlanta Journal Constitution*, Feb. 2, 1957; "Violence Must Be Stopped," *Americus Times-Recorder*, Feb. 20, 1957; "Special Report: Koinonia Updated," *Christian Century*, 868, AR 391.9; Auchmutey, *Class of '65*, 55–65.

99. Edgar Stoess, a voluntary service director, who was solicited to offer financial advice to Koinonia, estimated in a letter to Jordan that the Farm had suffered a 10,000 dollar loss for the past three years due to the boycott. On top of the economic distress caused by the boycott, the Farm had suffered severe financial losses from the violence destruction of their products. Estimations of losses from bombings, bullets, and arson from 1956–1957 add up to $12, 475, a significant sum (Letter from Stoess to Jordan, 1957, MS 756 4:3, Clarence L. Jordan Papers).

100. Lee, *Cotton Patch Evidence*, 111.

101. Koinonia Newsletter, quoted in Lee, 114.

102. Lee, *Cotton Patch Evidence*, 143

103. Nicholas von Hoffman, "Clarence Jordan: A Rights Hero in Faded Blue Denim," *Chicago Daily News*, August 7, 1965, MS 2341 3:6; Clarence L. Jordan Papers.

104. *Koinonia Farm Newsletter* 1957, Koinonia Archive; Various Correspondence, 1956 MS 756 3:8, MS 756 3:9, Clarence L. Jordan Papers; Various correspondence, 1957, MS 756 4:1, MS 756 4:2, Clarence L. Jordan Papers; Various Correspondence, 1963, MS 2341 1:1, Clarence L. Jordan Papers; "Freedom: The Christian Concept" George H. Wright, Report of the Council on Christian Relations to the 97th General Assembly, MS 2341 5:1, Clarence L. Jordan Papers; Lee, *Cotton Patch Evidence*, 111. The pecan business proved quite successful. The farm sent out mailings with requests to help them "ship the nuts out of Georgia!" and donations poured in. News of the farm's plight also increased sales, with stories appearing in the *Denver Post*, *Newsweek*, *Christian Century*, the *Southern Patriot*, the *Wall Street Journal*, and even an ABC news report.

105. See "Store Dynamited Here Monday Night," "Force and Coercion Not Condoned," *Americus Times-Recorder* July 24, 1956. "Bi-Racial Farm Project Blasted," *Washington Post*, July 25, 1956; "Exploding Bomb from Moving Vehicle Destroys Interracial Farm Store," *Pittsburgh Courier*, Aug. 4, 1956; "Other Cheek Is Turned in Georgia Bombing," *Christian Century* 73:34, Aug. 1956, 965; "An Open Letter from Koinonia Farm," *Americus Times-Recorder*, Aug. 2, 1956; "What Is Koinonia," *Americus Times-Recorder*, Aug. 8, 1956; "Solicitor Asks Revival of KKK at States' Rights Meet Here," *Albany Journal*, Aug. 3, 1956.

106. Lee, *Cotton Patch Evidence*, 117.

107. Interview with Jordan, Jan. 16, 1967, in Deatrick, "Koinonia," 60.

108. K'Meyer, *Interracialism and Christian Community*, 87.

109. Lee, *Cotton Patch Evidence*, 124.

110. Letter from Con Browne to Ashton and Marie, July 10, 1956, Letter from Con Browne, July 24, 1956, MS 756 3:7, Clarence L. Jordan Papers; *Koinonia Farm Newsletter*, July 26, 1956,

Nov. 23, 1956, Jan. 18, 1957; K'Meyer, *Interracialism and Christian Community*, 86; Chancey, "Restructuring Southern Society," 47.

111. "Special Report: Koinonia Updated," *Christian Century*, 868, AR 39 1.9, Clarence Jordan Collection.

112. "Local Ministers Attack Koinonia Farm Violence," *Americus Times- Recorder*, Jan. 17, 1957; "State Church Council Backs Americus Group," *Americus Times-Recorder*, Feb. 2, 1957; "Churches to Back Anti-Bias Groups," *New York Times*, March 1, 1957. "Violence Has No Place in Sumter's Problem," *Atlanta Constitution*, Feb. 2, 1957; "Violence Must Be Stopped," *Americus Times-Recorder*, Feb. 20, 1957; Koinonia Newsletter, Feb. 10, 1957, MS 2341 4:7, Clarence L. Jordan Papers.

113. *Americus Times-Recorder*, May 1957; Lee, *Cotton Patch Evidence*, 145–46.

114. At this point, the fellowship included around sixty people, forty-five of them white and fifteen of them black. This was likely the peak of Koinonia's population in the civil rights era, as violence limited activities, and deterred new members, particularly black ones (Clarence Jordan letter to Dwight D. Eisenhower, 1957, MS 2341 5:1, Clarence L. Jordan Papers).

115. Various correspondence, March 1957, MS 756 4:4; Letter from Jordan to Howard and Marion, March 29, 1957, MS 756 4:5, Clarence L. Jordan Papers.

116. Eugene Lipman, "By the Way: Report on a Siege," *The Christian Century*, Feb. 25, 1959, 233–235, AR 39:1.9, Clarence Jordan Collection; "Koinonia Farm under Siege," *Christian Century*, Feb. 20, 1957, 219; *Koinonia Farm Newsletter*, April 24, 1957, Koinonia Farm Archive; K'Meyer, *Interracialism and Christian Community*, 86.

117. "A Witness to History at Civil Rights Frontier," *Philadelphia Inquirer*, Aug. 2008, Koinonia Farm Archive.

118. Lee, *Cotton Patch Evidence*, 122.

119. Newsletter 1957, Koinonia Farm Archive.

120. Campbell, "Where There's So Much Smoke," *Soujourners*, 1979, 19, Koinonia Farm Archive.

121. The Koinonians corresponded with a number of other intentional communities—a Fellowship of Intentional Communities—including Koinonia Farm, Hidden Springs Community, Kingwood Community, Tuelumne Farm, Celebrook Cooperative Community, Cele Community, Quest, Tanguy Homesteads, Macedonia Cooperative Community, Haines Turner (MS 756 2:15, Clarence L. Jordan Papers). In many ways, those most affected were perhaps the children of Koinonia who faced ridicule in school each day (see Auchmutey, *Class of '65*).

122. Angry, *My Life Changing and Growing*, 13.

123. Day, "On Pilgrimage-May 1957," 3, 6.

124. Letter from Jordan to President Dwight Eisenhower, Jan. 1957, MS 2341 5:1, Clarence L. Jordan Papers; letter to Rev. Sam Brown from Maxwell Rabb, Aug. 7, 1957, MS 756 4:10, Clarence L. Jordan Papers.

125. Lipman, "By the Way," 233–35, AR 39:1.9, Clarence Jordan Collection; Lee, *Cotton Patch Evidence*, 120.

126. The Koinonians also contacted the Georgia Bureau of Investigations and the Federal Bureau of Investigation after discovering that some of the bullets from attacks on the farm were fired from a machine gun, necessarily government issue. "If United States weapons

were being used against citizens in peacetime" they thought, "it was a violation of federal law and the FBI could get involved." It turns out there was a connection between the guns and the National Guard, which was confirmed by the fact that many of the attacks occurred on Monday nights, following the weekly meetings of the local National Guard (K'Meyer, *Interracialism and Christian Community*, 89).

127. This delegation included J. R. Blair, Frank Bowen, Tom Clark, Charles Crisp, George Mathews, Frank Myers, Jimmie Lott, J. P. Luther, and J. H. Robinson representing (in no particular order) the president of the Bank of Commerce, president of the Chamber of Commerce, the leading attorneys, the mayor, the editor of the *Americus Times-Recorder*, and major businessmen.

128. This meeting was supposedly recorded on a cassette tape. See Faith Fuller, "Briars in the Cottonpatch"; Lee, *Cotton Patch Evidence*, 147–48.

129. Lee, *Cotton Patch Evidence*, 153.

130. Lee, 115, 39; letter to Claud, Billie, Marion, and Howard, March 30, 1956, MS 756 3:6, Clarence L. Jordan Papers; letter to Koinonia, Nov. 20, 1957, MS 756 4:13, Clarence L. Jordan Papers.

131. Author's interview with Sam Mahone.

132. "A New Venture: Koinonia Partners, Koinonia Farm," *The Baptist Student*, Nov. 1969, 42–43, AR 39:1.4, Clarence Jordan Collection.

133. Letter from Clarence Jordan to Hallock Hoffman, Nov. 27, 1957, MS 2340, Clarence L. Jordan Papers; K'Meyer, *Interracialism and Christian Community*, 97.

134. Quoted in Tuck, *Beyond Atlanta*, 176.

135. The local newspaper claimed Jordan used "peppery Dixie language," and that the translations were full of "quaint idioms" ("Jordan Publishes New Bible," *Americus Times-Recorder*, Feb. 9, 1965, MS 2341 1.14, Clarence L. Jordan Papers); Lee, *Cotton Patch Evidence*, 18; Hollyday, ed., *Clarence Jordan: Essential Writings*, 33; Jordan, *Cottonpatch Translations*; MS 756 7:1, Clarence L. Jordan Papers; "Jordan Publishes New Bible," *Americus Times-Recorder*, Feb. 9, 1968, 5; MS 2341 1:14, Clarence L. Jordan Papers. Many of the epistles are published several times and in different volumes. By the time of his death in 1969, Jordan had published *Cottonpatch* versions of Mark and John's Gospels and several of the Epistles of Paul.

136. Jordan, "Dipped in the Chattahoochee," *Cottonpatch Translations*, 40; Jordan, "And Laid Him in an Apple Box"; Hollyday, ed., *Clarence Jordan: Essential Writings*, 40. Some detested Jordan's liberties in translation. "The author should be shot for making such a mockery of the Scriptures," one particularly upset Illinois reader wrote. "If I were you I'd burn all copies—that way you might get a small idea of what it will be like in hell. For anyone who is an infidel to write such trash will end up in hell" (Lee, *Cotton Patch Evidence*, 184). Another man wrote a review which stated that Jordan's translation "literally violated" the Bible. He called it "propaganda," a "twisting and changing of the Holy Scriptures . . . characteristic of the liberal, leftist movement" (Carl McIntire, "New Version Destroys Christianity," *The Christian Beacon*, Mar. 14, 1968, MS 2341 1:13, Clarence L. Jordan Papers).

137. Jordan, *Cottonpatch Translations*, 54, 92, 100; Lee, *Cotton Patch Evidence*, 188–90.

138. Lee, *Cotton Patch Evidence*, 190.

139. Pieces from Jordan's translation appeared in the *Church Advocate*, the *Mennonite*, and many others. The play, performed by Tom Key, opened off-Broadway and has been

performed consistently for the last thirty years (Various records, MS 2340 3:11–16, MS 2340 4:1–3, 6, Clarence L. Jordan Papers).

Chapter Two

1. "Onward Christian Soldiers" (1865), Baptist Hymnal 1956 #412; author's interview with Ben Easterlin.

2. At the time, in the early 1960s, First Baptist had about 500–600 members according to one churchgoer. Author's interview with Marion Hicks and Kelso Gooden.

3. First Baptist meeting minutes; Alan Anderson, *Journey of Grace*, 144.

4. Interview with Roy Parker, Sumter County Oral History Project.

5. "Onward Christian Soldiers" (1865), Baptist Hymnal 1956 #412.

6. Williford, *Americus through the Years*, 282.

7. First Baptist was originally called Bethel Baptist. It changed its name to Americus Baptist in 1882, then to First Americus Baptist in 1897, and finally to First Baptist Church of Americus in 1898. For consistency and clarity's sake, I will use the current name of churches (Georgia Baptist Church records, Mercer University).

8. For more on antebellum churches and race, see Mathews, *Religion in the Old South*; Genovese, *Roll, Jordan, Roll*; Irons, *Origins of Proslavery Christianity*; Raboteau, *Slave Religion*.

9. Mission efforts targeted both foreign lands and other parts of America, including efforts to minister to rural blacks in 1852 and to Choctaw Indians in 1857. *First Baptist Records*, Lake Blackshear Library, Americus, Ga., 13.

10. C. F. Giddings, *Americus Times-Recorder*, Dec. 8, 1931; Williford, *Americus through the Years*, 34.

11. United States, 1840: Sumter County, Ga. (Microfilm #1352, vol. 8, Atlanta Public Library; Rev. George C. Smith, *History of Georgia Methodism*, 207; Williford, *Americus through the Years*, 35, 41).

12. Giddings, *Americus Times-Recorder*, Dec. 8, 1931; Williford, *Americus through the Years*, 252.

13. Burnett, *History of the Americus Presbyterian Church*; Mrs. Lillie N. Thurman "First Presbyterian Church of Americus, Georgia: Historical Summary: 1842–2008," First Presbyterian Church Archives, Americus, Ga., 2009.

14. Sherwood, *A Gazetteer of Georgia*, 122; Williford, *Americus through the Years*, 35. Mrs. Lillie N. Thurman, "First Presbyterian Church of Americus, Georgia: Historical Summary: 1842–2008," First Presbyterian Church Archives, Americus, Ga., 2009.

15. Mrs. Lillie N. Thurman, "First Presbyterian Church of Americus, Georgia: Historical Summary: 1842–2008," First Presbyterian Church Archives, Americus, Ga., 2009; *Americus City Record Book*, book 1, 358.

16. This church structure, including the original bell, is the oldest extant church building in Americus. Mrs. Lillie N. Thurman, "First Presbyterian Church of Americus, Georgia: Historical Summary: 1842–2008," First Presbyterian Church Archives, Americus, Ga., 2009.

17. Other denominations less common in the Black Belt of the South slowly won adherents in Americus as new residents settled in the area. In April 1853, Episcopalian Bishop Stephen

Elliot visited Americus, and eight Episcopalians "decided to band together and form a mission church," which met at the home of Ambrose Spencer. In 1921, a First Christian Church was formally organized, though it remained small. While most religious practitioners in Americus were Protestant, there were some Catholics. In the 1880s, several families began holding services in the home of Mr. and Mrs. Christopher J. Sherlock and a decade later, formally organized into St. Mary's Catholic Church, of the Savannah diocese (Williford, *Americus through the Years*, 63–64, 185, 282; Lawrence, *History of Calvary Church*, 13; Malone, *Episcopal Church in Georgia*, 91; *Americus Times-Recorder*, Dec. 8, 1931).

18. With news of World War II's end, Georgia Governor Ellis Arnall urged citizens to "thank God that victory has come." Americus residents did so by planning a joint service at First Methodist ("Arnall Urges 'Thank God'"; "V-J Plans for the City Revealed"; "V-J Church Service Time Is Explained," *Americus Times-Recorder*, Aug. 14, 1945).

19. Ketcham and Landis, eds., *Yearbook of American Churches*, in Hudnut-Beumler, *Looking for God in the Suburbs*, Table 2.1, 32. See May, *Homeward Bound*; May, "Cold War, Warm Hearth."

20. Letter from Pastor C. L. Leopard to Friends, First Baptist Church, Americus, Ga., March 19, 1957.

21. Author's interview with Ben Easterlin.

22. Author's interview with Martha Wood.

23. Crespino, *In Search of Another Country*, 277.

24. Crespino, *In Search of Another Country*, 66.

25. Marsden, *Fundamentalism and American Culture*.

26. James Hudnut-Beumler formalizes this split as one between popular religion, ecclesiastical religion, and elite religion, while Paul Harvey designates a separate ecclesiastical theology and "folk theology." See Hudnut-Beumler, *Looking for God in the Suburbs*, 79; Harvey, *Freedom's Coming*, 229–45. See also Dupont, *Mississippi Praying*, 80.

27. The Foundational Documents of the United Methodist Church, *Confession of Faith* (1962); *Articles of Religion of the Methodist Church*, V (1794); The Southern Baptist Convention, "Basic Beliefs," http://www.sbc.net/aboutus/basicbeliefs.asp.

28. Author's interview with Ben Easterlin.

29. Harvey, *Redeeming the South*, 1; Colossians 3:22; Ephesians 6:5.

30. Noll, *Civil War as a Theological Crisis*, 33.

31. Andrews, *The War-Time Journal of a Georgia Girl, 1864–1865*, 1908. During the war, Andrews actually lived near Americus in Southwest Georgia. See also Fox-Genovese and Genovese, *Mind of the Master Class*.

32. Harvey, "God and Jesus," 286.

33. Noll, *Civil War as a Theological Crisis*, 45.

34. Williford, *Americus through the Years*, 110.

35. See Blum, *Reforging the White Republic*; Blight, *Race and Reunion*.

36. Haynes, "Distinction and Dispersal," http://jsreligion.org/issues/vol17/haynes.html.

37. Some scholars, like David Chappell, claim that the arguments made to defend slavery "offered so little objective support" for segregation, and thus were not made as forcefully. Others, like Carolyn Dupont, Charles Marsh, and Steve Haynes, emphasize continuities in thought and interpretation. See Chappell, *Stone of Hope*, 112; Dupont, *Mississippi Praying*; Marsh, *Beloved Community*; and Haynes, "Distinction and Dispersal." See also Noll,

"Review of *Freedom's Coming*," *Journal of the American Academy of Religion* 75, no. 2 (June 2007): 473–77.

38. Genesis 6:10.

39. Genesis 9:18.

40. Genesis 9:24–27.

41. Genesis 10:6, 10:6–20.

42. The Hamitic hypothesis has a long history, both as anthropological and theological theory, first in the Talmudic tradition and then in the Christian. As Edith Sanders has written, since "ideas have a way of being accepted when they become useful as a rationalization of an economic fact of life," the Hamitic hypothesis increased in popularity as enslavement proved lucrative. It "clearly meant that the Negro was preordained for slavery . . . a state of the world created by the Almighty" (Sanders, "Hamitic Hypothesis," 523–24). See also Evans, "From the Land of Canaan to the Land of Guinea," 15–43; Fox-Genovese and Genovese, *Mind of the Master Class*, 521–26; Goldenberg, *Curse of Ham*; Graves and Patai, *Hebrew Myths*, 121; Haynes, *Noah's Curse*.

43. See Fox-Genovese and Genovese, *Mind of the Master Class*, 521–26; Graves and Patai, *Hebrew Myths*, 121; Sanders, "Hamitic Hypothesis," 522.

44. Haynes, "Distinction and Dispersal." Haynes catalogues important differences in interpretation surrounding Genesis 9–11.

45. Maston, *Segregation and Desegregation*, 99.

46. Ezell, *Christian Problem of Racial Segregation*, 14.

47. In both Psalm 105 and 106, Daniel exposited, Egypt and Africa are termed "the land of Ham" while Genesis chronicles that "Japheth and his posterity were given 'the isles of the Gentiles.'" Daniel explained: "the world 'isles' here means 'coasts' or 'settlements,' and the phrase 'the isles of the Gentiles' is further defined in Isaiah 41:1–5 and 49:1–6 as including all territories "to the end of the earth." In other words, Ham's descendants could have Africa and Egypt, and Japheth's children were to have all the rest of the world. This exegesis provided proof in Daniel's estimation that America, being one of the isles to the end of the earth, rightfully belonged to white people. Daniel explains that these biblical passages "also belie the vile slander that our forefathers 'stole' this country from the Indians, those wandering tribes who had no organized nation, and whom our ancestors were compelled to fight in defense of their wives and children" (Daniel, *God the Original Segregationist*, 9).

48. Daniel, *God the Original Segregationist*, 3, capitalization his.

49. Crespino, *In Search of Another Country*, 66.

50. Barnett in *New York Times*, Nov. 7, 1987; Crespino, *In Search of Another Country*, 69. This view extended across the Mason-Dixon line. Rev. M. William Trott of Ephart, Pennsylvania, affirmed the segregationist stance of the South, writing, "This is God's command—to keep the races segregated. We believe in segregation here at my church, but many churches here [in Pennsylvania] do not" (1965 Box Collection, First Methodist Church Archives, [hereafter FUMC box], 197).

51. FUMC box, 2. The letter is sent from Toledo but the author claims, "I am from Tennessee and I am white."

52. G. T. Gillespie, "A Christian View on Segregation," Address given to the Synod of Mississippi, Nov. 4, 1954; L. B. McCord, quoted in Crespino, *In Search of Another Country*, 67; Daniel, *God the Original Segregationist*, 6; Dailey, "Sex, Segregation, and the Sacred," 156.

53. This passage was invoked on both sides. Integrationists frequently cited Paul's statement that God "has made from one man every nation of mankind," while segregationists chastised them for failing to read the second half of the verse, which reads, "having determined allotted periods and the boundaries of their dwelling place" (Acts 17:22–28).

54. Gillespie, "Christian View on Segregation," 11.

55. Matthew 5:17–18.

56. Daniel, *God the Original Segregationist*, 11; Blum and Harvey, *Color of Christ*, 108.

57. Letter from Mrs. West to Virginia Gov. Thomas Stanley, in Dailey, "Sex, Segregation, and the Sacred," 133.

58. Since "the question of biblical provenance of their traditions and taboos was for many white southerners, a subject of great soul-searching," David Chappell has argued, Christian segregationism cannot be dismissed as "simply propaganda" (Chappell, "Disunity and Religious Institutions").

59. Crespino, *In Search of Another Country*, 64.

60. While the term "fundamentalist" comes with its own cache of connotations, for our purposes it primarily indicates a belief in certain dogmas thought to be essential to Christian faith and practice, as well as, as George Marsden put it, a "militant anti-modernist" form of Protestantism (Marsden, *Fundamentalism in American Culture*, 4). Also, though not the emphasis of the movement, fundamentalism undeniably interacts with race. As Bill Leonard aptly summarized: "While fundamentalism itself is not inherently racist, the southern fundamentalists . . . expressed their own racist sentiments largely through the medium of their fundamentalist theology" (Leonard, "Theology for Racism," 49). See also Ballmer, *The Making of Evangelicalism*; Martin, *With God on Our Side*; Marsden, *Fundamentalism in American Culture*; Carpenter, *Revive Us Again*; Dollar, *A History of Fundamentalism in America*; Hankins, *American Evangelicals*.

61. Torrey, preface to *Fundamentals*.

62. Martin, *With God on Our Side*, 11.

63. See Flowers, *Into the Pulpit*, 34–35.

64. See Larson, *Summer for the Gods*; Moran, *Scopes Trial*; Olasky and Perry, *Monkey Business*; *Americus Times-Recorder*, July 13, 1925; Mencken, "Scopes Monkey Trial," July 18, 1925; Marsden, *Fundamentalism and American Culture*, 185–88; Wood, *Flannery O'Connor*.

65. See Eighmy, *Churches in Cultural Captivity*, 157.

66. "Rev. Richard Simpson, Pastor Americus Presbyterian Church, Discusses Evolution," *Americus Times-Recorder*, July 22, 1925.

67. Crespino, *In Search of Another Country*, 64.

68. The National Council of Churches, which came out of the Federal Council of Churches, was established in 1950 and included thirty-three Protestant and Orthodox denominations (*Baptist Faith and Message* [1963]). See *Annual of the Southern Baptist Convention, 1963* (Nashville, Tenn.: Southern Baptist Convention, 1963), 269–81; Mohler, "Southern Baptist Convention and the Issue of Interdenominational Relationships," A Memorandum Prepared for the Great Commission Council of the Southern Baptist Convention, 2009.

69. Letter from Mr. W. E. Bell Smith Towson to Bishop John O. Smith, John O. Smith Papers, Emory University, MSS 242 box 7. See Crespino, *In Search of Another Country*, 156–57; Fried, *Nightmare in Red*; Kutler, *American Inquisition*; Schrecker, *Age of McCarthyism*; Whitfield, *Culture of the Cold War*.

70. Chappell, "Disunity and Religious Institutions," 141.

71. Baptists especially held this individualistic view of church governance. As Paul Harvey attests, Southerners "found in both their white and black Baptist churches a powerful theological and ecclesiastical tradition—congregational independence—that taught that God had sanctioned local men and women to run their own spiritual affairs and implied that they were meant to control their own destinies" (Harvey, *Redeeming the South*, 4; see also Eighmy, *Churches in Cultural Captivity*, xix–xx).

72. "MLK Question Response on Ministry and Segregation," the King Center Digital Archive, http://www.thekingcenter.org/archive/document/mlk-question-response-ministry -and-segregation.

73. Newman, *Getting Right with God*, 20–25.

74. *Americus Times-Recorder*, June 6, 1956; Williford, *Americus through the Years*, 333.

75. "Lee St. Methodist Warns against Mass Withdrawals in Church's New Policies," *Americus Times-Recorder*, Feb. 23, 1957, MS 756, Clarence L. Jordan Papers.

76. In 1861, the Southern Presbyterians split with their Northern brethren over slavery and secession; their different views on race and the role of the church and the nation carried on well into the twentieth century. In time, the Southern Presbyterians (PCUS) who remained separate from the National Presbyterian Church faced controversy within their own body. In 1954, the General Assembly, the official governing board of the Southern Presbyterian Church, stated that there should be no racial division within the church. This led, predictably, to controversy within the PCUS. Three factions emerged: a liberal faction that advocated adoption of civil rights initiatives, a moderate faction that wished to see agreement and consensus, and a conservative faction that strongly opposed any civil rights stance by the church, thus maintaining the segregated status quo. Eventually, the groups split, with the liberal wing joining the Northern Presbyterians in 1983 and the conservatives forming a new Presbyterian denomination in 1973. (See Alvis, *Religion and Race*; Blackwelder, "Southern White Fundamentalists and the Civil Rights Movement"; Lucas, *For a Continuing Church*.)

77. Dupont, *Mississippi Praying*, 41. See also Crespino, *In Search of Another Country*.

78. Author's interview with Ben Easterlin.

79. Feldman, *Politics, Society and the Klan*, 312–13, 318, 319.

80. First Baptist Church Bulletin, First Baptist Church Archive, Americus, Ga., Feb. 25, 1962.

81. Author's interview with Ben Easterlin.

82. First Baptist Church Bulletin, First Baptist Church Archive, Americus, Ga., Feb. 25, 1962.

83. Bill Rittenhouse, a native Georgian, World War II Air Corps bomber pilot, and former POW, was one of Americus's favorite preacher-evangelists. While in a prison camp, "he answered the call to preach the Christian Gospel" and went to UNC and Duke Divinity School upon his release. A Southern Baptist, Rittenhouse traveled throughout the state as a full-time evangelist. Frank Boggs, a musician from Texas, often traveled with these evangelists as a full-time "personal singer" (*First Baptist Church Bulletin*, May 9, 1965). Born in 1888, Arthur Moore is one of the most prominent religious figures in Georgia in the twentieth century. In addition to his work pastoring in the Methodist Church nationwide, Moore was highly sought after as a traveling evangelist. He wrote eight books, served on the board

of many ministries, began the retreat center Epworth By the Sea, and founded a devotional series, *The Upper Room*. See Gramling, *Ministry of Hope*; Moore, *Bishop to All Peoples*.

84. Author's interview with Ben Easterlin. "The Sinner's Prayer" is a short prayer prevalent in evangelical Protestantism that signals conversion to Christianity.

85. The term "born again" has its roots primarily in the Gospel of John when Jesus said, "Unless one is born of water and the Spirit, he cannot enter the kingdom of God. That which is born of the flesh is flesh, and that which is born of the Spirit is spirit. Do not marvel that I said to you, 'You must be born again'" (John 3:5–8).

86. From the early Puritans who hesitated to depict Christ physically to the explosion of mass-marketing images of Christ in the twentieth century, Americans' portrayal of Jesus has varied widely. Reflections of Jesus, from stoic to compassionate, brawny to effeminate, rugged to corporate, have reflected preferences and power in American life. (See Blum and Harvey, *Color of Christ*; Prothero, *American Jesus*; Fox, *Jesus in America*; Nichols, *Jesus*.)

87. Carter, *Race*.

88. Blum and Harvey, *Color of Christ*, 8, 10–11.

89. Author's interview with Kellete Heys.

90. Warner Sallman's 1941 work, *Head of Christ*, adorned the walls of Sunday school classrooms, sat on bedroom nightstands, and even came in a wallet size so Jesus could actually be physically with you "to the end of the age." By 1944, just three years after the portrait's creation, 14 million prints of *Head of Christ* had been distributed in the United States. By the 1990s, Sallman's portrait of Christ had been printed more than 500 million times and "had achieved global iconic status." So iconic was Sallman's Jesus that it was "the literal face of Jesus to many" (Blum and Harvey, *Color of Christ*, 12, 211).

91. Quoted in Marsh, *God's Long Summer*, 55–90. See also Sparks, *Religion in Mississippi*, 228–31.

92. Lee, *Cotton Patch Evidence*, 74–81; "Relationship with Community Churches," MS 2340, Clarence L. Jordan Papers; "Koinonia Members' Expulsion from Rehoboth Baptist Church," 1950; Ira B. Faglier to Clarence Jordan, Aug. 9, 1950, MS 756 2:13, Clarence L. Jordan Papers; "Recommendation to the Board of Deacons of Rehoboth Baptist Church," 1950; Deatrick, "Koinonia." Some Georgia Baptists disagreed with Rehoboth's decision, which caused a minor stir. An account of the incident was published in the *Christian Century*, Sept. 6, 1950, after which appeared a few letters of support. The following month, in September 1950, a group of faculty members at Mercer sent an open letter to be read to the Rehoboth congregation. It requested that action be taken to "rectify" the situation and to "establish reconciliation," though the letter also affirmed the congregation's autonomy, saying they "did not intend to interfere with your affairs" and "prized" the church's authority (MS 756 2:14, Clarence L. Jordan Papers).

93. K'Meyer, *Interracialism and Christian Community*, 60.

94. "Local Churched Hits Efforts Opposing Segregation Plan," *Americus Times-Recorder*, Koinonia Farm Archive.

95. "Lee St. Methodist Warns against Mass Withdrawals in Church's New Policies," *Americus Times-Recorder*, Feb. 23, 1957, MS 756, Clarence L. Jordan Papers.

96. Payne, *I've Got the Light of Freedom*, 418.

97. Author's interview with Ben Easterlin.

Chapter Three

1. Interview with Robertiena Freeman Fletcher, Sumter County Oral History Project. Albany is about forty miles from Americus.

2. Much of the debate revolves around what Fredrick Harris has called the opiate theory and the inspiration theory. While some maintain that Christianity placated the masses, functioning as an "opiate of the people," others have recognized the subversive possibilities Christianity offered blacks by inspiring resistance and freedom movements (Harris, *Something Within*, 4–5). See also Evans, *Burden of Black Religion*; Raboteau, *Canaan Land*.

3. Du Bois, *Souls of Black Folk*, 118; Mays and Nicholson, *Negro's Church*, 209–13.

4. Author's interview with Eddie Rhea Walker.

5. Interview with Robertiena Freeman Fletcher, Sumter County Oral History Project.

6. Du Bois, "Problem of Amusement," 1897, reprinted in Green and Driver, eds., *W. E. B. Du Bois*, 228, quoted in Evans, *Burden of Black Religion*, 152. See also Du Bois, *Souls of Black Folk*, 115–25.

7. Author's interview with Karl Wilson.

8. See Raboteau, *Slave Religion*; Genovese, *Roll, Jordan, Roll*; Du Bois, *Negro Church*; Harvey, *Through the Storm*; Woodson, *History of the Negro Church*; Mays, *Negro's God, as Reflected in His Literature*; Herskovitz, *Myth of the Negro Past*; Frazier, *Negro Church in America*; Wilmore, *Black Religion and Black Radicalism*; Frey, "Visible Church"; Lincoln and Mamiya, *Black Church in the African American Experience*.

9. See Du Bois, *Philadelphia Negro* (1899); Mays and Nicholson, *Negro Church*; Frazier, *Negro Church in America*; Hart, Yockley, and Nelsen, eds., *Black Church in America*; Morris, *Origins of the Civil Rights Movement*.

10. Morris, *Origins of the Civil Rights Movement*, 4.

11. Morris, 4.

12. Henderson, *First Baptist Church Americus, Georgia, 1831–1996*, First Baptist Church Archive, Americus, Ga., 6, self-published pamphlet.

13. Henderson, 9.

14. Henderson, 9. Another source states that this was in 1868. "Sumter County Church Chronology," Sumter County, Georgia Genealogy.

15. "History of Bethesda Baptist Church," Lake Blackshear Regional Library Special Collections.

16. Henderson, *First Baptist Church Americus, Georgia*, 9.

17. "History of Bethesda Baptist Church," Lake Blackshear Regional Library Special Collections.

18. "History of Campbell Chapel A.M.E. Church, 1869–1969," Karl Wilson Personal Collection.

19. "Sumter County Church Chronology," Sumter County, Georgia Genealogy. See also handwritten deed, Feb. 26, 1877, Deed Book, 549, Georgia, Sumter County, SC-VF 975, 8913, 342–44; *Sumter Republican*, Jan. 30, 1880, SC-VF 975, 8913.

20. "Campbell Chapel AME," *Americus Times-Recorder*, no date; "Annual Meeting of A.M.E. Group: Colored Ministers Attend Americus Conference in Large Numbers," *Americus Times-Recorder*, Oct. 13, 1922, Karl Wilson Personal Collection.

21. "500 Negro Workers to Attend Meeting: State Sunday School and League Convention to Meet at Campbell Chapel Wednesday," *Americus Times-Recorder*, May 16, 1924; "Prominent Negroes Attend Conference: Many Delegates Here to Participate in Annual Allen Christian Endeavor Meet," *Americus Times-Recorder*, March 26, 1926; "African Bishop Will Speak Here: White People Are Invited and Urged to Hear Negro Bishop Monday Night," *Americus Times-Recorder*, Feb. 2, 1929; "Revival Series at Campbell Chapel"; *Americus Times-Recorder*, Feb. 24, 1931; "Negro Drama Staged Here Moves Audience," *Americus Times-Recorder*, March 28, 1933; "Play at A.M.E. Church Friday," *Americus Times-Recorder*, Aug. 10, 1940; "Negroes Form Public Forum in Americus," *Americus Times-Recorder*, Dec. 14, 1940; "Rev. Wright at Campbell A.M.E. Church on Sunday," *Americus Times-Recorder*, April 8, 1950, Karl Wilson Personal Collection.

22. Author's interview with Eloise Paschal.

23. Some dates are approximate because, in many cases, congregations met before they appeared in official records. This is not an exhaustive list of every church in Americus; there is also at least one Colored Methodist Episcopal (C.M.E.) church in Americus and, since 1946, a black Catholic Church, St. Jerome's.

24. See Raboteau, *Canaan Land*; Logan, *Negro in American Life and Thought*.

25. Thurman, *Luminous Darkness*.

26. See Kidd, *George Whitefield*; Lawrence, *Feast of Tabernacles*; Owen, *Sacred Flame of Love*; Williams, *From Mounds to Megachurches*.

27. Raboteau, *Slave Religion*, 128, 96–150. See Smith, *Revivalism and Social Reform*; Dickson, *And They All Sang Hallelujah*; Stout, *Divine Dramatist*; Ahlstrom, *Religious History of the American People*; Noll, *Rise of Evangelicalism*.

28. Raboteau, *Slave Religion*, 128, 132; Benedict, *General History of the Baptist Denomination*, 739.

29. Harvey, *Through the Storm*, 6; Callahan, *Talking Book*, xiii.

30. See Harding, *There Is a River*; Hahn, *Political Worlds of Slavery and Freedom*; Speicher, *Religious World of Antislavery Women*; Andrews, *Sisters of the Spirit*; Peterson, "*Doers of the Word*."

31. Raboteau, *Slave Religion*, 136–137; Hopkins, "Slave Theology in the 'Invisible Institution,'" 792. See also Jones, *Religious Instruction of the Negro*; Woodson, *History of the Negro Church*; Brooks, "Evolution of the Negro Baptist Church."

32. See Mark, *Negro Songs in the United States*; Scarborough, *On the Trail of Negro Folk-Songs*; Thurman, "Negro Spiritual," 29–49; Thurman, *Deep River*.

33. Mays and Nicholson, *Negro's Church*, 2. See also Johnson, *Book of American Negro Spirituals*; Work, *Folk Songs of the American Negro*.

34. Cone, "Black Spirituals," 775.

35. Edwards, quoted in Rawick, *American Slave*, vol. 5, 6–7; Raboteau, *Slave Religion*, 218.

36. Cone, *Spirituals and the Blues*.

37. Higginson, "Negro Spirituals," *Atlantic Monthly*, June 1867.

38. Reverend Pearlie Brown, quoted in "Resurrection Remix," African American Lectionary, The African American Pulpit and American Bible College, 2008.

39. Thurman, *Deep River*, 36.

40. See Campbell, *Songs of Zion*; Higginbotham, *Righteous Discontent*; Schechter, *Ida B. Wells Barnett*; Angell, *Henry McNeal Turner*; Coan, *Daniel Alexander Payne*; Payne, *Recollections of Seventy Years*; Lewis, *W. E. B. Du Bois*.

41. Campbell, *Songs of Zion*; Gregg, *African Methodist Episcopal Church*; Cone, "God Our Father"; Bailey, *Race Patriotism*.

42. Dickerson, "African American Religious Intellectuals." See also Taylor, *Black Religious Intellectuals*; Young, *Major Black Religious Leaders*; Burkett and Newman, *Black Apostles*.

43. Dickerson, "African American Religious Intellectuals," 219.

44. Dickerson, 220.

45. "Whither the Negro Church?," Seminar at Yale Divinity School, New Haven, Conn., April 13–15, 1931, in Dickerson, "African American Religious Intellectuals," 220–21.

46. As early as 1921, W. E. B. Du Bois recognized the importance of Gandhi, writing about the "Indian saint" in *Crisis*. That same year, the A.M.E. *Church Review* also ran a piece highlighting Gandhi (Dickerson, "African American Religious Intellectuals," 221; Kapur, *Raising Up a Prophet*).

47. From 1935 to 1937, six black religious intellectuals, including Mordecai Johnson, Howard Thurman, and Benjamin Mays, went to India (Dickerson, "African American Religious Intellectuals," 222). See also Dickerson, "William Stuart Nelson."

48. Dickerson, "African American Religious Intellectuals"; Dickerson, lecture, Vanderbilt University, Spring 2010.

49. Dickerson, "African American Religious Intellectuals," 225.

50. Mays and Nicholson, *Negro's Church*, 291–292. This sociological study surveyed 749 rural and urban black churches.

51. Dickerson, "African American Religious Intellectuals," 225; Mays and Nicholson, *Negro's Church*.

52. Mays served as the dean of Howard Divinity School and president of Morehouse College. See Mays, *Born to Rebel*; Jelks, *Benjamin Elijah Mays*. Martin Luther King, James Farmer, and other civil rights leaders studied under the black religious intellectuals at Morehouse, Howard, and elsewhere.

53. This work was edited by William Stuart Nelson and sponsored by the School of Religion at Howard University, where Mays was dean.

54. Nelson, "Preface," Nelson, *Christian Way in Race Relations*, vii.

55. Nelson, "Crucial Issues in America's Race Relations Today," in Nelson, *Christian Way in Race Relations*, 15. Nelson, born in Kentucky in 1895, was educated at Howard University and later at Yale University. He became a professor and later dean at his alma mater, Howard University.

56. Nelson, "Crucial Issues in America's Race Relations Today," in Nelson, *Christian Way in Race Relations*, 25

57. Kelsey, "The Christian Way in Race Relations," in Nelson, *Christian Way in Race Relations*, 38; Robinson, "Social Practices and the Christian Way," in Nelson, *Christian Way in Race Relations*, 97.

58. Mays, "The Obligations of the Individual Christian," in Nelson, *Christian Way in Race Relations*, 223.

59. Thurman, "Judgment and Hope in the Christian Message," in Nelson, *Christian Way in Race Relations*, 233.

60. McKinney, "Judgment and Hope in the Nature of Man and Society," in Nelson, *Christian Way in Race Relations*, 244–45.

61. Thurman, "Judgment and Hope in the Christian Message," in Nelson, *Christian Way in Race Relations*, 235.

62. Dickerson, "African American Religious Intellectuals," 233.

63. Author's interview with Karl Wilson.

64. McKinney, "Judgment and Hope in the Nature of Man and Society," in Nelson, *Christian Way in Race Relations*, 239.

65. Kelsey, *Racism and the Christian Understanding of Man*, 25. While this particular volume was published rather late, in 1965, Kelsey had been teaching these ideas for many decades prior. In 1948, for instance, he wrote: "The concept of the image of God has significant implications for race relations." Kelsey, "Christian Way in Race Relations," in Nelson, *Christian Way in Race Relations*, 30–31.

66. Genesis 1:27, 31.

67. Kelsey, *Racism and the Christian Understanding of Man*, 87.

68. Kelsey, 87.

69. Kelsey, 86.

70. Thurman, "Judgment and Hope in the Christian Message," in Nelson, *Christian Way in Race Relations*, 230.

71. Romans 8:16–17.

72. Kelsey, *Racism and the Christian Understanding of Man*, 91.

73. Martin Luther King Jr., "Lecture at the University of Oslo" (1964).

74. King, "Chapel Address: The Church on the Frontier of Racial Tension," Apr. 19, 1961, Southern Baptist Theological Seminary.

75. King, Christmas sermon, 1967 in *Testament of Hope*, 255.

76. "Americus, GA Conference, 6th Episcopal District, Friday, May 9, 1952," in Official Minutes of the Thirty-Fourth Session of the General Conference of A.M.E Church in Chicago, Illinois, May 1952.

77. Thurman, *Luminous Darkness*, 687.

78. Kelsey, *Racism and the Christian Understanding of Man*, 25.

79. Mays quoted in Colson, *Dr. Benjamin E. Mays Speaks*, 61.

80. Kelsey, *Racism and the Christian Understanding of Man*, 56–57.

81. Kelsey, *Racism and the Christian Understanding of Man*, 72, 158.

82. Colson, *Dr. Benjamin E. Mays Speaks*, 61.

83. Kelsey, *Racism and the Christian Understanding of Man*, 176.

84. Kelsey, 146.

85. See Martin Luther King Jr., "Segregation Is Wrong," Greensboro, North Carolina, July 11, 1963, the King Center Digital Archive.

86. Martin L. King Jr., "Paul's Letter to American Christians," Nov. 4, 1956, Dexter Avenue Baptist Church, Birmingham, Ala. As George Kelsey himself later reflected on King's life and legacy, he asserted that his former student understood "that racism is an idolatrous contradiction of Christian faith," a truth King most certainly learned from the church men and women who taught him. See Kelsey, "Dr. King and the Civil Rights Struggle in Perspective," 28–30, Kelsey Papers, box 3 (notes undated), 2; Dickerson, "African American Religious Intellectuals."

87. "The American Dream," July 4, 1965, in *A Knock at Midnight*, 89. See also "Martin Luther King and the Meanings of Freedom," in King, *Civil Rights and the Idea of Freedom*, 104; Buber, *I and Thou*.

88. Author's interview with Eddie Rhea Walker.

89. See Walzer, *Exodus and Revolution*, 4–6.

90. See Joyner, *Down by the Riverside*, 142; Callahan, *Talking Book*, 83–137; Raboteau, *Fire in the Bones*, 17.

91. Davenport, quoted in Yetman, *Life under the "Peculiar Institution,"* 75.

92. Raboteau, *Fire in the Bones*, 33–34; 108–109.

93. Quoted in Callahan, *Talking Book*, 83.

94. King "The Birth of a New Nation," Dexter Avenue Baptist Church, Apr. 7, 1957, King Center Digital Archive.

95. Heschel, "Religion and Race"; Rieder, *Gospel of Freedom*.

96. Glaude, *Exodus!*, 81.

97. King "Birth of a New Nation."

98. Cone, "Black Spirituals."

99. King, *Where Do We Go from Here?*, 6.

100. Howard-Pitney, *African American Jeremiad*.

101. King "Birth of a New Nation."

102. See Selby, *Martin Luther King*, 168.

103. Glaude, *Exodus!*, 10.

104. Raboteau, *Fire in the Bones*, 33.

105. Winthrop, "Model of Christian Charity" (1630).

106. Glaude, *Exodus!*, 78. See also Moorhead, "American Israel."

107. Callahan, *Talking Book*, 112.

108. Some did advocate returning to Africa or establishing new homes at various moments and in various movements. See Barnes, *Journey of Hope*; Campbell, *Middle Passage*; Clegg, *Price of Liberty*; Jenkins, *Black Zion*.

109. Callahan, *Talking Book*, 118.

110. Walzer, *Exodus and Revolution*, 7, 9.

111. King, "Address by MLK at the Southern Baptist Theological Seminary," Apr. 19, 1961, the King Center Digital Archives; Selby, *Martin Luther King*, 2.

112. Interestingly, in this way, Exodus politics offered hope not just for blacks but for America itself—"that the true test of American democracy rested with the nation's darker sons and daughters" (Glaude, *Exodus!*, 111).

113. Colossians 1:17.

114. See Prothero, *American Jesus*.

115. Cone, *Black Theology and Black Power*, 99–100.

116. Cone, 34. "Christology is the sum and substance, the alpha and omega, the proton and eschaton, the capstone of Christian thought" (Carter, *Race*, 162).

117. See Raboteau, *Slave Religion*, 242; Callahan, *Talking Book*, 186–87; Du Bois, "Church and the Negro," 290.

118. Cone, *Black Theology and Black Power*, 30, 99.

119. Marsh, Review of Chappell, *A Stone of Hope*, 266–71.

120. Thurman, *Jesus and the Disinherited*, 15. This marks a core tenet of black theology as well, as Jim Cone emphatically exclaims: "Jesus was a Jew!" (Cone, *God of the Oppressed*, 109).

121. Thurman, *Jesus and the Disinherited*, 18. See also Cleage, *Black Messiah*, 3.

122. Thurman, *Jesus and the Disinherited*, 16–17.

123. Thurman, *Jesus and the Disinherited*, 13.

124. Cone, *Black Theology and Black Power*; Cone, *Black Theology of Liberation*; Cone, *God of the Oppressed*; Cleage, *Black Messiah*; Joseph, *Black Power Movement*.

125. Carter, *Race*, 92.

126. Cone, *God of the Oppressed*, 109; Thurman, *Jesus and the Disinherited*, 16.

127. Carter, *Race*, 378, 192.

128. Thurman, *Jesus and the Disinherited*, 29.

129. See Cullen, *Black Christ and Other Poems*; Cone, *Cross and the Lynching Tree*.

130. Galatians 3:13; Deuteronomy 21:23; Cone, *Cross and the Lynching Tree*, 9.

131. Cone, *Cross and the Lynching Tree*, 89.

132. Cone, *God of the Oppressed*, 97, 110.

133. Thurman, "Love," 49–61.

134. King, "Love in Action," Apr. 3, 1960, *Papers of Martin Luther King, Jr.*, vol. 6, 405–7.

135. King, "Loving Your Enemies," Nov. 17, 1957 in *A Knock at Midnight*, 315–24.

136. King, "Loving Your Enemies."

137. Matthew 5:44.

138. Thurman, "Love," 49–61.

139. King, "Loving Your Enemies."

140. Interview with J. R. and Mamie Campbell, Sumter County Oral History Project

141. Walton, "The Black Church Ain't Dead!" (Huffington Post, 2010), in response to Eddie Glaude, "The Black Church Is Dead."

142. Cone, *God of the Oppressed*, 115.

143. Mays and Nicholson, *Negro's Church*, cited in Dickerson, "African American Religious Intellectuals," 225.

144. John Lewis Correspondence, March 1964, SNCC Papers, in Marsh, *Beloved Community*, 3.

145. Chappell, *A Stone of Hope*, 97.

146. Interview with J. R. and Mamie Campbell, Sumter County Oral History Project.

147. See Savage, *Broadcasting Freedom*.

148. Interview with J. R. and Mamie Campbell, Sumter County Oral History Project.

149. Author's interview with Charles Sherrod.

150. Interview with J. R. and Mamie Campbell, Sumter County Oral History Project.

151. At one point, Freeman had to drop out of Morehouse for lack of funding. But "Daddy King went to Morehouse, used his influence, and got him back in school. That family meant a lot to him" (interview with Robertiena Freeman Fletcher, Sumter County Oral History Project).

152. *Bethesda History*, 17–18, Lake Blackshear Regional Library Special Collections.

153. Marshall Frady, *Southerners*, 233.

154. Interview with Robertiena Freeman Fletcher, Sumter County Oral History Project.

155. King, *Daddy King*, 82.

156. Interview with Robertiena Freeman Fletcher, Sumter County Oral History Project.

157. Chappell, *Stone of Hope*, 102.

158. Cone, *God of the Oppressed*, 108–37.

Chapter Four

1. WSBN clip 38840, WSB newsfilm collection, Walter J. Brown Archives and Peabody Awards Collection, University of Georgia Libraries, Athens, Ga., as presented in the Digital Library of Georgia [hereafter WSB-TV newsfilm collection]. The speaker is identified as Willie Bolden, but he may also be Benjamin Clark.

2. Fairclough, *To Redeem the Soul of America*.

3. King, "Montgomery Improvement Association Press Release," Jan. 7, 1957, *Papers of Martin Luther King Jr.*, vol. 4, 95.

4. Recent studies of "the long civil rights movement" are quite helpful in considering how change came to the South and across the nation and also how it did not. For more on *Brown*, see Klarman, *Brown v. Board of Education*; Patterson, *Brown v. Board of Education*; Bartley, *Rise of Massive Resistance*; Webb, *Massive Resistance*. For more on the Montgomery Bus Boycott, see Burns, *Daybreak of Freedom*; Robinson, *Montgomery Bus Boycott and the Women Who Started It*; Millner, *Montgomery Bus Boycott*; Williams, *Thunder of Angels*. For more on the SCLC, see Fairclough, *To Redeem the Soul of America*; Clayton, *The SCLC Story in Words and Pictures*; for more on the beginnings of the student movement, see Chafe, *Civilities and Civil Rights*.

5. See Bennett, "SNCC: Rebels with a Cause," *Ebony*, July 1965, 146–53.

6. King, "A Creative Protest," Feb. 1, 1960, *Papers of Martin Luther King Jr.*, vol. 5, 368.

7. See Houston, *Nashville Way*; Anthony Siracusa, "Disrupting the Calculation of Violence."

8. Lawson, "Who Speaks for the Negro?," Robert Penn Warren Center, Vanderbilt University, 15.

9. Letter from Jim Lawson to Martin King Jr., Nov. 3, 1958, *Papers of Martin Luther King Jr.*, vol. 4, 522–524.

10. Quoted in Williams and Dixie, *This Far by Faith*, 226.

11. Lawson, "From a Lunch Counter Stool," *Motive*, Feb. 1966. Lawson said this in reference to the nascent sit-in, which he believed symbolized a spirit of "judgment and promise." Beginning in February 1960 with students from Greensboro, then with students in Durham and Nashville, student sit-ins became one of the most effective nonviolent strategies for change and perhaps the most enduring image of the movement. While the Congress of Racial Equality (CORE) had actually conducted sit-ins in the 1940s, the 1960s sit-ins had a much larger impact on the movement and the public.

12. Author's interview with Charles and Shirley Sherrod.

13. "The Story of the Student Interracial Ministry," quoted in Cline, *From Reconciliation to Revolution*, xi.

14. *Student Voice*, 1.1, June 1960, SNCC Papers..

15. SNCC, *Statement of Purpose*, April 17, 1960, SNCC Papers.

16. Vivian, *Black Power and the American Myth*, 55.

17. Marsh, *Beloved Community*, 3.

18. King, "The Christian Way of Life in Human Relations," Address Delivered at the General Assembly of the National Council of Churches, Dec. 4, 1957, *Papers of Martin Luther King Jr.*, vol. 3, 136.

19. See: Marsh, *Beloved Community*, 3; King, "Statement to the Press at the Beginning of the Youth Leadership Conference," Feb. 15, 1960, *Papers of Martin Luther King Jr.*, vol. 5, 427.

20. Marsh, *Beloved Community*, 2.

21. Marsh, *Beloved Community*, 53; King, "I Have a Dream," March on Washington, August 28, 1963 (Washington, DC).

22. It was "an inspiration to blacks as much as an irritant to white supremacists" (Tuck, *Beyond Atlanta*, 178).

23. Lawson, "From a Lunch Counter Stool," *Motive*, Feb. 1966.

24. Marsh, *Beloved Community*, 2.

25. Marsh, 6.

26. Lawson, "From a Lunch Counter Stool," *Motive*, Feb. 1966.

27. Marsh, *The Beloved Community*, 3.

28. While the firm theological foundation was always present, it was explicitly invoked in much of the early movement. As SNCC's efforts spread, as more and more young people came into the movement from around the country, and as diffusiveness and impatience for change mounted, much of the original theology went overlooked. See Carson, *In Struggle*; Hogan, *Many Minds, One Heart*; Smith, "Who Speaks for the Negro?," Robert Penn Warren Center for the Humanities.

29. Hayden in Curry et al., *Deep in Our Hearts*, 342.

30. Marsh, *Beloved Community*, 6.

31. Davidson and Groffman, *Quiet Revolution in the South*, 71–72.

32. Author's interview with Charles and Shirley Sherrod.

33. SNCC Report, "Albany and South West Georgia Voter registration project," 1962, SNCC Papers. Marshall Frady elsewhere describes Albany as "a drab little city in the state's southwest sunstruck flatlands of cotton and peanut fields" (Frady, *King*, 87).

34. SIM Proposal, Sherrod Papers, Wisconsin Historical Society, folder 26.

35. Carson, *In Struggle*, 57.

36. See Walker, "American Dilemma in Miniature: Albany, Georgia," an address delivered at a Conference on Civil Disobedience and the American Police Executive, March 26, 1963.

37. In the early 1960s, the Albany Movement emerged as a touchstone for the larger civil rights struggle, providing a lesson in the intractability of Southern racism and uses of law enforcement. Many accounts see it as a loss for an ascendant King, though Sherrod vociferously objects to this synopsis and maintains that the movement was there before King, and thereafter (interview with Charles Sherrod, *Eyes on the Prize*; Branch, *Parting the Waters*; Tuck, *Beyond Atlanta*; Mussat, "Journey for Justice").

38. Walker, SCLC's executive director and one of Martin L. King's closest advisors, was also from Petersburg. There is no definitive biography on Sherrod. His name appears occasionally in accounts of the civil rights movement, especially in the episode on Albany, but the length and breadth of his activism has been woefully underresearched. More often, people recognize his wife, Shirley Sherrod, who served in the Obama Administration.

39. Carson, *In Struggle*, 57. Some accounts say five siblings.

40. Carson, 57.

41. Author's interview with Charles and Shirley Sherrod; Branch, *Parting the Waters*, 525.

42. Hogan, *Many Minds, One Heart*, 109.

43. Sherrod has a great singing voice and as a child was part of a traveling boys' choir that traveled with the Petersburg police force and sang for group meetings (author's interview with Charles and Shirley Sherrod).

44. Author's interview with Charles and Shirley Sherrod.

45. Tuck, *Beyond Atlanta*, 161.

46. Carson, *In Struggle*, 57. As one Georgia activist, Peter De Lissovoy, noted, "It's no accident that the early leaders like Martin Luther King and Charles Sherrod and Reverend Samuel B. Wells and others were Christian preachers. . . . It took a particular wholeness of spirit, vision, and strength beyond personal resources to start up something like the Movement in the American Deep South" (DeLissovoy, *Great Pool Jump*, 37).

47. One notable protest occurred at Thalhimer's Department Store (author's interview with Charles and Shirley Sherrod).

48. Halberstam, *Children*, 267–68.

49. Carson, *In Struggle*, 32–33.

50. Author's interview with Charles and Shirley Sherrod; Hogan, *Many Minds, One Heart*, 52.

51. Romans 8:38.

52. Author's interview with Charles and Shirley Sherrod.

53. Hogan, *Many Minds, One Heart*, 52.

54. Cordell Reagon, "the baby of the movement," worked with Charles Sherrod and other activists in Albany to conduct workshops and organize for many years. Originally from Nashville, Reagon had snuck into Lawson's workshops as a sixteen-year-old and participated in the first Freedom Rides. Despite his youth, Reagon was active in the movement and arrested over thirty times. He had a wonderful singing voice, and in 1962, at the behest of Pete Seeger, Reagon, along with wife Bernice Johnson Reagon, established the Freedom Singers, a national cultural treasure. Reagon continued his activism throughout his life, protesting the Vietnam War and labor issues, and he eventually moved to Berkeley, California. His life was tragically cut short, however, when he was the victim of an unsolved homicide in 1996 and died at the age of 53 (Hampton and Fayer, *Voices of Freedom*, 99; "Cordell Hull Reagon, Civil Rights Singer, Dies at 53," *New York Times*, Nov. 19, 1996).

55. Branch, *Parting the Waters*, 524.

56. Anderson, "Reflections on the Origins of the Albany Movement," 1–14, 8.

57. Branch, *Parting the Waters*, 526. Though not without his doubts, Boyd realized that "Sherrod was accomplishing what no Albany pastor, including himself, could do—he was attracting a growing number of teenagers into church, two, three, four times a week."

58. Sherrod, "Student Nonviolent Coordinating Committee Memorandum" (1961); Carson, *In Struggle*, 58; Branch, *Parting the Waters*, 526.

59. SNCC Report, "Albany and South West Georgia Voter Registration Project," 1962, SNCC Papers, 2.

60. Americus native William G. Anderson was elected president of the Albany Movement and Slater King vice president (Zinn, *New Republic*, July 20, 1963, 16; Tuck, *Beyond Atlanta*).

61. The handbill continued, "If we are of one blood, children of one common Father, brothers in the household of God, then we must be of equal worth in His family, entitled to equal opportunity in the society of men."

62. "Handbill, Albany Nonviolent Movement," Nov. 9, 1961, in *Debating the Civil Rights Movement 194–1968*, Lawson and Payne, 141. As Peter deLissovoy, a white volunteer in Albany, stated: "The Movement above all was an inner experience, an expression of the soul. . . . The SNCC kids and movement people in Albany, GA, had a peculiar wholeness and depth of spirit already intact, otherwise they would not have had the courage and joy to persevere" (deLissovoy, *Great Pool Jump*, 37).

63. SNCC "Song sheet," Veterans of the Civil Rights Movement.

64. Sherrod, "Student Nonviolent Coordinating Committee Memorandum" (1961); Anderson, "Reflections on the Origins of the Albany Movement," 2.

65. Prathia Hall, quoted in Bruns, *Martin Luther King Jr.: A Biography*, 70.

66. Sherrod, "Student Nonviolent Coordinating Committee Memorandum" (1961).

67. Author's interview with Charles and Shirley Sherrod.

68. Earlier that month, the Interstate Commerce Commission's ban on racial discrimination in interstate bus terminals took effect, providing an opportunity for the new Albany Movement to test the segregated structure. Sherrod said, "When this ruling came through, we were ready." Three high school students—Julian Carswell, Eddie Wilson, and Evelyn Toney—prepared to be arrested, beaten, or worse, armed only with their belief in nonviolent love. The bus station was "full of men in blue," Sherrod described, "but up through the mass of people past the men with guns and billies ready, into the terminal, they marched, quiet and quite clean." "They each understood that we would be nonviolent," Sherrod explained, "we'd been slapped around and kicked around and pushed around, so they—they were accustomed to what possibly might happen. And so they went in." The student protestors were arrested by Police Chief Laurie Pritchett and taken to jail. Though they were quickly bailed out, two other students from Albany State, Blanton Hall and Bertha Gober, came to the station later that day and were also arrested. Hall and Gober actually served time, spending their Thanksgiving break from school in jail, and winning the sympathies of local black Albany residents, some of whom "took plates of turkey down to the jail" (Hampton and Fayer, eds., *Voices of Freedom*; Branch, *Parting the Waters*, 531; Sherrod, *Eyes on the Prize*; Washington University Libraries, Film and Media Archive, Henry Hampton Collection; Jenkins, *Open Dem Cells*, 21.

69. Sherrod, "Student Nonviolent Coordinating Committee Memorandum" (1961).

70. With his name often included in the words of this freedom song, Albany Police Chief Laurie Pritchett "with his heavy bulk and cigar always stuffed in his mouth," is in some ways "the consummate caricature of a white Southern lawman," but he is also somewhat vexing. Unlike Bull Connor, Pritchett avoided spectacle. Underneath his slow drawl was an "amiable, possumlike wiliness, in which he had determined to answer the demonstrations by 'killin' 'em with kindness,'" as another Albany official recalled. The city on Albany opted to jail hundreds of people, draw out protests, and ultimately stifle them (Frady, *King*, 87–98; "Albany, Ga. Jails 267 Negro Youths," *New York Times*, Dec. 13, 1961; Branch, *Parting the Waters*, 536).

71. "Albany was a success," the NAACP's Ruby Hurley joked, "only if the goal was to go to jail" (Tuck, *Beyond Atlanta*, 150; Branch *Parting the Waters*, 536).

72. Author's interview with Charles and Shirley Sherrod.

73. Branch, *Parting the Waters*, 542.

74. Branch, 547.

75. Despite the men's personal friendship, King was resistant to the idea of coming to Albany in 1961. King "felt he was between a rock and a hard place, Wyatt T. Walker said. He "could not say at Dr. Anderson's invitation that it won't work into my schedule or I can't come . . . but without having organizational input and control it was a very difficult campaign for him." Anderson recalled being on the telephone with King, trying to convince him to come down. King was hesitating when Anderson interrupted. "Just a minute, Martin," he remembered saying, "I want you to hear these children singing." And, as Anderson recounted, "I hung the phone out the window so he could hear them singing as they filled up Shiloh Baptist Church. . . . I said, 'You hear that Martin?'" to which he simply responded, "Let me hear it some more." As the voices of the children of Albany singing "Oh Freedom, Oh Freedom" traveled across the lines of copper to Atlanta, King changed his mind. "I'll see you tomorrow,' he replied, and hung up the line (Anderson, "Reflections on the Origins of the Albany Movement," 9–10; Branch, *Parting the Waters*, 538–41; Interview with Wyatt Tee Walker, conducted by Blackside, Inc. on October 11, 1985, for *Eyes on the Prize*, Washington University Libraries, Film and Media Archive, Henry Hampton Collection).

76. Author's interview with Charles and Shirley Sherrod.

77. Anderson, "Reflections on the Origins of the Albany Movement," 10–11.

78. Anderson, 10–11. See Branch, *Parting the Waters*, 545.

79. Frady, *King*, 89.

80. Branch, *Parting the Waters*, 546.

81. King, "Address Delivered at Albany Movement Mass Meeting at Mt. Zion Baptist Church, Dec. 15, 1961, *Papers of Martin Luther King Jr.*, vol. 7, 342–343.

82. King, "Address Delivered at Albany Movement Mass Meeting," July 20, 1962, *Papers of Martin Luther King Jr.*, vol. 7, 541–44.

83. Frady, *King*, 89.

84. King, quoted in Branch, *Parting the Waters*, 548.

85. Branch, *Parting the Waters*, 549.

86. "I had sat down and looked at a map and went fifteen miles," Pritchett explained. "How many jails was in a fifteen mile radius. . . . I contacted those authorities and they assured us that we could use their facilities" (Hampton and Fayer, eds., *Voices of Freedom*, 105–11).

87. Chappell is a prototype of the racist Southern sheriff— the cigar-smoking, politeness-be-damned, profanity-spewing enforcer present in so many Southern towns. Chappell feared no retribution since members of his family held numerous governmental positions in Americus, including "home demonstration agent, sheriff, county court clerk (handles voter applications), public service commissioner, postmaster, county commissioners, and state highway patrolmen (three brothers in law)." The Chappell family had a "near-monopoly" of local power, including owning several thousand acres of farmland (Branch, *Parting the Waters*, 550; Perdew and Battle, "A Kitchen Table Conversation," Veterans of the Civil Rights Movement; Perdew, "Americus and Baker County," August 1, 1965, SNCC Research; Mahone, "Reflections on the Americus

Movement," in Lyman-Barner and Lyman-Barner eds., *Roots in the Cotton Patch*, vol. 1, 166).

88. Author's interview with Teresa Mansfield.

89. Stoper, "The Student Nonviolent Coordinating Committee"; one SNCC field-worker, Charles Black, even claimed, "Southwest Georgia was far worse than Mississippi" (*Pittsburgh Courier*, Aug. 8, 1962). See Payne, *I've Got the Light of Freedom*; Dittmer, *Local People*; Tuck, *Beyond Atlanta*, 160–61.

90. Perdew, "SNCC Report on Americus and Baker County," August 1, 1965, SNCC Field Reports.

91. Following his first arrest in South Georgia, Perdew elected to forgo Harvard and stay on SNCC's staff. He never left South Georgia. He married a black co-volunteer, Amanda Perdew, and the couple still lives in the area (Tuck, *Beyond Atlanta*, 163).

92. Zinn, *SNCC*.

93. Frier, "Letter to the Editor," http://digitalrepository.trincoll.edu/cgi/viewcontent .cgi?article=1618&context=tripod.

94. Tuck, *Beyond Atlanta*, 162; "Evaluation of Sumter County Project," Americus File, Mants Papers.

95. Tuck, *Beyond Atlanta*, 179.

96. Browning was a young Methodist woman who was involved with the freedom rides and also served with SNCC in Southwest Georgia from 1961 to 1965. Joan Browning, "Religion and Joining SNCC," Veterans of the Civil Rights Movement, 2004.

97. "Letter from Penelope Patch to Wiley Branton, Director of Voter Education," Dec. 8, 1962, SNCC Papers.

98. Hogan, *Many Minds, One Heart*, 151; Stoper, "Student Nonviolent Coordinating Committee," 28.

99. Hogan, *Many Minds, One Heart*, 72.

100. Braden, "Images Are Broken"; Hogan, *Many Minds, One Heart*, 72.

101. Charles Sherrod to Branton, Feb. 8, 1963, VEP 2-19, SNCC microfilm; Tuck, *Beyond Atlanta*, 178.

102. Letter from Dr. Martin Luther King Jr., to Clarence Jordan, Feb. 8, 1957, Koinonia Farm Archives.

103. Letter from Martin L. King Jr. to Clarence Jordan, Feb. 8, 1957, *Papers of Martin Luther King Jr.*, vol. 4, 122–123.

104. Lee, *Cotton Patch Evidence*, 162.

105. Marsh, Archives in *Project for Lived Theology*, http://archives.livedtheology.org /nodereference/thickbox/2395/thickbox_reference_full?width=700&height=500.

106. Letter to mother and sister, Jan. 16, 1963, Faith Holsaert Papers, box 4.

107. Letter to Faith Holsaert, Jan. 24, 1963, Faith Holsaert Papers, box 4.

108. Marsh, Archives in *Project for Lived Theology*.

109. "Koinonia: 20 summer workers orientation, June 11–15, 1963," SNCC papers; Tuck, *Beyond Atlanta*, 178; Letter from H. B. Munson, Dec. 6, 1663, MS 2341 1.1, Clarence L. Jordan Papers; K'Meyer, *Interracialism and Christian Community*, 152.

110. Letter to mother and sister, 1963, Faith Holsaert Papers, box 4.

111. Letter from H. B. Munson, Rapid City, S.D., Dec. 6, 1963; MS 2341 1:1, Clarence L. Jordan Papers.

112. Author's interview with Sam Mahone. In 1964, Koinonia was listed with only Barnum's Funeral Home as a hospitable contact for SNCC workers in Americus (Charles Sherrod Papers 1:9 [SNCC-Reports] Atlanta, Ga).

113. Quoted in K'Meyer, *Interracialism and Christian Community*, 151.

114. Letter from Zev Aelony, MS 756 6:8, Clarence L. Jordan Papers.

115. Letter from Zev Aelony, MS 756 5:7, Clarence L. Jordan Papers.

116. Interview with Charles Sherrod, *Project on Lived Theology*, Lived Theology Archive.

117. Mahone, "Reflections on the Americus Movement," in Lyman-Barner eds., *Roots in the Cotton Patch*, vol. 1, 134–140.

118. See: SNCC "Survey: Current Field Work, Spring 1963," Appendix A, 12–14, SNCC Records.

119. Campbell also reorganized the Americus chapter of the NAACP, which had existed since 1945 (interview with J. R. and Mamie Campbell, Sumter County Oral History Project).

120. In addition to Campbell and Freeman, others, like Rev. Daniel of Friendship Baptist, gave their support (author's interview with Jewel Wise Alaman).

121. *Sewanee Herald Tribune*, Oct. 13, 1960, 110.

122. *A City without Pity*.

123. *A City without Pity*.

124. Letter from Faith Holsaert, Nov. 18, 1962; Veterans of the Civil Rights Movement.

125. Author's interview with Charles and Shirley Sherrod.

126. *Circle of Trust*, 58; Hogan, *Many Minds, One Heart*, 74.

127. Letter from Faith Holsaert, Nov. 18, 1962; Veterans of the Civil Rights Movement..

128. Hasan Jeffries interview with Sam Mahone, Southern Oral History Program.

129. "We were so hot in Americus," John Perdew remembered, "that the cops would follow us around all the time, so we made a game of it. We knew the cops would arrest us if we did any slight thing wrong." Though the threats were real, the activists also managed to make a game out of the police scrutiny. "We drove around at ten miles an hour at most," Perdew laughed, "so we would have a slow, slow caravan through the projects and North Lee Street in Americus. And finally they would get tired of it. They would get tired of it before I would" (Perdew and Battle, "A Kitchen Table Conversation," Veterans of the Civil Rights Movement).

130. *A City without Pity*.

131. This occurred in April 1963; Americus and Sumter County Movement Remembered.

132. Mants, "Don't Stick Your Nose in Other Folks' Business: Remembrance of Southwest Georgia and Lowndes County Alabama," Veterans of the Civil Rights Movement, 1988.

133. Hogan, *Many Minds, One Heart*, 56.

134. Interview with J. R. and Mamie Campbell, Sumter County Oral History Project;

135. Mants, "Don't Stick Your Nose in Other Folks' Business."

136. Author's interview with Jewel Wise Alaman.

137. Mabel Barnum, quoted in interview with J. R. and Mamie Campbell, Sumter County Oral History Project.

138. Interestingly, Evans was not named president until July 17, 1963, and J. R. Campbell soon replaced him. The Barnum family, anchored by John and Mabel Barnum, operated

the successful Barnum Funeral Home and offered crucial financial support to the movement.

139. *Americus Times-Recorder*, July 12, 1963. Other accounts claim this action began at Friendship Baptist Church.

140. These students included Graham and Theresa Wiggins, Lorene Sanders, Lena Turner, Bobby Lee Jones, Sam Mahone, William Bowen, Phil Goober, and Barbara Jean Daniels, as well as two others (Americus and Sumter County Movement Remembered).

141. Hasan Jeffries interview with Sam Mahone, Southern Oral History Program.

142. Mants, "Don't Stick Your Nose in Other Folks' Business."

143. *Americus Times-Recorder*, July 15, 1963.

144. *Americus Times-Recorder*, July 15, 1963.

145. Author's interview with Sam Mahone. See also: Hasan Jeffries interview with Sam Mahone, Southern Oral History Program, Mahone stayed in Americus, his hometown, until 1966, when he went to Mississippi to attend Tougaloo College and do activist work in the Mississippi Delta. Mahone then went to Lowndes County, Alabama, with friend and fellow Americus volunteer Bob Mants. Then, in January 1969, Mahone was drafted, sent to Fort Benning, Georgia, for basic training, where he remained with a "hold-over company" doing manual labor. Mahone was sent to Germany, but he couldn't get a security clearance because of his arrest record. Stationed in an empty office, he got a camera and began a career as a photographer. In 1972, when Mahone returned to the United States, he got a job in Atlanta with the Georgia Department Archives of History and later with the High Museum.

146. *A City without Pity*.

147. Hogan, *Many Minds, One Heart*, 75.

148. Acts 16:25–26.

149. Roberts, "Visiting JoAnne Christian in Jail, Dawson, GA, 1963," Veterans of the Civil Rights Movement.

150. "Stolen Girls," *Essence Magazine*, Dec. 16, 2009.

151. Westbrooks-Griffin, *Freedom Is Not Free*, 16.

152. Westbrooks-Griffin, 14.

153. Westbrooks-Griffin, 15.

154. Westbrooks-Griffin, 16. Their crime, according to Americus Police Chief Ross Chambliss, was "disorderly conduct" (*Student Voice*, Oct. 1, 1963).

155. The girls kept at the Leesburg Stockade included Carol Barrier, Lorena Barnum, Pearl Brown, Bobbie Jean Butts, Agnes Carter, Pattie Jean Collier, Mattie Crittenden, Barbara Jean Daniels, Gloria Dean, Carolyn DeLoatch, Diane Dorsey, Juanita Freeman, Robertiena Freeman, Henrietta Fuller, Shirley Ann Green, Verna Hollis, Evette Hose, Mary Frances Jackson, Vyrtis Jackson, Dorothy Jones, Emma Jean Jones, Emmarene Kaigler, BarbaraAnn Peterson, Annie Lue Ragans, Judith Reid, Laura Ruff, Sandra Russell, Willie Mae Smith, Billie Jo Thornton, Gloria Breedlove Westbrooks, LuLu Westbrook, Ozellar Whitehead, and Carrie Mae Williams ("Leesburg Stockade," Veterans of the Civil Rights Movement).

156. Westbrooks-Griffin, *Freedom Is Not Free*, 16.

157. Mansfield, "Special Report: Stolen Girls Remember 1963 in Leesburg," WALB News 10, July 24, 2006; *Student Voice*, "Americus, GA: Police Smash Demonstrators," Oct. 1963.

158. Westbrooks-Griffin, *Freedom Is Not Free*, 18; Freeman, "Americus Rejects Americanism," *Christian Century*, Oct. 16, 1963, vol. 80.

159. Westbrooks-Griffin, *Freedom Is Not Free*, 35; Annie Lester and Sandra Mansfield in *A City without Pity*; interview with Robertiena Freeman Fletcher, Sumter County Oral History Project.

160. Kennedy, "Stubbornly Practicing His Principles of Photography," *New York Times*, April 24, 2009.

161. Danny Lyon, quoted in Westbrooks-Griffin, *Freedom Is Not Free*, 20.

162. Lyon was right to be afraid. Less than a year later, Michael Schwerner and Andrew Goodman, both Jews from New York, would be brutally murdered in Mississippi, along with James Chaney, a black man. See Kagan and Dray, *We Are Not Afraid*; Huie, *Three Lives for Mississippi*.

163. *Congressional Record*, 109, S18040-18041, daily ed. Sept. 25, 1963.

164. The girls, who were arrested on July 19, spent these weeks in prison while the judge went on vacation; their trial was not even scheduled until September 3, when he would return for the fall session (Sumter County Court Records).

165. The law was originally written in 1868, but it was amended to include attempt to incite insurrection in 1871.The law stipulates that insurrection "shall consist in any combined resistance to the lawful authority of the State" or "any attempt, by persuasion, or otherwise, to induce others to join in any combined resistance to lawful authority of the State." Insurrection or attempts at insurrection "shall be punished with death; or, if the jury recommend to mercy, confinement in the penitentiary" (*The Code of the State of Georgia*, prepared by Clark, Cobb, and Irwin; "Americus Ga., Stifles Negro Drive," *New York Times*, Sept. 29, 1963).

166. Zinn, *SNCC*, 183.

167. Letter from Zev Aelony, MS 756 6:8, Clarence L. Jordan Papers; Bryan, *These Few Also Paid a Price*, 53–54.

168. "In Americus, Ga," *Student Voice*, Oct. 1963, 2.

169. *Student Voice*, Oct. 1963, 2.

170. Sitton, "Special Report," *New York Times*, Sept. 29, 1963.

171. Americus and Sumter County Movement Remembered Timeline.

172. In many ways, the treatment of the girls in the Leesburg Stockade was significantly worse than that of the Americus Four (though, admittedly, the girls were not jailed under the threat of the death penalty). But in the same way that white college students brought national sympathy to the Freedom Rides and Mississippi Project, the imprisonment and possible death of educated adults (one even being white) brought on an increased level of concern. See also Roberts and Klibanoff, *Race Beat*.

173. At Williams's request, the Senate constitutional rights subcommittee started an investigation and asked Attorney General Kennedy and Georgia Attorney General Eugene Cook for reports (Shannon, "Free 4 in Americus, Solon Asks FRK," *Atlanta Journal*, Oct. 19, 1963). Two representatives from Colorado, John Perdew's home state, joined Williams in his request.

174. "New Jersey Senator Assails Rights Jailing at Americus," *Atlanta Journal*, Margaret Shannon, Washington correspondent, Sept. 26, 1963; Press Release 63/234, quoted in Anthony Manganaro, "HARRISON A. WILLIAMS, JR."

175. Shannon, "New Jersey Senator Assails Rights Jailing at Americus," *Atlanta Journal*, Sept. 26, 1963.

176. Original Draft of SNCC Chairman John Lewis's Speech to the March on Washington; Lewis and D'Orso, *Walking with the Wind*.

177. Fowle, "Riverdale Aiding Resident Jailed in Civil Rights Battle in Georgia," *New York Times*, Oct. 3, 1963. Harris's friends established "the Americus, Ga. Legal Defense Fund," which, in its first week raised over $1,200. Additionally, Harris's fellow students at Rutgers University raised $1,000 on his behalf.

178. Roberts, "Lawyers Petition Court to Release Six Students," *Harvard Crimson*, Oct. 10, 1963.

179. "350 Hear of Effort to Free Jailed Youth," *Hartford Times*, Oct. 11, 1963, Koinonia Farm Archive; "Ask Probe of 'Insurrection' Charge in GA," *United Press International*, 1963, Koinonia Farm Archive.

180. Raymond Coffey, "Race Rioting and Threat of Death Penalty: 4 in Dixie Jail Charged with Insurrection Attempt," Koinonia Farm Archive.

181. Perdew, "SNCC Report on Americus and Baker County," August 1, 1965, SNCC Field Reports.

182. *New York Times*, Sept. 29, 1963.

183. *New York Times*, Sept. 29, 1963.

184. WSBN clip 45411, WSB newsfilm collection.

185. See Roberts, "Remembering Attorney C. B. King," 119.

186. The three-judge panel included Frank Tuttle, Lewis Morgan, and Robert Elliot. Following this federal intervention loomed a near-endless line of appeals and retrials. Ralph Allen was held under new charges. A few weeks later, on November 26, 1963, Allen was indicted under the felony charge of "Assault with Intent to Murder a Police Officer." He pleaded not guilty. The case encountered many delays, brought by both the defense and the court, postponing a definitive ruling for months. On December 2, 1963, for example, C. B. King argued that the felony indictment was "violative of the Fourteenth Amendment," "vague, ambiguous, uncertain," and did not "provide a sufficiently ascertainable standard of guilt" (*State of Georgia v. Ralph Allen*, no. 1050, General Demurrer to Indictment, Dec. 2, 1963). The very same day the motion was "denied and overruled" (*State of Georgia v. Ralph Allen*, no. 1051, Dec. 2, 1963). The case went to court and a jury found Allen guilty on December 5, but that, too, was soon appealed (*State of Georgia v. Ralph Allen*, no. 1051, in Sumter Superior Court, Charge of Assault with Intent to Murder, "Charge of the Court," Dec. 5, 1963). The defense then filed a motion for a new trial, initially scheduled for February 14, 1964. Another March 30, 1964, plea for a new trial was overruled. On May 23, 1964, legal proceedings were still under way. By the end, both the plaintiff and defendant were "in error," and the trial had become so languorous and confusing that a 455-page review of events had to be filed to ensure that both the state and the defense remembered all the proceedings ("Case of Ralph W. Allen, defendant in error v. State of Georgia, Defendant in error" Sumter County Courthouse Records).

187. *New York Times*, Nov. 2, 1963; "Special Presentment," Sumter County Courthouse Records.

188. Clotfelter, "Rights Movement to Benefit from Americus Case Ruling," *Atlanta Journal Constitution*, 1963, Koinonia Farm Archive.

189. SNCC Field Report, Sept. 24, 1963, Mants Papers.

190. *Voice of Americus*, 1:1, Sherrod Papers, Wisconsin Historical Society.

191. John Perdew, Bob Mants, Graham Wiggins, Willie Ricks, and Sam Mahone were involved in this action on July 5, 1964 (Americus and Sumter County Movement Remembered).

192. Author's interview with Carl E. Sanders. Sanders himself, though by no means a promoter of civil rights initiatives, worked to keep Georgia from becoming a racial spectacle in the way of George Wallace's Alabama and Ross Barnett's Mississippi. See Buchanan, *Some of the People Who Ate My Barbeque Didn't Vote for Me*; Tuck, *Beyond Atlanta*.

193. See chapter 5 for a full discussion of school desegregation and its consequences in Americus.

194. Author's interview with Walter Lundy.

195. King and Williams, "Results of the Southern Christian Leadership Conference's Summer Community Organization and Political Education Project," Veterans of the Civil Rights Movement.

196. Interview with J. R. and Mamie Campbell, Sumter County Oral History Project.

197. Author's interview with Mamie Campbell.

198. Interview with J. R. and Mamie Campbell, Sumter County Oral History Project.

199. "Americus Target for Mass Invasion," *Americus Times-Recorder*, July 27, 1965. Comedian Dick Gregory also famously came to the city at this time.

200. Interview with J. R. and Mamie Campbell, Sumter County Oral History Project.

201. Movement Soul background notes, #36, Sherrod Papers, Wisconsin Historical Society.

202. Interview with Mark Pace, Sumter County Oral History Project.

203. WSBN clip 42203, WSB newsfilm collection; WSBN clip 48504, WSB newsfilm collection.

204. Anderson, *Remembering Americus*, 30.

205. Frady, "My Dream Came True: I was Mr. Maddox," *New York Review of Books*, April 6, 1972; Sokol, *There Goes My Everything*, 183. Some reports indicate that Mr. Maddox spoke at a recreational facility; see WSBN clip 48501, WSB newsfilm collection.

206. Some accounts mark this as July 26, 1965, and others July 29, 1965. Lester Maddox is a fascinating figure in Georgia history and politics. Elected governor in 1966, Maddox was a staunch segregationist whose campaign claim to fame was that he supposedly chased blacks away from his Pickwick restaurant with an axe handle. He used to sell and autograph these axe handles as a political symbol of his racial views.

207. "March on Mayor's Home Threatened in Americus," *Atlanta Journal*, Aug. 7, 1965.

208. Author's interview with Russell Thomas.

209. Interview with J. R. and Mamie Campbell, Sumter County Oral History Project.

210. Interview with Frank Myers, Sumter County Oral History Project.

211. Interview with Frank Myers, Sumter County Oral History Project.

212. Interview with J. R. and Mamie Campbell, Sumter County Oral History Project; "Negroes Continue Marches," *Americus Times-Recorder*, July 27, 1965.

213. "Negroes Renew Marches Today after Moratorium End," *Americus Times-Recorder*, July 30, 1965.

214. "Mayor Issues Statement; Press Headquarters Set Up," *Americus Times-Recorder*, July 30, 1965; "Mayor Again Pleads Negroes End Marches," *Americus Times-Recorder*, July 31, 1965.

215. Author's interview with Karl Wilson; author's interview with Teresa Mansfield.

Chapter Five

1. "Americus Negroes Begin Vigil at Court House," *UPI*, July 29, 1965; Interview with J. R. and Mamie Campbell, Sumter County Oral History Project. The students requested a police escort and spent the rest of the night at the Friendship Baptist Church ("Murder Charges Filed against Negroes in Death of Youth, 21," *Americus Times-Recorder*, July 29, 1965).

2. "Murder Charges Filed against Negroes in Death of Youth, 21," *Americus Times-Recorder*, July 29, 1965.

3. "Nightriders Gun Down Georgia Youth," *Delta Democrat-Times*, Greenville, Miss., July 29, 1965.

4. His mother, Mrs. Lyda Whatley, commented that her son suffered from "slight retardation," but had worked hard to overcome his deficiencies and had recently passed the entrance exam for the Marine Corps ("Whatley Had Just Joined Marine Corps, *Americus Times-Recorder*, July 29, 1965).

5. WSBN clip 38840, WSB newsfilm collection. Tom Brokaw moved to Atlanta in 1964 to work for WSB-TV, home of the Huntley-Brinkley Report, a program that focused on civil rights issues throughout the South. In this role, Brokaw was a news anchor on the eleven o'clock news with opportunity to cover civil rights issues for both WSB and occasionally NBC. The move to Atlanta exposed Brokaw to the subtle and resilient presence of race in the South. He recalled "seeing through our Midwestern eyes the depth and complexity of the place of race in the South." Brokaw remembered the events of that summer:

> In Americus, Georgia, an ugly confrontation between blacks and whites reached critical mass when a young white man was killed in a drive-by shooting. All hell broke loose inspired in part by a Klan rally and the racial rants of Lester Maddox. NBC News in New York dispatched me to Americus to cover events there until one of its regular correspondents could arrive. . . . I decided to see what the mother of the white victim had to say. Not quite knowing what to expect, I approached her house in a working class neighborhood. A small quiet woman in a plain, faded frock—what we used to call a housedress—opened the screen door just a crack and agreed to be interviewed. I asked her what she thought of all the trouble that had blown up in town, with threats of lynchings and shootings for any black who marched in protest. In soft tones she said it made no sense. It wouldn't bring back her son. She hoped it would end soon. I found her statement, in its simplicity, tremendously powerful, and an antidote to all the hate-filled rhetoric of the Klan. (Brokaw, *Boom!*, 15–16, 46)

6. *Americus Times-Recorder*, Aug. 1965.

7. *Americus Times-Recorder*, Aug. 2, 1965; WSBN 48501, WSBN 41882, WSB newsfilm collection.

8. "Negroes Beaten in Americus, GA," *New York Times*, Aug. 1, 1965; author's interview with Isabel Collins.

9. WSBN clip 38840, WSB newsfilm collection

10. "Negroes Renew Marches Today after Moratorium End; Sanders Watches," *Americus-Times Recorder*, July 30, 1965.

11. "Mayor Issues Statement; Press Headquarters Set Up," *Americus Times-Recorder*, July 30, 1965.

12. "Sanders Says Killing of Local Youth Tragic Result," *Americus Times-Recorder*, July 29, 1965.

13. "Sanders Says Killing of Local Youth Tragic Result."

14. "100 Additional Troopers Being Sent to Americus," *Americus Times-Recorder*, July 29, 1965. Most of these troopers were from Southwest Georgia

15. Interview with J. R. and Mamie Campbell, Sumter County Oral History Project.

16. "Mayor Issues Statement on Situation Here," *Americus Times-Recorder*, Aug. 3, 1965.

17. "Mayor Issues Statement."

18. *State of Georgia v. Charlie Hopkins*, "Motion for Change of Venue," Sumter County Superior Court, March 1, 1966.

19. See Jeffries, *Bloody Lowndes*; Joseph, *Black Power Movement*; Joseph, *Waiting Til the Midnight Hour*; Van Deburg, *New Day in Babylon*; Sitkoff, *Struggle for Black Equality*; Williams, *Negroes with Guns*.

20. Falwell, "Ministers and Marches," 1965 in Sutton, *Jerry Falwell and the Rise of the Religious Right*, 57–60.

21. Horne, *Fire This Time*; Conot, *Rivers of Blood, Years of Darkness*.

22. "Law and Order Will Be Kept, Chambliss Says," *Americus Times-Recorder*, Aug. 4, 1965.

23. The men were formally accused of killing and murdering Andy Whatley "with malice aforethought . . . by shooting him in the head with a pistol." *State of Georgia v. Charlie Lee Hopkins and Willie James Lamar* (Alias Willie Lamar Thomas), Case no. 1228, Sumter County Superior Court, Feb. Term 1966.

24. *State of Georgia v. Charlie Hopkins*, "Motion for Change of Venue," Sumter County Superior Court, March 1, 1966.

25. *State of Georgia v. Charlie Lee Hopkins*, Case no. 1228, Sumter County Superior Court, Feb. Term 1966. *Americus Times-Recorder*, Aug. 2, 1965; author's interview with Rev. Bill Dupree.

26. *State of Georgia v. Charlie Lee Hopkins*, Case no. 1228, Sumter County Superior Court, Feb. Term 1966.

27. There is a legal difference between a guilty verdict with a request for mercy and one without. The request for mercy officially indicates a recommendation for life in prison as opposed to the death penalty (K. L. Carpenter, foreman, March 3, 1966, Clerk Superior Court Records).

28. Felony Sentence, *State of Georgia v. Charlie Lee Hopkins*, Case no. 1228 (1966), Sumter County Court Records. Hopkins was paroled on March 19, 1976, and his civil and political rights were commuted on July 10, 1980.

29. *The State v. Willie James Lamar*, Case no. 1228 (1966), Sumter County Court Record.

30. *State of Georgia v. Willie Lamar*, "Motion to Quash the Indictment and Challenge to the Array of Traverse Jurors," Feb. 28, 1966, Sumter County Superior Court. Interestingly, King complains not only of blacks being excluded, but women as well, who he imagined would be more sympathetic to his clients.

31. *State of Georgia v. Charlie Hopkins*, "Motion for Change of Venue," Sumter County Superior Court.

32. See: Flamm, *Law and Order*; Alexander, *New Jim Crow*; Kendi, *Stamped from the Beginning*, 410–24.

33. "Mayor Hits Agitators, Urges Calm by Citizens," *Americus Times-Recorder*, Aug. 4, 1965.

34. Sanders, *Americus Times-Recorder*, Aug. 3, 1965.

35. "Keep Outsiders Out of Americus, Sanders Urges," *Americus Times-Recorder*, Aug. 2, 1965.

36. "Keep Outsiders Out of Americus."

37. *State of Georgia v. Charlie Hopkins*, "Motion for Change of Venue," Sumter County Superior Court, March 1, 1966.

38. Letter from "A Negro Citizen," "Voice of the People," *Americus Times-Recorder*, Aug. 2, 1965, FUMC box 25.

39. Letter from Wm. Harry Moore, *Americus Times-Recorder*, Aug. 4, 1965, FUMC box.

40. His eldest brother, Ben, served as Georgia's secretary of state for thirty-three years and had an illustrious political career. See http://www.georgiaencyclopedia.org/articles/government-politics/ben-fortson-1904-1979.

41. As county attorney, Fortson actually represented Americus High School in its1960 case against the Koinonia students.

42. Author's interview with Warren Fortson.

43. Author's interview with Warren Fortson. Clarence Jordan arranged for Robertiena to go to California. As her father, Rev. R. L. Freeman recalled, "While all of this was going on Dr. Clarence Jordan, in a prayerful manner, succeeded in getting the judge of court to turn my daughter over to him, and let him enroll her in a camp of their approval to spend the summer. This camp that he sent her to was very helpful and enjoyable to her. The prayers of Dr. Jordan and the people at the Koinonia Farm, my family and myself, and our many friends and her many friends and school mates—we believe God answered them all" (R. L. Freeman, Koinonia Archive).

44. Auchmutey, *Class of '65*, 60–62, 131.

45. "Americus the Beautiful," *Newsweek*, Sept. 1965, 30.

46. The story of the "hopeless" Americus biracial committee is a saga unto itself (Marshall Frady, "What Happened That Summer to Warren Fortson, *Southerners*). "At the appropriate time," Mayor Walker stated on July 31, 1965, "but certainly not now, meeting of a biracial committee can and will be recommended by myself and the Council." But, he continued, "I feel that it would be ineffective now because of the feeling generated in the hearts and minds of citizens of both races in the city of Americus." In the wake of tension and violence, the committee was postponed and deferred several times, and many in Americus were completely opposed to the formation of a political entity comprised of black and white citizens. Eventually, a group of eight white and eight black citizens was arranged and then met to discuss racial issues in Americus and come up with equitable solutions. Selection

of the committee members was decided by the mayor, City Council, and Board of Sumter County Commissioners and included the following white representatives: Warren Fortson, Mrs. Audrey Bass, Mr. R. D. McNeill, Sr., Lang Sheffield, Harold A. Collins, John Pope, Spencer Pryor, and W. E. Smith ("Community Relations Committee Named Here," *Americus Times-Recorder*, July 26, 1965). However, the committee never really came to fruition, as it was stymied by an issue at once completely superficial and yet deeply significant in the South. One of the women of the biracial committee, Mabel Barnum, was a prominent black citizen and member of Americus's small black middle class. She asked to be called Mrs. Barnum, which whites on the committee refused to do, signaling, as it did, equal status. "The whole damn thing broke up because they couldn't agree on what to call a woman they had known all their lives," Warren Fortson bemoaned (author's interview with Warren Fortson; see also WSBN clip 38840, WSB newsfilm collection).

47. Author's interview with Warren Fortson.

48. Author's interview with Warren Fortson.

49. There were exceptions. For example, "the most prominent" businessman in town, Charles Wheatley, once vociferously defended segregation, but he bent when his assets were threatened. A man whose "views [were] rarely disregarded," Wheatley controlled the hospital, bus station, four of the five grocery stores in town, the Manhattan Shirt Factory, a construction company, and he served influentially with a local bank, with the First Presbyterian Church of Americus, and as city engineer. But Wheatley's racial views "served to protect his economic and social capital at all costs." John Perdew recalled that in 1963, a group of black citizens sought an audience with the mayor, T. Griffin Walker. Wheatley "reportedly motioned aside the Mayor" and ensured that the city "refused adamantly to yield any concessions." Yet, the following year, fearing national retribution from organized labor, Wheatley quietly integrated the previously all-white labor force at his Manhattan Shirt Factory. Perdew, "SNCC Report on Americus and Baker County," August 1, 1965, SNCC Field Reports.

50. "Four Pickets Jailed in Georgia under Law with Penalty of Death, *Nashua Telegraph*, Nashua, N.H., Oct. 31, 1963.

51. "The Civil Rights Act: Compliance as Reported to the Georgia Council on Human Relations," July 15 and 20, 1964, Frances Freeborn Pauley Papers; *New York Times*, July 9, 1964; Sokol, *There Goes My Everything*, 41; Tuck, *Beyond Atlanta*, 158, 176. For more on Pauley, a remarkable woman and friend of Warren Fortson, see Nasstrom, *Everybody's Grandmother and Nobody's Fool*.

52. "Americus Whites Ask Peace Talks," Gene Roberts for the *New York Times*, Aug. 3, 1965, FUMC box.

53. "Americus the Beautiful," *Newsweek*, Sept. 1965, 30.

54. "Americus the Beautiful."

55. "Americus Whites Ask Peace Talks," Gene Roberts for the *New York Times*, Aug. 3, 1965, FUMC box.

56. "Americus Whites Ask Peace Talks."

57. For his part, Fortson claimed to be "less interested in defending his job than in seeing Americus recognize its racial difficulty as a 'human problem'" ("Americus Whites Ask Peace Talks," Gene Roberts for the *New York Times*, Aug. 3, 1965, FUMC box).

58. Author's interview with Warren Fortson.

59. Frady, "God and Man in the South," *Atlantic Monthly*, 1966.

60. "Racial Attorney Leaves Americus," *Ellensburg Daily Record*, AP Press, Sept. 16, 1965.

61. Letter from Anonymous, Athens, Ga., to FUMC, Aug. 16, 1965, FUMC box, 138. Although we cannot be entirely sure, this Athens man was likely white, as he was a member of the largely segregated Methodist denomination.

62. McGill, "The Devil Outscores Jesus," *Daytona Beach Morning Journal*, Sept. 25, 1965.

63. Letter from Anonymous, Athens, Ga., to FUMC, Aug. 16, 1965, FUMC box, 138.

64. "Racial Attorney Leaves Americus," *Ellensburg Daily Record*, Sept. 16, 1965 (AP Press). In some ways, Fortson was on those rapids the rest of his life. Having been kicked out of Americus for his racial stance, Fortson embraced racial activism, working briefly as a civil rights attorney in Mississippi and then taking up the cause in Atlanta. He worked tirelessly with the Atlanta School Board and Dr. Benjamin Mays and made many friends in the civil rights circles in Atlanta, where he still lives.

65. Interview with Robertiena Freeman Fletcher, Sumter County Oral History Project.

66. For more on the long history of conflict over education for religious reasons, see Peko, "Religious Schooling in America"; Carper and Hunt, eds., *Religious Schooling in America*; Rose, *Keeping Them Out of the Hands of Satan*; Nord, *Religion and American Education*; Blumhofer, *Religion, Education, and the American Experience*; Jorgenson, *State and the Non-Public School*; Jones, *Religious Schooling*; Peshkin, *God's Choice*; Hawkins and Sinitiere, eds., *Christians and the Color Line*.

67. Press release of speech, Aug. 9, 1958, box 13, Vandiver Papers; Roche, *Restructured Resistance*, 73.

68. HOPE and MASE exchanged a series of heated exchanges, including a notable bumper sticker war for the hearts and fenders of Peachtree Street. When HOPE declared, "We want Public Education," MASE responded, "Me too, But Segregated." Though not exactly clever, these slogans indicate how conflicted the city, and thus Governor Vandiver, was in the years following *Calhoun*. Roche, *Restructuring Resistance*, 60–63; Mertz, "'Mind Changing Time All over Georgia.'" It also bears mentioning that GUTS was lead and supported by Lester Maddox, the rabid segregationist, frequent Americus visitor, and later governor of the state.

69. John Sibley was an attorney at King & Spalding, a businessman, and prominent University of Georgia alum. See John Sibley Papers, Emory University, Atlanta, Ga.

70. McGill, "Slow Mills of Law," in *A Church, A School*, 92.

71. Judge Griffin Bell, Georgia's Political Heritage Program Oral History Interviews.

72. The weather was unseasonably cold in Americus. This was immortalized in a poem written to commemorate the commission: "There's mud on the backroads, / there's slush in the lane, / There's ice on the high roads, / From the freezing rain, / But, wait, Mister Weatherman, / Didn't you know / The Sibley Commission is on the go? / How about it, men / Of the Study Commission / Is the ice going to stop / Your fact finding mission? / No, says John Sibley. / Never, says Greer. / You can quote me, says Rankin—/ 'We'll let nothing interfere.' / So bring on your witnesses, / Call out the press. / We're going to get / To the bottom of this mess" (Al Kueltne, *Sibley Papers*, quoted in Roche, *Restructured Resistance*, 96).

73. The Americus and Sumter County Movement Remembered. See also transcript, Georgia General Assembly Committee on Schools, Hearing, March 3, 1960 (Americus

hearing transcript), Sibley Papers, Emory University, Atlanta, Ga.; Roche, *Restructured Resistance*, 105.

74. Roche, *Restructured Resistance*, 107. Many Georgians joked that they were tallying up the score.

75. In some ways this number is lower than expected. Most likely, this is due to geographical splits. In addition to the outlier of Atlanta in the state, many of Georgia's northern districts voted for compliance. These areas, while still mostly segregationist, were not demographically threatened by integration. Though they may have preferred segregated education, they did not want to see the schools shut down when the decision to integrate would have little local effect. In places like Americus, the percentage of those in favor of massive resistance was much higher.

76. Jeff Roche describes the story of the Sibley Commission as one of "how massive resistance ultimately failed in Georgia and why the Sibley Commission's restructured resistance succeeded." In avoiding dramatic displays of resistance, Georgia, under the direction of business and political elites like John Sibley and Griffin Bell, was able to attract commerce and stave off humiliation. They were also able to quietly preserve the racial status quo and leave a legacy of inequality in education. Roche notes that the commission created a "new form of segregation," one that "resembles the North's," which was a "deliberate new form of defiance—a restructured resistance—rooted in contemporary practicality and corporate pragmatism" (Roche, *Restructured Resistance*, xv–xvii).

77. See Roche, *Restructured Resistance*; Huff, "Sibley Commission."

78. These were the same students for whom Clarence Jordan had signed a recommendation letter. Judge Bootle's ruling over Hunter and Holmes's entrance to the University of Georgia was not the first time he had intervened in issues of who could attend public educational institutions. In 1960, Bootle overruled a city board decision that banned three white students from Americus High School, declaring that Will Wittkamper, Jan Jordan, and Lora Ruth Browne be admitted immediately. For this, Judge Bootle was burned in effigy in front of the courthouse.

79. See Crespino, *In Search of Another Country*, 176; *United States v. Jefferson County Board of Education*, 372 F.2d836 (1966), 856. Whether schools or institutions were in compliance with the Civil Rights Act was determined by the Department of Education, Health and Welfare.

80. Marian Wright Edelman of the Children's Defense League in Nevin and Bills, *Schools that Fear Built*, 9.

81. In order to receive federal funding, local school districts could submit a voluntary plan of desegregation—either a plan for designating school attendance by geographical area or by "freedom of choice," the choice of most Southern school districts. These plans had to be approved by the attorney general and the Department of Health, Education and Welfare.

82. Revised Statement of Policies for School Desegregation Plans under Title VI of the Civil Rights Act of 1964, 45.CRR, 181 (1966).

83. U.S. Commission on Civil Rights, Southern School Desegregation, 1966–1967, 45–46 (1967). Of school districts desegregating nonvoluntarily (under court order), freedom of choice plans were also favored, with 129 of the 160 Southern districts in this category implementing them.

84. There was great debate throughout the courts and public about what exactly was constitutionally mandated by *Brown*. Was the state required to "take affirmative action to remedy the inequality by mixing the races" or simply "precluded from requiring segregation but not forced to act affirmatively to achieve a certain degree of integration"? (See Brown, "Freedom of Choice in the South: A Constitutional Perspective.") The story of federal funding and school desegregation is very complicated. See *Brown v. Board of Education* (1954), *Brown II* (1955), *Briggs v. Elliot* (1955), *Goss v. Board* (1963), *Bell v. School Board, City of Gary* (1963), *United States v. Jefferson County* (1966), *United States v. Jefferson County II* (1967). See also Crespino, *In Search of Another Country*, 177–79.

85. Crespino, *In Search of Another Country*, 177.

86. The year after the plan went into effect, of a total 1,676 black students (to 1,812 white) only 15 (or .89 percent) were enrolled in white schools under freedom of choice (SNCC table, Sherrod Papers, King Center and Archive, Atlanta, Ga.).

87. In May, the county Board of Education opted to forgo federal money, a sum of $16,596.76, or 2.1 percent of their operating budget, rather than desegregate. But it seems they reconsidered. In July, the board decided to comply with state requests, adopting guidelines to integrate the schools in the fall and sending a plan to Washington for federal approval. See "Sumter School Board Set to Submit Plan," *Americus Times-Recorder*, July 1, 1965; "Sumter School Officials Changed Their Minds and Decided to Submit a Desegregation plan"; "50 Desegregation Plans Rejected from Georgia," *Americus Times-Recorder*, June 8, 1965.

88. "White Children Barred from Georgia School," *Christian Century*; MS 756 6:2, Clarence L. Jordan Papers.

89. "Court Orders Americus High to Admit Koinonia Students," *Macon Telegraph*, Oct. 26, 1960; MS 756 28:21, Clarence L. Jordan Papers; "Judge W. A. Bootle," *Mercer Lawyer*, Winter 2005, 4–7.

90. Western Union Telegram Collection (MUM0472), University of Mississippi, 3.13.14. TD. 28, Sept. 1962. 10:35 A.M. Citizens of Americus, Ga., to Ross Barnett and Lt. Gov. Johnson. Re: Support and praise.

91. Auchmutey, *Class of '65*, 90–91.

92. See Wittkamper, "Baptized in Spit," Clarence Jordan Symposium, Sept. 2012.

93. Dobbs Wiggins in *The City without Pity*.

94. *Voice of Americus*, 1:7, Sherrod Papers, Wisconsin Historical Society.

95. Author's interview with Jewel Wise Alaman.

96. See Auchmutey, *Class of '65*.

97. Schools in Americus were not meaningfully integrated until 1970. On Aug. 31, 1970, the school truly mixed racially, with an enrollment of 1,136 whites and 1,725 blacks. See "Americus School History," Sumter County, Georgia Genealogy.

98. The Lamar Society study estimates that as of the mid-1970s, 750,000 Southern students were being educated in such schools and that 3,000–4,000 of these institutions existed in the thirteen Southern states (Nevin and Bills, *Schools that Fear Built*, 9).

99. "Private School Applications Set," *Americus Times-Recorder*, July 22, 1966.

100. "Academy to Open in the Fall," *Americus Times-Recorder*, Aug. 9, 1966. Interestingly, no one can account for the name, as it does not owe to a benefactor, geographical area, or notable figure (author's interview with Ty Kinslow).

101. "Private School for Americus Proposed," *Americus Times-Recorder*, May 1966.

102. "Private School for Americus Proposed."

103. "Speaks to Rotary Club: McManus Outlines Plans for Southland Academy," *Americus Times-Recorder*, Aug. 16, 1967.

104. See Crespino, *In Search of Another Country*; Kruse, *White Flight*.

105. Skerry, *Public Interest*, quoted in Crespino, *In Search of Another Country*, 249; Nevin and Bills, *Schools that Fear Built*.

106. Nevin and Bills, *Schools that Fear Built*, 22–23, 37.

107. "Speaks to Rotary Club: McManus Outlines Plans for Southland Academy," *Americus Times-Recorder*, Aug. 16, 1967.

108. "Private School Meeting Friday," *Americus Times-Recorder*, July 20, 1966; "Private School Applications Set," *Americus Times-Recorder*, July 22, 1966. The Board of Trustees included Sumter residents Harry Entrekin (president), Tinley Anderson, Troy Morris, Henry Crisp, Pete Godwin, Ed Carson, and Roger Pollock.

109. Littlefield, "Ready for Fall Opening: Many Improvements at Private School Site," *Americus Times-Recorder*, July 7, 1967.

110. "On Tax Exempt Delay: Academy Officials Claim Discrimination," *Americus Times-Recorder*, July 28, 1967; "Private School Applications Set," *Americus Times-Recorder*, July 22, 1966; "On Tax Exempt Delay: Academy Officials Claim Discrimination," *Americus Times-Recorder*, July 28, 1967. The difficulties faced by Southland in 1967 emerged as hurdles that would face many private schools in the South in the late 1960s and into the 1970s. Although the federal government sought to block the funding of private, segregated schools from reinscribing separate and unequal educational systems in America, these schools countered that they were not primarily racial, but religious—a strong, historically unassailable argument. See *Green vs. Connally* (1971); *Bob Jones University v. United States* (1982); Balmer, *Thy Kingdom Come*.

111. "On Tax Exempt Delay: Academy Officials Claim Discrimination," *Americus Times-Recorder*, July 28, 1967.

112. "On the Tax Exempt Delay." Senator Talmadge even requested a hearing before the Senate Finance Committee in which Sheldon Cohen, commissioner of Internal Revenue Service, "will be called to appear and show cause for the delay in making a ruling in this case."

113. "Tax-Exempt Status Granted Southland Here," *Americus Times-Recorder*, Aug. 4, 1967.

114. "On Tax Exempt Delay: Academy Officials Claim Discrimination," *Americus Times-Recorder*, July 28, 1967; "Tax-Exempt Status Granted Southland Here," *Americus Times-Recorder*, Aug. 4, 1967.

115. Dierenfield, *Battle over School Prayer*, vii.

116. The prayer was "Almighty God, we acknowledge our dependence upon Thee, and we beg Thy blessings upon us, our parents, our teachers and our Country." Legal Information Institute, "Engel v. Vitale," Cornell Law School, Ithaca, N.Y.

117. Justice Hugo Black, *Engel v. Vitale* (1962).

118. A Gallup poll indicated that 85 percent of Americans disagreed with the ruling (Dierenfield, *Battle over School Prayer*, 138).

119. *Congressional Record*, June 26, 1962, p. 11675.

120. *Newsweek*, 1962, 44.

121. Talmadge in Dierenfield, *Battle over School Prayer*, 148.

122. Dierenfield, 149.

123. 1963 TV Interview; Dierenfield, *Battle over School Prayer*, 147.

124. Author's interview with Harry and Ann Entrekin.

125. Lott, interview in *Southern Partisan* (1984) 47, quoted in Dailey, "Theology of Massive Resistance," 171.

126. Falwell, *Jerry Falwell*, 99.

127. Falwell, "Ministers and Marches" (1965); see Winters, *God's Right Hand*; Harding, *Book of Jerry Falwell*.

128. Falwell, "Ministers and Marches."

Chapter Six

1. Author's interview with Kellete Heys.

2. Haynes, *Last Segregated Hour*, 3.

3. Dupont, *Mississippi Praying*, 156.

4. See Haynes, *Last Segregated Hour*, 3.

5. Haynes, 3; Frady, "God and Man in the South," *Atlantic Monthly*, 1967, 37–42.

6. Frady, "God and Man in the South," 37–42.

7. In recent years, some excellent works have rightly emphasized kneel-ins: Dupont, *Mississippi Praying*; Haynes, *Last Segregated Hour*; Kosek, "Just a Bunch of Agitators"; Lyon, *Sanctuaries of Segregation*; Cunningham, *Agony at Galloway*.

8. Haynes, *Last Segregated Hour*, 3.

9. Haynes, 3.

10. Haynes, 4.

11. *Student Voice*, vol. 1, no. 2, Aug. 1960, 3–4; "The New Phase: 'Kneel-Ins: 4 Atlanta White Churches Admit Colored Students, *Journal and Guide* (Norfolk, Va.) Aug. 13, 1960; *Student Voice*, Student Nonviolent Coordinating Committee, vol. 1, no. 2, Aug. 1960, 2.

12. *Student Voice*, Student Nonviolent Coordinating Committee, vol. 1, no. 2, Aug. 1960, 2.

13. Smith, "Why We Began the Kneel-Ins," *Atlanta Inquirer*, Aug. 14, 1960.

14. *Student Voice* 1, no. 2 (Aug. 1960): 3–4; see also Lonnie King in "Negro Leader Hails Churches," *Atlanta Journal*, Aug. 8, 1960.

15. Martin Luther King Jr., "The Negro and the American Dream," Excerpt from Address at the Annual Freedom Mass Meeting of the North Carolina State Conference of Branches of the NAACP, Sept. 25, 1960, in *Papers of Martin Luther King, Jr.*, vol. 5, 508–11.

16. "Let Us Kneel In Together!," *Christian Century*, Aug. 24, 1960, 963–64.

17. "Let Us Kneel In Together!"

18. "Let Us Kneel In Together!"

19. It is worth noting that not all black Americans supported the kneel-ins. J. H. Jackson, the president of the National Baptist Convention, deplored them as condescending, noting "when you 'kneel-in' you kneel in judgment of a segregated church." "Dr. Jackson Talks on Integration Battle," *Chicago Defender*, Nov. 5, 1960, 1.

20. Even though these coordinated kneel-ins as part of direct-action protests were unprecedented, black or interracial visitors to white churches were not. In fact, Martin King, Sr., apparently sought entrance at First Baptist Church in Atlanta in the 1950s. Intrigued by the

pastor Roy McLain, named by *Newsweek* as one of ten of the "Greatest American Preachers," King decided to go down Peachtree Street and hear him preach. Though King and his fellow visitors were greeted "very cordially," they were soon asked to move downstairs and, when they refused, were insulted, pushed, and made to leave (Mays, *Born to Rebel*, 244–47).

21. Mays, "Kneel-Ins: My View," *Pittsburgh Courier*, Sept. 10, 1960.

22. Commission on Religion and Race, *Minutes*, SNCC Papers, June 28, 1963, 2, folder 2; Findlay, *Church People in the Struggle*, 76.

23. King, "The Un-Christian Christian," *Ebony*, Aug. 1965.

24. "The New Phase," *Journal and Guide*, Norfolk, Va., Aug. 13, 1960.

25. The students, organized as the Committee on the Appeal for Human Rights (CO-AHR) were part of the Atlanta University Center and aided by Julian Bond and Lonnie King in their efforts ("An Appeal for Human Rights," March 9, 1960, Robert W. Woodruff Library, Atlanta University Center).

26. Gibson, "Why We Began the Kneel-Ins," *Atlanta Inquirer*, Aug. 14, 1960.

27. Gibson.

28. Not all the students were from Atlanta, but many were or were in school in the Atlanta system. Some of them include: Bonnie Kilstein, Frank James, Clarence Mitchell, R. Kenneth Davis, Jim Laue, Marion Barry, Ruby Doris Smith, Mary Anne Smith, Gwendolyn Harris, and Henry Thomas. The Atlanta churches visited that morning include First Baptist, Druid Hills Baptist, Grace Methodist, St. Mark Methodist, First Presbyterian, and the Episcopal Cathedral of St. Philip.

29. Gibson, "Why We Began the Kneel-Ins."

30. Only at First Baptist and Druid Hills Baptist were the students denied seating outright. "Negro Students Attend 6 White Churches Here," Jim Bentley, *Atlanta Constitution*, Aug. 8, 1960; Gibson, "Why We Began the Kneel-Ins."

31. "Negro Leader Hails Churches for Courtesy During Visits," *Atlanta Journal*, Aug. 8, 1960.

32. "Negro Students Attend 6 White Churches Here," Jim Bentley, *Atlanta Constitution*, Aug. 8, 1960.

33. "Negro Leader Hails Churches for Courtesy During Visits," *Atlanta Journal*, Aug. 8, 1960.

34. "Why We Began the Kneel-Ins," *Atlanta Inquirer*, Aug. 14, 1960; see also Lefever, *Undaunted by the Fight*, 56–58.

35. These churches were Grace Methodist, Westminster Presbyterian, and First Christian.

36. Owen, "Kneel-Ins," *Spelman Spotlight*, Dec. 16, 1960.

37. "Negro Leader Hails Churches for Courtesy During Visits," *Atlanta Journal*, Aug. 8, 1960.

38. See King, "Un-christian Christian," *Ebony*, Aug. 1965, 77–80.

39. "Ga. Pastor Asks Open Door Policy," *Baltimore Afro-American*, Sept. 6, 1960; Haynes, *Last Segregated Hour*, 14.

40. Dupont, *Mississippi Praying*, 156.

41. Owen, "Kneel-Ins," *Spelman Spotlight*, Dec. 16, 1960.

42. Kosek, "Just a Bunch of Agitators," 233.

43. These groups are the Baptist Convention (SBC), the Methodist Episcopal Church, South (until the Methodists reunified in 1936), and the Presbyterian Church (U.S.), often referred to simply as the Southern Presbyterian Church.

44. Historian Paul Harvey accounts for these divisions by making a distinction between "elite" and "folk" theologians. Elite theologians debated issues in seminaries and governed ecclesiastical bodies whereas folk theologians invoked tradition and dictated religious practice in local communities (Harvey, "God and Negroes and Jesus and Sin and Salvation").

45. "Liberal was the ecclesiastical equivalent of S.O.B."; quoted in Alvis, *Religion and Race*, 48.

46. See Findlay, *Church People in the Struggle*; Dupont, *Mississippi Praying*; Sledge, *Hands on the Ark*; Murray, *Methodists and the Crucible of Race*; Newman, "The Georgia Baptist Convention and Desegregation"; Newman, *Getting Right with God*; Willis, *All According to God's Plan*; Houck and Dixon, eds., *Rhetoric, Religion and the Civil Rights Movement*; Bartley, *Rise of Massive Resistance*.

47. See chapter 2. "Lee St. Methodist Warns against Mass Withdrawals in Church's New Policies," *Americus Times-Recorder*, Feb. 23, 1957, MS 756, Clarence L. Jordan Papers; letter from Frank L. Butler, Sr., Americus, Georgia, FUMC box. The vast majority of Southern congregations remained strictly segregated, with one 1963 survey postulating that 90 percent of Baptist churches officially excluded blacks from attending. See Newman, *Getting Right with God*, 154.

48. McGill, "Christianity on Trial," *Atlanta Constitution*, Aug. 20, 1960.

49. Bass, *Blessed Are the Peacemakers*, 86.

50. Kosek, "Just a Bunch of Agitators," 234; Chappell, *A Stone of Hope*.

51. Britton, "Candidate's Suit Aimed at Demonstrations Tossed Out," *Atlanta Daily World*, Sept. 14, 1960, 1; Haynes, *Last Segregated Hour*, 252.

52. One could imagine the judge was thinking of religious battles such as the Thirty Years' War, as well as the American Revolution, and, of course, the Civil War. Brown Nagin, *Courage to Dissent*, 234–51; Gillies, "Justice Southern Style," *Christian Century*, Jan 22, 1964, 112–14.

53. Grace Greene Pace (wife of Stephen Pace), to John Owen Smith, Sept. 7, 1965, John Owen Smith Papers, Emory University, box 5; "Petitions by Local Churches against Integration," General Board of Church and Society, Records in General Commission on Archives and History, United Methodist Church, Drew University, Patterson, N.J.; Harvey, *Freedom's Coming*, 243.

54. John Owen Smith Papers, MSS 242, box 5.

55. Haynes, *Last Segregated Hour*, 18.

56. Kosek, "Just a Bunch of Agitators," 238.

57. Questions of who can come to church and why are always theological questions, if more "practical" ones. Joseph Kip Kosek calls this a "practical theology of racial separation." Even when defenders of segregated congregations claimed their "decision to exclude visitors was understood not as a theological statement but as a simple reflection of congregational policy or social custom," this distancing mechanism was not as effective as its defendants may have imagined. For example, when one Southerner claimed that he "never heard a theological argument" for not seating the black visitors, he may have been speaking honestly. But this man undoubtedly had heard theological arguments about racial

separation, the separation of church and state, and the sanctity of the church during his years as a parishioner—all theological in some respects, and all used implicitly to bar African Americans from worship (Kosek, "Just a Bunch of Agitators," 245; Haynes, *Last Segregated Hour*, 17).

58. Haynes, *Last Segregated Hour*, 18.

59. It did not matter that many kneelers were actually motivated by religious sincerity. As Kip Kosek wrote, "Critics of kneel-ins refused to acknowledge that the actions had a religious dimension at all" (Kosek, "Just a Bunch of Agitators," 239). In many ways, this was the same tactic that the Americus residents had used in the 1950s in regard to Koinonia: if segregationists could convince the world (but most importantly themselves) that the Koinonians were communists, then their integrationist theology was nullified.

60. Author's interview with Harry and Ann Entrekin.

61. The usher was identified as F. Joe Vining. "Negroes Attend 6 Churches," *Atlanta Constitution*, Aug. 8, 1960; "Three Atlanta Churches Refuse Negroes Admission," 4, "3 Atlanta Churches Halt Kneel-In Demonstrations," *Norfolk Journal and Guide* (Sept. 3, 1960), 10; Haynes, *Last Segregated Hour*, 23.

62. Kosek, "Just a Bunch of Agitators," 233. Hoping "to avoid conflict and avoid disciplinary action" from their denominations, many opponents of the kneel-ins opted to "ignore segregation's theological or moral status and focus on impugning visitors' motives." Haynes, *Last Segregated Hour*, 19.

63. Haynes, *Last Segregated Hour*, 19; See MS 756 5:6, MS 756 6:9, Clarence L. Jordan Papers.

64. McGill, "World Christianity is on Trial," *Miami News*, Aug. 19, 1960.

65. Though the students did not attempt a kneel-in at First Presbyterian Church in Americus, the congregation had planned a course of action in the event of one. The session of First Presbyterian decided that the Rev. Rightmyer would present a written statement to be signed by any visitors:

> We realize and affirm that the church of our Lord and Savior, Jesus Christ offers a place of Worship and haven of refuge, to all who would enter the LORD'S house with a humble heart and Confession of Sin. Therefore, we welcome all who come in this spirit of reverence. We are aware also of the present trend on the part of some to use the church for other purposes than those which the Lord has intended. We therefore as His undershepherd and servants ask that you affirm that your purpose in coming to this house of worship, and this service of worship, today, is that of seeking the true spirit of worship and that you have no other motive in coming. The signing of this card will so confirm this truth to us (Burnett, "First Presbyterian Church of Americus, Georgia: Historical Summary: 1842–2008).

66. Carolyn Deloatch remembered that she wore a "pink dress, a black hat and patent leather pumps." She was, after all, heading to church (Author's interview with Carolyn Deloatch).

67. The group may have also included Willie Bolden, Benjamin Van Clarke, and Penny Patch.

68. Author's interview with Carolyn DeLoatch; author's interview with David Bell.

69. Some accounts report that the students split up, with half going to First Baptist and the other half going to First Methodist while others contend the group stayed together. "Two Churches Bar Civil Rights Groups in Americus Drive," *New York Times*, Aug. 2, 1965.

70. Author's interview with Marion Hicks and Kelso Gooden.

71. Author's interview with David Bell.

72. *Des Moines Register*, Aug. 2, 1965, FUMC box; *Plain Dealer*—Cleveland, "Americus Churches Bar Rights Units," Aug. 2, 1965, FUMC box.

73. Quoted in Frady, "God and Man in the South."

74. Frady. Russell Thomas, later the mayor of Americus, also recalled the usher at First Baptist bragging that he had "had what it takes to keep them out." Quizzically, Thomas asked him, "You had a gun at church?? Wasn't it uncomfortable sitting in the pew?" (author's interview with Russell Thomas).

75. Author's interview with Isabel Collins.

76. Frady, "God and Man in the South."

77. Frady. Bell said, "I knew that these people, even though you're standing in front of a church, I knew these people were prepared at any cost to keep us from coming to church." They told us, he continued, "you will not set your foot on church property." See *New York Post*, Aug. 3, 1965, 24.

78. It did not go unnoticed in later commentary that these words "ironically and tragically" echoed the "words an innkeeper addressed to a weary traveler many centuries ago." "There Was No Room," *Portland Evening Express*, Aug. 3, 1965, Portland, Minn, FUMC box.

79. "Americus Unrest," unidentified article in FUMC box.

80. Author's interview with Rev. Bill Dupree.

81. Actually, if you look closely at the photographs, David Bell does not bow his head when the others do. "They give me a hard time about that," Bell laughed, "I was the only one looking up!" In response to why, the humorous moment is sharply placed back into context, as Bell simply stated, "We were surrounded by the enemy. . . . I did know what they would do" (author's interview with David Bell).

82. The group was released on bond on Aug. 2, as news of the kneel-in was gracing the breakfast tables of people around the nation.

83. Obituary, "Vernard Robertson," Miscellaneous Clarke County Georgia Obituaries, 1998; "Preachers of First Methodist Church Americus,", Sumter County, Georgia Genealogy.

84. Author's interview with Martha Wood.

85. Author's interview with Rev. Bill Dupree.

86. Author's interview with Russell Thomas.

87. Author's interview with Rev. Bill Dupree; author's interview with Rev. Billy and Sunshine Key.

88. "Mayor Issues Statement; Press Headquarters Set Up," *Americus Times-Recorder*, July 30, 1965.

89. FUMC box; Associated Press, multiple articles, Aug. 2, 1965.

90. Frank Blair reported for NBC in New York while a young Tom Brokaw reported for the Atlanta affiliate. Letter to Vernard Robertson from Rev. Thomas M. Lee, Aug. 9, 1965, FUMC box.

91. Some letters even came from overseas, including some from Dover, England; Edinburgh, Scotland; Germany; Christ Church, New Zealand; Melbourne, Australia; and Wofgaugsee, Austria.

92. Various letters, FUMC box.

93. Letter from Elmer Hill, Sherman Oaks, Calif., Aug. 4, 1965, FUMC box.

94. Letter from the Armstrongs, the Methodist Church of New Zealand, Christchurch, New Zealand, Aug. 17, 1965, FUMC box.

95. Letter from Donald E. Walden, Minister First Methodist Church of Chicago Lawn, Chicago, Ill., Aug. 8, 1965, FUMC box.

96. Anonymous letter from San Diego, Calif., FUMC box.

97. He added, "I write this letter with the authority of Galatians 5:1–10." Charles O. Howard, Everett, Mass., Aug. 3, 1965, FUMC box.

98. Letter from Mrs. W. E. Pritchard, Longview, Wa., Aug. 4, 1965, FUMC box.

99. Letter from Mrs. H. B. Galaspere, Palos Verdes Peninsula, Aug. 2, 1965, FUMC box.

100. Letter from A Methodist Teenager, St. Paul, Minn., Aug. 3, 1965, FUMC box.

101. Popular verses include: Whosoever will, let him come"; "Come to me all ye that labour and are heavy laden, and I will give you rest"; "My house shall be a house of prayer for *all* people"; "So we, being many, are one body in Christ, and every one members of another"; "Having done it to the least of these you have done it to me"; "All have sinned and come short of the glory of God," Colossians 3:24–25. Some even included printed sermons, lest the wrongful stance derive from exegetical ignorance. Sermon delivered on Race Relations, Sunday, Feb. 10, 1963, First Congregational Church, Stratford, Connecticut, "God Speed the Day of Brotherhood," Colossians 3:1–11, included by Mrs. Thomas J. Matt, Aug. 3, 1965, FUMC box; "This I Believe" by Haywood N. Hill, M.D. (lesson at adult Sunday school at Trinity Presbyterian Church in Atlanta, Ga., on Jan. 1, 1961), submitted by Donald W. Lawson—Kingston, N.C., Aug. 10, 1965, FUMC box.

102. Letter to V. R. from Joseph F. Margolo, Aug. 9, 1965, FUMC box.

103. Letter from Ms. Penny H. Jenkins, Los Angeles, Calif., FUMC box.

104. Letter from Robert H. Morris, First Methodist Church, Endicott, N.Y., FUMC box.

105. Letter to V. R. from Joseph F. Margolo, Aug. 9, 1965, FUMC box.

106. Letter from H. A. Dennis, Tucson, Ariz., Aug. 2, 1965, FUMC box.

107. Letter from Melvin B. West, Missouri Methodist Areas Church and Community Office, Aug. 16, 1965, FUMC box.

108. Letter from Clyde R. Vaughn Jr., Farmington Community Methodist Church, Aug. 9, 1965, FUMC Box.

109. Letter from Eugene B. Tomlin, chairman of Commission for Social Concerns, First Methodist Church, Champaign, Ill., Sept. 13, 1965, FUMC box.

110. Letter from Donald A. Eagle, Aug. 2, 1965, FUMC box.

111. Anonymous letter from Mexico, N.Y., Aug. 12, 1965, FUMC box.

112. Letter from Mrs. Ethel King, Los Angeles, Calif., Aug. 3, 1965, FUMC box, emphasis hers.

113. Letter from Rev. Ross M. Haverfield, parish minister, Center Presbyterian Church, Canonsburg, Pa., Aug. 3, 1965, FUMC box.

114. Letter from H. A. Dennis, Tucson, Ariz., Aug. 2, 1965, FUMC box.

115. Letter from Lloyd C. Halverson, McLean, Va., Aug. 3, 1965, FUMC box.

116. Letter from Bessie Wilson, Des Moines, Iowa, Aug. 1965, FUMC box.

117. Letter from Julia White, Aug. 2, 1965, FUMC box.

118. Anonymous letter from Clayton, N.J., Aug. 2, 1965, FUMC box.

119. Letter from Estelle D. Clifton, Plymouth, Mass., Aug. 30, 1965, FUMC box.

120. Letter from Susie Fairchild, Freeport, Tex., Aug. 2, 1965, FUMC box.

121. Letter to V. R. from Alfred Achtert Jr., of Yeadon, Pa., Aug. 12, 1965, FUMC box.

122. Letter to V. R from Richard I. Hurley, Aug. 2, 1965, FUMC box.

123. Letter from Arthur L. McKenney, *Labor Magazine*, Joplin, Mo., Aug. 2, 1965, FUMC box.

124. Letter from Phillip Carroll, LaVerne, Calif., Aug. 3, 1965, FUMC box.

125. Letter from S. Rindner, feature writer and news reporter, *Star Newspaper*, Milwaukee, Minn., Aug. 9, 1965, FUMC box.

126. Letter from Mrs. Dean Upshaw, Condon, Ore., FUMC box.

127. Letter to FUMC from Mrs. Ruby D. (unreadable), Wenham, Mass., Aug. 15, 1965, FUMC box.

128. Letter to V. R. from John C. Soltman, Tacoma, Wash., Aug. 2, 1965, FUMC box.

129. Letter from Donald A. Eagle, the National Conference of Christians & Jews, Inc., Aug. 2, 1965, FUMC box.

130. Robert E. Cook, South Bend, Ind., Aug. 9, 1965, FUMC box.

131. Letter to V. R. from Mrs. D. M. Johnson, Worthington, Minn., FUMC box.

132. Letter to Vernard Robertson and J. O. Smith from Frank L. Butler, Sr., Americus, Ga., Aug. 19, 1965, FUMC box.

133. Letter from Sam B. Doughton, Columbia, S.C., Aug. 4, 1965, FUMC box.

134. Letter to V. R. from J. B. Hutchinson of Waycross, Ga., Aug. 3, 1965, FUMC box.

135. Letter to V. R. and the FUMC Church Board from Mr. and Mrs. Raymond Mills, Aug. 3, 1965, FUMC box; some grammatical alterations were made in these quotations to improve clarity when necessary.

136. Letter to V. R. from Mable, Rockford, Ill., Aug. 4, 1965, FUMC box.

137. Letter from Carl Liddle, Tallahassee, Fla., FUMC box.

138. Letter from C. C. James, Sequim, Wash., Aug. 15, 1965, FUMC box.

139. Letter from W. B. Dickson, Cincinnati, Ohio, Aug. 2, 1965, FUMC box.

140. Letter from H. Myers, Alhambra, Calif., FUMC box. Much of the pro-segregationist literature Myers sent is suffused with political and anti-communist sentiment as well as religious ideals. For example, one pamphlet quoted Woodrow Wilson, declaring: "The sum of the matter is this our civilization cannot survive materially unless it is redeemed spiritually." For many supporters of the Americus church, the "struggle to save our white race and our liberty" was both a material and a spiritual mission.

141. Letter from Rev. M. William Trott, Calvary Baptist Church, Ephart, Pa., FUMC box.

142. Letter to V. R. from Sarah LaVaughn, Lynmore Methodist Church, Macon, Ga., Aug. 3, 1965, FUMC box.

143. Letter to Vernard Robertson from James D. Reese, Macon, Ga., FUMC box.

144. Letter to Vernard Robertson from Rev. Thomas M. Lee, Aug. 9, 1965, FUMC box.

145. Letter to Vernard Robertson from Rev. Carlton Anderson, Savannah, Ga., Aug. 9, 1965, FUMC box.

146. Smith says he called several times over the previous weeks, but it seemed the minister, certainly under duress, had elected to go on vacation. Bishop Smith is an interesting figure in the struggle over civil rights in the Methodist Church. Born in South Carolina, Smith grew up less than ten miles from the infamous U.S. senator Strom Thurmond, who was a contemporary. Yet, Thurmond and Smith diverged sharply over the race question. A racial moderate who spoke for inclusion as early as 1960 at a conference at Lake Junaluska, Smith could be disliked by Methodists on both sides of the racial aisle. Some accused him of moving too slowly on integration, while others accused the bishop of trying "to ram church integration down our throats." Unlike his predecessor, Bishop Arthur Moore, Smith endured years of harsh criticism. Despite his reputation, Smith was a thoughtful, reasoned man, who also kept good records of his correspondence. Smith even had plans to release a book about the struggle he faced as bishop during the civil rights movement, but the work was never released due to his death in 1978. In 2009, though, Herschel Sheets, an acquaintance of Smith, edited and published the manuscript, *Letters Written in Turbulent Times* (see Smith, *Letters Written in Turbulent Times*, Sheets; South Georgia Methodist Archive, Epwoth by the Sea, St. Simons Island, Ga.).

147. Letter from J. Owen Smith to Vernard Robertson, Aug. 16, 1965, FUMC box.

148. It seems the Presbyterian, Baptist, and Catholic churches in Americus did the same, making statements "on radio and by publication concerning the Americus situation." Letter from Smith to Rev. W. Harry Moore, Aug. 25, 1965, MSS 242, box 17, 0812-31, John O. Smith Papers.

149. Smith, "A Reminder concerning the Open Door Policy of the Methodist Church," Aug. 14, 1965, MSS 242, box 17, 0812-31, John O. Smith Papers.

150. Smith, "The Bishop's Column," *Wesleyan Christian Advocate*, 1965, South Georgia Methodist Archive, St. Simons Island, Ga.

151. *Americus Times-Recorder*, Aug. 14, 1965.

152. Letter to Bishop J. O. Smith from Wm. Harry Moore, executive secretary, Magnolia Manor, Americus, Ga., FUMC box.

153. Letter from Bernard Smith, Aug. 8, 1965, MSS 242, box 7, 09, 1-7, John O. Smith Papers.

154. Letter from Smith to Rev. W. Harry Moore, Aug. 25, 1965, MSS 242, box 17, 0812-31; letter from Bishop J. Owen Smith to Mr. Carl A. Metzger, Aug. 30, 1965, MSS 242, box 17, 0812-31, John O. Smith Papers.

155. Letter from Bishop J. Owen Smith to Mr. Carl A. Metzger, Aug. 30, 1965, MSS 242, box 17, 0812-31, John O. Smith Papers; Smith, "Bishop's Column," *Wesleyan Christian Advocate*, 1965, South Georgia Methodist Archive, St. Simons Island, Ga.

156. Letter from Smith to Vernard Robertson, Aug. 16, 1965, FUMC box.

157. Haynes, *Last Segregated Hour*, 5.

158. Author's interview with Isabel Collins.

159. In the end, forty-six members of First Baptist left to found Fellowship Baptist (Anderson, *Journey of Grace*, 148–49). The church did, finally, integrate and open its doors, quietly and without fanfare, in 1977.

160. Author's interview with Marion Hicks and Kelso Gooden.

161. Haynes, *Last Segregated Hour*, 5.

162. Newman, *Getting Right with God*, 22.

163. Frady, "God and Man in the South," *Atlantic Monthly*, 1966.

Conclusion

1. Clarence Jordan to Phil Gailey, quoted in Millard Fuller, "The Incarnation, as Revealed in the Life of Clarence Jordan," Speech to the Atlanta Christian Council, Dec. 4, 1969, Fuller Center for Housing.

2. Frady, "Small Victories in Americus," *Life*, Feb. 12, 1971.

3. Frady, "Small Victories in Americus." One city leader actually claimed that the Christian segregationist academies "maybe have been a blessing," since "they've drawn off the reactionaries and allowed us to go about our business."

4. Author's interview with Teresa Mansfield.

5. Levanthal, "Personal Odyssey," article sent to Florence Jordan; MS 2341 5:13, Clarence L. Jordan Papers.

6. Interview with J. Frank Myers, Sumter County Oral History Project. That biracial committee included white members "John Davis, B. R. B. Davis, Mrs. Russell Thomas Jr., Homer Warren, Mrs. Langdon Sheffield" and black members "Mrs. Lucille Tyson, Mrs. Thelma Barnum, James Bryant, Rev. E. D. Sims, John Harris, Arthur Pless." "Local Black History Chronology," Sumter County, Georgia Genealogy.

7. Many felt that the blacks appointed simply did the bidding of the white establishment. As Bobby Fuse put it: "They had billy clubs, and they used them. . . . They were feared. They drove down the street, people would turn their lights and radios off because they almost had carte blanche in the black community, whooping heads, threatening, intimidating. They probably were some nice old guys who thought they were doing police work, they were policemen, but you know they were just what the whites wanted, you know. Y'all want some black police officers? We'll get you some black police officers" (Interview with Bobby Fuse, Sumter County Oral History Project).

8. Interview with Lewis Lowe, Sumter County Oral History Project; Anderson "Sumter County History Timeline," *Americus Times-Recorder*.

9. "A 'Mean' Town in Georgia in the '60s Sinks into Euphoria while Awaiting Carter Election," *New York Times*, Aug. 3, 1976.

10. Will Levanthal, "A Personal Odyssey, *New South*, fall 1972, MS 2341 5:13, Clarence L. Jordan Papers.

11. Sherrod Papers, Wisconsin Historical Society, folder 13.

12. Frady, "Small Victories in Americus," 51.

13. David Cline interview with Charles Sherrod, 2009; Sherrod Papers, Martin Luther King Center & Archive, Atlanta, Ga.

14. Author's interview with Charles and Shirley Sherrod.

15. SNCC Field reports, "Friends of SNCC," Charles Sherrod Papers, Martin Luther King Jr. 1:7.

16. Letter from Charles Sherrod to Assistant Attorney General John Doar, Sept. 18, 1965, Charles Sherrod Papers, "Georgia: Baker County," 3:2, Martin Luther King Jr. Library, Atlanta, Ga.

17. Mamiya, "SNCC, SIM and the Southwest Georgia Project," 2011, Veterans of the Civil Rights Movement. For years, tensions had simmered between Sherrod and the Atlanta SNCC offices over financial support, interracialism, and recognition (see Cline, *From Reconciliation to Revolution*, 97–98).

18. Cline, *From Reconciliation to Revolution*, xi.

19. Cline, 98–99.

20. Sherrod, SIM Proposal, Sherrod Papers, Wisconsin Historical Society, folder 26.

21. Sherrod; Cline, *From Reconciliation to Revolution*, 100.

22. Letter from Menzel to Sherrod, March 24, 1965, Sherrod Papers, Wisconsin Historical Society, folder 16.

23. These students included Bill and Ruth Minter, Jan Vrchota, Paul Menzel, and Ed Feaver. Sherrod, "From the Gator's Stronghold: SIM in Southwest Georgia," Sherrod Papers, SIM (1965) 4:16.

24. Sherrod, "From the Gator's Stronghold."

25. Cline, *From Reconciliation to Revolution*, 101.

26. Cline, 100.

27. Sherrod, in Cline, *From Reconciliation to Revolution*, 104.

28. Cline, *From Reconciliation to Revolution*, 107.

29. Mamiya, "SNCC, SIM and the Southwest Georgia Project," 2011, Veterans of the Civil Rights Movement.

30. Sherrod, "From the Gator's Stronghold."

31. Ed Feaver, Report to SIM, "From the Gator's Stronghold.".

32. Author's interview with Rev. Billy Key and Sunshine Key. As late as 1969, integrated worshippers were still being actively denied entry to First Baptist, as was the case when Koinonia resident Don Chappell, who was raised by Southern Baptist missionaries in the Congo, was turned away when he brought two friends, one black and one Puerto Rican, with him (Koinonia Newsletter, Oct. 27, 1969, Koinonia Farm Archive).

33. Cline, *From Reconciliation to Revolution*, 114.

34. "The doors never got opened, not really," stated Rev. Billy Key, who pastored First United Methodist from 1968 to 1972. Author's interview with Rev. Billy and Sunshine Key.

35. Godbold, *Jimmy and Rosalynn Carter*, 4–7.

36. Godbold, 13.

37. Carter biographer Peter Bourne estimated the wages were $1.00 per day for men, $.75 for women, and $.25 for children; Bourne, *Jimmy Carter*, 23.

38. Carter, *Hour before Daylight*.

39. Godbold, *Jimmy and Rosalynn Carter*, 15.

40. Carter, *Living Faith*, 11.

41. Interview with Lillian Carter, Sept. 26, 1978, Carter/Smith Family Interviews, 24, Jimmy Carter Presidential Library.

42. Balmer, *Redeemer*, 6.

43. Godbold, *Jimmy and Rosalynn Carter*, 20.

44. Godbold, 17.

45. Carter, *Turning Point*, 16.

46. Bourne, *Jimmy Carter*, 21–22.

47. Interview with Rachel Clark, Nov. 9, 1978, Carter/Smith Family Interviews, 14, Jimmy Carter Presidential Library.

48. Carter, *Hour before Daylight*, 23.

49. Carter, 23.

50. Godbold, *Jimmy and Rosalynn Carter*, 21.

51. Carter, *Hour before Daylight*, 41.

52. Interview with Rachel Clark, Carter Library.

53. Interview with Rachel Clark, Carter Library.

54. "Jimmy Carter's Early Life on a Georgia Farm," *Wall Street Journal*, July 7, 2015.

55. His Plains High School teacher Julia Coleman was another very strong influence. Significantly disabled but committed to education, travel, and culture, Miss Coleman dedicated her life to the children of Plains, revealing to them a wider world outside of South Georgia.

56. Interview with Rachel Clark, Carter Library.

57. Interview with Rachel, Carter Library.

58. Godbold, *Jimmy and Rosalynn Carter*, 18.

59. Quoted in Balmer, *Redeemer*, 6.

60. Carter, *Hour before Daylight*, 17.

61. Carter, 17.

62. Bourne, *Jimmy Carter*, 44–51.

63. Jimmy's uncle, Tom Gordy, was serving in the Pacific Theater and in December 1941 was captured by the Japanese in Guam. He remained a prisoner of war until September 1945; Godbold, *Jimmy and Rosalynn Carter*, 46.

64. Bourne, *Jimmy Carter*, 62.

65. Carter, *Living Faith*, 23.

66. Carter, 43.

67. Carter, 23.

68. He did this famously against Rosalynn's wishes. She was so mad, Carter recalled, that she "tried to quit me" (Bourne, *Jimmy Carter*, 81).

69. Carter, *Living Faith*, 24–26.

70. Carter, 64–64; Bourne, *Jimmy Carter*, 96, 99.

71. Godbold, *Jimmy and Rosalynn Carter*, 87.

72. Michael, *Jimmy Carter as Educational Policymaker*, 16.

73. In the end, Judge Bootle ruled that the children were being wrongfully barred and ordered them admitted. See chapter 5. Florence Jordan stated: "To my almost certain knowledge, none of Jimmy's family ever came to Koinonia. There is mention made of Rosalyn [*sic*] visiting the family of a man who at one time had been connected with Koinonia. This is true" (letter from Florence Jordan to Charles Kirsch, Feb. 1, 1977, correspondence Jan. 1977–Oct. 1977, MS 2341 2:9, Clarence L. Jordan Papers).

74. Michael, *Jimmy Carter as Educational Policymaker*, 16.

75. Michael, 20–21.

76. Carter lamented, "Only in Sumter County have the citizens failed their children," calculating that the vote cost the school $334,000 in state funds (handwritten notes, Sumter County consolidation speech, undated, box 62, Carter Family Papers, Jimmy Carter's Speech Files, Jimmy Carter Library).

77. Carter, *Turning Point*, 58–60.

78. Speech at Americus High School Graduation, undated, box 62, Carter Family Papers, Jimmy Carter's Speech Files, Jimmy Carter Presidential Library.

79. Carter, *Turning Point*, xix.

80. Years prior, Fortson and local radio host Charlie Smith had tried to get Jimmy to run against Tick Forrester for Congress. Fortson, with his characteristic sharp humor, claimed Forrester was an "abomination before the Lord and an embarrassment."

81. Quoted in Carter, *Turning Point*, 67.

82. Bourne, *Jimmy Carter*, 115; Godbold, *Jimmy and Rosalynn Carter*, 95.

83. *Baker v. Carr, 369 U.S. 186* (1962). Interestingly, the deciding vote in the Georgia case was cast by Griffin Bell, an attorney and Americus native. For more regarding the *Baker v. Carr* case, sometimes referred to as the "One Man, One Vote" case, see Smith, *On Democracy's Doorstep*.

84. Carter, *Turning Point*, 42.

85. Carter, 42.

86. Bourne, *Jimmy Carter*, 117.

87. See Melissa Fay Greene's account of Georgia's McIntosh County (Greene, *Praying for Sheetrock*).

88. Bourne, *Jimmy Carter*, 119.

89. Dan Carter, in "Jimmy Carter," PBS, *The American Experience*, http://www.pbs.org /wgbh/americanexperience/films/carter/.

90. Ben Fortson is the longest-serving secretary of state in Georgia's history, holding the position from 1946 until his death in 1979.

91. They were able to secure John largely because one of his fellow editors at the *Atlanta Journal* was Jimmy's cousin, Don Carter, who called on their behalf.

92. *Atlanta Journal*, Oct. 22, 1962, Oct. 29, 1962, Oct. 30, 1962, quoted in Bourne, *Jimmy Carter*, 124–26. The *Journal* also ran an editorial cartoon featuring a Quitman County official in a graveyard coping names on to blank ballots. Carter cheekily titled his chapter on the election "The Dead Voted Alphabetically."

93. Charles Kirbo would go on to be Carter's attorney as well as one of his most trusted advisors for the next several decades.

94. Moore dragged out the process in appeals, so much so that on inauguration day, Carter reported still being uncertain regarding the outcome. He did not know for certain that he was the state senator from the Fourteenth District until his hand was on the Bible, and the oath had been taken (Bourne, *Jimmy Carter*, 130–31).

95. In his spiritual memoir, *Living Faith*, Carter offers much more sympathy for moderate and even conservative whites than for the black Americans clamoring for their U.S. and yes, even human, rights. "Plains was and is a wonderful place to live," he stated. "As in all Southern communities, its white people were faced with a quandary during the civil rights days, but they struggled through the ordeal" (70).

96. "A 'Mean' Town in Georgia in the '60s Sinks into Euphoria while Awaiting Carter Election," *New York Times*, Aug. 3, 1976.

97. Bourne, *Jimmy Carter*, 136.

98. Article II, Section 7, Maranatha Baptist Church records.

99. 1 Timothy 3:8–13.

100. Carter, *Living Faith*, 120.

101. Unlike more hierarchical denominations—like the Roman Catholic or Episcopalian Churches, where doctrine and policy are determined by a bishop, or the Presbyterian churches, where they are determined by a group of elders—the session, in Baptist church

governance, is much more democratic; a recommendation is made from the church leadership, but it must be approved by the congregation (See chapter 2).

102. Bourne, *Jimmy Carter*, 146.

103. "Jimmy Carter Thinks He Could Be Elected Governor," *Atlanta Constitution*, June 7, 1966.

104. Five years earlier, Jimmy Carter and Bo Callaway had had a contest of their own over the establishment of a four-year college. In 1961, Carter petitioned for the college to be placed in Americus, while Callaway pressed for his hometown of Columbus, Georgia.

105. Georgia Official and Statistical Register, 1965–1966–1738. The remaining votes were split between Lt. Gov. Garland T. Gray and James H. Byrd.

106. Carter, "Foreward," in Jordan, *Boy from Georgia*, ix.

107. Powell would go on to be White House Press press secretary, and Jordan would become Carter's chief of staff. They would become known as Carter's "Georgia Mafia." See "The Georgia Mafia," PBS, *The American Experience*.

108. Actually, Clarence Jordan and Hamilton Jordan were first cousins, once removed, since Richard Lawson Jordan of Macon, Georgia, and Clarence Jordan of Talbotton, Georgia, were first cousins, but Hamilton considered Clarence his uncle.

109. Jordan, *Boy from Georgia*, 207.

110. Jordan, 132.

111. Jordan, 134.

112. Jordan.

113. Hamilton missed his Uncle Clarence's funeral six months after their final meeting—he was campaigning in Savannah. "I felt sad," Hamilton recalled, "not to be able to say goodbye to this great man I had barely known" (Jordan, *Boy from Georgia*, 219).

114. "Speech by Jimmy Carter, Plains," April 4, 1970, folder: Speech in Plains, box 63, Carter Family Papers, Jimmy Carter Speech Files, Jimmy Carter Library.

115. Hamilton Jordan had actually worked for Sanders previously.

116. Author's interview with Carl Sanders.

117. Georgia Government Documentation Project, Carl Sanders, Aug. 5, 1986, Aug. 12, 1986, Georgia State University Library digital collections.

118. Godbold, *Jimmy and Rosalynn Carter*.

119. Author's interview with Carl Sanders.

120. Carter, Inaugural address, January 12, 1971, Jimmy Carter Library.

121. Carter, Inaugural address.

122. Hatred toward Koinonia was still so pronounced that the Americus coroner and medical examiner would not even come out to the farm to pronounce him dead. Instead, Millard Fuller drove Jordan's body into town. "I smiled," Fuller recalled, "I knew that he would have gotten a terrific charge out of that scene. Incarnating the word, even after he was dead, incarnating the word and saying that the body is of no consequence after life has left it" (Fuller, "Incarnation, as Revealed in the Life of Clarence Jordan"; Coroner's Report, 1969, MS 2341 3:4, Clarence L. Jordan Papers).

123. Interview of Linda Fuller Degelmann by Angie Singletary, Dec. 4, 2013, Americus, Ga., First Person Project-0028, University of Georgia Richard Russell Library.

124. Fuller, *Theology of the Hammer*, 2.

125. Fuller and Scott, *Love in the Mortar Joints*, 57.

126. Fuller, *Theology of the Hammer*, 3.

127. Author's interview with Linda Fuller Degelmann.

128. Fuller, "Incarnation."

129. Letter from Edgar Stoess to Clarence Jordan, June 21, 1962, MS 2341 1:1, Clarence L. Jordan Papers.

130. Dorothy Swisshelm had left just prior. Auchmutey, *Class of '65*, 73.

131. Letter from Con Browne to Henlee Barnette, undated, MS 2341 3:8, Clarence L. Jordan Papers. The Brownes joined Myles Horton at Highlander Folk School in Monteagle, Tennessee.

132. While Jordan and Fuller were the visionaries for Koinonia Partners, they were not alone. In August 1968, Ned Coll, Bob Miller, Bob Wood, Ted Braun, Leroy Ellis, Richard Jones, Bob Swann, John Miller, Sam Emerick, Ladon Sheets, Doc Champion, and even Slater King came to Koinonia to serve as an advisory council of sorts.

133. Lee, *Cotton Patch Evidence*, 205.

134. Fuller and Scott, *Love in the Mortar Joints*, 68.

135. Millard Fuller, "Incarnation"; Lee, *Cotton Patch Evidence*, 215.

136. Tracy K'Meyer rightly highlights the broader historical context for this economic direction for the farm: the Great Society and the War on Poverty, both of which pushed economic reforms as the path for racial parity (K'Meyer, *Interracialism and Christian Community in the Postwar South*, 1997).

137. Fuller and Scott, *Love in the Mortar Joints*, 69.

138. Lee, *Cotton Patch Evidence*, 211–12. The fund raised money well, with $50,000 of donations in 1968 up to $250,000 in 1972 (Koinonia Memorandum, Sept. 29, 1972, Koinonia Farm Archive).

139. Dallas Lee's work, written concurrently with Koinonia Partners' founding, provides a foundational text for the farm's new season, so much so that Millard Fuller himself referenced it as definitional to Koinonia's vision in an internal memo: "I believe deeply in the rightness of the vision of Koinonia Partners as it is expressed in the brochure and chapter in the Cotton Patch Evidence" (Koinonia Memorandum, Sept. 29, 1972, Koinonia Farm Archive).

140. Lee, *Cotton Patch Evidence*, 220.

141. Lee, 198.

142. Lee, 197.

143. Hedgepeth, "American South," 31, MS 2341 5:8, Clarence L. Jordan Papers. Millard, like Clarence, was a son of the Deep South and had to have a conversion to racial justice. As a young man, despite his own moderate beliefs, Fuller had spoken to segregationist political groups and even taken the case of one of the men arrested for beating the Freedom Riders in Alabama in 1961. The fee Fuller accepted for the case was paid for by the Klan. But Fuller's racial politics radically shifted through a deep reckoning with theology and the teachings of Jesus (Fuller and Scott, *Love in the Mortar Joints*, 46–47).

144. Fuller, *Theology of the Hammer*, 7. Fuller later explained it to a neighbor this way: "It is a Christian venture, and building these houses is an expression of our faith. The houses are sold to the people with no profit added to the cost of construction and no interest charged. The people will pay low monthly payments over a twenty-year period. We get the money for the construction from gifts and noninterest loans from friends of Koinonia

around the country and from shared profits of the Koinonia farming operations and pecan-fruitcake-candy business" (Fuller and Scott, *Love in the Mortar Joints*, 70).

145. Hedgepeth, "American South," 31; MS 2341 5:8, Clarence L. Jordan Papers.

146. Dubay, "Queen E. White Remembers the Beginning," Koinonia Farm Archive..

147. Fuller, "Incarnation."

148. Starling, "Habitat for Humanity" *Ebony*, Nov. 1997, 207.

149. Koinonia Partners Fall Newsletter, Sept. 1970, Koinonia Farm Archive.

150. Hollyday, "Dream that Has Endured," *Soujourners*, Dec. 1979, 17.

151. Fuller and Scott, *Love in the Mortar Joints*, 71.

152. Letter from Florence Jordan to Harry and Ailene Atkinson, May 26, 1975, MS 2341 2:7, Clarence L. Jordan Papers.

153. Hollyday, "The Dream that Has Endured," *Soujourners*, Dec. 1979, 17.

154. Author's interview with Norman Race. By 1976, Race explained, there were about thirty-five "Resident Partners" living at Koinonia, and the farm was again thriving.

155. Koinonia Newsletter, Summer 1970, Koinonia Farm Archive.

156. Hollyday, "The Dream that Has Endured," *Soujourners*, Dec. 1979, 17.

157. Though they would return, this was a low moment for the Fullers and Koinonia. Millard wrote that he was "extremely unhappy about Koinonia and my involvement in the ministry here" (Koinonia memorandum, Sept. 29, 1972).

158. See Fuller, *Bokotola*.

159. Author's interview with Linda Fuller Degelmann.

160. In Habitat for Humanity, the lived theology of Koinonia Farm—the theology of the hammer—had gone global, and the world would never be the same. Over the following decades, largely through the publicity and support of Jimmy and Rosalynn Carter, Habitat for Humanity would become one of the most prominent and successful nonprofits in the world. As of 2016, Habitat operates in seventy different countries and has built or improved homes for 6.8 million people worldwide. Its headquarters is still located in Americus; see www.habitat.org.

161. Interview with Leila Barrett, Americus, Ga., June 27, 1989, Peanut Brigade Interviews by Jim Small, Ranger, National Park Service Interviews, National Park Service Interviews, Carter Presidential Library, box 1.

162. Interview with Rudy Hayes, Americus, Ga., June 27, 1989, Peanut Brigade Interviews by Jim Small, Ranger, National Park Service Interviews, Carter Presidential Library, box 2.

163. Balmer, *Redeemer*, xxii.

164. *Newsweek*, Oct. 25, 1976.

165. Interview with Rudy Hayes, Carter Library.

166. Flippen, *Jimmy Carter*; Balmer, *Redeemer*; Zwier, *Born Again Politics*; Hefley and Hefley, *Church that Produced a President*; Nielsen, *Religion of President Carter*.

167. Interview with Eloise Paschal, Sumter County Oral History Project.

168. Interview with Rachel Clark, Carter Library.

169. *New York Times*, Jan. 10, 1977.

170. Clennon King had notified Rev. Edwards of his intentions to apply for membership and attend Plains Baptist the following Sunday by affixing a note to his residence the previous Monday.

171. *New York Times*, Jan. 10, 1977.

172. *New York Times*, Jan. 10, 1977.

173. "Carter's Church Upholds Its Policy by Refusing to Admit Four Blacks," *New York Times*, Nov. 1, 1976.

174. "Carter's Church."

175. See "Carter's Ex-Pastor, Citing Opposition, Quits Plains Church," *Washington Post*, Feb. 21, 1977; "With a Foot in Each Church, Carter Finesses Baptist Split," *Washington Post*, Aug. 8, 1977; "Church Formed by Split Welcomes Carter Family," *New York Times*, Jan. 25, 1981.

176. Balmer, *Redeemer*, xxiii.

177. Lindsay, *Faith in the Halls of Power*, 17.

178. For his part, Carter claimed he was "dismayed" at the Right's takeover of the Southern Baptist Convention and their claim to orthodoxy, their insistence that they possessed a "special ordination from God to interpret the scriptures and to consider anyone who disagrees with us wrong and inferior" (Carter, *Living Faith*, 37).

179. Carter, *Living Faith*, 165.

180. Carter, 7.

181. Carter, 169.

182. Douthat, *Bad Religion*, 4, emphasis mine.

183. "The State of American Theology Study 2016," Ligonier Ministries, Lifeway Research; http://lifewayresearch.com/wp-content/uploads/2016/09/Ligonier-State-of-American -Theology-2016-Final-Report.pdf, accessed July 17, 2016.

184. See Hunter, *Culture Wars*; Putnam and Campbell, *Amazing Grace*; Walton, *Watch This!*; Bowler, *Blessed*.

185. See Barron, *Health and Wealth Gospel*; Walton, *Watch This!*; Tucker-Worgs, *Black Megachurch*; Bowler, *Blessed*.

186. Gladwell, "Generous Orthodoxy," Revisionist History, http://revisionisthistory .com/episodes/09-generous-orthodoxy, accessed July 13, 2016.

187. Anonymous, Sherrod Papers, Wisconsin Historical Society, folder 15.

Bibliography

Primary Sources

ARCHIVAL

Georgia

  Americus

    Church Archives

      Bethesda Baptist Church Archives

      Campbell Chapel AME Church History and Archives

      First Baptist Church Archives

      First Methodist Church Archives (FUMC box)

      First Presbyterian Church Archives

    Koinonia Farm Archive

    Lake Blackshear Regional Library, Special Collections

    Sumter County Court Records

    Karl Wilson Personal Collection

  Athens

    University of Georgia Libraries, the Walter J. Brown Media Archives & Peabody Awards Collection

      WSB Newsfilm Clips: 38840, 42203, 48502, 48454, 42982, 48497, 48455, 48457, 48435, 45411, 48501, 41882, 48504, 48397

    University of Georgia Libraries, Hargrett Rare Book and Manuscript Library

      Clarence L. Jordan Papers, MS 756, MS 2340, MS 2341

    University of Georgia Libraries, Richard B. Russell Library

      S. Ernest Vandiver, Jr. Papers

  Atlanta

    Emory University, Archives and Manuscripts Department, Pitts Theology Library

      John Owen Smith Papers, MSS 242

    Emory University, Stuart A. Rose Manuscript, Archives, and Rare Book Library

      Jimmy Carter Presidential Library

      Carter Family Papers, Jimmy Carter's Speech Files

      Frances Freeborn Pauley Papers, 1919–1992

      John A. Sibley Papers, MC 437

  Macon

    Mercer University, Georgia Baptist History Depository, Special Collections

      Georgia Baptist Church Records

  St. Simons Island

    South Georgia Methodist Collection, Epworth by the Sea

      South Georgia Conference of the United Methodist Church Papers

New Jersey
  Madison
    Drew University Archives
      George D. Kelsey Papers
      United Methodist Archives
Tennessee
  Nashville
    Southern Baptist Historical Library and Archives
      Thomas Buford Maston Collection, AR 704
      Christian Life Commission Administrative Files, AR 138
      Clarence Jordan Collection, AR 39
      Race Relations and Southern Baptists Collection, AR 788
      Southern Baptist Convention, Christian Life Commission Resource Files, AR 138-2

DIGITAL

Americus and Sumter County Movement Remembered, http://www.theamericus movement.org.

The Civil Rights Movement and the Federal Government, Records of the U.S. Commission on Civil Rights, School Desegregation in the South, 1965–1966, UPA Collection, Lexis Nexus, Bethesda Maryland, microfilm, https://searchworks.stanford .edu/view/8702281.

Congressional Record, the Library of Congress, Washington, D.C., https://www.congress .gov/congressional-record/archive.

Faith Holsaert Papers, 1950–2011, Duke University Archives, Durham, N.C., https: //repository.duke.edu/dc/holsaertfaith.

Film and Media Archive, Henry Hampton Collection, 1987, https://library.wustl.edu/spec /filmandmedia/collections/hampton/eop/.

Lived Theology Archive, the Project on Lived Theology, Charlottesville, Virginia, http: //archives.livedtheology.org.

The King Center Digital Archive, http://www.thekingcenter.org/archive.

Mants Papers, SNCC Digital Archives, https://snccdigital.org/people/bob-mants/.

Martin Luther King Jr., Papers Project, Stanford University, https://kinginstitute.stanford .edu/king-papers/about-papers-project.

Sherrod Papers (1961–1967), The King Library & Archive, Atlanta, Ga., http://www .thekingcenter.org/king-library-archive.

Sherrod Papers, Wisconsin Historical Society, http://digicoll.library.wisc.edu/cgi/f /findaid/findaid-idx?c=wiarchives;cc=wiarchives;view=text;rgn=main;didno=uw-whs -micro051.

SNCC Field Reports, Sherrod Papers, Martin Luther King Jr. Papers Project.

Southern Baptist Theological Seminary, the Boyce Digital Library, http://digital.library .sbts.edu.

Student Nonviolent Coordinating Committee (SNCC) Papers, 1959–1972, the King Center, Atlanta, Ga.

The Student Voice, Sherrod Papers, Wisconsin Historical Society, http://cdm15932
.contentdm.oclc.org/cdm/ref/collection/p15932coll2/id/50279.
Sumter County, Georgia, Genealogy: Alan Anderson and Robert Evans, http://www
.sumtercountyhistory.com.
Veterans of the Civil Rights Movement, http://www.crmvet.org.
"Who Speaks for the Negro?," Robert Penn Warren Center for the Humanities, Vanderbilt
University, https://whospeaks.library.vanderbilt.edu/interviews.

NEWSPAPERS

Americus Times-Recorder

Atlanta Daily World

Atlanta Inquirer

Atlanta Journal Constitution

Albany Journal

Chicago Daily News

Christian Century

Harvard Crimson

New York Times

Pittsburgh Courier

Washington Post

INTERVIEWS

Author's

Alaman, Jewel Wise. Aug. 2, 2012. Tape recording. Americus, Ga.

Argo, Malcolm. July 27, 2011. Tape recording. Americus, Ga.

Bell, David, Jr. Feb. 14, 2014. Tape recording. Phone Interview.

Bush, Paul. July 27, 2012. Tape recording. Americus, Ga.

Campbell, Mamie. July 26, 2012. Tape recording. Americus, Ga.

Collins, Isabel. Mar. 8, 2014. Tape recording. Americus, Ga

Crisp, Charles. Mar. 7, 2014. Tape recording. Americus, Ga.

Degelman, Linda Fuller, Aug. 9, 2012. Tape recording. Americus, Ga.

DeLoatch, Carolyn. Jan. 31, 2014. Tape recording. Phone interview.

Dupree, Rev. Bill. July 30, 2012. Tape recording. Americus, Ga.

Easterlin, Ben. Mar. 13, 2013. Tape recording. Atlanta, Ga.

Entrekin, Harry and Ann. Aug. 6, 2012. Tape recording. Americus, Ga.

Fortson, Warren. Jan. 20, 2012. Tape recording. Atlanta, Ga.

Green, Mike. Mar. 6, 2014. Americus, Ga.

Heys, Kellete. July 27, 2012. Tape recording. Americus, Ga.

Hicks, Marion, and Kelso Gooden. July 30, 2012. Tape recording. Americus, Ga.

Howard, Rev. William Moses. Oct. 3, 2013. Tape recording. Phone interview.

Key, Rev. Billy, and Sunshine Key. Aug. 7, 2012. Tape recording. Americus, Ga.

Kinslow, Ty. Mar. 6, 2013. Americus, Ga.

Lowery, Dr. Frank. Aug. 1, 2012. Tape recording. Americus, Ga.

Lundy, Walter. Sept. 27, 2013. Tape recording. Phone interview.

Lyman-Barner, Kirk. July 31, 2012. Americus, Ga.

Mahone, Sam. Aug. 9, 2012. Tape recording. Atlanta, Ga.

Mansfield, Teresa. July 27, 2012. Tape recording. Americus, Ga.

Paschal, Eloise. Aug. 1, 2012. Tape recording. Americus, Ga.

Race, Norman. Aug. 7, 2012. Tape recording. Americus, Ga.

Sanders, Gov. Carl. Oct. 10, 2013. Tape recording. Atlanta, Ga.

Sherrod, Charles. Jan. 6, 2016. Tape recording. Albany, Ga.

Thomas, Russell. Aug. 3, 2012. Tape recording. Americus, Ga.

Walker, Eddie Rhea. July 25, 2011. Tape recording. Americus, Ga.

Wilson, Karl. Jan. 19, 2012. Tape recording. Americus, Ga.

Wood, Martha. Aug. 8, 2012. Tape recording. Americus, Ga.

Carter Presidential Library

Barrett, Leila. June 27, 1989. Interview by Jim Small, Ranger. National Park Service. Americus, Ga.

Carter, Lillian. Sept. 26, 1978. Carter/Smith Family Interviews.

Clark, Rachel. Nov. 9, 1978. Carter/Smith Family Interviews.

Hayes, Rudy. June 27, 1989. Interview by Jim Small, Ranger. National Park Service. Americus, Ga.

Georgia State University, Special Collections

Frances Pauley, May 3, 1988. Interview No. 2 by Cliff Kuhn, Georgia Government Documentation Project.

Southern Oral History Program

Mahone, Sam. 2013. Interview by Hasan Jeffries, Southern Oral History Program. Albany State University, Albany, Ga.

Sumter County Oral History Project

Campbell, Rev. J. R., and Mamie Campbell. 2003. Interview by Sumter County Oral History Project. Tape recording. Georgia Southwestern University, Americus, Ga.

Cheokas, Anna. 2003. Interview by Sumter County Oral History Project. Tape recording. Georgia Southwestern University, Americus, Ga.

Fletcher, Robertiena Freeman. 2003. Interview by Sumter County Oral History Project. Tape recording. Georgia Southwestern University, Americus, Ga.

Fuse, Bob. 2003. Interview by Sumter County Oral History Project. Tape recording. Georgia Southwestern University, Americus, Ga.

King, William. 2003. Interview by Sumter County Oral History Project. Tape recording. Georgia Southwestern University, Americus, Ga.

Lowe, Lewis. 2003. Interview by Sumter County Oral History Project. Tape recording. Georgia Southwestern University, Americus, Ga.

Myers, J. Frank. 2003. Interview by Sumter County Oral History Project. Tape recording. Georgia Southwestern University, Americus, Ga.

Pace, Mark. 2003. Interview by Sumter County Oral History Project. Tape recording. Georgia Southwestern University, Americus, Ga.

Parker, Roy. 2003. Interview by Sumter County Oral History Project. Tape recording. Georgia Southwestern University, Americus, Ga.

Paschal, Eloise. 2003. Interview by Sumter County Oral History Project. Tape recording. Georgia Southwestern University, Americus, Ga.

Sabbs, Lorena Barnum. 2003. Interview by Sumter County Oral History Project. Tape recording. Georgia Southwestern University, Americus, Ga.

University of West Georgia, Irvine Sullivan Ingram Library

Bell, Judge Griffin, Sept. 24, 1997. Oral history interview. Annie Belle Weaver Special
　Collections.

Vanderbilt University, Robert Penn Warren Center for the Humanities

Campbell Will. Feb. 13–14, 1964. Interview by Robert Penn Warren. Tape recording.
　Nashville, Tenn.

Carmichael, Stokely. Mar. 4, 1964. Interview by Robert Penn Warren. Tape recording.
　[Atlanta, Ga.?].

Clark, Septima Poinsette. Mar. 18, 1964. Interview by Robert Penn Warren. Tape
　recording. Atlanta, Ga.

Forman, James. June 4, 1964. Interview by Robert Penn Warren. Tape recording.

Jordan Jr., Vernon E. Mar. 17, 1964. Interview by Robert Penn Warren. Tape recording.
　[Memphis, Tenn.?].

Lawson Jr., James M. Mar. 17, 1964. Interview by Robert Penn Warren. Tape recording.
　Memphis, Tenn.

King Jr., Martin L. Mar. 18, 1964. Interview by Robert Penn Warren. Tape recording.
　Atlanta, Ga.

King, Montgomery Wordsworth. Feb. 5, 1964. Interview by Robert Penn Warren. Tape
　recording. Atlanta, Ga.

Nelson, William Stuart. Mar. 3, 1964. Interview by Robert Penn Warren. Tape recording.
　Atlanta, Ga.

Smith, Kelly Miller. Feb. 13, 1964. Interview by Robert Penn Warren. Tape recording.
　Nashville, Tenn.

Tougaloo College Students, Feb. 11, 1964. Interview by Robert Penn Warren. Tape
　recording [Jackson, Miss.?].

Young, Andrew. March 17, 1964. Interview by Robert Penn Warren. Tape recording.
　Atlanta, Ga.

Washington University Libraries, Film and Media Archive, Henry Hampton Collection

Wyatt Tee Walker, Oct. 11, 1985. Interview by Blackside, Inc. for *Eyes on the Prize: America's
　Civil Rights Years (1954–1965).*

Secondary and Printed Sources

A City without Pity: Americus in the 1960s. Directed by John Hudson. (2007).

Ahlstrom, Sydney E. *A Religious History of the American People.* New Haven, Conn.: Yale
　University Press, 2004.

Alexander, Michelle. *The New Jim Crow: Mass Incarceration in the Age of Colorblindness.*
　New York: New Press, 2010.

Almond, Gabriel A., R. Scott Appleby, and Emmanuel Sivan. *Strong Religion: The
　Rise of Fundamentalisms around the World.* Chicago: University of Chicago Press,
　2003.

Alvis, Joel L. *Religion and Race: Southern Presbyterians, 1946–1983.* Tuscaloosa: University
　of Alabama Press, 1994.

Anderson, Alan. "Americus School History." Sumter County History, http://www
.sumtercountyhistory.com/history/AmSchHx.htm.

———. *A Journey of Grace: A History of the First Baptist Church in Americus, GA.* Americus,
Ga.: First Baptist, 2006.

———. *Remembering Americus: Essays on Southern Life.* Charleston, S.C.: History Press,
2006.

Anderson, William G. "Reflections on the Origins of the Albany Movement." *Journal of
Southwest Georgia History* 9 (Fall 1994): 1–14.

Andrews, Eliza Frances. *The War-Time Journal of a Georgia Girl, 1864–1865.* New York:
D. Appleton and Company, 1908.

Andrews, William. *Sisters of the Spirit: Three Black Women's Autobiographies of the
Nineteenth Century.* Bloomington: Indiana Press, 1986.

Angell, Stephen Ward. *Henry McNeal Turner and African-American Religion in the South.*
Knoxville: University of Tennessee, 1992.

Angry, Sue. *My Life: Changing and Growing.* Kennet Square, Pa.: Write Place, 2003

Annual Report of the Southern Baptist Convention, 1963. Nashville, Tenn.: Southern Baptist
Convention, 1963.

Ansbro, John. *Martin Luther King, Jr.: The Making of a Mind.* Maryknoll, N.Y.: Orbis
Books, 1982.

Arnesen, Eric. *Black Protest and the Great Migration.* Boston, Mass: Bedford/St. Martin's
Press, 2002.

Auchmutey, Jim. *Class of '65: A Student, a Divided Town, and the Long Road to Forgiveness.*
New York: PublicAffairs, 2015.

Augustine of Hippo, *City of God*, Book VIII.

Bailey, Julius H. *Race Patriotism: Protest and Print Culture in the AME Church.* Knoxville:
University of Tennessee Press, 2012.

Baker, Kelly J. *The Gospel according to the Klan.* Lawrence: University of Kansas Press, 2011.

Baldwin, Lewis. *To Make the Wounded Whole.* Minneapolis: Augsburg Fortress, 1992.

———. *Never to Leave Us Alone: The Prayer Life of Martin Luther King Jr.* Minneapolis,
Minn.: Augsburg Fortress, 2010.

———. *There Is a Balm in Gilead: The Cultural Roots of Martin Luther King, Jr.* Minneapolis:
Fortress Press, 1991.

Balmer, Randall. *The Making of Evangelicalism: From Revivalism to Politics and Beyond.*
Waco, Tex.: Baylor University Press, 2010.

———. *Redeemer: The Life of Jimmy Carter.* New York: Basic Books, 2014.

———. *Thy Kingdom Come.* New York: Basic Books, 2006.

Barnes, Kenneth C. *Journey of Hope: The Back-to-Africa Movement in Arkansas in the Late
1800s.* Chapel Hill: University of North Carolina Press, 2004.

Barnette, Henlee. *Clarence Jordan: Turning Dreams into Dreams.* Macon, Ga: Smyth and
Helwys, 1992.

Barron, Bruce. *The Health and Wealth Gospel: What's Going on Today in a Movement That
Has Shaped the Faith of Millions.* Downers Grove, Il.: InterVarsity Press, 1987.

Bartley, Numan V. *Rise of Massive Resistance: Race and Politics in the South during the 1950s.*
Baton Rouge: Louisiana State University Press, 1969.

Bass, S. Jonathan. *Blessed Are the Peacemakers: Martin Luther King, Jr., Eight White Religious Leaders, and the "Letter from Birmingham Jail."* Baton Rouge: Louisiana State University Press, 2001.

Beale, David O. *In Pursuit of Purity: American Fundamentalism since 1850.* Greenville, S.C.: Bob Jones University Press, 1986.

Benedict, David. *A General History of the Baptist Denomination in America.* Boston: Lincoln & Edmands, 1813.

Bennett, James B. *Religion and the Rise of Jim Crow in New Orleans.* Princeton, N.J.: Princeton University Press, 2005.

Bennett, Lerone, Jr. "SNCC: Rebels with a Cause." *Ebony*, July 1965, 146–53.

———. *What Manner of Man: A Biography of Martin Luther King, Jr.* Chicago, 1968.

Bestor, Arthur E., Jr. *Backwoods Utopias: The Sectarian Origins and the Owenite Phase of Communitarian Socialism in America, 1663–1829.* Philadelphia: University of Pennsylvania Press, 1950.

Blackmon, Douglas A. *Slavery by Another Name: Black Americans from the Civil War to World War II.* New York: Anchor Books, 2009.

Blackwelder, Julia Kirk. "Southern White Fundamentalists and the Civil Rights Movement." *Phylon* 40, no. 4 (1979): 334–41.

Blight, David. *Race and Reunion: The Civil War in American Memory.* Cambridge, Mass.: Belknap Press of Harvard University, 2001.

Blum, Edward J. *Reforging the White Republic: Race, Religion and American Nationalism, 1865–1898.* Baton Rouge: Louisiana State University Press, 2005.

Blum, Edward, and Paul Harvey. *The Color of Christ: The Son of God and the Saga of Race in America.* Chapel Hill: University of North Carolina Press, 2012.

Blumhofer, Edith L., ed. *Religion, Education, and the American Experience: Reflections on Religion and American Public Life.* Tuscaloosa: University of Alabama Press, 2002.

Bolster, Paul Douglas. "Civil Rights Movements in Twentieth Century Georgia." PhD diss. University of Georgia, 1972.

Bonhoeffer, Dietrich. *Life Together: The Classic Exploration of Faith in Community.* New York: Harper & Row, 1954.

Borstelmann, Thomas. *The Cold War and the Color Line: American Race Relations in the Global Arena.* Cambridge, Mass.: Harvard University Press, 2003.

Bourne, Peter. *Jimmy Carter: A Comprehensive Biography from Plains to Post-Presidency.* New York: Scriber, 1997.

Bowler, Kate. *Blessed: A History of the American Prosperity Gospel.* New York: Oxford University Press, 2013.

Boyer, Paul. "A Joyful Noyes: Reassessing America's Utopian Tradition." *Reviews in American History* 3, no. 1 (March 1975): 25–30.

Braden, Anne. "The Images are Broken: Students Challenge Rural Georgia." *Southern Patriot* 20 (Dec. 1962).

Branch, Taylor. *At Canaan's Edge: America in the King Years, 1965–1968.* New York: Simon & Schuster, 2006.

———. *Parting the Waters: America in the King Years, 1954–1963.* New York: Simon & Schuster, 1988.

——. *Pillar of Fire: America in the King Years, 1963–1965.* New York: Simon & Schuster, 1998.

Briars in the Cottonpatch. Directed by Faith Fuller. Cottonpatch Productions, 2005.

Brokaw, Tom. *Boom! Voices of the Sixties.* New York: Random House, 2007.

Brooks, Walter H. "The Evolution of the Negro Baptist Church." *Journal of Negro History* 7, no. 1 (Jan. 1922): 11–22.

Brown, Rev. Pearlie. as quoted in "Resurrection Remix," African American Lectionary, The African American Pulpit and American Bible College, 2008. http://www .theafricanamericanlectionary.org/PopupCulturalAid.asp?LRID=20.

Brown, Richard W. "Freedom of Choice in the South: A Constitutional Perspective." *Louisiana Law Review* 28 (1968). https://digitalcommons.law.lsu.edu/lalrev/vol28/iss3 /21/.

Brown-Nagin, Tomiko. *Courage to Dissent: Atlanta and the Long History of the Civil Rights Movement.* Oxford: Oxford University Press, 2011.

Bruns, Roger. *Martin Luther King Jr.: A Biography.* Westport, Conn.: Greenwood Press, 2006.

Bryan, G. Mcleod, ed. *These Few Also Paid a Price: Southern Whites Who Fought for Civil Rights.* Macon, Ga.: Mercer University Press, 2001.

Buber, Martin. *I and Thou.* Translated by Ronald Gregory Smith. Edinburgh: T&T Clark, 1937.

Buchanan, Scott E. *Some of the People Who Ate My Barbeque Didn't Vote for Me.* Nashville, Tenn.: Vanderbilt University Press, 2011.

Burkett, Randall, and Richard Newman. *Black Apostles: Afro-American Clergy Confront the Twentieth Century.* Boston: G. K. Hall, 1978.

Burnett, William G. *History of the Americus Presbyterian Church.* 1992.

Burns, Stewart, ed. *Daybreak of Freedom: The Montgomery Bus Boycott.* Chapel Hill: University of North Carolina Press, 1997.

Burns, Stewart, Susan Carson, Peter Holloran, and Dana L. H. Powell, eds. *The Papers of Martin Luther King, Jr.,* vol. 3, *The Birth of a New Age, December 1955–December 1956.* Berkeley: University of California Press, 1996.

Bush, L. Russ, and Tom J. Nettles, eds. *Baptists and the Bible.* Nashville, Tenn.: B&H, 1999.

Butler, Jon. "Jack-in-the-Box Faith: The Religion Problem in Modern American History." *Journal of American History,* 90 (March 2004): 1357–78.

Byron, Dora. "Courage in Action: Koinonia Revisited," *The Nation* 84 (March 16, 1957): N.p.

Callahan, Allen Dwight. *The Talking Book: African Americans and the Bible.* New Haven, Conn.: Yale University Press, 2006.

Campbell, James T. *Middle Passage: African American Journeys to Africa, 1787–2005.* New York: Penguin Press, 2006.

——. *Songs of Zion: The African Methodist Episcopal Church in the United States and South Africa.* New York: Oxford University Press, 1995.

Campbell, Will. "Where There's So Much Smoke," *Soujourners* 8, no. 12 (December 1979): 19.

Carpenter, Joel A. *Revive Us Again: The Reawakening of American Fundamentalism.* Oxford: Oxford University Press, 1999.

Carper, James C., and Thomas C. Hunt, eds. *Religious Schooling in America*. Birmingham, Ala.: Religious Education Press, 1984.

Carson, Clayborne, ed. *The Autobiography of Martin Luther King, Jr*. New York: Warner Books, 1998.

———. "Civil Rights Reform and the Black Freedom Struggle." In *The Civil Rights Movement in America*, edited by Charles W. Eagles, 19–32. Jackson: University Press of Mississippi, 1986.

———. *In Struggle: SNCC and the Black Awakening of the 1960s*. Cambridge, Mass.: Harvard University Press, 1981.

———, ed. *A Knock at Midnight: inspiration from the Great Sermons of Reverend Martin Luther King, Jr*. New York: Intellectual Properties Management in association with Warner Books, 1998.

———, ed. *The Student Voice, 1960–1965: Periodical of the Student Nonviolent Coordinating Committee*. Stanford, Calif.: Martin Luther King, Jr. Papers Project, 1990.

Carter, J. Kameron. *Race: A Theological Account*. Oxford: Oxford University Press, 2008.

Carter, Jimmy. *An Hour Before Daylight: Memories of a Rural Boyhood*. New York: Simon & Schuster, 2001.

———. *Living Faith*. New York: Times Books, 1996.

———. *Turning Point: A Candidate, a State and a Nation Come of Age*. New York: Crown, 1992.

Cash, W. J. *The Mind of the South*. New York: Knopf Press, 1941.

Chafe, William H. *Civilities and Civil Rights: Greensboro, North Carolina, and the Black Struggle for Freedom*. Oxford: Oxford University Press, 1981.

Chancey, Andrew S. "Restructuring Southern Society: The Radical Vision on Koinonia Farm." Master's thesis, University of Georgia, 1990.

———. "Race, Religion, and Reform: Koinonia's Challenge to Southern Society, 1942–1992." PhD diss., University of Florida, 1998.

Chappell, David L. "Disunity and Religious Institutions in the White South." In *Massive Resistance*, edited by Clive Webb, 136–50. New York: Oxford University Press, 2005.

———. *Inside Agitators: White Southerners in the Civil Rights Movement*. Baltimore: Johns Hopkins University Press, 1994.

———. "Religious Ideas of the Segregationists." *Journal of American Studies* 32 (August 1998): 237–62.

———. *A Stone of Hope: Prophetic Religion and the Death of Jim Crow*. Chapel Hill: University of North Carolina Press, 2004.

Clayton, Ed., ed. *The SLC Story in Words and Pictures*. Atlanta, Ga.: SCLC, 1964.

Cleage, Albert B. *The Black Messiah*. New York: Sheed and Ward, 1968.

Clegg, Claude A., III. *The Price of Liberty: African Americans and the Making of Liberia*. Chapel Hill: University of North Carolina Press, 2004.

Cline, David P. *From Reconciliation to Revolution: The Student Interracial Ministry, Liberal Christianity, and the Civil Rights Movement*. Chapel Hill: University of North Carolina Press, 2016.

Coan, Josephus R. *Daniel Alexander Payne: Christian Educator*. Philadelphia: A.M.E. Book Concern, 1935.

The Code of the State of Georgia, prepared by R. H. Clark, T. R. R. Cobb, and D. Irwin. Second Edition. Atlanta, Ga.: Jas. P. Harrison & Co., Printers and Publishers, 1882, King & Spalding Library.

Collier-Thomas, Bettye, and V. P. Franklin, eds. *Sisters in the Struggle: African American Women in the Civil Rights and Black Power Movement.* New York: New York University Press, 2001.

Colson, Freddie. *Dr. Benjamin E. Mays Speaks.* Lanham, Md.: University Press of America, 2002.

Cone, James H. "Black Spirituals: A Theological Interpretation." *Theology Today* 29. 1 (1972): 54–69.

———. *Black Theology and Black Power.* Maryknoll, N.Y.: Orbis Books, 1969.

———. *A Black Theology of Liberation.* Maryknoll, N.Y.: Orbis Books, 1970.

———. *The Cross and the Lynching Tree.* Maryknoll, N.Y.: Orbis Books, 2011.

———. *God of the Oppressed.* Maryknoll, N.Y.: Orbis Books, 1975.

———. "God Our Father, Christ Our Redeemer, Man Our Brother: A Theological Interpretation of the AME Church." *AME Church Review* 106, no. 341 (1991): 25–33.

———. *My Soul Looks Back.* New York: Orbis Books, 1985.

———. *The Spirituals and the Blues: An Interpretation.* Seabury Press, 1972.

Conot, Robert. *Rivers of Blood, Years of Darkness.* New York: William Morrow & Company, 1968.

Cox, Jack Frank. *History of Sumter County, Georgia.* Sumter, Ga.: Sumter Historic Preservation Society, 1983.

Crespino, Joseph. *In Search of Another Country: Mississippi and the Conservative Counterrevolution.* Princeton, N.J.: Princeton University Press, 2007.

———. *Strom Thurmond's America.* New York: Hill and Wang, 2012.

Cullen, Countee. *The Black Christ and Other Poems.* New York: Harper & Brothers, 1929.

Cunningham, W. J. *Agony at Galloway: One Church's Struggle with Social Change.* Jackson: University Press of Mississippi, 1980.

Curry, Constance, et al. *Deep in our Hearts: Nine White Women in the Freedom Movement.* Athens: University of Georgia Press, 2000.

Dailey, Jane. "Sex, Segregation, and the Sacred after *Brown.*" *Journal of American History* 91, no. 1 (June 2004): 119–144.

———. "The Theology of Massive Resistance: Sex, Segregation, and the Sacred after *Brown.*" In *Massive Resistance*, edited by Clive Webb, 151–80. New York: Oxford University Press, 2005.

Daniel, Dr. Carey. *God the Original Segregationist and Seven Other Segregation Sermons (1954).* First Baptist Church of West Dallas. *Citizens Council.* July 1957.

Dark, David. "Insert Soul Here." In *Lived Theology*, edited by Charles Marsh, Peter Slade, and Sarah Zaransky, 153–69. New York: Oxford University Press, 2016.

Davidson, Chandler, and Bernard Groffman. *Quiet Revolution in the South: The Impact of the Voting Rights Act, 1965–1990.* Princeton, N.J.: Princeton University Press, 1994.

Day, Dorothy. "On Pilgrimage-May 1957." *The Catholic Worker*, May 1957.

Deatrick, Juanita. "Koinonia: A Twentieth Century Experiment in Communal Living." Master's thesis, University of Georgia, 1968.

De Lissovoy, Peter, ed. *The Great Pool Jump & Other Stories from the Civil Rights Movement in Southwest Georgia*. Lancaster, N.H.: YouArePerfect Press, 2010.

De Tocqueville, Alexis. *Democracy in America*. Vol. 1. Translated by Henry Reeve. New York: Scatcherd and Adams, 1839.

Dickerson, Dennis C. "African American Religious Intellectuals and the Theological Foundations of the Civil Rights Movement, 1930–55." *Church History* 74, no. 2 (June 2005): 217–35.

——. "William Stuart Nelson: The Interfaith Origins of the Civil Rights Movement." In *Churches, Blackness, and Contested Multiculturalism*, edited by R. Drew Smith, William Ackah, and Anthony G. Reddie, 57–74. Cambridge: Cambridge University Press, 2013.

Dickson, Bruce, Jr. *And They All Sang Hallelujah: Plain Folk Camp-Meeting Religion, 1800–1845*. Knoxville: University of Tennessee Press, 1974.

Dierenfield, Bruce J. *The Battle over School Prayer: How* Engel v. Vitale *Changed America*. Lawrence: University of Kansas Press, 2007.

Dittmer, John. *Local People: The Struggle for Civil Rights in Mississippi*. Urbana: University of Illinois Press, 1995.

Dochuk, Darren. *From Bible Belt to Sun Belt: Plain-Folk Religion, Grassroots Politics, and the Rise of Evangelical Conservatism*. New York: W. W. Norton & Company, 2011.

Dollar, George W. *A History of Fundamentalism in America*. Greenville, S.C.: Bob Jones University Press, 1973.

Douthat, Ross. *Bad Religion: How We Became a Nation of Heretics*. New York: Free Press, 2012.

Du Bois, W. E. B. "The Church and the Negro." *Crisis*, no. 6 (October 1913).

——. *The Negro Church*. Atlanta, Ga.: Atlanta University Press, 1903.

——. *The Philadelphia Negro: A Sociological Study*. Philadelphia: University of Pennsylvania Press, 1899.

——. *The Souls of Black Folk*. Chicago: A.C. McClurg, 1903

Dudziak, Mary L. *Cold War Civil Rights: Race and the Image of American Democracy*. Princeton, N.J.: Princeton University Press, 2000.

Dupont, Carolyn Renee. *Mississippi Praying: Southern White Evangelicals and the Civil Rights Movement, 1945–1975*. New York: New York University Press, 2013.

Dyson, Michael Eric. *Making Malcolm: The Myth and Making of Malcolm X*. New York: Oxford University Press, 1996.

Eighmy, John Lee. *Churches in Cultural Captivity: A History of Social Attitudes of Southern Baptists*. Knoxville, Tenn.: University of Tennessee Press, 1987.

Escott, Paul D. *W. J. Cash and the Minds of the South*. Baton Rouge: Louisiana State University Press, 1992.

Evans, Curtis. *The Burden of Black Religion*. Oxford: Oxford University Press, 2008.

Evans, William M. "From the Land of Canaan to the Land of Guinea: The Strange Odyssey of the 'Sons of Ham.'" *American Historical Review* 85 (February 1980): 15–43.

Eyes on the Prize: America's Civil Rights Years 1954–1965. Washington University Libraries. https://library.wustl.edu/spec/filmandmedia/collections/hampton/eop/.

Ezell, Humphrey K. *Christian Problem of Racial Segregation*. New York: Greenwich, 1959.

Fairclough, Adam. *Martin Luther King, Jr*. Athens: University of Georgia Press, 1995.

——. *Race and Democracy: The Civil Rights Struggle in Louisiana, 1915–1972.* Athens: University of Georgia Press, 1995.

——. *To Redeem the Soul of America: The Southern Christian Leadership Conference and Martin Luther King, Jr.* Athens: University of Georgia Press, 2001.

Falwell, Jerry. "Ministers and Marches." In *Jerry Falwell and the Rise of the Religious Right: A Brief History with Documents,* edited by Matthew Sutton, 56–70. Boston: Bedford/St. Martin's Press, 2012.

Falwell, Macel. *Jerry Falwell: His Life and Legacy.* New York: Howard Books, 2008.

Feldman, Glenn. *Politics, Society and the Klan in Alabama, 1915–1949.* Tuscaloosa: University of Alabama Press, 1999.

Findlay, James F., Jr. *Church People in the Struggle: The National Council of Churches and the Black Freedom Movement, 1950–1970.* New York: Oxford University Press, 1993.

Flamm, Michael. *Law and Order: Street Crime, Civil Unrest and the Crisis of Liberalism in the 1960s.* New York: Columbia University Press, 2005.

Flippen, J. Brooks. *Jimmy Carter, the Politics of Family, and the Rise of the Religious Right.* Athens: University of Georgia Press, 2011.

Flowers, Elizabeth H. *Into the Pulpit: Southern Baptist Women and Power since World War II.* Chapel Hill: University of North Carolina Press, 2012.

Fowle, Farnsworth. "Riverdale Aiding Resident Jailed in Civil Rights Battle in Georgia." *New York Times,* October 3, 1963.

Fox, Richard Wrightman. *Jesus in America: Personal Savior, Cultural Hero, National Obsession.* San Francisco: HarperSanFrancisco, 2004.

Frady, Marshall. "God and Man in the South," *Atlantic,* January 1967, 37–42.

——. *Martin Luther King, Jr.* New York: Viking Penguin, 2002.

——. "My Dream Came True: I was Mr. Maddox." *New York Review of Books,* April 6, 1972.

——. "Small Victories in Americus: Discovering One Another in a Georgia Town." *Life,* February 12, 1971, 46B–52.

——. *Southerners: A Journalist's Odyssey.* New York: New American Library, 1980.

Franklin, John Hope. "Religious Belief and Political Activism in Black America." *Journal of Religious Thought* 43 (Fall/Winter 1986–87): 51–62.

Frazier, E. Franklin. *The Negro Church in America.* New York: Schocken Books, 1963.

Frey, Sylvia R. "The Visible Church: Historiography of African American Religion since Raboteau." *Slavery and Abolition* 29, no. 1 (March 2008): 83–110.

Fried, Richard M. *Nightmare in Red: The World of Joe McCarthy.* Oxford: Oxford University Press, 1990.

Frier, Bruce. "Letter to the Editor." *Trinity Tripod,* October 15, 1963. http://digitalrepository.trincoll.edu/cgi/viewcontent.cgi?article=1618&context=tripod.

Fuller, Millard. *Bokotola.* New York: Association Press, 1977.

——. "The Incarnation, as Revealed in the Life of Clarence Jordan." Speech to the Atlanta Christian Council, Dec. 4, 1969, Atlanta, Ga.: Fuller Center for Housing.

——. *Theology of the Hammer.* Macon, Ga.: Smyth & Helwys Publishers, 1994.

Fuller, Millard, and Diane Scott. *Love in the Mortar Joints: The Story of Habitat for Humanity.* El Monte, Calif.: New Win Publishing, 1990.

Furniss, Norman F. *The Fundamentalist Controversy, 1918–1931.* New Haven, Conn.: Yale University Press, 1954.

Gardner, Carl. *Andrew Young: A Biography.* New York, 1978.

Garrow, David J. *Bearing the Cross: Martin Luther King, Jr. and the Southern Christian Leadership Conference.* New York: William Morrow & Company, 1986.

Genovese, Eugene. "The Christian Tradition." In *African American Religious Thought,* edited by Cornell West and Eddie Glaude. Louisville, Ky.: Westminster John Knox Press, 2003.

——. *Roll, Jordan, Roll: The World the Slaves Made.* New York: Vintage Books, 1976.

Genovese, Eugene, and Elizabeth Fox-Genovese. *Mind of the Master Class: History and Faith in the Southern Slaveholders' Worldview.* Cambridge: Cambridge University Press, 2005.

Giddings, C.F. *Americus Times-Recorder,* Dec. 8, 1931.

Gillespie, G. T. "A Christian View on Segregation." Greenwood, Miss.: Association of Citizen Councils, 1954.

Gilmore, Glenda. *Defying Dixie: The Radical Roots of Civil Rights, 1919–1950.* New York: W. W. Norton & Company, 2008.

Glaude, Eddie S., Jr. *Exodus! Religion, Race and Nation in Nineteenth-Century Black America.* Chicago: University of Chicago Press, 2000.

Godbold, *Jimmy and Rosalynn Carter: the Georgia Years, 1924–1974.* New York: Oxford University Press, 2010.

Goldenberg, David M. *The Curse of Ham: Race and Slavery in Early Judaism, Christianity, and Islam.* Princeton, N.J.: Princeton University Press, 2003.

Goodwin, Everett. *Down by the Riverside: A Brief History of Baptist Faith.* Valley Forge, Pa.: Judson Press, 2002.

Gramling, Roger M. *A Ministry of Hope: Portrait of Arthur J. Moore.* Nashville, Tenn.: Upper Room, 1979.

Graves, Robert, and Raphael Patai. *Hebrew Myths: The Book of Genesis.* New York: McGraw-Hill, 1966.

Greenberg, Cheryl Lynn. *A Circle of Trust: Remembering SNCC.* New Brunswick, N.J.: Rutgers University Press, 1998.

Greene, Melissa Fay. *Praying for Sheetrock: A Work of Nonfiction.* New York: Ballantine Books, 1991.

Gregg, Howard D. *History of the African Methodist Episcopal Church: The Black Church in Action.* Nashville, Tenn.: AMEC Publishers, 1980.

Grem, Darren E. *The Blessings of Business: How Corporations Shaped Conservative Christianity.* New York: Oxford University Press, 2016.

Grossman, James R. *Land of Hope: Chicago, Black Southerners, and the Great Migration.* Chicago: University of Chicago Press, 1991.

Guarneri, Carl J. *The Utopian Alternative: Fourierism in Nineteenth-Century America.* Ithaca, N.Y.: Cornell University Press, 1991.

Hahn, Steven. *A Nation under Our Feet: Black Political Struggles in the Rural South from Slavery to the Great Migration.* Cambridge, Mass.: Belknap Press of Harvard University Press, 2003.

——. *The Political Worlds of Slavery and Freedom.* Cambridge, Mass.: Harvard University Press, 2009.

Halberstam, David. *The Children.* New York: Random House, 1998.

Hall, David D., ed. *Lived Religion in America: Toward a History of Practice*. Princeton, N.J.: Princeton University Press, 1997.

Hall, Jacquelyn Dowd. "The Long Civil Rights Movement and the Political Uses of the Past." *Journal of American History* 19, no. 4 (March 2005): 1233–36.

Hampton, Henry, and Steve Fayer, eds. *Voices of Freedom*. New York: Bantam Books, 1990.

Handy, Robert T., ed. *The Social Gospel in America, 1870–1920*. New York: Oxford University Press, 1966.

Hankins, Barry. *American Evangelicals: A Contemporary History of a Mainstream Religious Movement*. Lanham, Md.: Rowman and Littlefield, 2008.

Harding, Susan Friend. *The Book of Jerry Falwell*. Princeton, N.J.: Princeton University Press, 2001.

Harding, Vincent. *There Is a River: The Black Struggle for Freedom in America*. New York: Harcourt Brace Jovanovich, 1981.

Harris, Fredrick. *Something Within: Religion in African-American Religious Activism*. Oxford: Oxford University Press, 1999.

Harris, H. *The Tübingen School*. Oxford: Clarendon Press, 1975.

Harvey, Mazie Manson, ed. *The First United Methodist Church Records, 1843–1976*. Americus, Ga., 1976.

Harvey, Paul. *Bounds of Their Habitation: Race and Religion in American History*. Lanham, Md.: Rowman & Littlefield, 2017.

——. *Christianity and Race in the American South: A History*. Chicago: University of Chicago Press, 2016.

——. *Freedom's Coming: Religious Culture and the Shaping of the South from the Civil War to the Civil Rights Era*. Chapel Hill: University of North Carolina Press, 2007.

——. "God and Negroes and Jesus and Sin and Salvation: Racism, Racial Interchange, and Racial Interracialism in Southern Religious History." In *Religion in the American South: Protestants and Others in History and Culture*. Edited by Beth Barton Schwerger and Donald G. Mathews, 283–30. Chapel Hill: University of North Carolina Press, 2004.

——. *Redeeming the South: Religious Cultures and Racial Identities among Southern Baptists, 1865–1925*. Chapel Hill: University of North Carolina Press, 1997.

——. *Through the Storm, Through the Night*. The African American History Series. Lanham, Md.: Rowman and Littlefield Publishers, 2011.

Haselden, Kyle. *The Racial Problem in Christian Perspective*. New York: Harper & Brothers, 1959.

Hawkins, J. Russell, and Phillip Luke Sinitiere, eds. *Christians and the Color Line: Race and Religion after Divided by Faith*. Oxford: Oxford University Press, 2014.

Haynes, Stephen. "Distinction and Dispersal: Folk Theology and the Maintenance of White Supremacy." *Journal of Southern Religion* 17 (2015). http://jsreligion.org/issues /vol17/haynes.html.

——.*The Last Segregated Hour: The Memphis Kneel-Ins and the Campaign for Southern Church Desegregation*. New York: Oxford University Press, 2012.

——. *Noah's Curse: The Biblical Justification of American Slavery*. New York: Oxford University Press, 2001.

Hedgepeth, William. "The American South: Rise of a New Confederacy." *Look,* November 17, 1970.

Hefley, James C., and Marti Hefley. *The Church that Produced a President.* New York: Wyden Books, 1977.

Herskovitz, Melville. *The Myth of the Negro Past.* Boston: Beacon Press, 1941.

Heschel, Abraham Joshua. "Religion and Race." Speech, January 14, 1963. http://voicesofdemocracy.umd.edu/heschel-religion-and-race-speech-text/.

Higginbotham, Evelyn Brooks. *Righteous Discontent: The Women's Movement of the Black Baptist Church, 1880–1920.* Cambridge: Harvard University Press, 1994.

Hogan, Wesley. *Many Minds, One Heart: SNCC's Dream for a New America.* Chapel Hill: University of North Carolina Press, 2007.

Hollyday, Joyce, ed. *Clarence Jordan: Essential Writings.* Maryknoll, NY: Orbis, 1970.

Holsaert, Faith S., Martha Prescod Norman Noonan, Judy Richardson, Betty Garman Robinson, Jean Smith Young, and Dorothy M. Zellner, eds. *Hands on the Freedom Plow: Personal Accounts of Women in SNCC.* Urbana-Champaign: University of Illinois Press, 2010.

Holt, Thomas C. *The Problem of Race in the 21st Century.* Cambridge: Harvard University Press, 2000.

Hopkins, Charles Howard. *The Rise of the Social Gospel in American Protestantism, 1865–1915.* New Haven: Yale University Press, 1940.

Horne, Gerald. *Fire This Time: The Watts Uprising and the 1960s.* Charlottesville, VA: University Press of Virginia, 1995.

Houck, Davis and David Dixon, eds. *Rhetoric, Religion and the Civil Rights Movement.* Waco, Tex.: Baylor University Press, 2006.

———. *Women and the Civil Rights Movement, 1945–1965.* Oxford: University Press of Mississippi, 2009.

Houston, Benjamin. *The Nashville Way: Racial Etiquette and the Struggle for Social Justice in a Southern City.* Athens: University of Georgia Press, 2012.

Howard-Pitney, David. *The African American Jeremiad: Appeals for Justice in America.* Philadelphia: Temple University Press, 2005.

Hudnut-Beumler, James David. *Looking for God in the Suburbs: The Religion of the American Dream and its Critics, 1945–1965.* New Brunswick, NJ: Rutgers University Press, 1994.

Huie, William Bradford *Three Lives for Mississippi.* Jackson: University Press of Mississippi, 2000.

Hunter, James Davidson. *Culture Wars: The Struggle to Define America.* New York: Basic Books, 1991.

Hutchison, William R. and Hartmut Lehmann, eds. *Many are Chosen: Divine Election & Western Nationalism.* Minneapolis: Fortress Press, 1994.

Ingram, T. Robert. "Why Integration is UnChristian." *Citizen,* June 1962.

Jacobson, Matthew Frye. *Whiteness of A Different Color: European Immigrants and the Alchemy of Race.* Cambridge: Harvard University Press, 1998.

Jackson, Patrick. "Lost: American Evangelicals in the Public Square, 1925–1955." PhD diss. Vanderbilt University, 2012.

Jeffries, Hasan. *Bloody Lowndes: Civil Rights and Black Power in Alabama's Black Belt*. New York: New York University Press, 2009.

Jelks, Randal Maurice. *Benjamin Elijah Mays: Schoolmaster of the Movement*. Chapel Hill: University of North Carolina Press, 2012.

Jenkins, David. *Black Zion: The Return of Afro-Americans and West Indians to Africa*. London: Wildwood House, 1975.

Jenkins, Mary Royal. *Open Dem Cells: A Pictorial History of the Albany Movement*. Columbus, GA: Brentwood Academic Press, 2000.

Johnson, James Weldon. *The Book of American Negro Spirituals*. Binghamton, N.Y.: The Vail-Bollan Press, 1925.

Jones, Charles Colcock. *Religious Instruction of the Negro*. Savannah, Ga.: Thomas Purse, 1842.

Jones, Patrick D. *The Selma of the North: Civil Rights Insurgency in Milwaukee*. Cambridge: Harvard University Press, 2009.

Jones, Steven L. *Religious Schooling in America: Private Education and Public Life*. New York: Praeger Publishers, 2008.

Jorgenson, Lloyd P. *The State and the Non-Public School, 1825–1925*. Columbia, Mo.: University of Missouri Press, 1987.

Joseph, Peniel E. *The Black Power Movement: Rethinking the Civil Rights-Black Power Era*. New York: Routledge, 2006.

——. *Waiting Til the Midnight Hour*. New York: Henry Holt & Company, 2006.

Joyner, Charles. *Down by the Riverside*. Urbana-Champaign: University of Illinois Press, 2009.

Kagan, Seth and Philip Dray. *We are Not Afraid: The Story of Goodman, Schwerner, and Chaney, and the Civil Rights Campaign for Mississippi*. New York: Nation Books, 2006.

Kapur, Sudarshan. *Raising Up A Prophet: The African American Encounter with Gandhi*. Boston: Beacon Press, 1992.

Kelley, Robin D. G. *Hammer and Hoe: Alabama Communists During the Great Depression*. Chapel Hill: University of North Carolina Press, 1990.

——. *Race Rebels: Culture, Politics, and the Black Working Class*. New York: The Free Press, 1994.

Kelsey, George D. *Racism and the Christian Understanding of Man*. New York: Charles Scribner &Sons, 1965.

Kendi, Ibram X. *Stamped from the Beginning: The Definitive History of Racist Ideas in America*. New York: Nation Books, 2016.

Ketcham, G.F. and B.Y. Landis, eds. *Yearbook of American Churches*. Nashville: Abingdon Press, 1951–1961.

Kidd, Thomas S. *George Whitefield: America's Spiritual Founding Father*. New Haven: Yale University Press, 2014.

King, Jr., Martin Luther. *The Measure of a Man*. Pilgrim Press, 1959.

——. "Out of the Long Night of Segregation." *Presbyterian Outlook*, February 10, 1958.

——. *Strength to Love*. Cleveland, Ohio: William Collins+World Publishing Co., 1963.

——. "The Unchristian Christian," *Ebony* 20, no. 10 (August 1965): 76–80.

——. *Where Do We Go from Here?: Chaos or Community*. New York: Harper and Row. 1967.

King, Sr., Martin Luther. *Daddy King: An Autobiography*. New York: Harper & Row, 1980.

King, Richard. *Civil Rights and the Idea of Freedom*. Oxford: Oxford University Press, 1992.

Klarman, Michael. *Brown vs. Board of Education and the Civil Rights Movement*. Oxford: Oxford University Press, 2007.

K'Meyer, Tracy E. *Interracialism and Christian Community in the Postwar South: The Story of Koinonia Farm*. Charlottesville: University of Virginia Press, 1997.

Kosek, Joseph Kip. "'Just a Bunch of Agitators': Kneel-Ins and the Desegregation of Southern Churches." *Religion and American Culture* 23, no. 2 (Summer 2013): 232–61.

Kruse, Kevin M. *White Flight: Atlanta and the Making of Modern Conservatism*. Princeton, N.J.: Princeton University Press, 2005.

Kutler, Stanley I. *The American Inquisition: Justice and Injustice in the Cold War*. New York: Hill & Wang, 1982.

Larson, Edward J. *Summer for the Gods: The Scopes Trial and America's Continuing Debate over Science and Religion*. New York: Basic Books, 1998.

Lassiter, Matthew D. *The Silent Majority: Suburban Politics in the Sunbelt South*. Princeton, N.J.: Princeton University Press, 2006.

Lawrence, James B. *A History of Calvary Church, Americus, GA, 1858–1912*. Atlanta, Ga.: N.p., 1912.

Lawson, Jr., James M. "From a Lunch Counter Stool." *Motive*, February 1966.

Lawson, Sean. *Black Ballots: Voting Rights in the South, 1944–1969*. New York: Columbia University Press, 1976.

Lawson, Steven F. "Freedom Then, Freedom Now: The Historiography of the Civil Rights Movement." *The American Historical Review* 96, no. 2 (Apr. 1991): 456–71.

Lawson, Steven F., and Charles Payne, eds. *Debating the Civil Rights Movement, 1945–1968*. Lanham, Md: Rowman & Littlefield, 1998.

Lawton, Kim A. "Before He Was a Leader, King Was a Pastor." *The Seattle Times*, January 14, 2006.

Lee, Dallas. *The Cotton Patch Evidence: The Story of Clarence Jordan and the Koinonia Farm Experiment (1942–1970)*. Americus, Georgia: Koinonia Partners Inc., 1971.

Lefever, Harry G. *Undaunted by the Fight: Spelman College and the Civil Rights Movement, 1957–1967*. Macon, Ga.: Mercer University Press, 2005.

Leonard, Bill J. "A Theology for Racism: Southern Fundamentalists and the Civil Rights Movement." *Baptist History and Heritage* 34, no. 1 (Winter 1999): 33–48.

Lewis, David L. *King: A Biography of Martin Luther King, Jr.* Urbana: University of Illinois Press, 1978.

———. *W.E.B. Du Bois: Biography of a Race, 1868–1919*. New York: Holt Paperbacks, 1994.

———. *W.E.B. Du Bois: The Fight for Equality and the American Century, 1919–1963*. New York: Henry Holt and Company, 2000.

Lewis, John, and Michael D'Orso. *Walking with the Wind*. New York: Simon & Schuster, 1998.

Lincoln, C. Eric. *Martin Luther King, Jr.: A Profile*. New York: Hill and Wang, 1970.

Lincoln, C. Eric, and Lawrence H. Mamiya. *The Black Church in the African American Experience*. Durham. N.C.: Duke University Press, 1990.

Lischer, Richard. *The Preacher King: Martin Luther King, Jr. and the World that Moved America*. New York: Oxford University Press, 1995.

Logan, Rayford. *The Negro in American Life and Thought: The Nadir, 1877–1901*. New York: Dial Press, 1954.

Lucas, Sean Michael. *For a Continuing Church: The Roots of the Presbyterian Church in America*. Phillipsburg, N.Y.: P&R, 2016.

Luker, Ralph E. *Social Gospel in Black and White: American Racial Reform, 1885–1912*. Chapel Hill: University of North Carolina Press, 1998.

Lyon, Carter Dalton. "Lifting the Color Bar from the House of God: The 1963–1964 Church Visit Campaign to Challenge Segregated Sanctuaries in Jackson Mississippi." PhD diss., The University of Mississippi, 2010.

Lyon, Danny. *Memories of the Southern Civil Rights Movement*. Chapel Hill: University of North Carolina Press, 1992.

MacLean, Nancy. *Behind the Mask of Chivalry: The Making of the Second Ku Klux Klan*. Oxford: Oxford University Press, 1995.

———. *Freedom is Not Enough: The Opening of the American Workplace*. Cambridge, MA: Harvard University Press, 2006.

Malone, Henry Thompson. *The Episcopal Church in Georgia 1733–1957*. Atlanta, Ga.: N.p., 1960.

Mamiya, Larry. "SNCC, SIM and the Southwest Georgia Project." Poughkeepsie, N.Y.: Vassar College, 2011. http://www.crmvet.org/nars/mamiya.htm.

Manis, Andrew M. "'City Mothers': Dorothy Tilly, Georgia Methodist Women, and Black Civil Rights," *Politics and Religion in the White South*, 125–56. Edited by Glen Feldman and Kari Frederickson. Lexington: University of Kentucky Press, 2005.

———. *Southern Civil Religions in Conflict: Civil Rights and the Culture Wars*. Macon, Ga.: Mercer University Press, 2002.

Manuel, Frank ed. *Utopias and Utopian Thought*. Boston: Houghton Mifflin, 1966.

Marable, Manning. *Race, Reform, Rebellion: The Second Reconstruction and beyond in Black American, 1945–1984*. Jackson: University Press of Mississippi, 1984.

Marable, Manning, and Leith Mullings, eds. *Let Nobody Turn Us Around: Voices of Resistance, Reform, and Renewal; An African American Anthology*. Lanham, Md.: Rowman and Littlefield Publishers, 2000.

Mark, Miles. *Negro Songs in the United States*. Ithaca, N.Y.: Cornell University Press for the American Historical Association, 1953.

Marsden, George M. *Fundamentalism and American Culture*. Oxford: Oxford University Press, 2006.

Marsh, Charles. *The Beloved Community: How Faith Shapes Social Justice, From the Civil Rights Movement to Today*. New York: Basic Books, 2005.

———. "The Conference on Lived Theology and Civil Courage: A Collection of Essays." Charlottesville, Va.: The Project on Lived Theology, 2003.

———. *God's Long Summer*. Princeton, N.J.: Princeton University Press, 1997.

Marsh, Charles, Sarah Azaransky, and Peter Slade, eds. *Lived Theology: New Perspectives on Method, Style, and Pedagogy*. New York: Oxford, 2017.

Martin, William. *With God on Our Side: The Rise of the Religious Right in America*. New York: Broadway Books, 1996.

Masters, Victor I. *Making America Christian*. Nashville, Tenn.: Southern Baptist Convention Home Missions Board, 1921.

Maston, T. B. *The Bible and Race*. Nashville: Broadman Press, 1959.

——. *Segregation and Desegregation*. New York: Macmillan, 1959.

May, Elaine Tyler. "Cold War, Warm Hearth." In *The Rise and Fall of the New Deal Order*, edited by Steve Fraser and Gary Gerstle, 153–81. Princeton, N.J.: Princeton University Press, 1989.

——. *Homeward Bound*. New York: Basic Books, 1988.

Mayer, Milton. "The Jim Crow Christ: The Failure of Church and Churchmen." *Negro Digest*, February 1964.

Mays, Benjamin E. *Born to Rebel: An Autobiography*. Athens: University of Georgia Press, 1971.

——. "Kneel-Ins: My View," *Pittsburgh Courier*, September 10, 1960.

——. *The Negro's God, as Reflected in His Literature*. New York: Atheneum, 1938.

——. *Seeking to be Christian in Race Relations*. New York: Friendship, 1964.

Mays, Benjamin, and Joseph Nicholson. *The Negro Church*. New York: Arno Press, 1933.

McGill, Ralph. *A Church, A School*. Nashville, Tenn.: Abingdon Press, 1959.

——. "The Devil Outscores Jesus." *Daytona Beach Morning Journal*. September 25, 1965.

McGirr, Lisa. *Suburban Warriors: The Origins of the New American Right*. Princeton, N.J.: Princeton University Press, 2001.

McGreevy, John T. *Parish Boundaries: The Catholic Encounter with Race in the Twentieth-Century Urban North*. Chicago, Ill.: University of Chicago Press, 1996.

Meeks, Wayne A. *The First Urban Christians: The Social World of the Apostle Paul*. New Haven, Conn.: Yale University Press, 2003.

Meriwether, James, ed. *Lion in the Garden: Interviews with William Faulkner, 1926–1962*. Lincoln: University of Nebraska Press, 1980.

Merton, Thomas. *Faith and Violence*. South Bend, Ind.: University of Notre Dame Press, 1968.

Mertz, Paul E. "'Mind Changing Time all over Georgia': HOPE, Inc. and School Desegregation, 1958–1961." *The Georgia Historical Quarterly* 77, no. 1 (Spring 1993): 41–61.

Moore, Arthur J. *Bishop to All Peoples*. Nashville, Tenn.: Abingdon Press, 1973.

Moran, Jeffrey P. *The Scopes Trial: A Brief History with Documents*. New York: Bedford St. Martins, 2002.

Morris, Aldon. *The Origins of the Civil Rights Movement*. New York: Free Press, 1984.

Murray, Peter C. *Methodists and the Crucible of Race, 1930–1975*. Columbia: University of Missouri Press, 2004.

Nasstrom, Kathryn L. *Everybody's Grandmother and Nobody's Fool: Frances Freeborn Pauley and the Struggle for Social Justice*. Ithaca, N.Y.: Cornell University Press, 2000.

Nelsen, Hart M., Raytha L. Yockley, and Anne K. Nelsen, eds. *The Black Church in America*. New York: Basic Books, 1971.

Nelson, William Stuart, ed. *The Christian Way in Race Relations*. New York: Harper&-Brothers, 1948.

Nevin, David and Robert E. Bills. *The Schools That Fear Built: Segregationist Academies in the South*. Washington, D.C.: Acropolis Books, 1976.

Newman, Mark. "The Georgia Baptist Convention and Desegregation, 1945–1980." *Georgia Historical Quarterly* 83, no. 4 (Winter 1999): 683–711.

——. *Getting Right with God: Southern Baptists and Desegregation, 1945–1995.* Tuscaloosa: University of Alabama Press, 2001.

Nichols, Stephen J. *Jesus Made in America: A Cultural History from the Puritans to the Passion of the Christ.* Westmont, Ill.: Intervarsity Press, 2008.

Niels, Christian Nielson. *The Religion of President Carter.* Nashville, Tenn.: Thomas Nelson Publishers, 1977.

Noll, Mark A. *The Civil War as a Theological Crisis.* Chapel Hill: University of North Carolina Press, 2006.

——. Review of Paul Harvey, *Freedom's Coming. Journal of the American Academy of Religion* 75, no. 2. (June 2007): 473–77.

——. *The Rise of Evangelicalism: The Age of Edwards, Whitefield and the Wesleys.* Downers Grove, Ill.: Intervarsity Press, 2010.

Nord, Warren A. *Religion and American Education: Rethinking a National Dilemma.* Chapel Hill: University of North Carolina Press, 1995.

O'Connor, Charles. *A Rural Georgia Tragedy: Koinonia Farm in the 1950s.* Master's thesis, University of Georgia. 2003.

O'Connor, Flannery. *A Prayer Journal.* Edited by and with an introduction by W.A. Sessions. New York: Farrar, Strauss & Giraux, 2013.

Oates, Stephen B. *Let the Trumpet Sound: The Life of Martin Luther King, Jr.* New York: Harper & Row, 1982.

Ogbar, Jeffrey Ogbonna Green. *Black Power: Radical Politics and African American Identity.* Baltimore, Md.: Johns Hopkins University Press, 2004.

Olasky, Marvin, and John Perry. *Monkey Business: The True Story of the Scopes Trial.* Nashville, Tenn.: Broadman and Holman, 2005.

Ownby, Ted, ed. *The Role of Ideas in the Civil Rights South.* Oxford: University of Mississippi Press, 2002.

Painter, Nell Irvin. *The History of White People.* New York: W.W. Norton, 2010.

Patterson, James T. *Brown v. Board of Education: A Civil Rights Milestone and its Troubled Legacy.* Oxford: Oxford University Press, 2001.

Payne, Charles M. *I've Got the Light of Freedom: The Organizing Tradition and the Mississippi Freedom Struggle.* Berkeley: University of California Press, 1995.

Payne, Daniel Alexander. *Recollections of Seventy Years.* New York: Arno Press, 1968.

Perko, Michael F. "Religious Schooling in America: An Historiographic Reflection." *History of Education Quarterly* 40, no. 3 (2000): 320–38.

Peshkin, Alan. *God's Choice: The Total World of a Fundamentalist Christian School.* Chicago, Ill.: University of Chicago Press, 1986.

Peterson, Carla. *"Doers of the World": African-American Women Speakers and Writers in the North (1830–1880).* New York: Oxford University Press, 1995.

Pitzer, Donald E. *America's Communal Utopias.* Chapel Hill: University of North Carolina Press, 1997.

Prothero, Stephen. *American Jesus: How the Son of God became a National Icon.* New York: Farrar, Straus, and Giroux, 2003.

Putnam, Robert D. and David E. Campbell. *Amazing Grace: How Religion Divides and Unites Us.* New York: Simon & Schuster, 2012.

Raboteau, Albert J. *Fire in the Bones.* Boston: Beacon Press, 1996.

——. *Slave Religion: The 'Invisible Institution' in the Antebellum South*. New York: Oxford University Press, 1978.

Raines, Howell. *My Soul is Rested: The Story of the Civil Rights Movement in the Deep South*. New York: Putnam, 1977.

Ranier, Rev. John Jabez. *Kinship of God and Man*, Vol. 3, The American Church. New York: Thomas Whittaker, 1903.

Reddick, Lawrence D. *Crusader without Violence: A Biography of Martin Luther King, Jr*. New York: Harper, 1959.

Roberts, Gene and Hank Klibanoff. *The Race Beat: The Press, the Civil Rights Struggle and the Awakening of a Nation*. New York: Knopf Press, 2006.

Roche, Jeffrey. *Restructured Resistance: The Sibley Commission and the Politics of Desegregation in Georgia*. Athens: University of Georgia Press, 1998.

Roediger, David. *The Wages of Whiteness: Race and the Making of the American Working Class*. London: Verso, 1991.

Rose, Susan D. *Keeping Them Out of the Hands of Satan: Evangelical Schooling in America*. New York: Routledge, 1988.

Sanders, Edith R. "The Hamitic Hypothesis; Its Origin and Functions in Time Perspective." *The Journal of African History* 10, no. 4 (1969): 521–32.

Savage, Barbara Diane. *Broadcasting Freedom: Radio, War, and the Politics of Race, 1938–1948*. Chapel Hill: University of North Carolina Press, 1999.

Sayers, Dorothy L. "The Dogma is the Drama" (1938) in *Creed or Chaos?* New York: Harcourt, Brace & Co., 1949.

Scarborough, Dorothy. *On the Trail of Negro Folk-Songs*. Cambridge: Harvard University Press, 1925.

Schechter, Patricia A. *Ida B. Wells Barnett & American Reform, 1880–1930*. Chapel Hill: University of North Carolina Press, 2001.

Schrecker, Ellen. *The Age of McCarthyism*. Boston: Bedford St. Martin's Press, 1994.

Schulman, Bruce J. *From Cotton Belt to Sunbelt: Federal Policy, Economic Development, and the Transformation of the South, 1938–1980*. Oxford: Oxford University Press, 1991.

——. *The Seventies: The Great Shift in Culture, Society, and Politics*. New York: Free Press, 2001.

Schulman, Bruce J., and Julian E. Zelizer, eds. *Rightward Bound: Making America Conservative in the 1970s*. Cambridge: Harvard University Press, 2008.

Schultz, Debra L. *Going South: Jewish Women in the Civil Rights Movement*. New York: New York University Press, 2001.

Selby, Gary S. *Martin Luther King and the Rhetoric of Freedom: The Exodus Narrative in America's Struggle for Civil Rights*. Waco, Tex.: Baylor University Press, 2008.

Sernett, Milton. *Bound for the Promised Land: African Americans' Religion and the Great Migration*. Durham: Duke University Press, 1997.

Sherwood, Adiel. *A Gazetteer of Georgia*. Macon, Ga.: S. Boykin, 1860.

Siracusa, Anthony. "Disrupting the Calculation of Violence: James M. Lawson, Jr. and the Politics of Nonviolence." Master's thesis, Vanderbilt University, 2015.

Sitkoff, Harvard. *The Struggle for Black Equality, 1954–1980*. New York: Hill and Wang, 1981.

Sledge, Robert Watson. *Hands on the Ark: The Struggle for Change in the Methodist Episcopal Church, South, 1914–1939*. Lake Junaluska, N.C.: Commission on Archives and History, United Methodist Church, 1975.

Smith, Rev. George C. *The History of Georgia Methodism from 1786 to 1866*. Atlanta, Ga.: A. B. Caldwell, 1913.

Smith, Timothy L. *Revivalism and Social Reform: American Protestantism on the Eve of the Civil War*. New York: Harper and Row, 1957.

Sokol, Jason. *There Goes My Everything: White Southerners in the Age of Civil Rights, 1945–1975*. New York: Vintage Books, 2007.

Sparks, Randy J. *Religion in Mississippi*. Jackson: University Press of Mississippi, 2001.

Spercher, Anna. *The Religious World of Antislavery Women: Spirituality in the Lives of Five Abolitionist Lecturers*. New York: Syracuse University Press, 2000.

"Stolen Girls," *Essence Magazine*, December 16, 2009.

Stoper, Emily. "The Student Nonviolent Coordinating Committee." PhD diss., Harvard University, 1968.

Stout, Harry S. *The Divine Dramatist: George Whitefield and the Rise of Modern Evangelicalism*. Grand Rapids, Mich.: William B Eerdmans Publishers, 1991.

Sugrue, Thomas. *The Origins of the Urban Crisis: Race and Inequality in Postwar Detroit*. Princeton, N.J.: Princeton University Press, 1996.

———. *Sweet Land of Liberty: The Forgotten Struggle for Civil Rights in the North*. New York: Random House, 2008.

Sullivan, Patricia. *Lift Every Voice: The NAACP and the Making of the Civil Rights Movement*. New York: The New Press, 2009.

Sutton, Matthew Avery, ed. *Jerry Falwell and the Rise of the Religious Right: A Brief History with Documents*. Boston: Bedford/St. Martin's, 2012.

Taylor, Clarence. *Black Religious Intellectuals: The Fight for Equality from Jim Crow to the 21st Century*. New York: Routledge, 2002.

Thompson, E. T. *Presbyterians in the South*. Vol. 1. Louisville, Ky.: Westminster John Knox Press, 1963.

Thurman, Howard. *Deep River and the Negro Spiritual Speaks of Life and Death*. Richmond, Ind.: Friends United Press, 1975.

———. *Jesus and the Disinherited*. Boston: Beacon Press, 1949.

———. *The Luminous Darkness*. New York: Harper and Row, 1965.

Torrey, R. A., ed. *The Fundamentals: A Testimony to the Truth*. Los Angeles: Bible Institute, 1917.

Tuck, Steven G. N. *Beyond Atlanta: The Struggle for Racial Equality in Georgia, 1940–1980*. Athens: University of Georgia Press, 2001.

Van Deburg, William L. *New Day in Babylon*. Chicago, Ill.: University of Chicago Press, 1992.

Vivian, C. T. *Black Power and the American Myth*. Philadelphia, Pa.: Fortress Press, 1970.

von Eschen, Penny M. *Race Against Empire: Black Americans and Anticolonialiam, 1937–1957*. Ithaca, N.Y.: Cornell University Press, 1997.

Walton, Jonathan L. *Watch This!: The Ethic and Aesthetics of Black Televangelism*. New York: New York University Press, 2009.

Walzer, Michael. *Exodus and Revolution*. New York: Basic Books, 1985.

Warnock, Raphael. "Piety or Protest: Black Theology and the Divided Mind of the Black Church," Parks-King lecture, Yale Divinity School, New Haven, Conn., 2013.

Washington, James, ed. *Testament of Hope: The Essential Writings and Speeches of Dr. Martin Luther King, Jr.* New York: Harper Collins, 1986.

Washington, Joseph. *Black Religion: The Negro and Christianity in the United States.* Boston: Beacon Press, 1964.

West, Cornell, and Eddie J. Glaude, Jr., eds. *African American Religious Thought: An Anthology.* Louisville, Ky.: Westminster John Knox Press, 2003.

Westbrooks-Griffin, LuLu. *Freedom is Not Free: 45 Days in the Leesburg Stockade.* Rochester, N.Y.: George Eastman House, 1998.

Whalen, Charles, and Barbara Whalen. *The Longest Debate: A Legislative History of the 1964 Civil Rights Act.* Santa Ana, Calif.: Seven Locks Press, 1989.

White, Ronald C. *Liberty and Justice for All: Racial Reform and the Social Gospel, 1877–1925.* Louisville, Ky.: Westminster John Knox Press, 1990.

Whitfield, Stephen J. *The Culture of the Cold War.* Baltimore, Md.: Johns Hopkins Press, 1991.

Wilkerson, Isabel. *The Warmth of Other Suns: The Epic Story of America's Great Migration.* New York: Random House, 2010.

Williams, Beverly England. *By Faith and by Love: Martin and Mabel's Journey.* Eugene, Ore.: Wipf and Stock, 2014.

Williams, Johnny E. *African American Religion and the Civil Rights Movement in Arkansas.* Jackson: University Press of Mississippi, 2003.

Williams, Juan. *This Far by Faith: Stories from the African American Religious Experience.* New York: Harper Collins Publishers Amistad, 2003.

Williams, Robert. *Negroes with Guns.* New York: Marzani and Munsell, Inc., 1962.

Williams, S. *From Mounds to Megachurches: Georgia's Religious Heritage.* Athens: University of Georgia Press, 2008.

Williford, William Bailey. *Americus through the Years: The Story of a Georgia Town and Its People, 1832–1975.* Atlanta, Ga.: Cherokee, 1975.

Willis, Alan Scot. *All according to God's Plan: Southern Baptist Missions and Race, 1945–1970.* Lexington: University of Kentucky Press, 2005.

Wilmore, Gayraud. *Black Religion and Black Radicalism.* Maryknoll, N.Y.: Orbis, 1983.

Winters, Michael Sean. *God's Right Hand: How Jerry Falwell Made God a Republican and Baptized the American Right.* New York: HarperOne, 2012.

Winthrop, John. "A Model of Christian Charity." Sermon. *Arbella*, 1630.

Wood, Ralph C. *Flannery O'Connor and the Christ-Haunted South.* Grand Rapids, Mich.: William B. Erdmans, 2004.

Woodson, Carter G. *The History of the Negro Church.* Washington, D.C.: Associated, 1921.

Work, John W. *Folk Songs of the American Negro.* Nashville, Tenn.: Press of Fisk University, 1915.

Yetman, Norman R. *Life under the "Peculiar Institution": Selections from the Slave Narrative Collection.* New York: Holt, Rinehart, and Winston, 1970.

Young, Henry J. *Major Black Religious Leaders since 1940.* Nashville, Tenn.: Abingdon Press, 1979.

Youngs, Bettie B. *The House that Love Built.* Newburyport, Mass.: Hampton Roads, 2007.

Zepp, Ira G. *Search for the Beloved Community*. Lanham, Md.: University Press of America, 1986.

Zinn, Howard. *New Republic*, July 20, 1963.

———. *SNCC: The New Abolitionists*. Boston: Beacon Press, 1964.

Zwier, Robert. *Born Again Politics: The New Christian Right in America*. Downers Grove, Ill.: InterVarsity Press, 1982.

Index

Note: Information in figures is indicated by page numbers in *italics*.

Made in the USA
Middletown, DE
28 September 2023

39556474R00184